HEAVY STORM
AND
GENTLE BREEZE

HEAVY STORM
AND
GENTLE BREEZE

A Memoir of China's Diplomacy

TANG JIAXUAN

HARPER

An Imprint of HarperCollins*Publishers*
www.harpercollins.com

HEAVY STORM AND GENTLE BREEZE. Copyright © 2011 by Tang Jiaxuan. All rights reserved. Printed in the United States of America. No part of this book may be used or reproduced in any manner whatsoever without written permission except in the case of brief quotations embodied in critical articles and reviews. For information, address HarperCollins Publishers, 10 East 53rd Street, New York, NY 10022.

HarperCollins books may be purchased for educational, business, or sales promotional use. For information, please write: Special Markets Department, HarperCollins Publishers, 10 East 53rd Street, New York, NY 10022.

FIRST EDITION

Library of Congress Cataloging-in-Publication Data has been applied for.

ISBN: 978-0-06-206725-8

11 12 13 14 15   DIX/RRD   10 9 8 7 6 5 4 3 2 1

CONTENTS

FOREWORD

I WAS DEEPLY HONORED TO be one of the first readers of Mr. Tang Jiaxuan's book *Heavy Storm and Gentle Breeze*. I would like to extend my warm congratulations on its publication.

Mr. Tang is an esteemed leader on the diplomatic front who has had over forty years experience. His book covers a part of the major diplomatic events and state activities during the period from March 1998, when he became foreign minister, to March 2008, when he retired as state councilor.

During that decade, China's overall strength and international influence rose. China responded confidently to the vicissitudes of international situations and handled properly a series of major international events. Historic changes took place in China's relations with the rest of the world.

China's relations with major powers advanced. Despite the twists and turns caused by the bombing of the Chinese embassy in Yugoslavia, and the incident of collision over the South China Sea, China-US relations returned to the path of healthy and steady development and continuous progress. The China-Russia strategic cooperative partnership strengthened, and the two countries signed the Treaty of Good-Neighborliness and Friendly Cooperation. China and Japan broke the deadlock caused by Japanese leaders' visits to the Yasukuni Shrine, and opened up a new mutually beneficial relationship. China established various forms of strategic partnership with the European Union, the United Kingdom, France, and Germany as well as reinforcing its cooperation with major emerging countries, including India, Brazil, South Africa, and Mexico. China pursues a policy of fostering friendship and partnership with neighboring countries and actively expanding regional cooperation. ASEAN+1, ASEAN+3, and the East Asia Summit were fruitful. The founding, in 2001, of the Shanghai Cooperation Organization (SCO) bore good fruits. The Beijing Summit of the China-Africa Cooperation Forum concluded successfully. The China–Arab States Cooperation Forum was founded, and mutually beneficial cooperation between China and Latin American countries deepened. China played an active role in multilateral affairs, advocated peace, cooperation, and development, greatly contributing to the building of a harmonious world of lasting peace and common prosperity.

The splendid accomplishments in diplomatic work over the decade are attributable to the leadership of the Central Committee of the CPC and the State Council, the concerted efforts of relevant departments, and the firm support of the people nationwide. They also embodied the wisdom and energy of Mr. Tang Jiaxuan, foreign minister and state councilor in charge of foreign affairs.

In this book, Mr. Tang selects eleven representative events, and presents them with vivid narration and incisive analysis. The book is a skillful application of theory in practice. The patriotism shown in handling the bombing of the Chinese embassy in Yugoslavia, the diplomatic art of strict adherence to principles combined with strategic flexibility in facilitating win-win China-Russia and China-Vietnam boundary negotiations, the strong organization and coordination ability during the Beijing Summit of the China-Africa Cooperation Forum, the high sense of political responsibility in addressing the nuclear tests conducted by India and Pakistan, the strategic thinking in promoting the steady development of China's relations with major powers, and his style of telling truth from facts and keeping up with the times—all this constitutes a valuable treasure of our diplomacy. In a sense, the book is a true portrayal of Mr. Tang's diplomatic experience, as well as a valuable diplomatic document.

Mr. Tang has been a leader, a mentor, and a helpful friend. He is ready to listen to views from all. He is democratic and decisive. He is amicable and easy to approach. He is demanding and considerate. I have been deeply impressed by his leadership, diplomatic charisma, and great sense of responsibility. In early 2003, he visited New York four times in just over a month to attend the UN Security Council meetings, seeking a solution to the Iraq issue. Faced with complicated situations, he employed well-planned strategies and won praise for his prudent and pragmatic style. As ambassador to the United States at the time, I was deeply moved by his earnest devotion to the cause of world peace.

Writings are for conveying truth. *Heavy Storm and Gentle Breeze,* with its rich content and profound ideas, provides important guidance to the cause of diplomacy. Under the prevailing heavy storm in the international situation, we diplomats will benefit from the gentle breeze in China's diplomacy. The book will give us wisdom and strength, inspiring us to enrich China's diplomatic theory and practice, thus bringing new impetus to our work.

Yang Jiechi
September 27, 2009

PREFACE

I RETIRED AS A STATE councilor in March 2008 but, as a veteran diplomat, I am still concerned about and support China's diplomatic causes. Many colleagues suggested that I should write my recollections of the important events in my diplomatic career in order to record history, give advice, and impart knowledge. Some described it as a duty and obligation on my part to my country, to the cause of diplomacy, and to history.

Indeed, during the forty-plus years of my diplomatic career, particularly from March 1998, when I became foreign minister, to March 2008, when I retired as state councilor, complicated and profound changes took place in the international situation. By the beginning of the twenty-first century, major readjustments had emerged in international political and economic patterns, resulting in historic changes in China's relations with the rest of the world. Over this decade, under the correct leadership and direct guidance of the central authorities, China's diplomacy forged ahead with the times, transforming challenges into opportunities and opening up new prospects, thus achieving brilliant successes. During this period, there were indeed many events worth recording in China's diplomacy. Memories of these events linger in my heart. With the passage of time, I have gained an increasingly deep understanding of those events.

After thorough consideration, I decided to accept the suggestion to write and publish this book, because it is not an entirely personal matter of mine.

I have chosen eleven topics, all related to events significant to China's diplomacy over that decade. The book reflects not only the development of and changes in China's relations with major powers in the world, but also the dialogue and cooperation between China and other developing countries. Confucius said, "Recalling the past helps understand the present." Therefore, I strive to review history from a realistic point of view. In this way, I try to reveal the basis of historical truths, and the intentions and thinking, pains and gains of decision makers and participants, and present to the readers a comprehensive account of the essence, national interests, and work results. I hope this book will have a practical reference value. Owing to limited space and the diplomatic sensitivity of certain issues, the events related in this book constitute only part of my diplomatic experiences. I believe readers will understand.

I hope the book will help readers learn about the diplomatic history of that particular period and obtain some information to be passed on to future generations.

In the past decade, China had faced all kinds of diplomatic challenges; some were very severe and came like a heavy storm. China had adhered to an independent foreign policy of peace and the building of a harmonious world. This policy, along with China's firm yet flexible practices, has brought peace, friendship, cooperation, and development to the world like a gentle breeze. The title of this book, *Heavy Storm and Gentle Breeze,* roughly embraces the contents of the book and summarizes the international situation as well as the ideas and style of China's diplomatic policy.

Tang Jiaxuan
September 17, 2009

HEAVY STORM
AND
GENTLE BREEZE

CHAPTER I

The Tortuous Road of
Sino-Japanese Relations

OVER THE COURSE OF my diplomatic career of more than forty years, I have witnessed the diplomatic progress made by the People's Republic of China, and have experienced many significant historical events. I have kept in touch with my counterparts in most countries, but it is with Japan that my connections go deepest.

My involvement in Sino-Japanese relations began in 1958, when the Chinese government, with an eye to developing bilateral relations with Japan, decided to have a contingent of people learn Japanese. Selected as part of this group, I was transferred from the Department of Foreign Languages of Fudan University in Shanghai to the Department of Oriental Languages and Literature of Peking University. In 1964, I was assigned to work in the translation group of the Ministry of Foreign Affairs, which was the beginning of my connection with China's diplomacy and of my dealings with the Japanese.

During the course of two thousand years of friendly contacts, the Chinese and Japanese peoples have learned from each other, and thereby advanced their development and progress, but Japan is

May 21, 1979, Japan's Prime Minister Masayoshi Ohira receiving a Chinese delegation headed by Liao Chengzhi (2nd L) and Su Yu (1st L). Tang Jiaxuan (3rd L) was
the interpreter.

also the country that has done the greatest harm to China. From
the first Sino-Japanese War (1894–95) to World War II (1938–45),
Japan launched repeated wars of aggression against China, and colonized Taiwan. Consequently, how Japan looks at this history and
the Taiwan issue, and whether it can properly solve these historical
issues, remains a core problem in the rebuilding and development of
Sino-Japanese relations in the postwar period.

History has shown that Sino-Japanese relations will progress
smoothly provided that these two issues are properly handled. Otherwise, the political basis for the relationship will consequently be
damaged, and it will suffer a setback, if not a reversal.

Thanks to our protracted efforts and struggle, Japan has, in
bilateral political documents and speeches by its leaders, made a
series of positive promises and statements concerning the historical and Taiwan question, thus providing a political assurance to the
normalization and consequent sound development of Sino-Japanese
relations.

However, Prime Minister Junichiro Koizumi—in office from April 2001 to September 2006—breached the bilateral consensus regarding these issues, and persisted in making annual visits to the Yasukuni Shrine. This seriously damaged and destabilized the political basis for Sino-Japanese relations, thereby plunging them into the most difficult time since normalization.

During those years, the Yasukuni Shrine problem remained the focal point of Sino-Japanese relations.

Why Is the Yasukuni Shrine a Problem?

SHRINES ARE WHERE THE Japanese commemorate and worship various Shinto spirits. There are more than 80,000 shrines throughout Japan.

Built in 1869 in the Chiyoda district of Tokyo, and originally called the Tokyo Shokonsha, the Yasukuni Shrine commemorated soldiers who died for the emperor during the Meiji Restoration and resulting civil war. It was renamed Yasukuni Shrine in 1879. *Yasukuni,* a term chosen by the Emperor Meiji from the Chinese classic, *Zuo Zhuan*, means "pacifying the nation."

However, the shrine never played a pacifying role. On the contrary, it was used as a propaganda tool to imbue the Japanese people with militarism and obedience to the emperor during all of Japan's modern wars of invasion. For the purpose of invasion and expansion, the extreme rightists trumpeted ideas of loyalty to the emperor and dedication to the nation, promising that if one died for Japan and the emperor, one's spirit would return to the Yasukuni Shrine and rise to heaven as a *kami* (deity) to be worshipped forever.

It is important to point out that the Yasukuni Shrine has never been an ordinary shrine. Its priests had close links with political and official circles since its establishment, and enjoyed various privileges. Most of its *guji* (chief priests) were appointed by the emperor or the Ministry of Military Affairs; there was even a case of a serving general being appointed as a *guji*.

Soon after Japan's surrender in 1945, the US Occupation Authorities ordered the separation of religion and government. The shrine's priests were deprived of their political privileges, and the shrine became an ordinary religious institution. Yet it was not held to account for its criminal responsibilities, so the shrine has been kept intact. Enshrined there are 2,460,000 Japanese war dead since the Meiji Restoration, 80 percent of whom died in World War II. They include Hideki Tojo and thirteen other Class-A war criminals, and more than one thousand Class-B and Class-C war criminals.

Since the Yasukuni Shrine enshrines Class-A war criminals whose hands were stained with the blood of Chinese and other Asian peoples, the visits of Japanese leaders to the shrine are not an internal Japanese affair, nor is it an issue of religion or tradition. It is a significant matter of principle whether the Japanese government holds a correct attitude towards Japan's history of military invasion. Visits of Japanese leaders to the shrine are sure to damage the political basis for Sino-Japanese relations and seriously offend people in all the countries, China included, that were war victims. We have always firmly opposed such visits.

On August 15, 1985, Japan's Prime Minister Yasuhiro Nakasone led his entire cabinet to the shrine, an act that aroused strong criticism from the Japanese public itself, as well as from other Asian countries. China made great efforts to have the prime minister promise that there would be no more visits during his term. This was the first direct confrontation between China and Japan on the Yasukuni Shrine issue.

In July 1996, Prime Minister Ryutaro Hashimoto, as a private person, paid homage to his cousin enshrined there. As a result of solemn representation from China, he promised not to visit the site again during his term. The next two prime ministers did not visit the shrine.

Koizumi Takes Office, Says He Will Worship at Yasukuni

ON APRIL 18, 2001, Prime Minister Yoshiro Mori resigned. Six days later Junichiro Koizumi was elected president of the ruling Liberal Democratic Party (LDP) and took office as prime minister on April 26.

Koizumi was born into a family of politicians. His grandfather Matajiro Koizumi had been minister of Posts and Telecommunications, and his father, Junya Koizumi, had headed the Defense Agency. Junichiro Koizumi himself was a veteran politician. In the 1990s, he held such posts as minister of Health, Labor and Welfare in the cabinet of Noboru Takeshita, minister of Posts and Telecommunications in the cabinet of Kiichi Miyazawa, and minister of Health, Labor and Welfare in the cabinet of Ryutaro Hashimoto. In 1995, he was defeated by Ryutaro Hashimoto in a contest for the LDP presidency.

Junichiro Koizumi is known for his distinctive personality; his speeches were brief, lively, easily understood, incisive, and appealing.

When he took office, Japan had just experienced the so-called lost decade of the 1990s. Economic gloom dragged on, political scandals came to light, and feelings of loss, unease, anxiety, and depression permeated the country, which was desperate for reform.

Aware of public resentment and dissatisfaction, Koizumi proposed structural reform with no limits and new millennium reform under the banner of "reforming the LDP, reforming Japan," to arouse public hope for the future. His fresh style dazzled the mass of voters and created the Koizumi whirlwind. His approval rating soared to 90 percent.

When running for prime minister, Koizumi repeatedly promised to pay formal homage at the shrine on August 15, the date of Japan's defeat in World War II. He did so to gain the support of the Japan War Bereaved Association* and of rightist conservative forces. It was also deeply rooted in his wrong historical outlook and values.

Koizumi was born in 1942 and grew up after World War II. As the result of biased history education and family influence, he lacked a correct understanding of WWII history, and very much admired the Kamikaze Special Attack Corps (KSAC).† He once told the Japanese Diet that, when in difficulty, he would tell himself to model himself on the kamikaze suicide pilots. He regarded the shrine as an important place that embodied his sentiments, and visited there every year during his political career.

His repeated assertions that he would visit the shrine in future filled me with foreboding of a rough ride ahead for bilateral relations.

In fact, there were already signs of trouble for the relationship, engendered by the rightist trend in Japanese politics. On April 3, 2001, Japan's Ministry of Education, Culture, Sports, Science and Technology published a history textbook compiled by rightist forces that distorted the history of Japan's aggression against China and other Asian countries. The Chinese government lodged a strong protest and demanded that the Japanese government correct its mistake. On April 20, despite China's repeated protests and disapproving voices in Japan, the caretaker government of Yoshiro Mori obstinately allowed Lee Teng-hui (a former president of the Republic of China who had volunteered as a Japanese Imperial Army officer) to visit Japan on the excuse of medical treatment. The Chinese government lodged a solemn representation to Japan, and also sus-

---

*A national organization of the families of service personnel who died in WWII. It supports visits by officials to the Yasukuni Shrine.

†After Japan's defeat at Midway Islands in June 1942, Admiral Takijiro Onishi proposed that the Kamikaze Special Attack Corps be formed to counter the powerful US Air Force. Armed by the bushido spirit, the aviators launched suicide attacks on US ships, landing troops, and fixed group targets.

pended bilateral high-level contacts, a visit to Japan by ships of the Chinese navy, and dialogues on security.

Koizumi's visits to the Yasukuni would cause even worse problems for our relations. Many Japanese were worried by this gloomy prospect and called for efforts to curb the decline in bilateral relations.

Under these circumstances, we decided to make clear to Japan China's opposition to Koizumi's declared intention to visit the shrine.

In line with the unified arrangement of the central leadership, we proactively contacted many sectors of Japanese society, hoping through their influence to get Koizumi to change his mind. China's Ambassador to Japan Chen Jian and his successor Wu Dawei made extensive, in-depth contacts with the Japanese people. Wu Dawei also took his chance to work on Koizumi when visiting him as China's newly appointed ambassador

Japan's foreign minister at the time was Makiko Tanaka, daughter of former Prime Minister Kakuei Tanaka. She was a straightforward and capable person and her great service in helping Koizumi to election victory had made her a most influential member of his cabinet. Her father had been witness to the normalization of diplomatic ties, and she herself was fairly clear about the sensitive issues in our bilateral relations.

On May 24, one month after Koizumi took office, Makiko Tanaka came to Beijing to attend the third Asia-Europe Foreign Ministers' Meeting. She had visited China several times before, but this was her first as foreign minister. When we met, I talked about the Japanese history textbook, Lee Teng-hui's visit to Japan, and other issues, particularly Koizumi visiting the Yasukuni.

I pointed out that problems over the shrine had occurred both in the 1980s and the 1990s, had seriously affected Japan's relations with Asian neighbors, including China, and had damaged Japan's image overseas. Japan should learn from these lessons. Given the

With Japanese Foreign Minister Makiko Tanaka in Beijing, May 24, 2001.

already serious harm done to bilateral relations, if Japanese leaders insisted on visiting the Yasukuni Shrine, it would undoubtedly exacerbate the situation and make it more difficult to resume and improve bilateral relations. I stressed that Japan should fully understand the feelings of the people who had been subjected to Japanese militarist aggression, and that Japan's new cabinet should take concrete measures consistent with its declaration of "enhancing international coordination" and sincerely honor its solemn commitments to face up to and reflect on Japan's history.

Tanaka said she was very troubled by the textbook issue, as well as other problems. She also said that the new cabinet would honor the commitments made by former Prime Minister Tomiichi Murayama* in 1995, about recognizing Japan's history of aggression

---

*In August 1995 Japan's Prime Minister Tomiichi Murayama spoke on behalf of the Japanese government, at the fiftieth anniversary of Japan's defeat in WWII, saying, "Japan once followed an erroneous state policy and launched wars against oth-

and handling relevant historical issues, and that she herself would not visit the Yasukuni Shrine. She also said that Japan would handle the issue of Taiwan strictly in line with the Japan-China Joint Statement.

Our efforts through various channels put Koizumi under pressure. He wrote letters to China's President Jiang Zemin and Vice President Hu Jintao. The two letters expressed, from different perspectives, the same message, namely that he had always regarded Japan-China relations as one of Japan's most important bilateral relationships, that this belief had remained unchanged, and that he would continue to take full account of China's stance and endeavor to advance bilateral relations.

On July 24, I met with Makiko Tanaka at the ASEAN Regional Forum Foreign Ministers Meeting in Hanoi. Apart from discussing the regional situation and bilateral relations, I made a point of raising the Yasukuni Shrine issue. I stressed that the core of the issue was whether the Japanese government would sincerely recognize and reflect on Japan's history of aggression, and whether it would respect the feelings of the victim countries. I expressed my earnest hope that the Japanese leaders would think twice and make a wise decision.

As Japan's prime minister, Koizumi's every action would reflect the policies of his government and the national will of Japan, the weight of which he should be fully aware. To be frank, his perspective on the Yasukuni issue was very blinkered, and he had proceeded from Japan's domestic needs only, which was inconsistent with his repeatedly stated principle regarding international coordination, and also revealed his lack of differentiation between culprit

---

ers, which was disastrous for the nation and the people. Japan's colonial rule and aggression brought tremendous harm and suffering to many countries, especially in Asia. To avoid any recurrence of such wrongdoings, Japan will humbly recognize this undeniable historical fact, and again express deep remorse and a sincere apology to the victims."

and victim. Such behavior would fail internationally, especially in dealing with Asian neighbors. I hoped Koizumi would have second thoughts as to which acts would serve Japan's national interests and be conducive to improving bilateral relations with its Asian neighbors. Not much time remained before August 15, and I hoped Koizumi would consider seriously the concerns of his Asian neighbors and come to a wise decision. Otherwise, many of the programs scheduled for the second half of the year, programs intended to develop Sino-Japanese relations, would be seriously impacted. I also hoped that Foreign Minister Tanaka, as an influential cabinet member, would play an important role in dissuading Koizumi from visiting the shrine.

My words made Tanaka fully aware of the sensitivity and gravity of the Yasukuni Shrine issue. She said that the Yasukuni Shrine was a vital issue in Japan's relations with its neighbors and that Tokyo needed to take a discreet approach. In a later media interview, she for the first time publicly opposed the prime ministerial visit to the shrine.

Defiant Koizumi Makes First Visit to the Shrine

THE STRONG OPPOSITION FROM China, the Republic of Korea (ROK), and other countries forced Japan to give serious thought to the Yasukuni Shrine issue. As the August 15 anniversary approached, many opinions were voiced in Japan about Koizumi's visit to the war shrine, and more disapproving voices were being heard. The *Asahi Shimbun* newspaper and other media carried editorials opposing his visit.

During that time, China and Japan had frequent contacts through various channels in the hope of finding a solution.

In early August, Koizumi sent a secret envoy to Beijing to discuss possible solutions, and I met with him.

The Japanese envoy laid out their exploratory proposal. He said that Prime Minister Koizumi, in the light of strong criticism from China, the ROK, and other countries, had decided, after careful consideration, not to visit the Yasukuni Shrine on August 15. However, since he had promised several times to visit the place, he had to honor his word to the Japanese public. After much thought, therefore, the prime minister decided that he would pay homage at the shrine as a private visitor sometime after August 15, and talk on the spot, as prime minister, on Japan's understanding of its history. He hoped China would understand this decision.

I immediately told the envoy of China's opposition to visits by Japanese leaders to the shrine, and asked him to report this statement verbatim to Prime Minister Koizumi.

I made it clear that the Yasukuni Shrine issue was the most prominent problem in the current stage of our relations. Since August 15 was fast approaching, China hoped that Japan would handle this issue and avoid further damage to our relations. Our view had always been that the chief culprits for the war of aggression were a small number of Japanese militarists, as represented by the Class-A war criminals enshrined in the Yasukuni Shrine, and that the Japanese people had also been victims of aggression. Based on this understanding, the Chinese government had for a long time guided its people to look to the future, and to get along well with the Japanese. We Chinese were tolerant and had never opposed the Japanese public's visiting their dead family members or relatives enshrined in the Yasukuni Shrine. It was a different matter, however, if Japanese officials were involved, since their acts embodied the will of the Japanese government and directly reflected the attitude of the Japanese government towards Japan's history of aggression. We had noted Japan's proposal that Prime Minister Koizumi would visit on a day other than August 15, but China's position was that Koizumi would be wise to drop that plan.

A farsighted politician, I pointed out, would not merely follow the Japanese way of thinking and consider domestic factors alone; rather, he should consider the feelings of the people of the victim countries. I demanded that Koizumi realize this and handle this problem properly.

The Japanese envoy listened carefully. Before his departure, he said he would proceed straight to Prime Minister Koizumi's residence upon arriving in Tokyo and report to him in person.

However, almost at the same time, we learned that Koizumi might visit the shrine before August 15.

On obtaining this information, I instructed Vice Foreign Minister Wang Yi, who was in charge of Asian affairs, to urgently summon the Japanese ambassador, Koreshige Anami, and make solemn representations, demanding that Japan fully understand the gravity of the issue and handle it prudently.

Ambassador Anami, who had just taken up his post, was an expert on China. He told Wang Yi that he fully understood China's stance, and that, as far as he knew, no final decision had been made in Japan. He would work right away for a solution.

Around midday on August 13, Japan's Chief Cabinet Secretary Yasuo Fukuda requested an immediate telephone conversation with Wang Yi. Given the happenings of the previous days, I had a foreboding that problems were brewing.

Fukuda told Wang Yi that Prime Minister Koizumi had decided to pay a personal visit of homage to the shrine that very afternoon. Wang Yi immediately voiced strong opposition to the decision.

Fukuda argued that it was very difficult for the prime minister to give up his visit planned for August 15, and he had thought of postponing it. However, due to the recent changes in Japan, many Japanese had criticized Koizumi for postponing the visit as the result of Chinese pressure. As Japan saw things, postponement would stir up nationalist sentiment and therefore harm Japan–China relations. Fukuda reiterated that the prime minister valued Japan's relations with China and hoped China would judge him by his actions henceforward.

Wang Yi told Fukuda that the Chinese people and other Asian neighbors were highly concerned about Koizumi's decision to visit the shrine. At this critical juncture, Japan should be prudent about any action taken. China's stance that Prime Minister Koizumi should give up this visit remained unchanged. We advised that Japan's leaders should proceed from the overall situation of Sino-Japanese relations and make a wise decision.

Our advice had no effect on Koizumi whatsoever. At four-thirty that afternoon, he appeared at the Yasukuni Shrine, wearing a black swallowtail suit. Before paying homage, he gave a speech, acknowledging that Japan's colonial rule had brought immeasurable disasters to its Asian neighbors and reiterating Japan's deep reflection on this. Afterward, he told the media present that his visit was to commemorate the ordinary officers who had died in World War II, not the Class-A war criminals.

China's Foreign Ministry spokesman released an immediate statement expressing strong resentment and indignation at Koizumi's obstinacy. Meanwhile, we lodged solemn representations to Japan through diplomatic channels in Beijing and Tokyo.

Koizumi Visits China

CHINA'S STRONG REACTION BROUGHT home to Koizumi the serious damage his visit had caused to Sino-Japanese relations. Soon afterward, he asked former Prime Minister Morihiro Hosokawa, who was to visit China, to pass on to President Jiang Zemin a personal letter that contained relevant explanations.

Morihiro Hosokawa, Japan's prime minister from August 1993 to June 1994, was the first Japanese prime minister to clearly acknowledge and apologize for Japan's wars of aggression against its

Asian neighbors during World War II. One of the initiators of the Boao Forum for Asia, he remained positive towards China and was an influential politician in Japan.

Mr. Hosokawa visited China from September 2 to 5. He handed to Vice President Hu Jintao Koizumi's letter to President Jiang Zemin. According to Hosokawa, Koizumi was giving hard thought as to how to solve the difficulties his Yasukuni visit had brought to Japan-China relations. Koizumi hoped to visit Beijing en route to the upcoming October Asia-Pacific Economic Cooperation (APEC) meeting in Shanghai so that he could explain to President Jiang in person.

Vice President Hu replied that China had expected Koizumi to contribute to bilateral relations once he came into office, but he had in fact disregarded our repeated representations and obstinately paid a visit to the shrine. This had not only offended the Chinese people, but also damaged the political foundation of Sino-Japanese relations. Although China always valued the friendship between the two countries and believed that direct leader-to-leader contact would benefit bilateral relations, for such high-level visits to succeed the conditions and environment had to be right. We hoped the Japanese could fully understand the grave situation in bilateral relations, and take concrete and effective measures to improve them.

A week later, on September 12, at the invitation of the China-Japan Friendship Association, Yoshiro Hayashi, a former minister of finance who was also an LDP congressman, led a Japan-China Friendship Parliamentary Union delegation to China. It was the first Japanese parliamentary delegation to visit China after Koizumi's visit to Yasukuni Shrine.

On September 13, President Jiang received them in Zhongnanhai, seat of the central government. He earnestly told them that history was made up of objective facts that could never be erased or forgotten. We valued history to consolidate the political basis of China-Japan relations and ensure the sound progress of bilateral relations. Japan should recognize the historical facts and draw lessons from them.

President Jiang quoted a saying that "it is for the doer to undo what he has done." He hoped Koizumi would take concrete action to solve the current problem.

Jiang's remarks apparently moved the Japanese delegation.

In the spirit of Jiang's speech, we kept up the pressure through various channels, and demanded that Japan appreciate the gravity of the issue and take the initiative in moving ahead.

Prime Minister Koizumi became aware of the gravity of the issue, and wrote to President Jiang on August 30 and September 4, each letter bearing his signature. The prime minister stressed that he attached importance to relations with China and would endeavor to effect a recovery in bilateral relations. He repeatedly raised the idea of visiting China as soon as possible, so he could convey to President Jiang in person how much he valued Japan-China relations.

On September 21, Ambassador Anami formally reported to China's Vice Foreign Minister Wang Yi his government's proposal for Koizumi to visit China. What Japan had in mind, he said, was a one-day informal visit on October 7 or 8, to show how Japan valued its relations with China. Prime Minister Koizumi would visit the Museum of the War of Chinese People's Resistance against Japanese Aggression at Beijing's Lugouqiao to mourn Chinese war victims and make a public announcement of his reflection on Japan's history of aggression. He would also explain to Chinese leaders his own understanding of relevant historical issues and that of the Japanese government.

Prime Minister Koizumi suggesting a visit to the Lugouqiao Museum and mourning Chinese war victims was a positive development. If we consented, it would help him further understand the harm caused to the Chinese people by that war of aggression, and the harm caused by his erroneous deeds to Sino-Japanese relations and to the Chinese people.

One point had to be made clear: Koizumi's first destination after arriving in Beijing had to be the Lugouqiao Museum, where he should apologize to Chinese war victims and reflect on Japan's history of aggression. When meeting with Chinese leaders, he should fully and clearly spell out his own perception of history and that of the Japanese government, and state whether he would visit the shrine in future.

The central leadership soon approved these ideas, and the Japanese side also consented to our requirements. So, we agreed to Koizumi's working visit to China.

On the morning of October 8, Koizumi arrived in Beijing for a one-day working visit. As China's foreign minister, I accompanied him throughout the visit.

Koizumi headed for Lugouqiao straight from the airport. At the museum, he first presented a wreath, in the name of Japan's prime minister, to the Chinese victims who had died in Japan's war of aggression against China, then bowed in mourning. Written on the wreath were the words "Praying for eternal peace and friendship for generations."

Having gone through the museum displays, Koizumi wrote down two Japanese characters that mean "loyalty" and "forgiveness." He also delivered a speech at the museum saying that the visit had made a vivid impression on him of the miseries caused by the war, and he sincerely apologized to and mourned the Chinese whose lives had been taken by the aggression.

Koizumi said that Japan should face up to and reflect on history, never again start wars, learn from history, and follow the path of peaceful development. To develop friendly relations with China would benefit not only the two countries, but also Asia and the rest of the world. As prime minister of Japan, he would do his utmost to promote friendship between our two nations.

Before leaving, he told the museum curator Mr. Chen Qigang that the visit had taught him a great deal.

He then headed for the Diaoyutai State Guesthouse to meet with Premier Zhu Rongji. In the afternoon, President Jiang Zemin received him in Zhongnanhai. In these meetings, Koizumi again expressed his sincere mourning and apology to the Chinese war dead. He said that Japan should deeply examine its history and firmly hold to the road of future development. He sincerely hoped that the two countries could develop a solid friendship.

Following his meeting with President Jiang, Koizumi concluded his brief visit and left for the airport.

During his visit, he had evaded the question of whether he would visit the shrine again. This was an important issue that could not be ignored, so I instructed Wang Yi, who was accompanying him to the airport, to make clear China's stance on this. Mr. Wang conveyed this to Ambassador Anami, who replied that, though Koizumi had not been explicit, he and the Japanese government alike had already made it clear that they would handle the issue with great prudence next year, given the criticism his act had provoked from China and the ROK.

After Koizumi's visit, there was some relaxation of the strain in bilateral relations caused by the Yasukuni issue. During the APEC meeting in Shanghai and the 10+3 meeting in Brunei later that year, President Jiang and Premier Zhu both held talks with Koizumi.

In early April 2002, Li Peng, chairman of the Standing Committee of the National People's Congress (NPC), paid a formal friendly visit to Japan. He attended the opening ceremony of China Culture Year and Japan Culture Year, two events commemorating the thirtieth anniversary of the normalization of diplomatic ties.

In the same month, the first Boao Forum for Asia was held in Hainan. Prime Minister Koizumi declared at the forum that China's economic growth posed no threat at all, but brought more opportunities to Japan and to the world. That was the first public and formal statement of his position regarding China's development.

An Unheralded Second Visit

SOON AFTER THE BOAO Forum, I accompanied Premier Zhu Rongji to Turkey, Egypt, and Kenya. It was in Egypt that I learned Koizumi had visited the shrine at eight in the morning Beijing time on April 21, in the name of annual spring worship.

That was just nine days after his remarks at the Boao Forum: I could still hear his words in my ears and he was suddenly paying a second visit! Obviously, his erroneous stance about the historical issues was deeply rooted and his attitude quite obstinate.

Our Foreign Ministry immediately reacted strongly. Vice Minister Li Zhaoxing and Ambassador Wu Dawei lodged urgent representations to the Japanese side in Beijing and Tokyo. The ministry spokesperson delivered a speech on China's firm opposition to Japanese leaders visiting the Yasukuni Shrine where the Class-A war criminals were enshrined, no matter how and no matter when. We suspended military-to-military exchanges, including the visits to China of Japan's head of the Defense Agency scheduled for late April, and of Chinese Navy fleets to Japan arranged for mid-May.

Koizumi's second shrine visit plunged the recovering bilateral relationship back into difficulties.

The two sides had already agreed on a formal visit to China by Koizumi to take place in September 2002, but his sudden action forced us to suspend any specific talks with Japan about this visit.

They tried various means to find out our attitude to the proposed formal visit, but we insisted that first they should provide explanations about relevant historical issues and the second shrine visit.

In July that year, during the 10+3 meetings in Brunei, I held talks with Yoriko Kawaguchi, Japan's new foreign minister.

Kawaguchi, formerly Koizumi's minister of environment, had succeeded Makiko Tanaka in February. She was a prudent and very able administrator. When she held the environment portfolio, she was highly acclaimed for her diplomatic skills in persuading certain countries to accede to the United Nations Framework Convention on Climate Change Treaty, and other environmental diplomacy.

She said that the historical issues involved domestic and foreign relations and were very difficult to handle. She had been thinking about how to appropriately handle the two since assuming her new post. Then she argued Koizumi's case, saying that Koizumi had avoided visiting the Yasukuni in the sensitive month of August, which had been a hard decision, made in consideration of Japan's relationship with China. She said that Koizumi was looking forward to visiting China at a time when he would be welcome.

I informed her that China always set store by the visits of high-level leaders, but that Koizumi's second shrine visit had greatly hurt the feelings of the Chinese people. Right now, what was needed was a good atmosphere and favorable environment, for which Japan should take the necessary action.

With Japanese Foreign Minister Yoriko Kawaguchi at the Great Hall of the People, Beijing, April 4, 2004.

After several explorations, Koizumi finally came to understand China's firm stand on the shrine issue, which made the prospect of a China visit within the year quite distant. So he announced that such a visit was not absolutely vital and that he would wait for the time to be ripe.

Though we did not agree to a Koizumi visit, we did not shut the door on contact. Since the Asia-Europe meeting (ASEM) was to take place in Denmark in late September, Japan suggested a meeting of the two prime ministers there. It was agreed that Premier Zhu Rongji would meet with Koizumi during the course of the meeting, so as to work with him regarding the historical issues.

Koizumi's Third Visit to the Shrine

AT MIDDAY ON JANUARY 14, 2003, Japan's Chief Cabinet Secretary Yasuo Fukuda telephoned Chinese Ambassador Wu Dawei to tell him that Koizumi would pay a third visit to the shrine that very afternoon.

Wu Dawei responded in a very tough tone, saying that Koizumi's two previous visits had greatly harmed Sino-Japanese relations and that a third would result in even greater damage that might affect bilateral relations for years. The Japanese should understand this very clearly.

He hoped Fukuda would play a political role at this critical moment and persuade Koizumi to drop his plan.

Fukuda said he had already tried his best and asked the Chinese to understand his dilemma.

At two o'clock in the afternoon, Koizumi visited the Yasukuni for the third time. He told the media that he came in the spirit of cherishing peace and never launching a war, that he had made repeated explanations of his shrine visits to China and the Republic of Korea, and that he hoped the two countries could understand him.

That same day, a spokesperson for our foreign ministry made an immediate speech expressing strong indignation. Meanwhile, through diplomatic channels, we lodged solemn representations to Japan and expressed China's position, demanding that Koizumi correct his mistake and attempt to undo the negative impact it was having. Popular reaction in China was extremely vehement and many expressed condemnation on the Internet.

The New Komeito Party, the Social Democratic Party, and other opposition parties in Japan also lodged criticisms of Koizumi's third visit.

President Hu Meets Koizumi in St. Petersburg

IN LATE MAY 2003, China's President Hu Jintao visited Russia, Kazakhstan, and Mongolia. During the visit he attended celebrations in St. Petersburg marking the three-hundredth anniversary of the founding of the city.

Once informed of the visit, in late April, the Japanese embassy in Beijing contacted us and suggested that Prime Minister Koizumi could hold talks with President Hu in St. Petersburg. Koizumi was good at dealing with the media. While making the suggestion to China, he was trying to prepare the ground at home. He told the media he had always valued friendship between Japan and China, and expected to reach consensus with President Hu on pushing forward friendship and cooperation.

The Japanese media believed that if China agreed to it, a Japan-China meeting in St. Petersburg would be the first summit with the new Chinese leadership. The ruling party and opposition in Japan anticipated the meeting with enthusiasm.

Through various channels, Japan indicated the importance Koizumi attached to the meeting and hoped for a positive response.

My colleagues and I gave the matter serious study. We agreed on the significance of the meeting for stabilizing, gradually improving, and developing bilateral relations.

Once, after a foreign affairs event, President Hu asked my opinion about the meeting. I explained to him relevant information and my own ideas.

In mid-May, we replied through diplomatic channels that President Hu had consented to a meeting in St. Petersburg.

On May 30, President Hu arrived in St. Petersburg. That night, the Russian hosts arranged a concert at the Mariinsky Theater followed by dinner on a pleasure boat on the River Neva for the state leaders. It was arranged that President Hu would sit in the same concert row and at the same dinner table as Koizumi.

Koizumi took the initiative in greeting President Hu, and said he was very happy to meet him.

He told President Hu that he had visited Beijing, Nanjing, and Xi'an in the early 1970s. Since then he had developed a strong interest in Chinese opera. He liked Chinese food, and especially favored Shaoxing rice wine. He also praised the organization of the Shanghai APEC meeting in October 2001, saying how amazed he had been by the fireworks, the dinner, and the Chinese performances.

Judging from appearances, he intended to have further talks with President Hu.

President Hu said that the people of China and Japan shared the same origin in Eastern culture, and maintained more than two thousand years of friendly contact.

"Except for just one period of miserable history," Koizumi interposed.

It was because of this, President Hu continued, that we should summarize good experience in our friendly contacts, draw lessons from the miserable history, and look to the future. In the early 1980s, he had organized some bilateral friendly activities and kept in touch with many people on both sides, who had done a lot for friendship between us. Both sides should treasure the hard-won fruits and prevent any disruption.

Koizumi said he had learned much from President Hu's remarks and believed the bilateral friendship would grow stronger.

The following day, President Hu met Koizumi at his hotel. They exchanged views on such hot topics as the Korean Peninsula nuclear issue and the SARS epidemic, but what they talked about most was bilateral relations.

Koizumi said he had looked forward to his first meeting with President Hu, and that it had made his St. Petersburg visit worthwhile. China's rapid growth brought no threat to Japan, but rather an opportunity that would benefit Japan and stimulate its own economy.

President Hu, for his part, appreciated Koizumi's reiteration of the importance of the bilateral relationship, his remarks that China's development would be an opportunity rather than a threat to Japan, and his advocacy of pushing forward bilateral cooperation on a win-win basis.

President Hu said that, as close neighbors separated by a strip of water, the Chinese and the Japanese peoples had more than two thousand years of friendly exchanges. There had also been miseries that caused serious harm to both, but the dominant theme of the relationship had been one of friendly neighborliness and mutually beneficial cooperation. Over more than thirty years since the normalization of diplomatic ties, with the nurturing, persistent efforts of several generations of leaders of both countries, Sino-Japanese relations had achieved all-around and in-depth development, and China-Japan friendship had become deeply rooted in people's hearts. "History tells us that harmonious coexistence and mutually friendly cooperation between China and Japan not only bring concrete benefits to both peoples, but make important contributions to Asian and world peace, stability, and development," he said.

China and Japan bear important responsibility in safeguarding world peace and promoting Asian stability and development, President Hu continued. Chinese and Japanese leaders needed to handle bilateral ties from such a strategic perspective, grasp the general direction of development of bilateral relations, seize the historical opportunity, and push forward their sound and stable advancement for the long term.

He also stressed that, to develop Chinese-Japanese relations in the new millennium, the two sides must be mindful of the historical pains and gains of their friendly ties, and cherish the hard-won achievements. Both sides should adhere to the China-Japan Joint Statement (1972), the China-Japan Treaty of Peace and Friendship (1978), and the China-Japan Joint Declaration (1998), expand areas of common interest, and pay attention to and properly address each other's concerns. China especially hoped that Japan would handle the historic issues and the Taiwan issue with prudence, since they were the political basis for bilateral relations, and that Japan should do no further harm to the Chinese people's feelings. The two sides should take history as a mirror to guide future development, and take into account the overall situation from a long-term perspective, so as to write a new chapter of friendly relations.

At the end of the meeting, Koizumi got up to leave and said he hoped for reciprocal high-level visits at a convenient time, that he would welcome President Hu to visit Japan and he himself hoped to visit China.

President Hu answered meaningfully, "Let us work together to this end."

The following September, Chairman of the NPC Standing Committee Wu Bangguo paid a formal goodwill visit to Japan. In October, when Premier Wen Jiabao attended the Seventh ASEAN

10+3 meeting in Bali, Indonesia, and when President Hu attended the 11th APEC meeting in Bangkok, Thailand, they each held talks with Koizumi.

Koizumi Willfully Makes a Fourth Visit

APPARENTLY, KOIZUMI FAILED TO fully comprehend President Hu's remarks. Just a few months later, as the whole world was greeting New Year's Day 2004, he visited the Yasukuni Shrine for the fourth time.

We later learned that Koizumi thought whatever time he visited the shrine it would elicit criticism from China, hence the earlier, the better. He had deliberately chosen the New Year's Day holiday to reduce domestic media coverage.

My ministry and the Chinese embassy in Japan immediately lodged solemn representations to Japan. Our attitude was clear: We firmly opposed visits by Japanese leaders to the Yasukuni Shrine, where Class-A war criminals were enshrined, in any form and at any time.

Koizumi's obduracy triggered great controversy in Japan, too. With the exception of the ruling LDP, most political parties showed unprecedented unanimity in criticizing his action, which came under more and more questioning from the media and the public.

Sadly, all these criticisms, at home or abroad, moved Koizumi not one jot. He was reported as saying, when asked by the Diet budget committee, that he did not oppose the Yasukuni Shrine's enshrinement of the Class-A war criminals, that "lashing the dead" was not part of Japanese culture, and that "other countries' hackneyed tune" would not change his mind in the slightest.

This was Koizumi's first public statement of his attitude towards the Class-A war criminals. It was nothing but undisguised exoneration of those internationally acknowledged war criminals.

Koizumi's insistent visits to Yasukuni posed a problem for Japan itself. Calls went up for resolution of the issue, the two influential representatives being Yasuhiro Nakasone and Yasuo Fukuda. Yasuhiro Nakasone suggested removal of the Class-A war criminals for enshrinement elsewhere. He had suggested the idea as prime minister in the 1980s, but had met with opposition from Tojo's family and the shrine's head priest.

When the Yasukuni Shrine became an outstanding issue under Koizumi, Nakasone repeated the separated enshrinement proposal on different public occasions, in the hope that this might resolve the disputes around the shrine issue between China and Japan.

The other suggestion was raised by Yasuo Fukuda's private policy consultancy in late 2002, based on a year of studying the issue. They proposed the creation of a state cemetery, like Arlington National Cemetery in the United States, to include those who had died in Japan's civil or overseas wars in modern times, and those Self-Defense Force soldiers who had died on global peace missions in recent years. Such a cemetery would have no religious associations whatsoever.

According to Fukuda, this would avert diplomatic friction with neighbor countries and hush domestic debate on the separation of government and religion in the Japanese Constitution. Japanese leaders, including the emperor, could come freely, and foreign visitors, too, could go and present wreaths.

However, the complexities of the shrine issue made it hard to solve, and both proposals met with domestic opposition.

It was in such conditions that Sino-Japanese relations went into 2005.

The Eventful Sixtieth Anniversary Year

THE YEAR 2005 MARKED the sixtieth anniversary of the end of World War II. It was an important and sensitive year for relations between our two countries.

It proved an eventful year indeed.

Early in the year, Japan had increased its efforts to seek UN Security Council permanent membership. The fact that Japanese leaders had not changed their erroneous attitude towards historical issues incensed popular opinion in China, and millions of Chinese signed Internet petitions expressing strong opposition to Japan's attempt at Security Council permanent membership. By early April, people were staging street demonstrations in several cities, with violence erupting in isolated instances.

The Japanese reaction was vehement. The government and politicians made public statements on their position: Some even accused the Chinese government of instigating the anti-Japan demonstrations. It was constantly reported in the media, and TV stations repeatedly broadcast footage of the demonstrations and the violent behavior of a small minority. Our embassy and consulates in Japan suffered attacks by anti-China right-wing factions.

It was an all-time low in bilateral relations since the normalization of ties. Though economic and trade exchanges continued, Japan's prolonged, erroneous attitude toward historical issues had dragged political relations to the depths, and caused emotional conflict between the two peoples. Political cold and economic heat were the characteristics of the bilateral ties.

Hu Jintao and other senior leaders took this very seriously, and were constantly issuing important relevant instructions.

I was enormously busy during that time, often working around the clock. Whenever I had time, I would think about the issues related to Sino-Japanese relations.

How could Japan and Germany, the two instigators of World

War II, behave so differently in the postwar era? Germany had long
since enacted laws that prohibited exculpating the Nazis, but Japan
had permitted rightist history textbooks to whitewash its own history of aggression. Back in the 1970s, West Germany's Chancellor
Willy Brandt had knelt at the monument to the victims of Warsaw
Ghetto Uprising, whereas the Japanese prime minister kept paying
homage every year at the Yasukuni Shrine where the Class-A war
criminals were enshrined. What a great difference! There was no
way Chinese popular opinion could accept as a UN Security Council permanent member a country unable to correctly reflect upon its
history of aggression, unable to correctly comprehend the feelings
of the people of the victim countries! Why in recent years had there
been frequent demonstrations against Japan in China, the Republic
of Korea, and elsewhere? Why was Japan always in trouble with its
major neighbors? The essential reason lay in Japan's failure to treat
history correctly.

In the early postwar era, the Japanese government had, in retrospect and with an apologetic manner, expressed its understanding
of and respect for the feelings of the people of the victim countries.
The normalization and gradual improvement in Sino-Japanese relations had been based on the then Japanese leaders' correct treatment
and handling of historical issues. Today, however, the Japanese
leaders one-sidedly stress domestic factors, ignore the feelings of
their neighbors, justified prime ministerial visits to the shrine on
the grounds of cultural traditions, and totally reject as foreign interference the sentiments of neighboring peoples.

In mid-April, Toyohiko Yamauchi, president of *Kyodo News*,
visited China. When meeting him in Zhongnanhai, I expounded
all my thoughts on relevant issues, going deeply into some issues of
particular concern to the Japanese. My hope was that Japan's largest news agency would convey my remarks to the Japanese readers
objectively and completely.

With regard to the Chinese protests and demonstrations, I said that the Chinese government had paid attention to and called on the public to express their emotions by calm, reasonable, and legal means, rather than with violent behavior. The relevant authorities had done much and assigned a large police presence to prevent the situation from escalating and to protect the safety of Japanese organizations and citizens in China. All this was to uphold bilateral relations. There was some excessive action, which the Chinese government neither supported nor welcomed. We had already taken and would continue to take various measures to protect in accordance with the law the safety of Japanese diplomatic missions, enterprises, and citizens in China.

I emphasized the grave and complicated situation in bilateral relations to which both sides should give due attention. In particular, they should delve deep into the origins of the problems and tackle them properly. Looking at problems individually rather than

With *Kyodo News* President Toyohiko Yamauchi in Zhongnanhai, Beijing, April 12, 2005.

as a whole would only complicate things further, and not benefit long-term relations.

Unfortunately, however, the word in Japan was that the Chinese demonstrations had government support and were the result of anti-Japan education here. I told him that such claims were groundless, a serious distortion of fact, and harmful to bilateral relations. It was quite normal for a government to give patriotic education to its people, but China's patriotic education had never been anti-Japan. We had consistently abided by the principle of drawing lessons from history and looking to the future, and had never instilled hostility toward, or hatred of, Japan. Rather, we had encouraged the Chinese to learn from history to avoid any recurrence, to look to the future and cherish bilateral friendship for generations. China had never grouped the broad mass of Japanese together with the handful of militarists, nor did we want the Japanese of today to take the blame for Japan's aggression in the past.

Two days later, *People's Daily* published my remarks to Yamauchi in full.

Not long after, Foreign Minister Nobutaka Machimura visited China. He took office in September 2004, and held a tough attitude towards China. When the demonstrations took place and marches started, he urgently summoned our Ambassador Wang Yi, and expressed a strong protest at the regrettable events and demanded an apology, compensation, and a promise of more police to ensure the safety of Japanese missions and citizens in China.

This time Machimura had come to denounce us with anger. We would not show deference, since his visit offered us a chance to teach him a lesson.

After arriving in Beijing on the afternoon of April 17, Machimura held diplomatic talks with Foreign Minister Li Zhaoxing.

Usually, once the host and the visitor had exchanged greetings, the media would be dismissed. However, Machimura, apparently forgetting this protocol, began showering criticism on Mr. Li while the reporters were still present. He said that Japan deplored the violent attacks on Japanese diplomatic missions, companies, and citizens in some Chinese cities, and that Japan was surprised to have received no explanation from China, and demanded China's apology.

His questioning caught the ear of reporters, who stayed to jot down his words. When he finished some were about to leave, but Mr. Li invited them to stay and hear what China had to say.

Li then told his Japanese counterpart that, as foreign minister, Machimura could hardly understand what huge injury Japan's erroneous approach to historical issues had caused to this country of 1.3 billion people. To solve these issues, we must review the events of the past, not putting the cart before the horse. We hoped Japan would correctly understand the history, and tackle the root causes that had produced these troubles.

Li also expounded upon China's stance on the demonstrations criticized by Machimura.

Around the time of Machimura's visit, the residence of China's ambassador to Japan and the general consulate in Osaka were damaged by Japanese rightists, and the Bank of China in Yokohama received threats. Li Zhaoxing lodged representations to Machimura and strongly demanded that Japan take practical steps to prevent any recurrence.

The following afternoon, I met Machimura in the Diaoyutai State Guesthouse, where he once more raised his concerns. He said he had seen smashed glass and stained walls at the Japanese embassy and ambassadorial residence. In the previous day's talk with Foreign Minister Li, he had received no apology or expression of concern from China, but if some signs were forthcoming, they would help to mitigate public sentiments in Japan.

To stop him from further haggling I decided to talk history.

The late Premier Zhou Enlai had encapsulated the history of Sino-Japanese relations as "two thousand years of friendship and fifty years of hostility." By "hostility," Zhou was referring to the enmity that had existed at certain times. In the half century between the First Sino-Japanese War (1894–95) and the end of World War II, Japanese militarists had repeatedly launched atrocious attacks on China and brought catastrophe to the Chinese people. The Japanese people had been victims, too. Only on the basis of a clear settlement of this wretched history would it be possible for our two nations to resume our previous friendship and look forward to a hopeful future. This historic task had been fulfilled in the negotiations of 1972 around the normalization of diplomatic ties, thus turning hostility into friendship and ushering in a new chapter in bilateral relations.

I went on to say that China had always adhered to the principles of good-neighborly partnership and wanted to increase strategic mutual trust, expand exchanges and cooperation, and continuously push forward long-term and stable friendship with all China's neighbors, including Japan. The disappointment had been that, in recent years, Sino-Japanese relations had suffered serious damage, and that it was Japan that had lit the fuse. Japan had repeatedly gone back on its commitment on the historical issues and the Taiwan issue, thereby provoking an eruption of the long-accumulated resentment and indignation of the Chinese public. As a veteran diplomat who had been engaged in promoting bilateral friendship, I found the current situation extremely painful.

"You may not agree with me, or may even think this is the result of 'anti-Japan education' in China," I said. "But I can tell you that China has no 'anti-Japan education' at all. Chinese textbooks are consistent in their statements about Sino-Japanese relations, including relevant historical issues. When in Yan'an, the first generation of communist leaders instructed us to differentiate Japanese militarists from the Japanese ordinary people. We have always educated the people in the spirit of 'past experience, if not forgotten, is a guide for the future' and 'taking history as a mirror and looking into the future,' and have never demanded that today's Japanese take blame for the crimes committed by militarism in the past. On the contrary, we have always looked to the future."

I pointed out to Machimura that the results caused by Japan's erroneous attitude and acts on a series of issues were now very clear to all: Serious harm had been done to the friendly relations restored and developed through the painstaking efforts of the elder generations of statesmen; serious harm had been done to the hard-won restoration of friendly sentiments between the two peoples; even the efforts to promote peace, stability, and development in East Asia had been hindered. These results benefited neither country.

I reminded him that 2005 marked the sixtieth anniversary of the victory of the world antifascist war and the Chinese people's war of resistance against Japanese aggression, and was therefore a very sensitive year for bilateral relations. I hoped Japan would be prudent in its remarks concerning the sensitive issues of history, Taiwan, Diaoyu Island, and the East China Sea, avoid remarks that would harm the feelings of the Chinese people, and take no actions that would intensify bilateral conflicts. Imprudence would bring untold consequences. The two sides should proceed from the basis of safeguarding bilateral relations, increasing communication and consultation, and handling any issues in a calm, pragmatic, and reasonable manner.

Machimura's visit did not get Japan the result it expected, but rather a lesson from us.

Another Meeting in Jakarta

WHILE IN CHINA, MACHIMURA conveyed Koizumi's wish to meet President Hu to exchange views during the Asia-Africa Summit on April 22 in Jakarta.

Seemingly, Japan wished, by means of this goodwill gesture,

to soften the current hostility between the two peoples, to avert a further deterioration of relations, and to ease both domestic and overseas pressure.

Should we agree to their suggestion? We gave it much thought and deliberation.

In my view, problems left over by history should be resolved not by obstruction but by productive means. Japan-related demonstrations in early April had further increased resentment towards Japan. If President Hu were to meet with Koizumi during the multilateral Jakarta meeting and warn him of the possible consequences, it might help find proper solutions to the sensitive issues in our relations, help the Japanese people to acquire a correct understanding of China's policies towards Japan, and benefit bilateral relations and stable friendship.

However, there must be conditions. We told the Japanese that the meeting should send out a positive message to the world, and that Koizumi in particular should make a positive statement of his stance regarding the historical issues and Taiwan issue and on the bilateral relationship as a whole. They replied that Koizumi might accept these demands.

On April 20, President Hu left for Jakarta. On the plane, he called together relevant staff to discuss his meeting with Koizumi. His words impressed us all deeply. He said that now the relationship was in difficulty, but the more difficult the situation, the more effort we should make. The meeting between the two leaders would help overcome the present difficulties, increase mutual understanding between the two peoples, and push forward good-neighborly friendship.

Over the following days, my ministry and our embassy in Japan made appointments with Japanese officials, and Foreign Minister Li Zhaoxing made direct contact with the Japanese delegation in Jakarta. Finally, the Hu-Koizumi meeting was arranged for the evening of April 23 at President Hu's hotel.

When Koizumi arrived, the two shook hands and sat down. President Hu maintained a serious expression throughout the meeting.

President Hu told Koizumi that he had a tight schedule, but had decided, in the interest of steady development of bilateral ties and friendship, to find time to meet Koizumi for a further frank exchange of views on Sino-Japanese relations. He hoped this meeting could serve to move bilateral relations onto a sound and stable development track.

President Hu's words were weighty. If Koizumi were a sensible person, he should understand the profound meaning they carried.

Koizumi responded that he wanted to reaffirm, by meeting President Hu, the importance of bilateral friendship. It served the interests of both countries and was conducive to Asian peace, stability, and development. This, he said, was the spirit in which he had come to meet China's president.

Despite the existence of problems of one kind or another right now, he continued, looking ahead ten, twenty, or even fifty years into the future, we would understand the importance of friendly relations between China and Japan. Since becoming prime minister, he had repeated his view that China's development was not a threat, but an opportunity that would boost Japan's development. He had expressed that opinion not only to China, but on many international occasions. Several years had gone by and his belief had been proven true and many Japanese who had regarded Chinese development as a threat to Japan had now changed their minds.

When Koizumi had finished, President Hu said there was no denying that Sino-Japanese relations were currently facing difficulties and that the situation called for serious handling by the two nations' leaders. The leaders of the two nations should be farsighted and responsible so as to find a proper solution and safeguard China-Japan friendship as well as stability and development in Asia.

He mentioned their previous talks about the sixtieth anniversary, in 2005, of the victory of the world antifascist war and Chinese people's war of resistance against Japanese aggression. Thus, he said, 2005 would be an important and sensitive year for Sino-Japanese relations, so we needed to deal appropriately with some important issues, including the historical issues, the visits to Yasukuni Shrine and the Taiwan question.

President Hu reminded Koizumi of his positive response at the time, asserting that he would draw lessons from history, and that Japan should consider how to push forward China-Japan friendship while reflecting on its past wrongdoings. He had promised to be prudent about visiting the shrine, and said that it had been Japan's consistent position not to support Taiwan independence, a position that would not change.

"China set store by your words. However, Japan's recent actions regarding the issues of history and Taiwan have violated its own commitments," President Hu said. "I mention these today not in order to argue with you on specific issues, but to show that your deeds have disrupted the political basis for bilateral relations, and offended the people of China and other Asian countries. This will surely spark dissatisfaction among the people of China and other Asian countries. Taking all these things together, many Chinese have started to ask whether Japan's China policies are shifting to the right, and whether Japan is starting to reverse its stance regarding the issues of history and Taiwan. Such views and comments are also being voiced by international scholars. In my view, the strong public reaction in China and other Asian countries should provoke the deep thought of Japan's leaders.

"Under the current circumstances, we need to take practical steps to reverse the troubled state of Sino-Japanese relations and push forward the sound and stable development of bilateral relations," he concluded.

He then put forward five points for the development of bilateral relations.

First, strict adherence to the principles of the three political documents, namely, the China-Japan Joint Statement, the China-Japan Treaty of Peace and Friendship, and the China-Japan Joint Declaration, and continued deeds to develop friendly, cooperative relations oriented to the twenty-first century.

Second, adherence to the principle of taking history as a mirror to guide future development. To correctly understand and deal with history, Japan needed to earnestly reflect on the wars of aggression with actual deeds and never again do anything harmful to the feelings of the people of China and other Asian countries. The hope was that Japan would take a serious and prudent attitude and properly solve historical issues.

Third, proper handling of the Taiwan issue. Taiwan represents China's core interest and concerns the feelings of 1.3 billion Chinese people. The Japanese government had indicated on a number of occasions its adherence to the one-China policy and that it did not support Taiwan independence. China expected Japan to honor those commitments with actual deeds, and when handling relevant issues, to take into full consideration China's principled stance.

Fourth, appropriately addressing bilateral differences through dialogue and consultation on an equal footing, actively exploring ways to settle differences, and avoiding new disturbance to, and impact on, Sino-Japanese friendship.

Fifth, further strengthening of bilateral exchanges and cooperation in a wide range of areas, and boosting people-to-people exchanges in order to enhance mutual understanding, expanding common interests, and pushing forward the sound and stable development of Sino-Japanese relations.

These five points had been formulated in advance by President Hu.

Koizumi thanked President Hu for his frankness, and said that Japan would actively promote Japan-China friendly cooperative relations in line with these five points. As for the history issue and the

Taiwan issue, Japan would abide by the principles set by the three political documents; its position had not changed.

After their meeting, Hu met with journalists and shared with them the views he had stated.

The Hu-Koizumi meeting was a hot topic in both countries. Chinese public opinion overwhelmingly praised President Hu's five proposals. The Japanese mainstream newspapers gave the reports front-page headline coverage with considerable comment, describing the meeting as a helpful first step toward improving bilateral relations. They also noted that differences on a series of major issues remained unresolved and that the prospects for improved relations remained somewhat not optimistic. The meeting drew attention in Asia and the world at large.

Koizumi's Fifth Visit to the Shrine

IN 2005, WITH THE advent of the sixtieth anniversary of Japan's defeat on August 15, more domestic and international attention was directed to the stance of Koizumi and the Japanese government.

Japanese public opinion regarding the shrine visit was changing. At the urging of House of Representatives speaker Yohei Kono, eight former prime ministers unanimously urged Koizumi to make a wise decision, and Yasuhiro Nakasone even stated his own position publicly.

Most Japanese media opposed Koizumi's visit. *Asahi Shimbun, Mainichi Shimbun, Tokyo Shimbun,* and *Nihon Keizai Shimbun* all stressed that the Yasukuni Shrine issue was the root cause of the difficult situation in Japan–China relations, urging Koizumi to move to improve bilateral relations. An editorial in *Yomiuri Shimbun,* previously a supporter of Koizumi, questioned his action and suggested a new national cemetery be built. It also published articles by scholars calling on Koizumi to change his approach in Japan's own interest.

Public opinion polls in May and June showed a disapproval rate exceeding 50 percent. They revealed dissatisfaction with his diplomatic gesture towards China, and criticized him for not taking necessary measures to improve bilateral relations. People worried that continued visits would make the relationship even worse.

Koizumi disregarded these opinions and kept harping on the tune that his was a personal visit, not made in his official capacity; that the Class-A war criminals were indeed guilty, but it was not to them that he was paying respects, and so on. The subtext was that he intended to keep on visiting.

On August 15, Koizumi released a written statement regarding the sixtieth anniversary of the end of WWII. He said that Japan's past colonial rule and aggression had caused catastrophic damage and harm to countries in Asia and elsewhere, and that Japan acknowledged these historical facts and would deeply reflect on and sincerely apologize for them. Japan hoped to build cooperative relations with other countries on the basis of mutual understanding and mutual trust. Japan would never forget the painful lessons of the war, never follow the path of war, but would contribute to world peace and prosperity.

Facts later proved this to be mere lip service: Koizumi's actions were at complete variance with his words.

In September and October, there was more talk about a possible visit to the shrine. Some media predicted he would take the chance of an autumn memorial ceremony and visit after mid-October.

Thereupon, we immediately began our work in Beijing and Tokyo. Ambassador Wang Yi met with several Japanese politicians and earnestly asked them to play a positive role in dissuading Koizumi from visiting, so as to avoid greater harm to bilateral relations. The Japanese side expressed their agreement to Ambassador

Wang and their worries about the problems created by the Yasu-kuni Shrine issue. They promised to try their best to stop Koizumi.

However, the stubborn Koizumi would not listen to anyone. On October 17, he visited the shrine for the fifth time.

Politicians of all parties except his own voiced disagreement or criticism. The media also criticized him for worsening bilateral relations.

China's Foreign Ministry released an immediate statement severely condemning the visit. Foreign Minister Li Zhaoxing and Ambassador Wang Yi took up the matter with Japan's Ambassador Anami in Beijing and Foreign Minister Machimura in Tokyo, and read the ministry statement to them.

On the day of the fifth shrine visit, Executive Vice Foreign Minister Dai Bingguo was holding a strategic dialogue in Bei-jing with Japan's Vice Foreign Minister Shotaro Yachi, and one of the agenda items was how to solve the Yasukuni Shrine problem. Learning about Koizumi's visit, Mr. Dai made a point of meeting with Yachi to express China's solemn stance. Yachi looked very embarrassed, apparently ignorant of what had happened back home.

Despite China's utmost forbearance, Koizumi's stubborn insis-tence on visiting the Yasukuni Shrine for a fifth time led to the complete suspension of contacts between the leaders of the two countries.

New Proposals for an Old Problem

KOIZUMI'S OBSTINACY STRUCK MANY countries, including the United States.

Howard Baker, a former US Ambassador to Japan, on a sight-seeing visit to the Yushukan military hall at Yasukuni, had been surprised at its lavish displays of the personal effects of WWII Japa-nese military. The exhibits, materials, and audiovisual displays all trumpeted Japan's view of imperial history. Some even praised the so-called merits of Japan's wars of aggression, asserting that Japan had been forced to launch war against the United States because of an American "embargo," "to defend its own survival," and "to break white man's rule." In Baker's view, these displays left visitors with just one impression, namely that Japan had been the victor.

Another US diplomat told *Mainichi Shimbun* that the United States could not ignore the Yushukan, because it did not tell people the truth.

Koizumi's fifth visit resulted in greater pressure from the United States, according to Japanese media insiders. President George W. Bush, when visiting Japan that November, sternly addressed the issues of the Yasukuni Shrine and Sino-Japanese relations, at which Koizumi is said to have appeared agitated and embarrassed.

As Japan's government was facing elections in September 2006, more US politicians and scholars started questioning and criticizing Koizumi's visits to the shrine. Henry Hyde, chairman of the US House Committee on International Relations, wrote to Koizumi twice within half a year urging him to desist. As a result, many Koreans, American WWII veterans, and some overseas Chinese called Hyde's office with expressions of support and thanks.

A trend toward reflecting on and reexamining the shrine issue emerged in Japanese society as a whole. The dialogue between Tsuneo Watanabe, president of *Yomiuri Shimbun*, and Yashibumi Wakamiya, president of *Asahi Shimbun*, caught wide public attention.

These two influential newspapers had the biggest readership in Japan, but their opinions on historical issues had differed for quite a long time in the postwar years. Now Watanabe, a leading conservative and traditionalist, explicitly opposed Koizumi's visits to Yasukuni, which stirred a strong public reaction.

In their dialogue, Watanabe said that he was seventy-nine years old, and feared that once his generation had passed away, the younger Japanese would have little knowledge of the cruel wars, so he must leave behind messages about his own experience and tell people the true history.

Around that time, Yasukuni was a constantly recurring topic of debate in Japan's political circles. Various proposals were put forward, three of which were influential. One was to expand the Chidorigafuchi national cemetery, where the unknown dead of WWII were worshipped, into a park to include all war dead for worship by the Japanese public and foreigners. The second was to build a new national facility mourning the fallen. The third was to put the Yasukuni Shrine under state management and move the Class-A war criminals out.

On July 20, *Nihon Keizai Shimbun* published a handwritten note by the late Emperor Hirohito, which revealed his strong dissatisfaction that the tablets of the Class-A war criminals had been put in the shrine, and that he stopped visiting there as a result.

This report drew wide attention. Because of the emperor's unique influence in Japan, some thought it might sway Koizumi. To their surprise, Koizumi told the press that same day, "Shrine worshipping is a personal decision. The report won't affect me."

A Sixth Visit on the Anniversary of Defeat

KOIZUMI'S TERM OF OFFICE was to expire in September 2006. Since he had said he would visit the Yasukuni Shrine once a year, we inferred that he would pay a sixth visit before then.

On August 6, the Hong Kong Phoenix TV website carried a report from *Chosun Ilbo*, a major South Korean newspaper, saying that Koizumi would visit the shrine on August 15, the day of defeat, in defiance of opposition at home and abroad.

True to the report, on the morning of August 15, Koizumi appeared at Yasukuni, in formal attire and accompanied by his secretary. He made salutation and worshipped in the main hall, and left his signature "Junichiro Koizumi, Prime Minister of Japan." It was a gloomy day in Tokyo.

Koizumi brazenly defended his reckless visit, saying, "No matter what day I choose to go, China and the Republic of Korea will protest, so why not go on the day of the anniversary?" Koizumi indeed had no scruples.

Our foreign ministry and embassy in Japan lodged solemn representations to both Japan's embassy in China and their foreign ministry in Tokyo.

At home, Koizumi came under criticism on an unprecedented scale. Several politicians deemed his act unforgiveable, and the Association of Bereaved Families for Peace* also demanded that he stop visiting. Except for *Sankei Shimbun*, the major media heaped criticism on him.

Throughout his time in office, Koizumi visited the shrine every year, defying opposition from all quarters. His actions not only met firm opposition from China, the Republic of Korea, and other Asian countries, but also aroused strong reactions from the international community. Like China, the Republic of Korea lodged a strong protest every time Koizumi visited the shrine. Major media in the United States, United Kingdom, France, Germany, Australia, Russia, Singapore, and Algeria condemned his behavior.

Of all Japan's postwar prime ministers, Koizumi was most controversial in developing relations with China. In office, he voiced his valuing of Japan-China relations time and time again; labeled himself an advocate of Japan-China friendship; publicly criticized the China threat concept, saying that China's development presented opportunity rather than threat to Japan; and stressed a win-win approach in bilateral cooperation.

---

*An organization made up of families of Japanese service personnel who died in WWII. It stands for peace, and has close to twenty branches throughout Japan. It has expressed willingness to reflect on Japan's wars of aggression and is opposed to Japanese leaders visiting the Yasukuni Shrine.

On the other hand, he obstinately visited the Yasukuni Shrine every year in the face of our strong opposition, thus causing the explosion of conflicts, old and new, between China and Japan, and pushed Sino-Japanese relations to their most difficult point since normalization.

During that period, we engaged in bitter struggles with Japan centering on the Yasukuni Shrine issue. Besides the personal factor of Koizumi, these struggles had a deep-rooted complicated background, and to some extent, were unavoidable in the transitional period of bilateral relations.

First, Koizumi's insistence on these visits reflected the right-ist trend in Japan's currents of thought. With the end of the Cold War, Japan's left wing declined in strength, while conservatism grew stronger, and the trend of thought and public opinion moved to the right. Over 70 percent of Japan's population was born after WWII, and young politicians held a majority of the seats in the Diet. Having only a dim awareness of Japan's overseas aggression, some with a wrong concept of history, they wished to shrug off the historical constraints a defeated country must bear, and become an ordinary country. Koizumi tried to use the shrine visits as a break-through point hoping to force the international community, includ-ing China and the Republic of Korea, into accepting the fact, thus serving to accelerate Japan's progress toward the status of a major political power.

Second, changes in our nations' relative strength were exert-ing a subtle influence on the Japanese. Since China's reform and opening up, its economy had developed swiftly, with conspicu-ous achievements that had drawn global attention. Japan, by con-trast, had experienced the so-called lost decade of the 1990s. The economic strength of the two nations witnessed a historic change. Japan's GDP in 1990 was eight times that of China, but in 2006, that ratio was 1.65 times. It was the first time since Japan's Meiji Restoration of 1867 that there had been two powers in Asia. Meanwhile, there was a profound change in international status, that of Japan declining while China's was rising. The trend was in favor of China. In the opinion of some Japanese scholars and media, Japan was uncomfortable with this and not psychologically ready for such changes.

On the other hand, along with China's sustained economic growth and rise of its overall national strength, Japan was also benefiting. Japan's ruling group and elite were coming to accept this reality and realized that only by stabilizing and improving Japan's relations with China, and by seeking rational coexistence and coordinated cooperation with China, could Japan's interests be better safeguarded. By the end of our tussles with Koizumi, such ideas prevailed in Japan.

China Endeavors to Turn the Situation Around

THE POLITICAL DEADLOCK IN bilateral relations was always of concern to the central leadership. President Hu Jintao spoke to me on the topic as early as February 2005.

Describing Sino-Japanese relations as standing at a crossroad, and Japan as an important neighbor and economic and trade partner of China, he said we should perceive, from a strategic height, the importance of stabilizing our relations.

"You can't clap with one hand," he said. "China's efforts alone will not be effective in achieving the stable development of bilateral relations. We need to get the Japanese to act."

In March, Premier Wen Jiabao, at the press conference at the end of the annual National People's Congress and the Chinese People's Political Consultative Conference, set out the three principles governing China-Japan relations: taking history as a mirror and looking forward, adherence to the one-China principle, and strengthening cooperation for common development.

He also made three concrete proposals: joint efforts to create the necessary conditions for exchange of high-level visits, both sides' foreign ministries to start strategic studies on strengthening China-Japan friendship, and proper handling of the problems left over from history.

To implement these instructions, I several times summoned ministry staff to my office to study our next moves. The meetings often ran late into the night.

It was a critical moment, and a most difficult period in Sino-Japanese relations. Decades of contact with Japan told me we should take the long-term view in handling bilateral ties, and not feel elated or dismayed at any individual event. Rather, we should firmly uphold the national interest, maintain a sense of proportion, and not lose confidence in face of periodic difficulties. The end of Koizumi's term in September 2006 would provide an objective opportunity for improving bilateral relations. While continuing our tussles with him, we should concentrate our efforts on Japanese in other walks of life, and create conditions conducive to improved relations by means of economic, cultural, and nongovernmental contacts and exchanges.

While China was doing its part, Japanese society also showed a strong desire to improve the status quo.

In Japan there were numerous organizations promoting friendship with China. The seven major ones were: Japan-China Friendship Association, Japan-China Association for the Promotion of International Trade, Japan-China Cultural Exchange Association, Japan-China Economic Association, Japan-China Friendship Parliamentary Union, Japan-China Association, and Japan-China Friendship Center. They were the pillars in building nongovernmental friendship, and had done concrete work in promoting the normalization of diplomatic ties, the signing of the China-Japan Treaty of Peace and Friendship, and increasing bilateral exchanges and cooperation in various fields.

We suggested that the China-Japan Friendship Association should invite the leaders of these seven organizations to China, where President Hu would meet them and elaborate on China's views on bilateral relations and policies toward Japan, thus paving the way for a break in the political deadlock.

On March 30, 2006, a delegation composed of members of the seven Japanese organizations visited China. Headed by Ryutaro Hashimoto, a former prime minister and president of the Japan-China Association for the Promotion of International Trade, the visit was the subject of great attention in both countries.

On March 31, President Hu Jintao received the heads of these seven organizations: Ryutaro Hashimoto, Masahiko Komura, Ikuo Hirayama, Takashi Tsujii, Takeshi Noda, Yoshiro Hayashi, and Akira Chihaya.

Hu said that the difficult situation in bilateral relations in recent years had become a matter of concern to the Chinese people and to the world at large. This, he said, was not what China wanted to see. To be candid, the responsibility did not lie with China, nor with the Japanese people, but with the insistence of certain Japanese leaders on visiting the Yasukuni Shrine where Class-A war criminals were enshrined. Their behavior had offended the peoples of the victim countries, including the Chinese, and had harmed the political basis of China-Japan relations.

He continued, "I have reiterated that we should take a highly responsible attitude towards history, the people, and the future in handling the problems that have emerged in our bilateral relations. Being responsible to history means respecting the facts and drawing lessons from it so as to prevent the recurrence of historical tragedy. Being responsible to the people means always taking the friendship of the two peoples and their tangible benefits as the starting point and end result for developing bilateral ties. Being responsible to the future means seeking peaceful coexistence, lasting friendship, good-neighborly relations, and mutually beneficial cooperation."

The Chinese government had maintained a clear, consistent, and firm stance in its relations with Japan, he continued. It would always treat the relationship from a strategic height and long-term perspective, and seek peaceful coexistence, friendship over the generations, mutually beneficial cooperation, and common development. It would abide by the principles set in the three political documents signed by the two countries, properly handle the existing problems, and maintain the momentum of friendship. It would adhere firmly to the principle of "friendship and partnership with neighboring countries," actively promote exchanges and cooperation in extensive fields, and enhance the friendly sentiments of the two peoples.

President Hu's concluding words were emphatic. "Provided the Japanese leaders make a definite decision to stop visiting the Yasukuni Shrine where the Class-A war criminals are enshrined, I will be ready to hold talks and dialogues with them on improving and developing bilateral relations."

I could see that the Japanese guests were touched by these remarks. At the banquet I arranged for them at the Diaoyutai State Guesthouse that night, Ryutaro Hashimoto commented to me that President Hu's speech had been rich in content and profound in meaning and had made clear the direction both sides should take.

President Hu's closing remarks were significant. At that time, leadership-level contacts had been completely suspended. He took the opportunity to deliver a message to the Japanese leaders and people that upon the resolution of the Yasukuni Shrine issue, meetings between leaders could be resumed. This demonstrated the sincerity of China's top leader regarding bilateral relations. It also put an end to delusions harbored in some Japanese quarters about the Yasukuni Shrine issue.

The Japanese media gave the meeting wide coverage, highlighting President Hu's remarks on bilateral relations, and running such headlines as "Talks to be Resumed Once Shrine Visits Stop." Edi-

Tang holding a banquet for the leaders of seven Japanese organizations at the Diaoyutai State Guesthouse, Beijing, March 31, 2006.

torials recognized that China was looking to post-Koizumi leaders with its explicit information on the Yasukuni Shrine issue, that China was looking towards Japan's general public, and had a strong desire for improved relations.

To make the best of the opportunity and help the Japanese public better understand President Hu's remarks, I met with Tsutomu Takebe, visiting LDP secretary general, on May 1, 2006.

I explained to him my understanding of President Hu's remarks in four areas.

One, the Chinese government not only saw Sino-Japanese relations as important, but perceived and handled the relationship from a strategic and long-term perspective. It would make unremitting efforts to end the abnormal political situation as soon as possible and get it back onto the track of sound and steady development.

Two, the Chinese would further strengthen friendly exchanges and mutually beneficial cooperation in all sectors, improve and consolidate the friendship of the two peoples, and deepen their understanding and trust of each other.

Three, President Hu had pointed out the causes and symptoms of the current difficult situation, suggested effective countermeasures, and mapped out the development direction and prospects.

Four, China would continue to firmly follow the path of peaceful development, and China's development would only bring about new development opportunities to the world including Japan, rather than any threat.

Regarding historical issues, President Hu pointed out two differentiations. One was to differentiate between ordinary soldiers who were forced to the battlefields and the handful of militarists who had plotted, launched, and commanded the wars of aggression that had brought untold suffering and catastrophe to the Chinese people as well as the Japanese people; the other was to differentiate between the bereaved who visited Yasukuni to commemorate and worship their dead relatives and the state leaders who visited the place where the Class-A war criminals were enshrined.

By responsibility, President Hu meant that, as a state leader, one should be more mindful of the impact and consequences of one's actions rather than arguing for one's own personal sentiments, and must accept corresponding responsibility in political, social, and international spheres.

I told Tsutomu Takebe that we hoped Japanese society could fully understand the sincerity and goodwill implied in Hu's remarks and do more to turn bilateral relations in a better direction.

He replied that he was impressed by Hu Jintao's positive attitude and firm determination to advance bilateral relations. He agreed that both sides should strictly abide by the spirit of the three political documents signed by the two countries. He further summarized President Hu's message into one line: mutual understanding and mutual accommodation from both sides. Japan and China should have frank and sincere dialogue on the basis of a correct understanding of their disputes. This was very important, he said.

As the result of our efforts, the majority of Japanese politicians and media expressed agreement with President Hu's remarks, and in particular their understanding of China's resolute opposition to Japanese leaders visiting the Yasukuni Shrine.

Preparing for the Post-Koizumi Era

POLITICAL RELATIONS WITH PRIME Minister Koizimu had reached their nadir, but our two countries had become closely intertwined through long-term economic and trade cooperation. In 2004, China had become Japan's biggest trading partner. Furthermore, close cultural connections and deep-rooted friendship at a nongovernmental level served as important conditions for the development of bilateral relations. In early 2006, China's central leadership set the guidelines of promoting political and official contacts through economic, cultural, and nongovernmental contacts, with a view to ameliorating bilateral relations without delay once Koizumi left office.

In conformity with these guidelines, we put a lot of work into expanding and pioneering exchanges in various fields.

We actively supported bilateral economic and trade cooperation. In March 2006, the China–Japan Finance Ministers' Dialogue framework was initiated. In May, the first China–Japan Energy Saving and Environmental Protection Forum was held in Tokyo. In September, when receiving the Japan–China Economic Association delegation, Premier Wen Jiabao reiterated that China valued bilateral economic and trade relations, and hoped to expand the fields of cooperation.

In 2006, we also put in a major effort into promoting cultural exchanges to strengthen people-to-people friendship. The China Cultural Festival held in Japan increased understanding of Chinese culture there. Close contacts between Chinese and Japanese media created a favorable environment for objective, friendly debate.

Bilateral exchanges went on between legislative bodies and political parties. Direct contacts with Japanese politicians reduced strategic suspicions and increased mutual trust. A youth exchange system was established to organize visits between senior high school students from each country.

Facts clearly proved the effectiveness of these measures in creating the right conditions for improved bilateral relations in the post-Koizumi era.

New Leader, New Hope

THANKS TO CONSTANT WORK on our part and to the efforts of friendly Japanese, favorable conditions were created for breaking the standoff in the political situation. The upcoming change of Japanese leadership in September also offered an important opportunity for resolving the Yasukuni Shrine issue and for improving bilateral relations. Both sides were looking forward to this moment as the turning point.

Before Koizumi stepped down, it seemed virtually certain that Chief Cabinet Secretary Shinzo Abe would succeed him as Japan's new prime minister.

Abe came from a family of politicians. His maternal grandfather, Nobusuke Kishi, and paternal grandfather, Eisaku Sato, had each been prime minister, and his father, Shintaro Abe, had been LDP secretary general and foreign minister. Shintaro Abe, sincere in character, had enjoyed wide support among the LDP and had been regarded as the best candidate to succeed Prime Minister Noboru Takeshita. His sudden death caused LDP members and the electorate to transfer their love and sympathy to his son Shinzo. In 1993, the thirty-eight-year-old Shinzo Abe took over his father's constituency and was elected to the House of Representatives. Thus began his political career as prince of the LDP.

The good-looking Abe was once honored for his graceful dress by a Japanese men's fashion association. Eloquent and, like his father, good at coordinating and listening to others, he maintained wide contacts with all sectors of life. He paid attention to his public image, and was good at using television, the Internet, and other modern media to spread his ideas.

Around that time, Abe had repeatedly stressed the importance of Japan's relations with China, promising to maintain both political and economic contacts, and to bring bilateral relations to a new level.

On August 3, 2006, Abe attended the second Beijing-Tokyo Forum held in Tokyo and stated that China's economic growth posed no threat to Japan but offered opportunities, that the relationship with China was one of Japan's most important bilateral relationships, and that the two should not let political issues impair their economic ties.

One anecdote concerning Abe's goodwill message to China illustrates this attitude. September 2 was the first day of the LDP presidential election. That evening, his wife hosted a dinner in Tokyo for Lin Liyun, visiting vice president of China International Culture Exchange Center. Ms. Lin had invited Ms. Abe to a Peking Opera performance the year before during her visit to China.

During the dinner, Abe suddenly appeared and went to greet Ms. Lin. Seeing the prime-minister-in-waiting, the congressmen present cried "Long Live Abe!" but Abe corrected them, saying "Long Live Japan-China Friendship!"

Abe knew that bilateral ties could not be resumed unless the Yasukuni Shrine issue was resolved. So, before and after taking office, he promised that he would follow the 1995 speech by Tomiichi Murayama on historical issues, acknowledge the harm Japan had inflicted on its Asian neighbors, and work to improve Japan-China relations. He also proposed a visit to China at the earliest possible date after taking office.

Strategic dialogues constituted the main diplomatic channel for bilateral discussions on how to solve the Yasukuni Shrine issue. Both sides were in favor of holding one such dialogue to clear the political obstacles and change bilateral relations for the better. However, they differed regarding the conditions under which relations might be improved.

During the LDP presidential election, the Japanese side proposed September 22–23 for the sixth round of strategic dialogues to be held in Tokyo.

The timing—right after the LDP presidential election and before the prime ministerial election—was a deliberate choice, one that made apparent their wish to reach consensus with China on the improvement of bilateral ties before the new prime minister took office, and thus prepare the ground for his smooth administration.

On September 20, Abe was elected president of the LDP.

On September 22, Vice Foreign Minister Dai Bingguo went to Japan for the sixth round of strategic dialogues to be held with his Japanese counterpart Shotaro Yachi.

We had had several strategic dialogues in the past, but none to compare with the significance of this one. Besides the intensity of the daily negotiations, the psychological trial of strength was the toughest. The Japanese proposals varied greatly, and the two sides broke up several times.

Since ancient times, diplomatic negotiations were, so to speak, wars without gunpowder. To a certain extent, diplomats can be compared to military generals. They are sent to defend the national interests, but armed only with words, or perhaps one sheet of paper, to decide a country's fate. In other words, diplomatic negotiations are a contest of mentality, wisdom, resourcefulness, and tenacity.

After much wrangling, Dai Bingguo fulfilled his mission in the end. The two sides reached agreement on overcoming the political obstacles for healthy development of bilateral friendly cooperation.

On this proviso, we agreed on Prime Minister Abe's formal visit to China on October 8 and 9, 2006.

Abe's Ice-Breaking Visit

AT MIDDAY ON OCTOBER 8, Abe's special airplane arrived at Beijing's Capital Airport, thus beginning the first visit to China by a Japanese prime minister after five years of deadlock in bilateral relations. It attracted wide global interest. Long before the plane landed, reporters from the world's media had gathered at the airport to await the historic moment.

It rained all morning, not stopping until noon, when the skies started to clear. We were all relieved that the welcoming ceremony could be held outdoors.

At three o'clock, Premier Wen Jiabao held a welcome ceremony for Prime Minister Shinzo Abe outside the east entrance to the Great Hall of the People. The national flags of the two countries hung from the lamp poles around Tiananmen Square. In line with protocol, nineteen-gun salutes were fired. The two prime ministers reviewed the guard of honor while the national anthems of the two nations were played.

In line with protocol, I did not attend the ceremony. When I watched the scenes on television, I could not help recalling the past. Five years before, Koizumi's obstinate visit to the Yasukuni Shrine had seriously jeopardized the political basis of bilateral relations, so his visit to China had involved no ceremonial welcome and no gun salute. One other reason was that Koizumi's had been a working visit, not a formal one. Now the chilly years were over, Sino-Japanese relations were finally turning for the better, and the ceremonial welcome contributed to the historic significance of the occasion.

After the ceremony, formal talks were held between Premier Wen Jiabao and Prime Minister Abe in the Great Hall of the People.

On behalf of the Chinese government, Premier Wen first welcomed Mr. Abe and congratulated him on his election as prime minister. He described the two countries as neighbors "separated by a strip of water that a boat can cross." For well-known reasons, the previous five years had seen a suspension of visits by state leaders, and bilateral relations remained in an abnormal state. Thanks to concerted efforts, consensus had been reached on overcoming the political obstacles and promoting the stable and sound development of bilateral relations. This had led to Prime Minister Abe's visit and opened the window on improving such relations.

He quoted an ancient Chinese poem, "Unblocked by the green hills, the water flows on," to describe China-Japan friendship as keeping up with the trend of the times and serving the fundamental interests of the two peoples.

Prime Minister Abe said that his China visit had been settled on very quickly. He felt grateful for the considerate and hospitable arrangements China had made and for Premier Wen's welcome ceremony, especially given the tight schedule of Chinese senior leaders around the October 1 (National Day) and the Sixth Plenary Session of the 16th CPC Central Committee (October 8–11). He believed that Sino-Japanese relations would be like that day in Beijing, with the sun coming out once the rain had stopped.

He continued that the timing of his visit straight after taking office showed how both sides valued their relationship, and that the Japanese public and the international community were taking a keen interest in this visit. He would earnestly exchange views with Premier Wen on bilateral relations.

Looked at in a historical perspective, Sino-Japanese relations were at a crossroads, he said, and the attitudes of both sides would determine the direction of its development over the next century. It was a lofty mission and solemn duty for the leaders of the two countries to push bilateral relations to a higher stage and make constructive contributions to Asian and global peace, stability, and prosperity. Bilateral relations should not only be friendly, but mutually beneficial and based on common strategic interests. Therefore, both sides should keep the political and economic wheels turning, and take forward-looking bilateral relations to a higher level.

This was the first time that Japan had described its relationship with China as one of "mutual strategic benefit." It was a positive sign, one that manifested Japan's putting its relations with China on a strategic level, facing up to the realities of China's development, and valuing bilateral relations. Prior to the visit, diplomats of both sides had held close talks and reached consensus in this regard.

Regarding the historical issues that had attracted wide attention, Premier Wen said that to maintain long-term sound and stable development of Sino-Japanese relations, the two sides should properly settle the Yasukuni Shrine issue in line with their agreement, and remove the political obstacles that might affect bilateral ties. "We appreciate your decision to visit China soon after taking office as Japan's prime minister," he said. "This decision complies with Japan's own interests and will gain support from the two peoples and the international community as well. We sincerely hope and have confidence that your visit will be a historic one and help restore bilateral relations onto the track of normal development."

Abe replied that Japan would look humbly at history and continue to follow the road of peaceful development. Japan had brought tremendous disasters and sufferings to Asian people, and inflicted countless traumas on them. For this Japan felt deep remorse, and on this basis had chosen the path of development in the sixty years since the end of the war. The Japanese and he personally felt this way, something that would never change.

After a brief explanation of his previous visit to Yasukuni, he went on to say that since the shrine had become a diplomatic and political issue, he would not make public whether he had visited or would again visit the place. He would properly handle the case in line with the consensus on overcoming the political difficulties and promoting the sound development of bilateral ties.

These words indicated that Japan had taken a step forward concerning the historical issues. In the joint press communiqué issued later, the Japanese side agreed for the first time to include the words "face up to history and look forward to the future."

China was also very concerned about Japan's attitude toward the Taiwan issue. Abe said that Japan would continue to abide by the principles and spirit set in the three political documents between the two countries, and that it would not support "two Chinas," or "one China, one Taiwan," or "Taiwan independence."

During their talks, the discussions ranged widely over bilateral relations. Prime Minister Abe invited Premier Wen to visit Japan at an early date. It had not been an easy process to get the leaders of the two nations sitting down together and talking calmly about the future, given the suspension of such talks for more than a year.

Following the meeting between the two premiers, Chinese President Hu Jintao met with Abe, also at the Great Hall of the People. I was present and witnessed a friendly atmosphere that had not been seen for several years.

President Hu first welcomed Abe's visit to China. "Making China your first official visit after taking office shows the value you put on improving and developing relations with China. I've made positive comments on this," he said to Abe. "Yours is the first China visit by a Japanese prime minister in five years, and it marks a turn in our bilateral relations. I hope your visit will be a new starting point for us to improve our relations."

In reply, Abe said that his decision to visit, though sudden, had been warmly received by the Chinese side. His choice of China as the destination of his first official overseas trip had been a surprise both at home and abroad. The realization of the visit reflected the common will of the two countries in promoting bilateral relations.

He said the two nations were at a new starting point. At this critical juncture, the judgments made by their leaders, the success or otherwise in building mutual trust would affect the development of bilateral relations for the coming century. The two sides should look forward and push bilateral ties to new heights. This is of supreme importance for our two peoples, for the bright future of the younger generation, and for regional and global peace. It is also the common responsibility of the leaders of both sides.

President Hu said he shared his sentiments, also hoping for bright prospects in bilateral relations, like clear skies after rain. He pointed out that while bilateral ties had been deepening and expanding in the twenty-first century, difficulties had remained because of his predecessor's persistent visits to the Yasukuni Shrine where Japanese Class-A war criminals in WWII were enshrined. His actions had offended the peoples of China and other Asian victim countries, damaged the political basis of bilateral relations, led to the suspension of reciprocal visits between state leaders, and disturbed bilateral exchanges and cooperation in various sectors.

"This is not something we wanted," said Hu. "We put in great efforts to turn the situation around and bring bilateral ties back to the path of normal development. Unfortunately, it did not succeed. Since you came into office, you have showed serious regard for our concerns and taken positive measures to respond to China's efforts. We appreciate that highly."

Abe said that Japan attached great importance to the guidelines put forth by Hu (peaceful coexistence, friendship for generations, mutually beneficial cooperation, and common development). They embodied the strong wish of Chinese leaders to strengthen China-Japan friendship. Abe also made positive statements regarding the historical issues and Taiwan issue.

Abe invited President Hu to visit Japan in early 2007, and said he was looking forward to seeing Chinese leaders during the APEC meeting in November and at the 10+3 meeting in December.

Abe left Beijing the following morning to continue to South Korea. His trip to China had been short but fruitful, and welcomed by the two peoples and the international community. This "ice-breaking visit," as the media termed it, marked the initial breaking of the five-year-long political deadlock.

It was a win-win result. Japan shook off the heavy diplomatic burden left behind by Koizumi, and normalized its relations with neighboring countries. For China, it created conditions for stabilizing our good-neighborly relations and invigorating our diplomatic moves in northeast Asia.

Premier Wen's Ice-Melting Visit to Japan

ABE'S VISIT USHERED IN a new stage for bilateral relations. High-ranking visits were exchanged. President Hu met with Prime Minister Abe during the APEC summit, and Premier Wen also met with him during the 10+3 meeting. A succession of Japanese politicians visited China, the business world sought cooperative opportunities with China, in Japan understanding of and public opinion toward China improved, there was a new outlook in mutually beneficial cooperation, and bilateral relations showed signs of warming.

Abe's visit had broken five years of ice. But, as the saying goes, "It takes more than one cold day to freeze three feet of ice," and bilateral relations were still very fragile, like a convalescent after a severe illness.

To maintain good momentum, it was necessary to maintain high-level contacts and exchange of visits and to increase mutual trust. In early 2007, the two sides decided that Premier Wen's visit to Japan at the invitation of Prime Minister Abe would take place in April.

Mr. Abe attached great importance to the visit. He conveyed to

Premier Wen two letters with his signature expressing his anticipation of Wen's visit.

One of the letters was brought by Toshihiro Nikai, who had visited China at the invitation of the China-Japan Friendship Association.

Toshihiro Nikai was chairman of the LDP Diet Policy Committee. He had previously been minister of Economy, Trade and Industry, minister of Transportation, and director of the General Affairs Bureau. He was friendly toward China, and had visited China several times and been received by senior Chinese leaders.

Nikai and I were about the same age and had stayed in touch for years, since we were both devoted to bilateral friendship.

He arrived in Beijing on January 22, 2007, and I met with him when he delivered Abe's letter to Premier Wen.

In the letter, Abe expressed a sincere welcome for Premier Wen's upcoming visit to Japan, when they could exchange views

With Toshihiro Nikai in Zhongnanhai, Beijing, January 22, 2006.

on bilateral ties in celebration of the thirty-fifth anniversary of the normalization of diplomatic relations.

Premier Wen wrote back to say that he would join Prime Minister Abe in unremitting efforts for the long-term, healthy, and steady development of bilateral ties.

In February, Abe asked Yuya Niwa, another director of the General Affairs Bureau, to deliver a second letter to Premier Wen. This showed how highly Japan anticipated Wen's visit. The Japanese media also began running reports on the subject.

Premier Wen himself also set store by the visit. At the press conference following the annual NPC session in March, he told reporters, "If Prime Minister Abe's China visit can be described as an ice-breaker, I hope mine will be an ice-melter." He called it his most important visit as China's prime minister.

It would be the first visit to Japan by a Chinese leader after five years of deadlock in bilateral relations and also the first in seven years by a Chinese premier. The visit got wide attention in both countries and the world at large because of its far-reaching significance in maintaining the good momentum of bilateral relations, promoting exchanges and cooperation in all fields, and outlining the long-term development of international ties.

We started preparing for the visit from the beginning of the year, hoping it would produce the following results: In the political field, enrich mutually beneficial strategic relations and push forward bilateral ties; in economy, improve the cooperative mechanism, push bilateral economic and trade cooperation to a new high, and launch a high-level economic dialogue mechanism; in security, increase trust and reduce suspicion, and increase high-ranking military exchanges and contacts; and in the social field, on the occasion of the China-Japan Culture and Sports Year, further promote exchanges in youth, culture, and sports, and facilitate medium and long-term planning in this regard.

To ensure these results, we agreed on the following schedule with Japan: holding talks with Prime Minister Abe; meeting Emperor Akihito, the speaker of the House of Representatives, the president of the House of Councilors, and leaders of various political parties; attending welcome banquets from the business world and friendly organizations; and making a speech to the Diet.

To create a good atmosphere for the visit, a week before leaving, Premier Wen gave an interview to the Japanese press corps in China.

He told the Japanese reporters that he expected to reach consensus with Japanese leaders and increase mutual trust on several major issues vital to the development of bilateral relations, that he expected to learn more about Japan's latest developments, and do his part to promote bilateral friendship, and that he expected his visit to be a successful ice-melter.

His speech to the Diet was the highlight of his trip. He took it seriously, and did a lot of homework for it. While spending the Spring Festival in Liaoning Province, he had learned from the locals that not long after WWII, the Chinese had helped 1.05 million Japanese expatriates to return home via Liaoning's Huludao Port. Back in Beijing, the premier had asked the Foreign Ministry to supply the relevant historical records. Their inclusion in his speech won a positive response from the Japanese.

On that day, about 480 people, including Prime Minister Abe and other cabinet members, were present to hear his address. Japan Broadcasting Corporation (NHK) and China Central Television broadcast it live. Entitled "For Friendship and Cooperation," Wen's speech centered on the theme of "drawing lessons from history and looking forward to the future." It listed many persuasive facts, recalled and summarized bilateral contacts in history, and elaborated on China's principle and stance regarding bilateral relations, especially certain historical issues. Wen also outlined his vision for bilateral relations.

The Japanese public hailed the speech. As Prime Minister Abe put it, the speech "can be written in history," and in the words of Chikage Oogi, president of the House of Councilors, "the ice between Japan and China has melted today at the Diet."

Besides formal talks and political meetings, the premier also visited Japanese farmers, college students, and a teahouse to have close contact with the general public and increase mutual understanding and trust.

His appearance at Ritsumeikan University baseball stadium attracted great attention. The initial plan was a talk with the students, but Premier Wen said how much he had loved baseball when he was young, and that he'd like to join the students in the game that enjoyed great popularity in Japan. When selecting a jersey for him, a young Foreign Ministry functionary suggested number thirty-five to mark the thirty-fifth anniversary of bilateral diplomatic relations. It proved a clever decision.

The game and other anecdotes from the premier's Japan trip were later included in an illustrated book, *Wen Jiabao, Pitcher No. 35,* published by the Duan Press.

On the afternoon of April 13, the premier visited Yoshikazu Nagahama, a Kyoto farmer, and joined his host in planting tomato seedlings in the fields. When interviewed, Nagahama said, "Premier Wen is an amiable chap. He knows a lot about farming. I feel he's just one of us."

Later, Nagahama wrote to Wen that the tomatoes they had planted together had thrived and were bearing fruit. The premier wrote a warm reply, and Nagahama and his family were invited to China to attend the reception in September celebrating the thirty-fifth anniversary of the normalization of relations.

Premier Wen's Japan trip, though only fifty-two hours long, was quite productive and successful. It maintained the momentum of improvement in bilateral relations.

Fukuda Becomes Prime Minister

FOLLOWING PREMIER WEN'S VISIT to Japan, bilateral exchanges and cooperation in various fields continued. The improvement and progress in Sino-Japanese relations was the highlight of Abe's short administration.

Abe had conspicuous achievements in foreign relations, but not in domestic affairs, where he became mired in difficulties. Public support to the Abe cabinet dropped to 30 percent at one point.

At midday on September 12, 2007, Abe resigned, citing health reasons.

His resignation triggered an election contest within the LDP, and on September 23, Yasuo Fukuda was elected party president, taking office two days later as Japan's prime minister.

I had known him for years. Two years older than I, he had grown up in a political family. When his father, Takeo Fukuda, was prime minister, he worked with China's Vice Premier Deng Xiaoping to conclude the China-Japan Treaty of Peace and Friendship.

Yasuo Fukuda rose swiftly on the political ladder. He became chief cabinet secretary in the cabinet of Yoshiro Mori in 2000, and continued in post in the Koizumi cabinet, where he demonstrated excellent political balance and coordination. He was the longest-serving chief cabinet secretary of the postwar era.

Fukuda valued Japan's relations with China, and played a positive role in time of difficulties. He had a profound awareness of the historical issues. He explicitly supported Tomiichi Murayama's speech, and promised not to visit the Yasukuni Shrine during his term as prime minister.

On September 23, Premier Wen sent Fukuda a congratulatory message on his election as prime minister of Japan. Four days after Fukuda took office, Premier Wen talked to him on the phone by previous arrangement. This was the first telephone conversation between the leaders of the two countries.

Fukuda told Wen that Japan's relationship with China was one of Japan's most important bilateral ties and that Japan valued it highly. He would work further to strengthen mutually beneficial strategic relations and reinforce bilateral cooperation on the basis of the consensus reached so far.

Premier Wen said that over the past year, the two countries had resumed frequent contacts and exchanges, reached important consensus regarding the proper settlement of the sensitive historical issues and the Taiwan issue, established China-Japan strategic relations of mutual benefit, and realized the broad objective of "peaceful coexistence, generation-long friendship, mutually beneficial cooperation, and common development." Bilateral ties had seen an important change for the better. Because the current situation had been hard earned it should be cherished all the more. "Based on these fruits, I will make joint efforts with you to maintain and consolidate the momentum of improvement and development so as to push bilateral relations forward."

Fukuda expressed his wish to visit China within the year so that he could have an in-depth exchange of views with Premier Wen face-to-face.

Premier Wen invited him to visit China at a convenient time, since contacts between the state leaders were important for increasing mutual understanding and friendly cooperation.

Later, Fukuda's China visit was set for December 27 to 30, 2007.

Prior to his visit, Prime Minister Fukuda was interviewed at his residence by Xinhua News Agency and other Chinese media. He told them he would exchange detailed ideas with Chinese leaders on building strategic relations of mutual benefit, so as to hasten the improvement since autumn 2006, and bring bilateral relations to new heights.

Fukuda Arrives for a Spring-Greeting Visit

AT NOON ON DECEMBER 27, Fukuda arrived in Beijing, accompanied by his wife. He called it a "spring-greeting" visit.

We devoted a great deal of thought as to how to receive the new prime minister. Given his family's close connections with China, we treated him as an old friend and arranged high-level receptions, including a small banquet hosted by President Hu Jintao.

When Fukuda's father visited China in 1981, he left a calligraphic inscription, "Japan-China friendship contributes to world peace," to Xingqing Park in the ancient city of Xi'an. We made a replica of this calligraphic work. When Premier Wen presented it after the luncheon, Fukuda was surprised and delighted at such a considerate gift and thanked his host repeatedly.

The Japanese are sensitive to subtle details, and they immediately noticed our careful arrangements. Their media all highlighted

Japan's Prime Minister Yasuo Fukuda speaking at Peking University during his formal visit to China, December 28, 2007.

the warm treatment from China, describing many of the arrangements as unprecedented.

On the morning of December 28, the two premiers held a talk in a cordial atmosphere. Fukuda began by saying that he would take this opportunity for a thorough exchange of views with Premier Wen on bilateral relations—a heart-to-heart, so to speak—with a view to making 2008 a year in which bilateral relations could leap forward.

During their talk, Fukuda was the first to bring up the historical issues. "The more difficult our history is to look back on, the more important it is to face it up. Passing on this knowledge to the next generation is the responsibility of our generation. Only on this basis can we avoid any recurrence of our past mistakes," he said. "Japan will continue to follow the road of a peaceful country, and on this basis to build a relationship with China that is oriented toward the future."

In the afternoon, I accompanied Fukuda to Peking University, my alma mater, where he delivered a speech entitled "Join Hands to Create Our Future."

It was an outstanding speech imbued with traditional Chinese culture.

He started with an amusing play on words, saying, "As the New Year is around the corner, Fukuda has come with fortune." Applause and laughter rang through the auditorium at this witty remark— the Japanese name Fukuda contains a character "Fu," meaning fortune.

He quoted several familiar Chinese sayings. When stressing the desirability of reciprocal sincerity, deeper mutual understanding, recognition of differences, and getting a true picture of the other, he quoted the Confucius saying, "Say you know when you know and you don't when you don't know; that is knowledge." Recommending that both sides look fifty or even one hundred years ahead in order to build a long-term stable bilateral relationship, and train personnel capable of deepening mutual understanding, respecting differences and learning from each other, Fukuda quoted the Chinese proverb "It takes ten years to grow a tree, but one hundred years to cultivate a man" to describe the long time needed to bring up people of talent.

He also put forth some ideas on developing bilateral relations. "There is no alternative but peace and friendship for our bilateral relations," he reiterated. This notion under the Japan–China Treaty of Peace and Friendship had transcended time and space as the cornerstone of friendship between the two nations. On the historical issues, he said, "Only if we face up to the history with the courage and wisdom to examine wherever self-examination is needed, can we anticipate that such mistakes will not happen again in the future." He named four concepts as the pillars for developing mutually beneficial strategic relations: beneficial cooperation, international contribution, understanding, and trust.

That evening, President Hu Jintao held a small banquet for Fukuda at the Yangyuan Studio in the Diaoyutai State Guesthouse. I was present at the dinner, where the atmosphere was relaxed.

The conversation was wide ranging: from the craze in Japan for the *Analects of Confucius* to the juvenile education of the from individual interests to China's development. I was impressed when Fukuda said that it would not be good news for Japan if China met setbacks in its development, because, in a sense, our destinies were indivisible.

Fukuda invited President Hu to visit Japan in spring, at cherry blossom time. "It's getting harder to predict when exactly the cherry will blossom, but once President Hu sets the date of his visit it will surely relax and start flowering," he said. His humor made everyone laugh. President Hu replied that he too would look forward to a visit in spring.

The Japanese media ran constant reports about Fukuda's spring-greeting trip to China, describing it as a successful start for Fukuda's

China diplomacy, which marked a new stage and a welcome spring in political relations. The political parties also commended the positive outcome of his visit.

Meditation on the Tokyo-Bound Flight

AT JAPAN'S REPEATED INVITATION, President Hu decided to pay a state visit to Japan in the spring of 2008, the first such visit in a decade by a Chinese head of state. It was also the first official visit by a Chinese president since the 17th National Congress of the Communist Party of China in 2007. It was a significant diplomatic event at a time of global complexity and a vital moment in the improving and developing bilateral relationship. I visited Japan in advance of the visit to make political preparations. Japan was the last country on an itinerary involving the United Kingdom and the Republic of Korea, where, as President Hu's special envoy, I attended the inauguration of President Lee Myung-bak. It was my last official overseas visit as a state councilor.

On the night of February 19, I left London for Tokyo on board a Japanese plane. During the flight, I recalled my contacts with Japan more than forty years earlier, when Japan had been the destination of my first visit abroad. That was in 1964, when I accompanied a Ministry of Agriculture delegation to study Japan's farming science and technology. Over the years, I had worked two terms in the Chinese embassy in Japan, for a total of nine and a half years. I had also engaged in nongovernmental contacts and done much important work as executive of the China-Japan Friendship Association, and had witnessed the resumption, improvement, and development of bilateral relations.

From years of working with Japan I was keenly aware that the good results and current situation in Sino-Japanese relations had not come easily. After New China was founded in 1949, the toil and sweat of the older generation of Chinese leaders and their historic contributions had laid a solid foundation for bilateral relations. Since the normalization of diplomatic ties in 1972, notable progress had been achieved in bilateral contacts in various fields, thanks to the efforts of insightful persons from both sides.

There was no denying the sensitive and unique nature of the relationship between our two countries, given the historical traumas and current conflicts. However, we had to be conscious that bilateral friendly contacts over the previous two thousand years had already laid a deep foundation among the people, and that this always played a positive role at difficult times when bilateral relations ran into trouble. At such times, it was always those friendly people who made unremitting endeavors and played a significant role in turning the situation around. Historical pains and gains had taught us that the only choice for our two countries was to embark on the road of peace, friendship, cooperation, and mutual benefit.

In practical terms, the development of friendly cooperation serves the interests of both China and Japan. As the world's largest developing country and the second-largest economy, respectively, we each had our own highly complementary strengths. We shared interests in maintaining peace and stability in northeast Asia, promoting East Asian regional cooperation, cooperating on such global issues as energy security, environmental protection, and climate change, as well as combating terrorism and transnational crimes, and preventing the proliferation of weapons of mass destruction. Joint efforts were needed to safeguard common interests.

In terms of the global situation, the international balance of power was in the process of change, and the global situation and systems were facing a new cycle of readjustment. Asia had entered an era of overall rejuvenation. It became a historical task shared by China and Japan as to how to safeguard peace, promote development, and greet the new era together with other Asian members. We both bore important responsibilities and had to strengthen dialogue, coordination, and cooperation.

Thanks to the ice-breaking, ice-melting, and spring-greeting trips by our national leaders, relations between China and Japan had reached a new, historic starting point with an important opportunity for further development. With the removal of the political obstacles that had troubled us for so many years, bilateral relations had climbed out of the low ebb, gotten back to normal, and started to build strategic partnership of mutual benefit.

Under such circumstances, President Hu's state visit to Japan was highly significant as a comprehensive embodiment of the progress of our bilateral relations since the normalization of ties, particularly in recent years, significant too regarding creating a new strategic relationship of mutual benefit.

These thoughts made me feel the heavy responsibility of my visit to Japan.

My Last Official Mission

ON THE AFTERNOON OF February 20, 2008, I arrived at Tokyo's Narita Airport and began my formal visit to Japan.

My task was to work with my Japanese counterparts on the contents of the fourth political document to be released by our two countries. The three previous political documents had acted as the cornerstone of Sino-Japanese relations, summarizing the past relationship in terms of politics, law, and historical facts, and outlining the future of bilateral relations.

Over the last decade, both China and Japan had experienced great changes, and bilateral relations had undergone unprecedented ups and downs. We thought it necessary to release a joint document

With Prime Minister Yasuo Fukuda at his residence in Tokyo, February 21, 2008.

during the course of the presidential visit. The document would mark a new starting point, a new consensus, lay out the new prospects for cooperation, and clearly point out the new direction of bilateral relations.

The visit gave me the opportunity to work with Prime Minister Fukuda himself.

On the afternoon of February 21, I went to the prime ministerial residence where we exchanged views on President Hu's forthcoming visit. I said that the visit would be an important opportunity for both countries and that ensuring its success would truly move bilateral relations onto a long-term, stable, development track in the real sense.

Fukuda agreed, saying that he also wished it to prove a total success and an important milestone in bilateral relations.

I told him our view, based on thorough study, that the two sides should give serious consideration to issuing a new document at the right time. Its theme would be to look forward and create a future for bilateral relations, especially in the field of cooperation, so that our two peoples could be inspired by the bright prospects mapped out in the document.

"Thirty years ago, Mr. Deng Xiaoping and your father together made a political decision to sign the China–Japan Treaty of Peace and Friendship," I said. "Just as you said at Peking University, this treaty acted as an iron bridge between our two countries. We hope you will make your decision and sign a new document as a new bridge leading to the future. Our respective diplomatic staffs are in contact about this. We hope that the new document could come to represent a shared asset of our two peoples."

Fukuda replied that Japan had begun preparations to receive President Hu, and would heed Chinese suggestions and requirements. He would pay close attention to progress regarding the fourth political document, and provided both sides made concerted efforts, he was confident they would produce a very good document.

During my stay in Japan, I met with House of Representatives

With Japan's Foreign Minister Masahiko Komura, February 21, 2008.

Speaker Yohei Kono, House of Councilors President Satsuki Eda, Foreign Minister Masahiko Komura, and leaders of political parties, and exchanged views on President Hu's visit, bilateral economic and trade cooperation, East Asia regional cooperation, and other international issues. I also attended a welcome breakfast hosted by Japan Business Federation President Fujio Mitarai. From them I learned that Japanese society was earnestly anticipating President Hu's visit, and would greet him with summer warmth.

On my second day, China's Ambassador Cui Tiankai held a luncheon in my honor at Tokyo's New Otani Hotel, where many friendly personages were present.

Over the past forty years or so, I had made numerous Japanese friends across a wide spectrum. They included prime ministers, Diet heads, political party leaders and executives, entrepreneurs, writers, performers, lawyers, professors, reporters, religious people, and corporation staff.

Addressing the reception held in the author's honor by China's Ambassador Cui Tiankai at the New Otani Hotel, Tokyo, February 21, 2008.

There were more than six hundred people there, many of whom had made a special journey to the reception. I was touched by their friendliness.

When addressing the gathering, I recalled, in Japanese, my close connection with Japan and my experience of significant events in bilateral relations. Referring to the Chinese adage "the past has vanished like smoke," I told them that for me, the past had not vanished, but remained fresh in my memory. Over the years, we had been delighted by progress in our friendship and concerned over setbacks. We had made painstaking efforts for healthy and stable development and formed profound friendships.

The year 2008 marked the thirtieth anniversary of the signing of the China-Japan Treaty of Peace and Friendship. In my speech, I recalled the considerable progress over the past thirty years and said from the bottom of my heart that the current good situation and progress in bilateral relations had been hard won, and should be valued and cherished. This was the duty of both sides. Bilateral friendship was the will of the people and an unstoppable historical trend. We should never waver from this conviction. The development of friendly, cooperative relations served the interests of both China and Japan, and was conducive to regional and global peace and development. These things I had come to understand during the course of thirty years since the normalization of diplomatic ties.

I also told my old friends that my main mission this time was to have an in-depth exchange of views with the Japanese side on how to develop a forward-looking strategic relationship of mutual benefit, and to prepare the political ground for President Hu's imminent visit. We expected that during his visit the two sides would together map out the blueprint for bilateral relations and establish a new framework for the long-term sound and stable development of a mutually beneficial strategic relationship.

At a reception held on September 28, 1997, to mark the twenty-fifth anniversary of the normalization of Sino-Japanese diplomatic relations. Left to right: Mrs. Etuko Minamimura, whose husband did much for bilateral friendship; the author; former NPC Standing Committee Vice Chairman Huang Hua; Mr. Masao Shimizu.

While in Tokyo, I visited the family of Masao Shimizu and the Matsuyama Ballet Company, which had made a notable contribution to bilateral friendship.

Masao Shimizu was director of the Matsuyama Ballet Company, and his wife, Mikiko Matsuyama, had been a celebrated ballerina and teacher. In 1948, they founded the Matsuyama Ballet troupe and an affiliated ballet school, which had nurtured their son Tetsutaro Shimizu and his wife, Yoko Morishita, both internationally renowned ballet dancers.

My friendship with the family stretched back more than forty years. We had stayed in touch.

The Shimizu family and the ballet company gave me a warm welcome. More than one hundred dancers in costume lined up at the entrance to the company and greeted me in Chinese. Despite the cold of early spring outside, I felt warm at heart.

I quickly walked forward and shook hands with Masao Shimizu. Several years had passed since last we met, and I was moved by the passage of time shown by the wrinkles etched on his face.

In 1958, Masao Shimizu and his wife, then both in their prime, had brought to China their ballet version of the popular Chinese revolutionary opera *The White-Haired Girl*. Theirs was the first ballet adaptation of the opera. Having performed in many places across Japan, they were warmly received by audiences in Beijing, Chongqing, Wuhan, and Shanghai.

Since then, the company had visited China several times and Shimizu himself had made over a hundred trips to China as leader of the Japan–China Friendship Association, and had been received by Chinese leaders Mao Zedong, Zhou Enlai, Deng Xiaoping, and Jiang Zemin.

Masao Shimizu was a witness to and active promoter of bilateral friendship and cultural exchange. Four decades had passed without any letup in his efforts.

In the reception room, his son Tetsutaro delivered a speech of welcome on behalf of the family. He said that the ballet company had, since 1955, enjoyed friendship with several generations of Chinese leaders and had done its part in artistic exchanges with China. "Your visit today will greatly encourage Japanese people who are friendly toward China," he said to me.

Then I was invited upstairs to the rehearsal hall to watch a documentary on the company's contacts with China. The dancers also performed the ballet *Ode to the Yellow River*, choreographed to the music of Xian Xinghai, a famous Chinese composer. It was indeed a feast for the eyes and ears.

Afterward, I went up to the stage to shake hands with and thank the performers. I recalled to the young dancers the Matsuyama Ballet's close links with China, and told them the Chinese

Presenting a gift to Masao Shimizu, together with China's Ambassador Cui Tiankai (1st L) and Vice Foreign Minister Wu Dawei (1st R), February 20, 2008.

people would never forget these old friends. Many of them were moved to tears.

Sadly, four months thereafter, Masao Shimizu passed away, and this meeting was our last. But, while his state of health still allowed, this old man, in his late eighties, took his company to the Chinese embassy to express condolences and make donations for the victims of the Sichuan earthquake of May 12, 2008.

After Tokyo, I went on to Nara and Osaka. In Nara, I visited the Horyu-ji and the Toshodai-ji temples. The former, Nara's first UNESCO World Heritage site, was built at the decree of Prince Shotoku, who dispatched envoys to China's Tang Dynasty, following the introduction of Buddhism from China. The Toshodai-ji was built in 759 by the Chinese monk Jianzhen, and was a symbol of cultural exchange between the two countries.

Addressing the welcome reception, the Nara governor Shogo

Visiting the Toshodai-ji Temple in Nara, February 23, 2008.

Arai remarked, "Mr. Tang looks jolly, just like the Laughing Buddha." At this, the guests all burst out laughing.

I replied in Japanese, "You're flattering me. As a matter of fact, all Chinese diplomats have an affable smile, because we pursue peace diplomacy, harmony diplomacy, and smile diplomacy." My words were warmly applauded in the banquet hall.

Back in Beijing, I immediately held a meeting of the departments concerned.

Based on my talks in Japan, I analyzed the situation and problems in bilateral relations, arranged for the preparations for President Hu's visit, and demanded that everyone should work earnestly to make the visit a success.

In March 2008, during the 11th National People's Congress, I retired from the State Council.

I was pleased that I had fulfilled an important diplomatic mission before stepping down, playing a humble part in ensuring a successful state visit, and in the continued improvement and development of Sino-Japanese relations.

The Warm-Spring Visit by Hu Jintao

PRESIDENT HU JINTAO PAID a five-day state visit to Japan from May 6 to 10, 2008. It was his first official visit as president to a single country.

The trip, known as the "warm-spring visit," was a great success. Several highlights impressed me.

The trip was extremely productive politically. In terms of increasing mutual trust, consolidating friendship, deepening cooperation, and planning the future, President Hu made extensive contacts with the Japanese government and people from of all walks of life, and achieved positive results.

The two sides issued the Joint Statement on Pushing Forward the Strategic and Mutually Beneficial Relations between China and Japan. Building on the spirit and principles of the previous three political documents, it focused on planning future growth of bilateral ties, defining the guiding principles for the development of bilateral relations in the twenty-first century, and making overall and long-term plans for bilateral cooperation. It was the fourth important political document between China and Japan since the establishment of diplomatic relations. It was also the first political document signed by the highest leaders of the two countries.

The Joint Press Communiqué on Strengthening Exchanges and Cooperation between the Chinese and the Japanese Governments was released. This covered seventy concrete measures for implementing the Joint Statement, involving high-level contacts, mutual political trust, exchanges in the fields of culture and defense, economic cooperation, and environmental protection.

During the visit, President Hu did not forget the old friends of China.

At his hotel, he received the offspring of Kenzo Matsumura, Koichi Saionji, Tokuma Utsunomiya, and Kaheita Okazaki, who had been dedicated to China-Japan friendship, and relatives of former Japanese leaders Kakuei Tanaka, Takeo Fukuda, Masayoshi Ohira, and Sunao Sonoda, who had made significant contributions to bilateral relations. President Hu encouraged them to carry on the will of their predecessors and continue to support China-Japan friendship.

He also met with Kiichiro Onodera, Yoko Seri, Kazunari Hozumi, and other friendly personages who had been part of the three-thousand-strong Japanese delegation to China in 1984. The 1984 visit was an unprecedented event that had sown the seeds of friendship among the youth of both countries.

At that time, Hu Jintao was secretary of the Secretariat of the Central Committee of the Communist Youth League of China and chairman of the All-China Youth Federation. He had overseen the entire process of the massive event, joined the visitors all day long, and developed a deep friendship with them. Many of the delegates later became strong supporters of China-Japan friendship.

During his stay in Japan, President Hu made extensive contacts with Japanese youth. The year 2008 was China-Japan Youth Friendly Exchange Year and, on the afternoon of May 8, President Hu and Prime Minister Fukuda attended the event's opening ceremony. They went on to Waseda University's International Exchange Center, where President Hu played table tennis with players from China (Wang Nan) and Japan (Ai Fukuhara). His skills won applause from the young audience.

Other details also won him plaudits from the Japanese people.

Not long previously, the giant panda Ling Ling, a gift from China, had succumbed to old age, and many people had gone to Ueno Park Zoo to mourn it. Japan expressed the hope of obtaining more giant pandas from China.

During his stay, President Hu announced the Chinese government's decision to present a pair of giant pandas to Japan for research purposes. I read about the Japanese people's gratitude, hailing this as a wonderful gift from President Hu.

The president also called on the family of Masao Shimizu, founder of the Matsuyama Ballet. When I saw this on television, I felt warm at heart.

When interviewed later, Shimizu said, "I've devoted my life to Japan-China friendship and cultural exchange. I'm much honored that the Chinese leader has chosen to visit our Matsuyama Ballet Company and delivered an inspiring speech. This is a great encouragement and confirmation of all who are devoted to bilateral friendship." One might say that these were not just Shimizu's sentiments but those of everyone dedicated to Sino-Japanese friendship.

President Hu's warm-spring visit pointed out the development direction for bilateral relations, mapped out the blueprint, and opened a new chapter for Sino-Japanese strategic relations of mutual benefit.

Under the impetus of the ice-breaking, ice-melting, spring-greeting, and warm-spring visits by the leaders of the two countries, Sino-Japanese relations returned to the track of stable development and stood at a new starting point. Straight ahead were important new opportunities and broader prospects.

In the spring of 2009, I was elected chief Chinese member of the China-Japan Friendship Committee for the 21st Century. This is a consultancy organ for the two governments, founded in 1984, and is composed of experts, scholars, and renowned personages. Since its establishment, and in particular when bilateral ties were in trouble, its members have provided insight to the governments and made positive contributions to the turnover, improvement, and advancement of bilateral relations.

I am really happy that, though now in my seventies, I am still able to do my bit for the development of Sino-Japanese relations. I also feel the weighty responsibility. I hope and believe that bilateral strategic and mutually beneficial relations will surely move on, and the guidelines (peaceful coexistence, generation-long friendship, mutually beneficial cooperation, and common development) will surely bear fruit in the lands of China and Japan, bring more blessings to the two peoples, and make a great contribution to world peace, stability, and development.

CHAPTER 2

The New Foreign Minister's First Overseas Visit

Indonesia

On December 11, 2008, a colleague from the Foreign Ministry called to inform me that Ali Alatas, the former foreign minister of Indonesia, had passed away in the early morning in Singapore, due to illness.

I was deeply grieved by this news.

Ali Alatas was a highly respected friend of long standing. We had had a close friendship, particularly since my visit to Indonesia in April 1998, when we made a deep impression on each other.

It was a working visit to Indonesia conducted within a month of my taking office as foreign minister.

In March that year, I was appointed the eighth foreign minister of the People's Republic of China. In my new appointment, I was keenly aware of the heavy weight of my mission and responsibility.

Generally speaking, the first visit of a foreign minister is an important diplomatic activity, seen by the outside world as manifesting to a certain extent the new administration's foreign policy. As the foreign minister of China, I knew that my every gesture would be closely watched.

A meeting with former Indonesian Foreign Minister Ali Alatas at Zhongnanhai, May 14, 2005.

The main reason I chose Indonesia as my first visit after assuming office was that the Southeast Asian countries were going through a severe financial crisis. Though only a working visit, it nevertheless drew great attention from the rest of the world.

The Rampant Financial Crisis

I BELIEVE THE FINANCIAL crisis of that time still remains fresh in the memory of many Chinese, especially those in the commercial and financial sectors. It was a severe test of China's economy after the country's reform and opening up.

The crisis began in Thailand and spread like wildfire. Starting in July 1997, it soon engulfed all of Southeast Asia, including the

Philippines, Malaysia, and Indonesia; even Singapore, which had a rather developed economy, was badly battered.

The financial crisis severely hit the economies of various countries, and was of a severity and duration far beyond the expectations of all concerned. Its impact surpassed that of any previous financial crises since the Second World War.

Within just a few months, currencies plummeted, their values down by as much as 40 to 70 percent against the US dollar, foreign exchange reserves shrank drastically, the burden of external debt suddenly increased, stock markets and other financial sectors were fraught with perils, many banks and securities firms collapsed one after another, and the number of jobless soared.

The rest of the world was not immune to the impact of the crisis. One after the other, stock markets in the United States, Europe, Latin America, East Asia, and Australia started fluctuating violently. The turmoil in the financial and capital markets was spreading to regions beyond Southeast Asia.

Before the crisis, Southeast Asia was a vigorous and booming region enjoying worldwide admiration. Thailand, Malaysia, Indonesia, and the Philippines were referred to as the Asian "four tiger cub economies," having long maintained economic growth of between 6 and 8 percent, and became an economic legend. As one of the tiger cubs, Indonesia was one of the most flourishing economies in the Asia-Pacific region. The prospects for its further development had been bright.

It is fair to say that, despite the severity of the financial crisis, Indonesia and other Southeast Asian countries were universally recognized for their economic achievements.

Indonesia was seen as the big brother of ASEAN countries and was also the biggest Islamic country in terms of population. It was also of strategic importance, guarding crucial shipping routes, including the Malacca Straits. This being the case, China's Central

Authorities decided to send me to Indonesia. A visit to Indonesia would provide a firsthand lesson on the impact of the crisis on the Southeast Asian region; more important, it would make clear to the world that China sympathized with the Southeast Asian countries in their economic plight, and was ready to help steer the boat through troubled economic waters.

Land of a Thousand Islands, Battered by an Economic Storm

INDONESIA WAS TO BE affected by the financial crisis relatively late, but it was stricken the hardest.

This was primarily due to intrinsic problems in Indonesia's economy, including a flawed financial supervisory system, unrestrained development of private banks, and persistently high deposit and loan interest rates. Furthermore, the country was loaded with weighty external debt, with the short-term debt owed by private enterprises accounting for too much of the total; also, the economy was structurally flawed, protectionist, excessively monopolistic, and overly subject to influence from political factors and the privileged classes. In the financial storm, such complex factors quickly dragged the economy into the abyss.

Confronted with this situation, the Indonesian government adopted a series of rescue measures, including drawing on a large amount of foreign exchange reserves in order to stabilize its currency. The effect was minimal, however.

On August 14, 1997, the Indonesian government announced its decision to stop exchange rate intervention and to allow the Indonesian rupiah to move freely against other currencies, so as to ensure its flexibility and reduce the impact of foreign speculation. On the day of this announcement, the rupiah plunged 112 points.

In order to save the economy, on September 3 President Suharto announced ten further measures aimed at national economic recovery. These included: prudent relaxation of restrictions on currency circulation, cutting interest rates, canceling or suspending certain engineering projects, increasing non-oil and gas exports, injecting government capital into well-run state-owned banks, lifting the 49 percent cap on foreign shareholding in a company, and ensuring the market supply of daily necessities.

On September 4, Indonesia's central bank announced the decision to cut interest rates, reducing rates on its negotiable securities to an average of 3 percent and reducing the interbank rate from 40 to 25 percent in an effort to mitigate the adverse effects of high interest rates.

Despite the government's prompt launching of urgent rescue measures, the public still lacked confidence.

By the end of September, intensifying social panic and declining public confidence in the government led to another dive in the value of the rupiah. The government's repeated pledges to stabilize the currency only led to frequent bank runs and arbitrage trading.

Recalling this situation, I naturally turn to the financial crisis we are experiencing today. Premier Wen Jiabao has repeated many times that in the face of crisis, it is crucial to maintain confidence, which is more precious than gold. He could not be more right. In the throes of an economic crisis, public panic is often the biggest danger, furious enough to instantly exacerbate the economic problems to the extreme, bringing about consequences far more serious and damaging than the original economic issues.

At that time, Indonesian society across the board was in panic. After repeated consultations with the economic sector, the Indonesian government concluded that it must turn to the International Monetary Fund (IMF) for help. However, this move proved to be ineffective.

After several rounds of bargaining, the IMF decided to provide an aid package of 23 billion US dollars, which was intended for the recovery of healthy financial operations, the adjustment of fiscal policy, monetary policy and economic structure, and so on. The plan, a large-scale one covering a wide range of fields, needed three years to implement.

Under pressure from the IMF, the Indonesian government had to change its previous policies. It liberalized the financial sector and ended subsidies on daily necessities, which led to price hikes and intensified inflation.

However, the IMF prescription did not cure the patient.

The rupiah continued to fall. Prior to the crisis, the exchange rate was 2,700 rupiahs to the US dollar; by 1998, it was 10,000; and at its worst, 17,000. Indonesia's purchasing power fell drastically.

According to Indonesian media, by 1998 the domestic inflation rate was running at 77.63 percent, its stock markets had halved in value, assets had seriously shrunk, and debts had shot up, with foreign debt soaring to 109.3 billion US dollars, amounting to 48 percent of the country's GDP.

As the financial crisis spread, social and political conflicts started to emerge, and the situation became volatile.

At that time, Indonesian President Suharto had been in power for over thirty years. He was a legendary figure. In 1921, he was born in Yogyakarta on the island of Java, the most densely populated region of Indonesia. Biographies record that Suharto was born poor and had just a few years of primary education, but that he was avid for knowledge, and would eagerly read any written material he could get his hands on, even a discarded newspaper. This tough background had shaped his strong character and unyielding style.

In his adulthood, Suharto enjoyed a happy family life. He and his wife, Siti Hartinah Suharto, enjoyed a lifetime partnership, and together raised six children.

In his early years, Suharto served in the army, and had a successful military career: By the age of forty-one, he was promoted to head of the Army Strategic Reserve Command. After the 30th

September Movement* in 1965, Suharto had replaced Sukarno and became the de facto president of Indonesia. Elected president seven times in succession, he ruled Indonesia for over thirty years, from 1968 to 1998.

Suharto practiced military despotic rule. He controlled the country and society by expanding the role of the military, and established absolute authority. At the same time, he appointed experts in different fields to ministerial positions and strove to develop the economy. During his thirty-odd-years rule, Indonesia had achieved fairly rapid economic growth, and Suharto himself was acclaimed Indonesia's Father of Development.

In the later years of Suharto's governance, his children and cronies controlled Indonesia's major economic arteries; they abused their powers and amassed personal wealth through corruption, thereby arousing discontent from all sectors of Indonesian society. There was a yawning gap between rich and poor, public grievances were accumulating, and domestic conflict was becoming more acute. By this time, Suharto was already advanced in years, and his grip on power became shaky. Since he had been in power for so many years, there was no immediate contender to take over his position.

In March 1998, Suharto was reelected for the seventh time. Upon reelection, however, he brazenly packed the cabinet with his own daughter and members of his clique, thereby further increasing public discontent.

The financial crisis added to political instability. Calls for reform were becoming more strident, and antigovernment forces

---

*According to Indonesian media, the term refers to the events of September 30, 1965, when a number of officers of the Presidential Guard, accusing the army's Generals' Council of plotting a coup d'état, arrested and killed six generals including the army commander. Several generals of the Indonesian army immediately adopted countermeasures, and frustrated their actions. A severe suppression and purge of Indonesian Communists and pro-Sukarno political forces followed.

stronger. Students everywhere organized frequent, vociferous protests pressing for immediate government reform. College students in Jakarta, Yogyakarta, Medan, and elsewhere brandished slogans such as "Suharto Step Down" and "Reshuffle the Cabinet" in rallies and demonstrations. Medan and other places also saw continuous outbursts of mass violence. The country was on the verge of sweeping social turmoil.

As an important power, Indonesia played a special and important role in regional and international affairs.

If the situation of such a country kept deteriorating, it would inevitably threaten the stability of all Southeast Asia. For this reason, the international community attached great importance to Indonesia's troubles.

Help Steer the Boat Through Troubled Waters

CHINA ALWAYS PAID CLOSE attention to its Southeast Asian neighbors, in particular to changes in Indonesia's domestic situation.

The financial crisis greatly impacted the Chinese economy: Exports declined and foreign investment shrank. But, despite the pressure, China refused to devalue its currency. Had China chosen otherwise, it would have boosted its exports, which could have won a greater share of the European and American markets. However, the measure would have been disastrous for China's neighbors in Southeast Asia.

As a responsible country, China did not let others take the brunt of trouble; instead, we tried our best to aid our hard-stricken neighbors in mitigating the damage caused by the crisis.

With a strong sense of responsibility, in the spirit of helping steer the boat through troubled waters, and out of consideration for regional stability and development, China made a crucial strategic decision not to devalue the RMB. This decision played a crucial role in weathering the Asian financial crisis and restoring regional financial stability.

Moreover, China, through the IMF, provided affected countries with some four billion US dollars in the form of bilateral aid: About 400 million dollars went to Indonesia, in addition to medical supplies worth three million dollars.

China provided aid money second only to that of the US and Japan, two big developed countries. China's aid figures may seem insignificant today, ten or more years after the event, yet given the economic environment and situation of the time, especially as China too was suffering from the financial crisis, its aid was indeed commendable.

China's charitable action won praise from its neighbors, and moved many people who had had misgivings about China.

Indonesia greatly appreciated China's positive role in the Asian financial crisis, attaching greater importance to China's status and hoping to enter into deeper cooperation with China.

It was under such circumstances that Indonesia saw my visit as quite important and I was accorded a very warm welcome.

Visiting at a Crucial Moment

WITHIN A WEEK OF the decision, we set out for Indonesia. I was no stranger to the country, yet preparing for the visit in such a short time was still quite a challenge.

Determining the itinerary was the first problem. My schedule was already full except for April 11 and 12, which, as a weekend, was the only possible time for my visit. By convention, Indonesia never held official events on weekends. The Indonesian people observed very strict rules of protocol, which they seldom broke. My colleagues in the Department of Asian Affairs were not sure that the Indonesian side would break the rule.

Once our embassy in Indonesia explained to the Indonesian Foreign Ministry our thoughts on the visit and the difficulties of the schedule, they readily agreed to our proposal, which showed that the Indonesian side did indeed attach great importance to my visit.

This was the first high-level governmental visit by China's new administration to the Southeast Asian region since the onset of the region's financial crisis. Therefore, our central government leaders attached great weight to the visit. President Jiang Zemin specially asked me to deliver to President Suharto a personally signed letter expressing China's willingness to aid Indonesia through these hard times and deepen the relationship between the two countries.

Generally speaking, reading a letter is like meeting the person who wrote it. Delivering the president's personally signed letter was equivalent to facilitating an exchange of ideas between the two heads of state. It was too important a matter to be handled casually.

My colleagues in the Foreign Ministry devoted a great deal of energy to produce a precise translation of the content into fluent, standard Indonesian. Through meticulous revision, they strove to make the translation faithful, expressive, and elegant, so as to fully convey the message of the Chinese version.

Furthermore, they called on Mr. Xie Zhiqiong, an Indonesian-language expert in the International Department of the CPC Central Committee. Mr. Xie was a returned Chinese national, born in Indonesia, and a first-class speaker of Indonesian. After his polishing and revision, the translation was indeed more faithful, expressive, and elegant.

With the timing decided, our embassy personnel in Indonesia started busying themselves with the details. They and their Indonesian counterparts quickly finalized the specific itinerary and a series of protocol matters.

After several days of hectic preparations, I left as planned for a working visit to Indonesia.

Since there were no direct flights between Beijing and Jakarta, I had to transfer at Singapore. At five-thirty in the evening, on March 11, I arrived at Soekarno-Hatta International Airport in Jakarta, the Indonesian capital. Here I was greeted by the Chinese ambassador to Indonesia, Chen Shiqiu, and two officials from Indonesia's foreign ministry, director of the protocol department and director of the department of Asia-Pacific affairs. They accompanied me to the Shangri-La Hotel, where I was going to stay.

I was deeply impressed by what I saw between the airport and the downtown area. We drove on expressways all the way, passing through several very modern overpasses, which then were still a rare sight in developing countries. Along the midline of the wide main road, tall palm trees had been planted at regular intervals; on either side rose forests of high buildings. It was plain that Indonesia had indeed achieved great economic growth during the past decades. What a pity, then, to see a random scattering of abandoned, unfinished buildings among the densely built edifices, but that was an apt reflection of Indonesia's current economic situation.

That evening, Indonesia's Foreign Minister Alatas held a reception banquet for me in the Java Hall of the Shangri-La.

It is worth mentioning that Chen Shiqiu, our ambassador to Indonesia, also attended the banquet. He had just taken up his post, but had not yet presented his credentials.* According to international practice, an ambassador cannot attend official events in the country to which he is accredited until his credentials have been presented. It was clear that the Indonesian side had indeed made special arrangements for my visit.

---

*Credentials are the documents needed when a head of state sends an ambassador extraordinary and plenipotentiary to another country. *Presenting credentials* refers to the act of an ambassador handing the documents to the head of state of the country to which he or she is accredited. Until credentials have been presented, an ambassador is not officially recognized under international law.

The Heavy-Hearted Veteran Diplomat

THIS WAS NOT MY first meeting with Foreign Minister Alatas; during my time as deputy foreign minister, I had met him twice on multilateral occasions.

A seasoned diplomat, Ali Alatas served as Indonesia's foreign minister for thirteen years. He stressed developing Indonesia's relationship with China. In 1990, it was he who, together with Qian Qichen, China's then foreign minister, started working toward reestablishing diplomatic ties between China and Indonesia, which played an important role in the normalization of relations between our two countries. He visited China many times both during and after his tenure as foreign minister, either on official visits or attending international conferences, and contributed much to the deepening of Sino-Indonesian relations. It is fair to describe him as an old, dear friend of the Chinese people.

Seated at the banquet, my first words to Alatas were that his experience and seniority as foreign minister for a dozen years made him the professor while I, just a dozen days in office, was the student, there to learn from him.

Alatas appeared quite moved by my words. Smiling, and removing his glasses, he said with deep emotion that in such a hard time Indonesia had been deeply touched by China's offer of sincere help. The fact that I, just appointed foreign minister, had chosen to visit Indonesia first was a clear indication of the importance attached by the Chinese government to relations between the two countries, and a manifestation of China's warm spirit of friendship.

The atmosphere at the banquet was cordial and friendly throughout, and attendees from both countries had a pleasant time. It boded well for the following day's meeting.

My meeting with Foreign Minister Alatas was scheduled for two o'clock at the Indonesian Foreign Ministry.

As I walked towards the meeting room, ushered in by a protocol officer, I saw Alatas already standing by the door waiting for me, and, behind him, dozens of Indonesian officials in a long row ready to welcome their guests from China.

It was only after being introduced by Alatas that I learned that the meeting was being attended by all their Foreign Ministry directors-general, even including the director-general in charge of administration and logistics (directors general were equivalent in rank to a vice minister; at that time Indonesia's Foreign Ministry had no vice ministerial titles). There were twenty or thirty Indonesian attendees at the meeting, far outnumbering the Chinese.

After the meeting officially started, Foreign Minister Alatas and I exchanged views on matters concerning the Southeast Asian financial crisis.

I first expressed the intimate concern shared by China's leaders about Indonesia's hardships.

I told Alatas most sincerely that the great achievements and abundant experience in economic development made by Southeast Asian countries during the past decade could not be denied just because of the financial crisis. Although Indonesia and some other countries had met with some difficulties, the main factors driving economic growth were still present.

I also said some encouraging words that, although the crisis was not yet past, the worst of it was over. Provided the countries concerned united, built up confidence, adopted proper measures, and kept on striving to overcome the difficulties, they, with the help of the international community, would definitely overcome the hardships and bring the economy back onto a healthy track. China was very confident about the economic outlook for this region.

I described in detail the measures adopted by the Chinese government to tackle the financial crisis and the efforts it had made to help stabilize financial markets in Southeast Asia. I told him that, in the interests of Southeast Asian financial stability, China was willing to bear losses and make sacrifices, refusing to devalue the RMB.

The aid offered by China to affected countries was sincere, with no conditions attached.

I told him that I fully understood Indonesia's adherence to a realistic, national-conditions-based approach in its discussions with the IMF on terms and forms of cooperation, and that we welcomed their new agreement with the IMF, in the belief that Indonesia's reforms in its financial system and economy would be successful.

Foreign Minister Alatas was very glad that I had come to visit at such a critical time. He described the visit as demonstrating "China's brotherly friendship" with Indonesia.

He frankly admitted that Southeast Asian countries, although stricken by the crisis by external factors, actually had all kinds of internal problems in their economic and financial systems. The major problem for Indonesia was that private enterprises had too much foreign debt. He said that governmental foreign debt could be reined in and resolved, but private company debt was always hard to control.

He also told me about the agreement between Indonesia and the IMF, explaining that during the negotiations, the IMF had disregarded the terrain of Indonesia's numerous scattered islands, and compelled Indonesia's Logistics Bureau to terminate unified food prices and remove subsidies on all main daily necessities except rice. He said that it might lead to soaring prices and even social turbulence.

Mr. Alatas expressed his gratitude for China's sympathy and support, and praised the policies and measures adopted by our government in the crisis. He said it greatly helped Indonesia that China, in addition to joining the IMF's aid program for affected countries, had explicitly committed not to devalue the RMB, and had given Indonesia support and aid in the form of tangible funds and goods.

He added sincerely that Indonesia was very clear about the great economic sacrifices China was making by these actions. We also exchanged views on specific bilateral issues and on international and regional issues of common concern, such as reducing processing time for visa applications, simplifying formalities for mutual visits, deepening fishery cooperation, and reestablishing the Bank of China's Jakarta branch.

Our talks were candid and deep. Covering many subjects, the meeting was prolonged twice, from the planned two hours to four hours, not ending until almost six o'clock. The joint foreign ministers' press conference was also postponed accordingly.

Through my talk with Foreign Minister Alatas, I better understood that the Southeast Asian financial crisis had seriously damaged Indonesia's economy. The country was at a critical moment. If the situation was not properly handled, and the economic downturn not brought to a halt in time, the result might be intensified domestic conflict, even political and social upheaval.

I noticed that Foreign Minister Alatas was deeply worried; every time the question came up his furrowed brow betrayed his grave concern.

My talk with Alatas was highly beneficial, as it not only promoted mutual understanding and trust between our two countries, but also deepened the personal friendship between us.

I still remember an episode following the meeting. Since we had talked for too long, after the meeting Foreign Minister Alatas and I went to the restroom at the same time. As I was about to wash my hands, he personally pushed the faucet button for me—Indonesia already used push-button faucets—then handed me a towel.

Such an act was rare in the diplomatic world. It not only reflected his respect for and amicable feelings towards China, but also showed his heartfelt wish to establish a personal friendship with me. In diplomatic work, sincere personal friendship developed through working contact is always helpful in promoting cooperation between two countries.

For many years after the meeting, the two of us remained in contact. After he was relieved of his duty, we met on many occasions and whenever he visited China, I would reschedule my diary so as to meet him and refresh our friendship.

When he passed away in 2008, I sent a message of condolence to his family, and asked Zhang Qiyue, Chinese ambassador to Indonesia, to send a wreath and attend the memorial meeting at the Indonesia Foreign Ministry on my behalf, and to reiterate my deep condolences and heartfelt sympathy to his widow.

After the meeting, Foreign Minister Alatas and I held a joint press conference, and gave an account of our talks. The Indonesian media paid close attention to my visit, and a great many reporters were waiting patiently, despite the delay caused by repeated prolongation of the meeting.

They raised many questions about the financial crisis. Some asked about detailed matters such as the total volume of aid provided by China, and the impact of the crisis on China; some asked about the Taiwan Strait situation. I replied to every question. Later, I found that many Indonesian newspapers had reported my visit, and that the media had responded with positive and friendly coverage.

The Iron-Fisted President, Brimming with Confidence

ON THE MORNING OF the 13th, I headed for Istana Merdeka, the residence of Indonesia's president, in order to meet President Suharto.

Despite its location in the center of Jakarta, the compound, shaded by luxuriant trees, was quiet and peaceful, the sounds of birds and insects audible from time to time. The Istana Merdeka is a European-style, predominantly white building with a majestic and elegant frontage. Inside, the decoration is mostly in valuable local hardwood, and the eye falls everywhere on exquisite hand carving; on the wall hung a giant oil painting of scenes in local rural areas.

At first sight Suharto looked like a scholar; with his silver hair, he appeared rather more composed and easygoing than one would expect of an iron-fisted man with years of military life. He usually had a smile on his face, but that day he appeared rather serious.

During our conversation, his appearance was unruffled and his thinking precise. I felt that he was very bullish about Indonesia's situation, and quite confident of smoothly emerging from the financial crisis. Unfortunately, the way things later developed proved him overly optimistic about the country's situation and overconfident about his own ruling position.

First, I delivered the letter personally signed by President Jiang Zemin. In this letter, President Jiang expressed his solicitude for and sympathy with Indonesia in its economic difficulties, his support for Indonesia's adherence to an approach based on national conditions, and his certainty that Indonesia would overcome the temporary hardships. The Chinese government was willing to make efforts, together with the Indonesian government, to advance to a new level of relationship of good-neighborliness, mutual trust, and friendly cooperation.

President Suharto opened the envelope, took out the letter, and read it carefully. Afterward, he looked up and solemnly said to me that he was very grateful for the letter. He said that China's president sending his foreign minister to visit Indonesia at such a special time would surely lead to a significant advancement of friendship and mutual understanding between the two countries, and to strengthening of mutually beneficial cooperation in various fields.

I briefed President Suharto on the meeting I had with Foreign Minister Alatas. Once more, I expressed my confidence that, through its efforts, Indonesia would overcome its difficulties and regain economic vitality. I reassured him that China would stick to its policy of not devaluing the RMB, in the interests of regional economic development and financial stability and the restoration of confidence in the region.

President Suharto expressed his gratitude for the hard decision made by China, praising China as a major power with a strong sense of responsibility.

He told me that the financial storm had indeed inflicted severe damage to Indonesia's economic achievements won over the preceding thirty years. He said that Indonesia's economy had only limited capability to defend against risks, and that there was already a crisis of confidence in society. The Indonesian government was working hard to restore confidence. Finally, he said that the fundamental way for Indonesia to overcome the crisis was to rely on itself.

I strongly agreed with Suharto's view that Indonesia needed to rely on its own efforts and said that China was willing, based on Indonesia's actual needs, to provide tangible help to the best of its ability. Suharto restated his gratitude.

Shortly after my return to China, President Suharto sent President Jiang a reply. In this letter he described Indonesia's domestic situation and expressed his strong desire to further Indonesia's cooperation with China.

At the time, he surely did not expect to be forced out of office a month later.

During my stay in Indonesia, I also called on the entire staff of our Indonesian embassy, visited some Chinese-funded institutions, and met some representatives of Chinese students studying in Indonesia.

Our diplomats, arduously working on overseas front lines year in year out, constantly face unpredictable and ever-changing international environments. In defending China's national interests and dignity, not only must they overcome many difficulties in their living environment and the loneliness of being away from family and friends, but in some cases their security is threatened by conflicts, turmoil, and warfare. The hardships they endure, the pressure they bear, and the sacrifices they make are inconceivable to outsiders.

Therefore, over many years on every foreign visit, I would call on the staff of the local Chinese embassy.

Communications then were far behind what they are today, and the Internet was not as reliable as it is now. Embassy staff were always keen to know China's latest domestic news, especially in the context of a worsening financial crisis and rapidly changing situation. Because of the drastic drop of the rupiah against the US dollar, many of the embassy staff had suffered economic losses, to the extent that their livelihood in Indonesia had been affected. This being so, I decided to use this opportunity to raise morale and boost their confidence that the financial crisis would be overcome.

I gave them a detailed account of the international and regional political and economic situation, and also of the measures taken by China to tackle the financial crisis, encouraging everyone that the more trying the situation, the more they should hold on to their confidence, work with enthusiasm, strive to turn challenges into opportunities, and contribute to the development of Sino-Indonesian relations.

Considering the unique background to the relationship between our two countries and the sensitive issue of ethnic Chinese in Indonesia, I laid particular emphasis on the importance of consular protection during this special time.

I stayed in Indonesia for less than forty-eight hours in total; it was a pure working visit. Despite its brevity, the visit allowed me a deeper understanding of the country's volatile situation. Indonesia was deeply moved by my option to visit in its hour of deep crisis, when I talked about our policies and offered our support and aid. Though China's aid was limited, it was sincere and without conditions. China's policy of not devaluing the RMB also enabled Indonesian society to see a new, flourishing China, and made many influential people there see China in a new light and reconsider Indonesia's policies toward our country.

The visit also had an unforeseen yet positive and important

effect. It laid a good foundation for proper settlement later of the issue of ethnic Chinese in Indonesia, an issue brought to a head by the riots of May 1998.

The May Riots and a New President

ALTHOUGH PRESIDENT SUHARTO WAS confident of stabilizing the political situation and of economic recovery, the situation was heading in a direction most unfavorable to his administration.

In order to demonstrate to the outside world that his hold on power was firm and steady, in early May 1998, Suharto decided to attend the G-15 Summit* in Egypt, even though the Indonesian domestic situation was extremely turbulent.

With Suharto out of the country, the activities of Indonesian antigovernment organizations intensified.

On May 12, some eight hundred students of Trisakti University in West Jakarta clashed with the army ·and the police outside the university. Wearing civilian clothes, several policemen had infiltrated student ranks, but were discovered by the students and beaten. The conflict thus escalated. The army started firing at the students from overpasses and vantage points across the highway. Four were shot dead, and eighteen injured. In Indonesia, the incident became known to as the May 12th Incident.

The next day, students stormed off campus and confronted the

---

*G-15, also known as "Summit Level Group for South-South Consultation and Cooperation," is another cooperation organization of developing countries formed after the Non-Aligned Movement and Group of 77. It was established at the Non-Aligned Movement Summit Meeting in Belgrade in September 1989, and is aimed at encouraging South-South cooperation and North-South dialogue through more concrete measures and enhancing economic development and people's living standards in developing countries. Although membership later grew to seventeen countries, the G-15 name has remained unchanged.

police on the streets. The bloody tragedy had intensified the public's discontent with the government.

According to Indonesian media reports at the time, after the May 12th Incident, quite a few urban youngsters, vagrants, and migrant workers took over the streets and alleys of Jakarta, venting their dissatisfaction with the government. Violent incidents erupted in different parts of the city, as cars were destroyed, shops and banks robbed, and shop owners assaulted. Gradually, the violence escalated into large-scale mass looting and burning of Jakarta's main commercial streets, and culminated in severe riots. The Indonesian media referred to these events as "the May 1998 riots."

Having received authorization from Suharto in Egypt, on the evening of May 14 the Indonesian army launched a crackdown operation. According to Indonesian media reports at the time, the army regained complete control of the capital by that night.

Suharto cut short his visit and returned to Indonesia on May 15 in the hope of continuing his overall control of the country and gradually pacifying the situation, but things did not turn out that way.

Later, the Suharto-led Sekber Golkar party started to split, and both Harmoko, who had always been loyal to Suharto as chairman of Golkar, and the Indonesian parliament for the first time made a public call on Suharto to take the blame for the riots and to resign. Students staged all-night demonstrations. Surrounding the parliament building, they pressed Suharto to resign and the government to reform without delay.

May 20, or National Awakening Day, commemorates Indonesia's struggle for independence, and is an official holiday. On May 20, 1998, the anti-Suharto demonstrations reached a climax. According to reports, over seven thousand students rushed into the square outside the parliament building and occupied it for the whole night. Furthermore, Indonesian opposition parties launched massive anti-Suharto marches in major cities including Jakarta, Yogyakarta, Surabaya, Bandung, Surakarta, and Medan; as many as seven hundred thousand people joined the demonstrations.

On May 21, 1998, Suharto solemnly announced on television that he was resigning as president and that he would be succeeded by Bacharuddin Jusuf Habibie, the vice president.

The history of Indonesia changed course there and then. The turbulent domestic political situation also began gradually to calm down.

Ethnic Chinese in Indonesia Attacked

ETHNIC CHINESE IN INDONESIA were severely affected by the riots of May 1998.

It is estimated that about seven million ethnic Chinese and over two hundred thousand Chinese nationals were living in Indonesia at the time. They were mainly involved in commercial activities, and, through their hard work, had made important contributions to Indonesia's economic and social development.

Unfortunately, in the May riots, ethnic Chinese became targets of attack. Most of the shops looted and burned were owned by ethnic Chinese. A comprehensive and precise assessment of the grievous losses they suffered is still impossible today.

According to statistics released later by the Indonesian National Commission on Human Rights and by humanitarian volunteer organizations, of the over five thousand houses and shops robbed and burned, the majority belonged to ethnic Chinese. Even more shocking were the rapes of some 168 ethnic Chinese women, twenty of whom died.

At that time, however, it was the society-shaking fall of Suharto that monopolized Indonesian media attention. It was only a month later, when Indonesia's new leaders began investigating the facts of the riots, that the tragic rapes of ethnic Chinese women were gradually exposed by local media and women's organizations. In June and July, following further exposure in the Western media, immense indignation was aroused among ethnic Chinese around the globe.

Strenuous Efforts and Active Rescue

ALL EYES WERE ON China, the country of origin of overseas Chinese, to see what position it would take and what measures it would adopt.

When the rioting flared up, the Central Committee of the CPC and China's State Council regarded it as extremely important, and paid close attention throughout to the safety of ethnic Chinese in Indonesia. In this spirit, the Foreign Ministry held many meetings with relevant departments to deliberate on solutions and offer advice. The Chinese embassy in Indonesia did a great deal of work to rescue ethnic Chinese in distress.

I should explain that the term *ethnic Chinese* includes both expatriate Chinese nationals and foreign citizens of Chinese origin. Expatriate Chinese nationals are Chinese citizens holding Chinese passports and living overseas; foreign citizens of Chinese origin have been legally naturalized as citizens of their countries of residence.

Foreign citizens of Chinese origin, though legally citizens of other countries, are our blood relatives. Premier Zhou Enlai described them as "married daughters," a vivid metaphor implying blood ties despite physical distance.

The Chinese government could not and would not turn a blind eye to the sufferings of ethnic Chinese. We promptly expressed our concern to the Indonesian government, pointing out that the Indonesian government was responsible for protecting the basic rights of the ethnic Chinese.

The legal status of Chinese Indonesians made it impossible for us to evacuate them. Their protection, therefore, had to be conducted mainly through the Indonesian government.

It was our urgent duty to do everything possible to rescue the ethnic Chinese in distress. I asked the staff of our embassy in Indonesia to try by every means to help those ethnic Chinese who had been attacked. Time and again, we demanded through diplomatic channels that the Indonesian government adopt effective measures to protect the legal rights and interests of the ethnic Chinese, to properly handle issues concerning them, to investigate the facts of the riots, to prosecute and punish the criminals according to law, and to avoid the recurrence of such a tragedy.

Ambassador Chen Shiqiu made special visits to President Habibie and senior cabinet members including the minister of Investment and the minister of Industry and Trade, urging them to deal with these matters with all possible speed and to effectively protect the personal safety and legal rights and interests of the ethnic Chinese.

Senior Foreign Ministry officials in Beijing also made repeated representations to the Indonesian embassy in China, in which they demanded that the Indonesian government ensure the ethnic Chinese the same peaceful life as that of other ethnic groups in Indonesia, reminding them that proper and fair handling of ethnic Chinese issues would be in the interests of Indonesia's own stability and development.

Staff of the Chinese embassy in Indonesia worked around the clock, skipping meals and sleep. Ambassador Chen Shiqiu and members of his staff paid many visits of comfort to severely affected Chinese districts in Jakarta and Kalimantan. As for ethnic Chinese whom they were unable to visit, they telephoned them to ask about their situations. Even when conditions were still quite turbulent, at the risk of their own safety they drove to ethnic Chinese areas to visit and help the people trapped there. As for the Chinese people, including Hong Kong and Taiwan compatriots, the Chinese embassy, even at night, arranged for cars and escorted them to the airport to be evacuated from the country.

In the light of developing events, I twice instructed the Foreign Ministry spokesperson to deliver a statement concerning the riots, in order to make clear the Chinese government's solemn stance, and to stress the Chinese government's deep solicitude and concern for the suffering of ethnic Chinese in Indonesia.

Departments other than the Foreign Ministry in China also cooperated actively. We relaxed and simplified entry formalities for Chinese Indonesians wishing to come to China, extended the time limit for them to stay, and even helped them organize schooling for their children in China. Through various channels, we did a great deal of work to comfort ethnic Chinese in distress. According to border inspection authorities, in May and June alone, over 10,800 Chinese Indonesian refugees arrived in China.

A Speech at Kai Tak Airport

TWO MONTHS AFTER THE riots, the ASEAN Regional Forum Foreign Ministers' Meeting took place in Manila, capital of the Philippines.

Aware that Indonesian Foreign Minister Alatas would attend, I decided to meet with him during the meeting in order to have a serious face-to-face talk about the riot-affected ethnic Chinese in Indonesia.

On July 28, I met with Alatas in Manila. Despite our friendly working and personal relationship, I approached him bluntly on a major problem of principle concerning the vital interests of the ethnic Chinese.

I pointed out that the assaults on ethnic Chinese in Indonesia had provoked an intense response and indignation among Chinese all over the globe. Chinese Indonesians were the same as Indonesian citizens, and their legitimate rights and interests should be protected according to law. As the country of origin of Chinese Indonesians, China demanded that the Indonesian government take the situation seriously, adopt concrete measures to properly handle the issue, and ensure that no further such incidents would occur.

Heavy-hearted, Foreign Minister Alatas expressed that the incident was a disgrace to Indonesia. He told me that President Habibie had ordered the establishment of a special committee to investigate the incident. Alatas pledged that the Indonesian government would certainly bring the criminals to justice.

During my stay in Manila, the reaction of overseas Chinese around the globe to the attacks on ethnic Chinese became increasingly vehement. Quite a few political figures in Hong Kong sent a joint letter to President Habibie, and some people even took to the streets, calling on the Indonesian government to treat the ethnic Chinese well.

The Central Authorities attached great importance to the incident, and demanded that departments involved should speed up related work so as to further protect the legal rights and interests of ethnic Chinese overseas. Deputy Foreign Minister Wang Yingfan made a special telephone call to me from Beijing to communicate the instructions of the Central Authorities.

With an upsurge of overseas public opinion, the Indonesian situation and the ethnic Chinese issue gradually became the focus of worldwide attention. I felt it necessary to make the whole world aware of our government's position on these matters and the measures taken.

After the Manila meeting, I went to Malaysia for a brief visit, during which I spent time thinking about how to convey the Chinese government's stance to the world.

I was going to stop at Hong Kong on my way back to China. Taking into account the concentration of media in Hong Kong, and in particular the intense reaction of the people there to the suffering of ethnic Chinese in the Indonesian riots, I decided, after consulting colleagues, to adjust my schedule in Hong Kong. Right after getting off the plane at Kai Tak Airport, I would hold a press conference at which I would personally give a comprehensive speech systematically expounding on the issue of the ethnic Chinese and the May 1998 riots.

From Kuala Lumpur, I instructed staff of the Commissioner's Office of China's Foreign Ministry in Hong Kong SAR to promptly inform the major media in Hong Kong, in particular the Chinese media, about my speech.

Wu Hongbo, then information counselor in the Commissioner's Office and later to become assistant foreign minister of China, immediately called different media in Hong Kong, informing them that I would arrive at Kai Tak Airport in a few hours and give an important speech there.

The media responded with enthusiasm and instantly dispatched reporters to the airport. Before my arrival, the airport lobby was packed with waiting reporters.

On the afternoon of August 3, I took a Cathay Pacific flight from Kuala Lumpur to Hong Kong. Since I had decided to make a speech just before my departure, I had to grab what time was available on the flight to prepare it. I dictated the intended content of my speech for my colleague to produce a draft. I personally revised it over and over, and the speech was finalized just before we landed.

When I disembarked at eight o'clock, I already knew my speech by heart, so I decided to give it without reading notes.

I addressed the media for thirty-five minutes without a break. First, I expressed that the people of China and Chinese societies and communities around the world had every reason to air their indignation at the violence against ethnic Chinese during the May riots

Talking to the press at Kai Tak Airport on August 3, 1998, about the Chinese government's stance on the attacks on ethnic Chinese during riots in Indonesia that May.

in Indonesia, and that the Chinese government, attaching great importance to the incident and being extremely concerned over the plight of ethnic Chinese in Indonesia, had repeatedly demanded through diplomatic channels that the Indonesian government punish the criminals, ensure the life and property security and the legal rights and interests of the ethnic Chinese, and prevent any recurrence of such incidents.

I also told the press that Foreign Minister Alatas had candidly described the events as a disgrace to Indonesia, telling me that President Habibie, deeming the incident extremely inhumane, had given orders to set up a special committee of investigation, and that the Indonesian government had pledged to bring the criminals to justice and adopt measures to avoid any recurrence. We were looking forward to the fulfillment of their promises.

After the speech, I answered questions from reporters.

Some were interested in whether China would continue its aid to Indonesia after the incident. I told them that China's aid to

Indonesia was aimed at helping the numerous Indonesian people, that lending a helping hand to a neighbor stricken by the Southeast Asian financial storm was only right and proper, and that China would not cut off its economic aid to Indonesia.

Shortly after my speech, Radio Television Hong Kong (RTHK) was the first to carry the news, with a newsflash at ten-thirty; later, TV stations, including TVB and ATV, aired the detailed contents of my speech. Over a dozen Hong Kong newspapers including *Wen Wei Po, Ta Kung Pao, South China Morning Post,* and *Ming Pao* carried a number of prominent reports and comments on my speech, which made a positive impression on the international community, especially on overseas Chinese.

I had planned to go directly from the press conference to the Commissioner's Office of China's Foreign Ministry in the Hong Kong SAR in order to meet with Mr. Tung Chee Hwa, the first chief executive of the Hong Kong SAR. However, since my speech ended late, Mr. Tung, having seen the news on television, asked his secretary to call the commissioner's office and suggested inviting me to the Hong Kong Government House instead. Government House was the official residence of the chief executive of Hong Kong, and had originally been the official residence of Hong Kong governors. By the time I arrived, it was already around midnight, and so the dinner banquet originally proposed by Mr. and Mrs. Tung was replaced by a night snack.

Thus, I had the honor of being Mr. Tung's first guest from the Chinese central government hosted at the Government House and sharing a night snack with him. Although it was my first meeting with Chief Executive Tung, we had a very agreeable talk. His wife, who specially prepared Japanese-style refreshments for me, was also very hospitable.

The day of my speech at Kai Tak Airport, *People's Daily* printed "The Legal Rights and Interests of Chinese Indonesians Should Be

Protected," a commentary on the May riots. The article urged the Indonesian government to promptly adopt concrete, forceful measures to severely punish the criminals and protect the legal rights and interests of Chinese Indonesians.

My speech in Hong Kong and the commentary in *People's Daily* found a strong echo in the ethnic Chinese community in Indonesia. Exhilarated and heartened, many ethnic Chinese called the Chinese embassy in Indonesia to express their gratitude for the Chinese government's moral and practical support.

The Chinese government's position statement on the riots was also given great weight and treated seriously by the Indonesian government. Almost all the Indonesian media excerpted the statement, and started carrying reports encouraging ethnic harmony. The local newspapers printed some articles affirming the contributions of ethnic Chinese to Indonesia, analyzed the in-depth historical causes of the riots, and criticized Suharto's policy towards the ethnic Chinese. An Indonesian private TV station also aired public service announcements calling for ethnic harmony.

For quite some time after the riots, China and the rest of the world kept a close watch on ensuing events; at the Foreign Ministry we continued with our efforts on related matters.

On September 3, I met with Foreign Minister Alatas while attending the 12th Non-Aligned Movement Summit in Durban, South Africa, where I once more urged Indonesia to eliminate interference and speed up investigations into the riots. Alatas expressed that the Indonesian government had set up a special investigation committee that would get to the bottom of matters, bring the criminals to justice, and ensure that no such incidents would recur.

Learn from History; Look to the Future

CHINA HAS HAD LONG-TERM, friendly contacts with Indonesia. Even two thousand years ago, there were trade contacts between China and the Indonesian area. Back in the Jin Dynasty (around 5th century AD) there was regular shipping back and forth, and by the Tang and Song dynasties (618–1279), close relations had already been established. In the Ming dynasty (1368–1644), Zheng He stopped at Indonesia on each of his seven maritime expeditions; in Semarang on the island of Java, there is still a temple commemorating the famous navigator.

Indonesia was the first country in Southeast Asia to establish diplomatic relations with the People's Republic of China. Our bilateral relations, however, experienced several major setbacks. The issue of ethnic Chinese in Indonesia has always been a sensitive issue for both sides.

When diplomatic relations were established in 1950, the Indonesian government raised the issue of the dual nationality of Chinese Indonesians. After many rounds of negotiations, the two

Meeting with Indonesian President Megawati in Jakarta, May 17, 2002.

governments reached agreement on how to resolve the issue: The ethnic Chinese in Indonesia could freely choose the nationality of either country. Most of them chose naturalization as citizens of Indonesia, while some chose to return to China.

After the September 30 Movement in Indonesia, the Indonesian military had unwarrantedly accused Chinese Indonesians of being a fifth column.* During the thirty-odd years of Suharto's rule, the Indonesian government had implemented policies restricting and assimilating ethnic Chinese. The identification certificates of Chinese Indonesians carried a distinctive mark. They were barred from joining the army and entering politics, and their career options were subject to many restrictions.

Since Chinese Indonesians had long been economically prosperous but politically powerless, in all previous social conflicts in Indonesia they had become the main target of attack, their life and property suffering severe losses.

To be objective, the eruption of the May 1998 riots resulted from years of accumulated political, economic, and social conflicts. They were not targeted exclusively at ethnic Chinese nor at China itself, but, sadly, it was the ethnic Chinese who suffered the most during the riots.

Alleviating the plight of ethnic Chinese in Indonesia hinged to a great extent on the domestic political situation there. Therefore, while paying attention to the ethnic Chinese issue and striving to protect their legitimate rights and interests, we also had to strive to maintain normal relations with Indonesia and to step up official

---

* The term *fifth column* first appeared in the Spanish Civil War just before WWII. In October 1936, Franco, leader of the Spanish rebel armed forces, with the backing of Nazi Germany, approached Madrid and prepared to launch an attack. When a reporter asked Franco which column would first occupy the city, a commander under him conceitedly replied "the fifth column." Actually, Franco only had four columns, and by the fifth column, the commander was referring to spies hidden in Madrid. Afterwards, the term came to refer generally to defectors instigated by and infiltrators sent by an enemy to facilitate subversion from within.

Talking to Indonesian media in 2004.

contacts, so as to facilitate improvements in the living environment of ethnic Chinese in the country.

Given these considerations, we could neither turn a blind eye to the suffering and losses of ethnic Chinese in Indonesia, nor could we act impetuously and in disregard of the overall situation, thereby damaging Sino-Indonesian relations. Still less should we exacerbate the difficulties of the ethnic Chinese by adopting inappropriate measures.

I visited Indonesia again in 2002 and 2004. On each visit, I could see through the car window Jakarta's orderly layout, busy streets, and newly built skyscrapers. All Indonesian society presented an appearance of prosperity. I had the clear impression that Indonesia's economy had gradually emerged from the shadow of the financial crisis.

During the past several years, the living environment of ethnic Chinese in Indonesia had greatly improved. The Wahid government started to relax policies toward Chinese Indonesians. President Wahid himself publicly declared that he had Chinese blood, and, after leaving office, even went to Quanzhou in China's Fujian Province in search of his roots.

President Megawati designated the Spring Festival (Chinese lunar New Year) as an official Indonesian holiday on the first day of the first lunar month. From then on, Chinese Indonesians had the same right as enjoyed by other ethnic groups in Indonesia to celebrate their own traditional festival.

In Indonesia, Chinese-language newspapers, TV stations, and schools also mushroomed. Chinese Indonesians not only merged into Indonesian mainstream society, but also started to enter politics. Along with the appearance of a Chinese party, Chinese ministers, and Chinese assemblymen, ethnic Chinese started making headway in the Indonesian political arena. None of this would have been imaginable during the Suharto years.

Under the administration of President Susilo Bambang Yudhoyono, a new Indonesian Nationality Act was passed in 2006, and the Elimination of Ethnic Discrimination Act in 2008. With the elimination of racially discriminatory clauses from legal statutes, Chinese Indonesian and other ethnic minorities in Indonesia were officially granted legal status equal to that of other Indonesian citizens.

Improvements of the social status and living environment of Chinese Indonesians are inseparable from the efforts of the Chinese community in Indonesia, in particular those of governmental officials and assemblymen of Chinese ancestry. They are inseparable, too, from the development of China, their country of origin, and the improvement in Sino-Indonesian relations. In recent years, with the continuous growth of its overall national strength and international influence, China has established close ties with its neighbors in political, economic, cultural, and other fields, and has been expanding friendly exchanges and cooperation.

Meeting Indonesian President Susilo Bambang Yudhoyono in Jakarta, November 5, 2004.

All recent Indonesian administrations—those of President Wahid, President Megawati, and President Yudhoyono—have all come to realize China's influence and the great importance for Indonesia to develop friendly relations with China.

In 2005, President Hu Jintao paid a successful state visit to Indonesia. He and President Yudhoyono together signed the Joint Declaration on Strategic Partnership between China and Indonesia. Thus, Indonesia was the first of the ASEAN countries to become China's strategic partner, and a new chapter opened in our bilateral relations.

Over the past several years, I have been paying close attention to the situation in Indonesia and the development of Sino-Indonesian relations. It is commendable that the Indonesian government has actively carried out policies promoting ethnic harmony.

The promotion of ethnic harmony, social stability, and economic development in Indonesia is in keeping with the country's realities and long-term interests, and also conducive to the long-term, healthy development of Sino-Indonesian relations.

I have always encouraged the ethnic Chinese to abide by the laws and national traditions of Indonesia, to live in peace and harmony with all the other ethnic groups there, to contribute to Indonesia's economic and social development, and to play the role of a bridge in friendly cooperation between our two countries.

CHAPTER 3

Four Trips to New York in Four Weeks

Diplomatic Struggles
Before the Iraq War of 2003

O N THE NIGHT OF January 20, 2009, I watched the inaugural speech of Barack Obama, forty-fourth president of the United States. His speech touched upon US traditions, as well as the challenges Americans were facing. On Iraq, one sentence in particular caught my attention. He said, "We will responsibly begin to leave Iraq to its people . . ." Though short, the sentence was a signal that the US government would make a major adjustment to its Iraq policy.

At the time of the speech, the war in Iraq had lasted for six years, and rather than making Iraq a "model democratic country" as American government had claimed, it had thrown Iraq into turmoil. The United States itself had become inextricably bogged down, and Iraq had become a heavy burden on the Bush administration. It was reasonable that President Obama wanted to change US policy towards Iraq.

As the saying goes, "Don't start what you can't finish." In fact, the war, then in its sixth year, could have been avoided completely.

The international community had done its utmost to stop it, and many people, including myself, had gone about canvassing support for peace.

The Wind Before the Storm

SEPTEMBER IS ALWAYS THE busiest month for the United Nations, because state leaders and foreign ministers of all countries gather at the UN headquarters beside the East River to attend the annual general debate of the UN General Assembly. Although termed a *debate*, the occasion is, in fact, a succession of state leaders and foreign ministers delivering speeches, expressing the stand and positions of their respective governments.

The fifty-seventh session of the UN General Assembly came in 2002, on the first anniversary of 9/11.*

Over the previous year, the international situation had undergone great changes, as opposing and combating terrorism had become the main subject for changes in international relations. The United States had launched the military operation known as "Enduring Freedom" in Afghanistan, overthrown the Taliban regime, and struck at al-Qaeda. The Americans' next target in its antiterrorism war was Iraq.

On September 12, President George W. Bush delivered a speech at the 2002 general debate of the UN General Assembly. Because of the UN's location on US soil, it is usual for the US president to deliver a speech every year at the start of the UN General Assembly, but, this year in particular, the eyes of the world were watching,

---

*On the morning of September 11, 2001, nineteen terrorists hijacked four commercial passenger jet airliners. The hijackers intentionally crashed two of the planes into the twin towers of the World Trade Center in New York, and a third into the Pentagon on the outskirts of Washington, DC. The fourth crashed in Pennsylvania. Thousands of civilians died in the terrorist attacks, referred to as the September 11th attacks or 9/11. Afghanistan-based al-Qaeda claimed responsibility for the attacks.

since the media generally believed that President Bush was about to show his cards vis-à-vis Iraq.

Just as anticipated, President Bush devoted much of his speech to expounding on the Iraq issue. He said that, twelve years previously, Iraq had invaded Kuwait, and was stopped by the will of the United Nations. In order to suspend hostilities and to spare himself, Iraq's dictator had made a series of commitments, and had agreed to prove his compliance with every one of those obligations. Instead, however, he had proven only his contempt for the United Nations, and for all his pledges.

President Bush then enumerated the violations of UN Security Council resolutions by the Iraq regime. He said that if the regime wished for peace, it should immediately destroy all weapons of mass destruction (WMD), end all support for terrorism, cease persecution of its civilian population, release all Gulf War prisoners, and end all illicit trade.

Bush then emphasized that the United States would work with the UN Security Council to meet their common challenge. He said, "If the Iraq regime defies us again, the world must move deliberately, decisively to hold Iraq to account. We will work with the UN Security Council for the adoption of necessary resolutions."

President Bush's tough speech hit the headlines in the world's media that very day.

I was head of the Chinese delegation to the 57th UN General Assembly. Sitting in the General Assembly Hall, I could sense that Iraq stood once again at the crossroads of war or peace.

In August 1990, Iraq invaded Kuwait, in serious breach of the purposes and principles of the United Nations Charter. Authorized by the UN Security Council, multinational forces led by the United States launched Operation Desert Storm, driving Iraqi forces out of Kuwait. That was the first Gulf War.

From August 1990 to September 2003, the UN Security Council passed nearly sixty resolutions, imposing the strictest all-around sanctions on Iraq. Iraq was urged to unconditionally destroy or remove all its chemical and biological weapons as well as ballistic missiles with a range over 150 kilometers, and renounce all involvement in and end all support for terrorism. The United Nations even set up the United Nations Special Commission (UNSCOM) to investigate nuclear weapons in Iraq. These sanctions made the life of innocent Iraqi citizens quite miserable. They paid a heavy price for Saddam Hussein's policies.

Inspection of nuclear weapons in Iraq went on and off for twelve years since May 1991. During this period, there had been three US presidents: George H. W. Bush, Bill Clinton, and George W. Bush. There were three UN secretaries-general: Javier Perez de Cuellar, Boutros Boutros-Ghali, and Kofi Annan. Iraq and UNSCOM were at loggerheads and many crises arose during those twelve years.

After May 1997, Iraq several times refused UNSCOM's demand to inspect Iraq's presidential palace, and even stopped cooperating with UNSCOM several times.

In December 1997, the United States and the United Kingdom launched the military action called Desert Fox against Iraq, after which Iraq stopped all cooperation with UNSCOM.

In December 1999, the Security Council founded, through Resolution 1284, the UN Monitoring, Verification and Inspection Commission (UNMOVIC) to replace UNSCOM for weapons inspection in Iraq in collaboration with the International Atomic Energy Agency (IAEA). Iraq did not accept the resolution. However, with the development of the situation, Iraq had to admit UNMOVIC inspection in Iraq.

After the attacks of 9/11, the relationship between the United States and Iraq further worsened. The US criticized Iraq for being involved with al-Qaeda, for violating Security Council resolutions, and for WMD research and development. The United States stated that Iraq had posed a direct threat to its national security and to its strategic interests in the Middle East, so it had listed Iraq at the head of a so-called axis of evil. The United States even threatened a pre-emptive strategy in launching military attacks against Iraq.

The United States' attempt to resort to force against Iraq was opposed by an overwhelming majority of nations, as well as by UN Secretary-General Kofi Annan. Even some US allies disapproved. The international community called for a political settlement under the framework of the UN Security Council. Pressure from different sides forced the Bush administration to table the issue for discussion at the Security Council. The UN Security Council is one of the six principal organs of the United Nations.* Its fifteen-strong membership consists of five permanent members (China, France, Russia, the United Kingdom, and the United States) and ten non-permanent members elected through geographical distribution to serve a two-year term.

The main functions of the Security Council as stipulated in the UN Charter are: to investigate any dispute, or any situation which might lead to international friction or give rise to a dispute; to make recommendations for peaceful resolution of a dispute; to determine the existence of any threat to the peace, breach of the peace, or act of aggression; and to enforce its decisions by economic, diplomatic, or military means.

Thus it can be seen that the Security Council is the core institution of the international collective security system, assuming the primary responsibility for the maintenance of international peace and security. It is the only organ of the United Nations that can call for mandatory action, including the use of force. Its resolutions are binding on UN member states.

If the Security Council determines the existence of threat to or breach of peace, it can authorize UN member states, in compliance with provisions of the UN Charter, to restore international peace

---

*The other five organs are the General Assembly, the Economic and Social Council, the United Nations Trusteeship Council, the International Court of Justice, and the Secretariat.

and security by resorting to force. In this case, according to international law, the use of force by a nation or nations against another would be lawful.

However, if a country resorts to the use of force against another that is neither in self-defense nor authorized by the Security Council, the action would be deemed illegal, and would be neither approved nor supported by the international community.

In view of the importance and authority of the Security Council in maintaining international peace and security, all countries in the world attach great importance to the functions of the former. That was why US President George W. Bush brought the Iraq issue back to the Security Council for further deliberation.

Bush's speech put pressure on Iraq. On September 16, 2002, Iraq's Foreign Minister Naji Sabri sent a letter to UN Secretary-General Kofi Annan indicating that Iraq would unconditionally accept the resumption of nuclear weapon inspections by the UN.

However, the US gave no credence to Iraq's decision, and accused Iraq of trying to evade sanctions. The US insisted that a new resolution should be passed by the Security Council to force Iraq to fully comply with all the resolutions and to cooperate with the United Nations unconditionally.

That same day, while in New York, I had an arranged telephone conversation with the Iraqi Foreign Minister Naji Sabri, whom I had met in Beijing a month before and had tried to persuade to cooperate with the UN.

During our telephone discussion, Naji Sabri informed me about Iraqi perspectives and thinking, and hoped that China could continue to make efforts for a political settlement of the Iraq issue within the UN framework.

I told him that China welcomed Iraq's decision to unconditionally accept the return of the UN nuclear inspectors, and praised Iraq for its wise decision at such a critical moment, a decision that made it more likely for the international community, including China, to achieve a political settlement of the issue.

On September 26, 2002, when I was accompanying Premier Zhu Rongji in Paris on a formal visit to France, the US Secretary of State Colin Powell asked to talk to me on the phone.

Wondering why Mr. Powell was so anxious to call me, I assumed it was because the US was seeking Chinese support to pass a new resolution at the Security Council.

However, I had no idea about the content of the draft resolution the Americans were preparing. If the draft contained articles on authorization of the use of force, China would by no means support it, for it was contrary to our foreign policy of resolving regional disputes in a peaceful way. I had to clarify our position.

Before replying, I wanted to hear what Powell had to say.

As anticipated, the secretary of state told me that the United States was discussing with the United Kingdom a new draft resolution on the Iraq issue. The United States maintained that a determined and tough new resolution should be passed by the Security Council, so that Iraq would be forced into cooperation with the United Nations for serious compliance with Security Council resolutions.

He said, regarding the detailed content of the draft, the US side would inform Zhou Wenzhong, China's assistant foreign minister, who was then visiting Washington, DC, and the five permanent members of the Security Council could discuss it.

After he finished, I first commented positively on the US attitude of resolving the Iraq issue politically under the UN framework. I told him that it had become the common aspiration of the international community to see the UN play a dominant role and to maintain the authority of the Security Council on this issue. Since the issue had entered a critical stage of war or peace, its influence and consequences must be considered in an all-around way before any action was taken. China's attitude on this issue was known to the US side. I continued that China held that nuclear weapon inspections should be resumed in the first place, and that appropriate actions should then be taken in the light of the inspection results. The act would gain more support from the international community, and also demonstrate that the Security Council wished to try every peaceful means to resolve the issue. Therefore, the return of UN nuclear inspectors was the top priority.

Before long, a draft resolution by the United States and the United Kingdom was distributed to the five permanent members of the Security Council, which proposed tough conditions and means of nuclear inspections on Iraq. On September 30, William Erhman, a special envoy from the British foreign secretary, came all the way to Beijing to present the draft to China. William Erhman was a senior British diplomat, who later became the British ambassador to China.

The essence of the draft was simple: Iraq must hand in a report on its WMD R&D to the Security Council within thirty days of the date of adoption of the resolution; Iraq must immediately and unconditionally allow inspectors from UNMOVIC and IAEA to undertake unhampered inspections in any place and in any way; if there were any concealment or cheating on the Iraqi side, or failure of complete cooperation, all UN member states had the right to resort to any necessary means to maintain regional peace and security.

Of course, the phrase "any necessary means" covered the use of armed force. If the draft resolution was passed, it meant that as long as the United States was dissatisfied with Iraq's cooperation with the United Nations, it could take any kind of action against Iraq, including the use of force. It was, in fact, a draft authorizing automatic direct recourse to armed force by the United States.

On the same day that the British presented their draft, Russia's Foreign Minister Igor Ivanov also called me to talk about Russia's opinion of this draft.

Mr. Ivanov said that Russia had carefully studied the draft and found it unacceptable because of the articles allowing the United States to automatically resort to force against Iraq. He told me that France too favored the Russian stand.

It seemed that Russia saw eye to eye with us. I told Mr. Ivanov that the Chinese attitude was clear: We would strive for a political settlement of the Iraq issue under the UN framework. The Security Council could try a two-stage approach: first, sending the UN nuclear inspectors back to work in Iraq as soon as possible; second, deciding on further action in the light of the inspection's findings.

Automatic Authorization Refused

FROM WHAT WE KNEW, the five permanent members of the Security Council were split into two camps centering on the US-UK draft resolution.

The United States and the United Kingdom backed direct recourse to military action, whereas China, France, and Russia stood for a two-stage solution; France and Russia were very insistent, going as far as to declare that if the United States and the United Kingdom did not accept the two-stage approach, they would not hesitate to exercise their veto when the matter was put to a vote at the Security Council.

This put the United States and the United Kingdom under great pressure. According to the provisions of the UN Charter, if even one permanent member of the Security Council votes against a draft resolution on a nonprocedural issue, the draft will not be passed. This is known as *veto power* and the principle of *great power unanimity*. Now that France and Russia had declared that they would veto the draft resolution, it could not be passed at the Security Council.

At the insistence of China, France, and Russia, the United States and the United Kingdom revised the draft several times. After more than a month of consultations, division still persisted among the five permanent members. China, France, and Russia were still dissatisfied with the expression of "automatic authorization," but the United States could not wait any longer.

On the morning of November 6, 2002, US Secretary of State Colin Powell asked to speak with me urgently on the phone.

I came to the telephone room of the Chinese Ministry of Foreign Affairs at the appointed time.

Diplomatic telephone calls are different from ordinary ones. Normally, they take place at a designated time with one party speaking first, the words being translated into the language of the other party before the other replies.

During our exchange, Mr. Powell informed me that the US was going to formally distribute the latest draft resolution at the Security Council and would ask for it to be voted on forty-eight hours later. He said that he sincerely hoped China could continue to play an important role in promoting consensus among the five permanent members, so that the Security Council could pass the new draft resolution as early as possible after consultations.

Several hours later, we received the new draft resolution. The United States and the United Kingdom had deleted "automatic authorization," and the draft was basically in conformity with our two-stage concept. It could be said that since our biggest concern had been resolved, it would not be so difficult for us to pass this new draft resolution.

It happened to coincide with China's presidency of the Security Council.

The presidency is taken in turn by each of the fifteen member states of the Security Council. Each country serves for a one-month term, in English alphabetical order of their names. The president is responsible for chairing meetings of the Security Council and for other routine work, and represents the Security Council in its rela-

Meeting UN Secretary-General Kofi Annan at the UN headquarters in New York on September 13, 2002.

tions with other organizations. When taking the presidency, countries usually use the advantage of chairing meetings to influence the organization of meetings and the discussion of certain subjects.

At that time, the international community was concerned about whether Iraq was developing WMD, and generally supported the resumption of inspections in Iraq. If a resolution could be passed at the Security Council demanding Iraq's complete cooperation with the United Nations, it would alleviate international concern and promote a political settlement of the issue under the UN framework.

Therefore, we should make good use of our advantage as president of the Security Council to coordinate discussion of the draft resolution by the permanent members, so as to arrive at a consensus. In this way, China could send a clear message to Iraq on behalf of the international community, make clear the just stand of China, and play a constructive role on the issue.

Therefore, on the day the United States distributed the newest draft resolution, I called the Russian and French foreign ministers and UN Secretary-General Kofi Annan.

I emphasized in each of these conversations that, after prolonged consultation, the five permanent members had reached important consensus on many aspects of the draft resolution. The United States had also made some revisions to the draft in the light of consultation, which had taken care of the concerns of relevant countries. This was good for unanimity of the five permanent members.

I said that at present all parties wished to settle the issue politically under the UN framework, and all thought it a critical moment. We hoped that all parties could continue to take a flexible and cooperative attitude in the ensuing consultations, and strive for unanimity among the Security Council members.

All parties agreed with my point of view and made positive responses.

Russia thought that some adjustments and concessions had been made to the draft, but it still had concerns about certain aspects. Russia hoped that representatives from the five permanent member states could further negotiate in order to reach unanimity.

France also said that, following the revisions, the new US draft was in general conformity with the two-stage concept. France also hoped that all member states could reach a consensus at the final stage and send a strong and clear message to Iraq.

The UN secretary-general had high praise for China's stand and constructive role on the Iraq issue. He maintained that if the Security Council could pass the important resolution in full or near unanimity, it would be the best result at the current time. He told me that as China was president of the Security Council, he would actively assist China's work with a constructive and cooperative attitude, push for approval of the new resolution, and make sure the resolution would be effectively implemented.

Addressing the concerns of Russia and France, the United States

Resolution 1441 being unanimously passed at the UN Security Council on November 8, 2002.

made a quick revision to the draft, and distributed the final version on the afternoon of November 7. With this, the five permanent members finally reached unanimity on the draft resolution.

On November 8, under the chairmanship of Ambassador Zhang Yishan, Chinese deputy permanent representative to the United Nations, the resolution on the Iraq issue was passed unanimously at the Security Council. Being the 1441st resolution since the founding of the United Nations in 1945, it was called Security Council Resolution 1441.

It was stipulated in the resolution that Iraq must allow UN inspectors to return to Iraq immediately, and allow them to undertake large-scale and unhindered nuclear inspections. The UN inspectors would leave for Iraq within forty-five days of the adoption of the resolution, and present their preliminary report to the Security Council within sixty days thereafter. The Security Council would then consider what actions to take in the light of the report and the actual situation in Iraq. It was also stipulated that if Iraq refused to fulfill the resolution, it would face severe consequences.

It could be seen that the resolution contained no automatic authorization of the use of force, thus the UN inspectors could return to Iraq immediately, which guaranteed that the Security Council could take the initiative in taking further actions.

It was a resolution acceptable to all parties. The international community including UN Secretary-General Kofi Annan commended the resolution and considered it conducive to maintaining the authority of the Security Council. The resolution provided new opportunities for Iraq to resume cooperation with the United Nations, and was conducive to a political settlement of the Iraq issue. It can be said that the resolution eased tension, and gained more time and opportunities for peace.

After the Security Council approved Resolution 1441, Iraq immediately announced its acceptance and, before long, Iraq presented to the United Nations a 12,000-page report on WMD and missile R&D, as required by the resolution.

The full report was distributed only to the five permanent members of the Security Council, with some sensitive content deleted from the version given to other member states. The purpose was to prevent the proliferation of some technical materials on WMD. At that time, aware of our responsibility, we assigned a colleague in the Chinese permanent mission to the United Nations to personally escort the report to China.

On November 27, 2002, the UN inspectors arrived in Iraq and resumed the UN inspections.

War Clouds Gather over the Gulf

As THE UN RESUMED inspections in Iraq, the United States was on the one hand speeding up military deployment and marshaling troops in the Gulf area, and on the other setting up an anti-Saddam alliance in preparations for war against Iraq.

According to reports, by the end of 2002, the United States had about 60,000 navy, army, and air force troops deployed in the Gulf area. The forces were mainly at United States military bases around Iraq, including Turkey in the north; the Persian Gulf in the south; Israel and Saudi Arabia in the southwest; and Kuwait, Bahrain, Qatar, the United Arab Emirates (UAE), and Oman in the southeast. The United States also dispatched the aircraft carriers USS *Constellation CV-64* and USS *Harry S. Truman CVN-75*, one submarine, nearly twenty surface vessels, and about four hundred advanced aircraft for multiple uses.

For a moment, war clouds gathered over the Gulf area and the situation became tense.

However, the United States and the United Kingdom did not take action immediately, but stepped up diplomatic efforts. They still reckoned on getting legitimate authorization from the Security Council to wage war on Iraq, thereby legalizing their military actions.

Within the Security Council there were serious divisions as to whether to authorize the United States and the United Kingdom to use force against Iraq, and a fierce struggle unfolded on war or inspections.

In this context, I went to New York four times within one month, striving for peace.

The First Visit: Sounding Out

SHORTLY AFTER NEW YEAR'S Day in 2003, France's Foreign Minister Dominique de Villepin sent me a message through the French embassy in China.

He said that France held the presidency of the Security Council that month. Mr. de Villepin suggested that a ministerial meeting on counterterrorism be held at the Security Council in New

York on January 20 to summarize the fight against terrorism under the UN framework, so as to carry out the fight against terrorism more effectively.

This was of course a good suggestion, but an awkward one for me.

According to normal practice, I visited Africa at the beginning of every year. At the time, I had decided to visit Mauritius, Botswana, Congo (Brazzaville), and Congo (Kinshasa) from January 16 to 26, then visit Italy. France's suggestion was obviously not convenient.

On the other hand, after 9/11, antiterrorism had become an issue of great concern to the international community, and the Security Council had achieved a lot in this regard. That said, there had been a series of terrorist incidents in Bali in Indonesia, Moscow, and Mombasa in Kenya. France's purpose in convening the foreign ministers' meeting was to maintain the momentum of international cooperation in combatting terrorism.

China had actively participated in international antiterrorist cooperation after the 9/11 attack and had won high praise from the international community. If I could attend the meeting, the international community could see our positive attitude on countering terrorism and China's constructive role in international affairs.

At that time, Iraq concerns were making the situation in the Gulf area very tense. I estimated that the issue would probably become a hot topic at the meeting. Foreign ministers from major powers including the United States, the United Kingdom, France, and Russia all agreed to the meeting, and decided to attend in person. They all valued China's role, and hoped that I could also take part.

It seemed I had to make a special trip to New York. After getting approval from the central government, I decided to take a day from my African trip in order to attend the meeting in New York.

On January 18, having completed my visit to Botswana, I left

Gaborone at that night aboard a plane chartered from a French company. After a short technical stop in Conakry, capital of Guinea, I flew to New York.

On the morning of January 19, I arrived at John F. Kennedy International Airport in New York after a nine-hour flight.

I stayed in New York for thirty-five hours. During that time, apart from attending the foreign ministers' meeting on combatting terrorism, I met with the US Secretary of State Colin Powell, Russian Foreign Minister Igor Ivanov, German Vice Chancellor and Foreign Minister Joschka Fischer, and UN Secretary-General Kofi Annan.

The Iraq issue was the central concern of all these consultations.

Just four days before, the UN inspectors had found twelve chemical warheads in an Iraqi ammunition depot, and more than three thousand pages of documents on nuclear technology in the homes of two Iraqi scientists.

The United States insisted that the matter was a serious example of Iraq's material breach of the UN resolutions, but France, Russia, and Germany held a different point of view and urged hearing the inspectors' report before making a judgment.

At my meeting with Colin Powell, he said clearly that time was nearly up for Iraq, who must take the final opportunity to cooperate with the international community and comply with Security Council Resolution 1441.

He also said that President Bush had not yet made any decision as to whether military actions should be taken against Iraq, and still wished to settle the Iraq issue by peaceful and political means. He said that American military deployment in the Gulf area was to address problems that might arise.

He told me that UNMOVIC and IAEA would report to the Security Council a week later on their inspection findings. President Bush had instructed the US permanent mission to the United Nations to carefully study the report and the reactions of other

Meeting US Secretary of State Colin Powell at the UN headquarters in New York on September 14, 2002.

Security Council members. Later, President Bush would discuss with Chinese President Jiang Zemin and leaders of other countries before deciding what to do next.

Obviously, the United States thought it had obtained the evidence, and was really tough in its attitude.

I stressed to Mr. Powell that resolving the Iraq issue under the UN framework would be the least costly option and that the priority for the time being was to continue the UN inspections and let the facts speak for themselves. As to what to do next, the Security Council would decide. It should respect the viewpoints of UNMOVIC and IAEA.

Russia's view was similar to ours on the issue. Both Mr. Ivanov and I held that if doubts existed on the Iraq report concerning the WMD, the parties concerned could ask Iraq for explanations and clarifications. All parties should support UNMOVIC and IAEA

At a luncheon held by UN Secretary-General Kofi Annan for foreign ministers of the five permanent member states of the Security Council at the UN headquarters in New York on September 13, 2002.

in carrying out objective and just inspections, give them enough time, and respect their assessment. It was the Security Council that should decide what to do next.

Germany was also against the use of force against Iraq. Joschka Fischer said that in Germany's opinion, Security Council Resolution 1441 could be enforced by nonmilitary means. Resorting to force would only bring humanitarian disasters and even the revival of terrorism. The adverse impact could not be overestimated.

He spoke highly of the United Nations' inspection work on the Iraq issue, and considered that UNMOVIC and IAEA had done a very good job. He said that if the goal of all parties was really to remove Iraq's WMD, they should not obstruct the continuation of the inspection work. Having heard the report from the two organizations, the Security Council should act carefully to prevent things from going in the wrong direction.

Finally, he told me expressly that he and German Chancellor Gerhard Schröder both thought that Germany should do its best to seek a political settlement, and would not participate in any war against Iraq.

As president of the Security Council, French Foreign Minister Dominique de Villepin held a luncheon for the foreign ministers and Mr. Kofi Annan in the official residence of the French permanent mission to the United Nations on January 20, 2003. The luncheon, however, turned out to be a heated debate. Everybody was talking about work, mainly centering on the inspection findings from UNMOVIC and IAEA, and how the international community should handle the Iraq issue. In fact, the Security Council member states were trying to sound out each other's real intentions.

Mr. Powell insisted that the report submitted by Iraq had not told the whole truth on its WMD, emphasizing repeatedly that, despite the importance of the briefing to be given by UNMOVIC and IAEA to the Security Council on January 27, inspections in Iraq could not be carried on indefinitely. He even said that if Iraq continued to breach Resolution 1441, the United States would not deny the possibility of resorting to force against Iraq in the near future. The United States was concerned about Iraq's economic development and social stability, which would bring the Iraqi people a new government and help them develop oil resources.

British Foreign Secretary Jack Straw echoed that history had proved that Iraq would implement the Security Council resolutions only under great military pressure and that diplomatic efforts would be effective only under pressure. He said that the United Kingdom would not tolerate Iraq's continued evasion of its obligation to destroy its WMD.

UN Secretary-General Kofi Annan spoke of the necessity to put pressure on Iraq so that Iraq would not misread the situation or play tricks. Without the previous pressure from the United States, Iraq probably would not have allowed the UN inspectors to return,

Meeting British Foreign Secretary Jack Straw at the UN headquarters in New York on September 14, 2002.

and the nuclear inspections on Iraq would not have been implemented and strengthened. Kofi Annan also said that we should give the UN inspectors enough time to finish their tasks.

France, Russia, and Germany's position was clear: They were for further inspection and against the use of force.

Russian Foreign Minister Igor Ivanov maintained that the recent visit to Iraq by the two organizations had produced positive results. All parties should support further inspections in Iraq and give the inspectors more time to make sure that the Security Council resolutions were fully complied with. He pointedly stressed that the United Nations' policy towards Iraq was disarmament, not regime change.

French Foreign Minister Dominique de Villepin stated that the use of force against Iraq would negate all the previous achievements and the meaning of inspections. Interested parties should consider the serious consequences that military actions might cause, which would be disastrous not only for Iraq, but also for the region and for neighboring countries. He said frankly that since there were serious divisions on whether to use force against Iraq, it would impair the authority and function of the Security Council if some countries went their own way.

Other countries also took their stand. German Foreign Minister Joschka Fischer agreed with Igor Ivanov in believing that the purpose of the United Nations was to disarm Iraq. Germany supported the continuation of inspection work. Pakistan was worried that a war against Iraq would arouse greater hostility in the Islamic world against the United States.

Syria's foreign minister was not present, so he appointed the Syrian permanent representative to the UN to attend the meeting. The representative told us that his foreign minister had just visited Saudi Arabia, Iran, and Turkey. Opinion in all three countries was that since Iraq had destroyed great quantities of WMD, it no longer posed a threat to neighboring countries, and that Israel was the biggest threat to the entire Middle East. Syria maintained that the primary task for the international community was not to fight against Iraq, but to solve the current Palestinian-Israeli conflict at an early date. The Syrian representative's speech to some extent represented the attitude of the entire Arab world.

I also made a speech at the luncheon. I said that until now the inspections on Iraq had been going well, without serious problems. UNMOVIC and IAEA had reached a ten-point joint statement with Iraq, hoping to get more time for the inspection. The Security Council should value and respect their views.

I also said clearly that, on January 27, the Security Council would hear the most recent inspection briefing, but that this did not mean the conclusion of the inspections. All parties should respect the information and assessment provided by the two organizations with an objective and practical attitude. As to whether Iraq had complied with Security Council resolutions or still held WMD, we should let the facts speak for themselves rather than jump to conclusions. If the situation required further actions by the Security Council, a prudent decision should be taken after hearing the views of the two organizations and after full consultations in the Security Council.

That night, I took a chartered plane from New York to Brazzaville in the Republic of Congo to continue my interrupted African itinerary.

As JFK International Airport receded in the distance, I recalled the intensive diplomatic activities around the Iraq issue at the foreign ministers' meeting. Reflecting on the different positions of all parties, I had the feeling that this was just the beginning and that ahead lay even fiercer struggles and disputes on Iraq within the Security Council.

A Second Visit to New York: American Cards on the Table

ON JANUARY 27, 2003, UNMOVIC and IAEA presented a report to the Security Council, saying they had so far discovered no solid evidence that Iraq was developing WMD, and asking to continue their inspections.

The international community supported the request of the two organizations, but the United States insisted that as long as Saddam Hussein was in power, it would be meaningless to prolong the nuclear inspections.

The next day, President Bush delivered a State of the Union address in Washington, criticizing Iraq again for noncompliance with Resolution 1441, and saying that Iraq had connections with al-Qaeda. He explicitly announced that the United States was going to lead an international coalition to disarm Iraq.

In his speech, Mr. Bush suggested that a foreign ministers' meeting should be held on February 5 to discuss the Iraq issue.

I immediately asked our embassy in Washington to find out the United States' true intentions and what were its specific considerations. The United States revealed that Colin Powell was going to share with all participants certain information obtained by the United States, which would constitute solid evidence of Iraq's non-compliance with Security Council resolutions and its possession of WMD.

The United States also said that it valued highly the position of, and role played by, China and hoped that the Chinese foreign minister could attend the meeting. Later, the United States side repeatedly expressed the same ideas to us through various channels.

At the same time, we learned that foreign ministers of the United Kingdom, France, Russia, Germany, and other major countries had decided to attend the meeting.

In view of these circumstances, I decided to leave for New York for a second time.

The meeting fell on the Spring Festival holidays, a traditional Chinese festival. February 1 was the lunar New Year's Day. On that morning, I summoned Foreign Ministry colleagues to study issues that might be involved in the forthcoming foreign ministers' meeting.

Actually, many of my Foreign Ministry colleagues had been working overtime those days; some had even spent New Year's Eve in the office. Of course, they would have preferred to be with their families for the holiday, but the job required them to stay at their post. This is an experience shared by many diplomats.

Prior to the meeting, we carefully studied and analyzed the situation and various possible scenarios.

At that time, the United States was taking a series of diplomatic actions. US President Bush and Secretary of State Colin Powell

An open meeting on the Iraq issue being convened within the Security Council at the UN headquarters in New York on February 5, 2003.

made personal phone calls to the state leaders and foreign ministers of Security Council members, urging support for the passing of a resolution at the Security Council to authorize military action by the United States against Iraq.

Although the United States repeatedly expressed its determination to resort to force even without Security Council authorization, it actually wished to make every effort to get the resolution passed. Colin Powell would attend the meeting in person, with a view to proving the solidness of the evidence of Iraq's noncompliance with Security Council resolutions, and pushing forward the process on the Iraq issue at the Security Council. The United States was, in fact, forcing a showdown on Iraq.

While others were celebrating the Spring Festival, my colleagues and I boarded a plane for New York. It was usually very difficult to get visas for the United States, but this time, the United States was very generous. When one of our diplomats went to the American embassy in China about visas for the Chinese delegation, the US visa officer was there waiting, even though it was a holiday for embassy staff, too. He welcomed our diplomat and got all the visas ready immediately.

On February 5, the Security Council convened an open meeting on the Iraq issue. Open meetings, as the name implies, are open to the rest of the world besides the fifteen member states of the Security Council. Other UN members and the media may all attend and listen to the proceedings.

At that time, the Iraq issue was a matter of prime importance in the world. All parties, the United States in particular, paid great attention to it. The size of the US delegation was unprecedented, including Secretary of State Colin Powell, and high-ranking officials such as the director of the CIA and the chairman of the Joint Chiefs of Staff.

The US delegation made meticulous preparations for this meeting. They installed various advanced video and audio equipment in the Hall of the Security Council, the venue for the meeting. The equipment was for Colin Powell's address.

With the exception of Angola, Guinea, and Syria, the foreign ministers of all fifteen member states of the Security Council attended the meeting, namely, China, Russia, the United States, the United Kingdom, France, Germany, Bulgaria, Spain, Cameroon, Mexico, Chile, and Pakistan. UN Secretary-General Kofi Annan, Chairman of UNMOVIC Dr. Hans Blix, and IAEA Director-General Mohamed ElBaradei also attended the meeting.

The Hall of the Security Council was very crowded on that day. Every seat was taken; many diplomats from other UN member states were obliged to stand in the aisles, since the seats reserved for them had been occupied by journalists arriving early. The hall was packed to bursting.

According to colleagues who had long worked in the United Nations, that day's spectacle was a rare one in its history.

The event was broadcast live by international media.

Colin Powell was the first to speak.

Wearing a dark suit, white shirt, and purplish necktie, Mr. Powell happened to be seated diagonally opposite me. I could tell from his heavy-hearted look that his speech would be very important for both him and the United States.

Later, his aide told us that Mr. Powell had rehearsed a lot for the presentation and could practically recite it. This reflected how much importance he attached to it.

His speech lasted about ninety minutes. With the assistance of many video clips, recordings, and slides, he enumerated case after case of Iraq's breaches of Security Council resolutions

Mr. Powell solemnly stated that evidence showed that Iraq had concealed WMD, cheated the UN nuclear inspectors, and even obstructed their work surreptitiously. Iraq was developing ballistic missiles and other means of delivering WMD. The Saddam regime had connections with international terrorist organizations; it financed Palestinian terrorists and harbored al-Qaeda members who had fled Afghanistan. He also claimed that al-Qaeda terrorists hiding in Iraq were implicated in the assassination of a high-ranking US diplomat in Jordan.

Mr. Powell concluded that Iraq's actions had been in material breach of its obligations under Security Council Resolution 1441. According to him, the problem lay not in allowing the UN inspectors more time, but in how much more the Security Council would tolerate Iraq. In the light of Iraq's invasion of other countries in the past, its attempt to control the whole of the Middle East, and its determination to keep and develop WMD, the United States would not and could not let Saddam Hussein keep and use WMD at the risk of world security.

Mr. Powell finally said that Resolution 1441 had given Iraq one last chance. However, the inspections of the last two months had proven that Iraq had no intention of seizing this chance, but continued to breach its obligations under the Security Council resolu-

Attending the high-level Security Council meeting held at the UN headquarters in New York to mark the 1st anniversary of the 9/11 attacks, on September 11, 2002.

tions. In this situation, the Security Council must not shrink from its responsibilities.

Mr. Powell's statement actually kicked off a new round of diplomatic initiatives and media support for America's eventual declaration of war on Iraq.

The United States did indeed present new things at this meeting, and to some extent, these gave the impression that Iraq was holding and concealing WMD. However, later facts proved that the so-called information and evidence were faulty, and Mr. Powell's presentation at the Security Council became his Waterloo.

In September 2005, retired Secretary of State Colin Powell publicly admitted, in an interview given to American ABC TV, that his presentation at the Security Council was inaccurate. Describing it as "a blot" on his record, he said, "It's painful for me."

After Powell's presentation, foreign ministers from other participating nations began to deliver speeches. The order of speaking had been decided by drawing lots, and I was the first to speak.

I made five points in my speech. First, I noted that foreign ministers from a majority of the Security Council member states were present, which indicated that all parties valued the authority and function of the Security Council and supported the political settlement of the Iraq issue under the UN framework. It would be of critical importance for the proper settlement of the Iraq issue if the Security Council member states could maintain unity and cooperation. It was also the common aspiration of the international community.

I then said that China welcomed the information and evidence provided by the United States to the United Nations about Iraq's possession of WMD. We hoped that all parties would hand their information and evidence to UNMOVIC and IAEA, so that their inspections and assessment could be carried out more effectively, while the two organizations should present their inspection findings to the Security Council on schedule.

I also affirmed the achievements of the two organizations. For as long as they maintained that the inspections should not be concluded but continued, we should respect and support them. Not long before, the two organizations had pointed out some problems encountered in the inspection, so we had urged Iraq to take a more positive attitude and make further explanations and clarifications to help the inspection.

I especially pointed out that the Security Council members shared the same opinion on removing Iraq's WMD, as reflected in the relevant Security Council resolutions, Resolution 1441 in particular. The priority at present was to implement the resolution in earnest. As for further actions of the Security Council, these should be decided by all member states after deliberation on the basis of the inspection results.

Finally, I stressed the strong desire of the international community to achieve a political settlement of the Iraq issue under the UN framework and to avoid war. The Security Council must attach great importance to this common aspiration. As long as there was a ray of hope, we should make every effort to seek a political settlement. China was ready to work hand in hand with other parties to this end.

After my speech, foreign ministers of France, Russia, Germany, and other countries then delivered their speeches. Their views were still at odds with those of the United States and the United Kingdom. The positions of the member states were sharply divided on this issue.

After the meeting, I met with the foreign ministers of the United States, Russia, the United Kingdom, France, Germany, Mexico, Spain, and Pakistan as well as UN Secretary-General Kofi Annan.

Judging by the atmosphere at the meeting and my conversations with the foreign ministers, I could tell that on the one hand, Saddam Hussein's regime was indeed unpopular and all nations had been prepared for the United States to resort to force against Iraq. On the other hand, the United States and the United Kingdom were still trying to pass a new authorization resolution at the Security Council to legitimize military action against Iraq. They were doing their best to win international support for passing an ambiguous resolution at least, which they could interpret in a way favorable for further action on their part.

However, the United States and the United Kingdom were unwilling to spend too much time on this. If the United States thought consensus would not be reached in a short period of time, it might unite some countries in taking military action of their own accord.

A Third Visit: War and Peace in the Balance

ACCORDING TO UN ARRANGEMENTS, UNMOVIC and IAEA would hand in another inspection report to the Security Council on February 14, 2003.

On February 11, French President Jacques Chirac discussed the Iraq issue on the phone with Chinese President Jiang Zemin. President Chirac said that Iraq's situation was at a critical point and that in order to solicit support from other Security Council member states for a political settlement, the foreign ministers of France, Germany, and Russia would leave for New York to attend the relevant Security Council meeting on February 14. President Chirac desired that President Jiang ask the Chinese foreign minister to attend.

In order to demonstrate China's constructive role on the Iraq issue and in support of diplomatic efforts to avert war, the central government decided to send me to the meeting. Therefore, within ten days, I left for New York to attend the foreign ministers' meeting on the Iraq issue once again.

On February 14, the UN Security Council held an open meeting to hear the report from inspectors of the two organizations. Ten of the fifteen Security Council member states sent their foreign ministers, including China, France, Russia, the United Kingdom, and the United States.

This time, the inspectors of the two organizations primarily presented their inspection findings to the Security Council. On the one hand, they said that WMD had not been found in Iraq; on the other, they could not confirm that Iraq was not holding WMD. While recognizing that Iraq had provided some new cooperation to the UN inspection organizations, the report criticized the documents supplied by Iraq for not clarifying the problems found in the inspections, and demanded that Iraq provide substantive cooperation.

With regard to the critical issue as to whether Iraq was in mate-

Arriving in New York on February 13, 2003, ready to attend an open meeting on the Iraq issue to be held the next day within the UN Security Council.

rial breach of its obligations under UN resolutions, whether inspections should be continued, and whether the inspection mechanism should be strengthened, the two organizations stressed that these were decisions for the Security Council to make.

It was clear that the two organizations were addressing the concerns of all the parties.

All participants delivered speeches on the report.

The United States criticized Iraq for failing to cooperate with the UN inspection work and not fulfilling Resolution 1441. It maintained that Iraq was still cheating the United Nations and that any increase in the number of inspectors or prolongation of inspections would be pointless. The Security Council should take action in the near future.

The United Kingdom, Spain, and Bulgaria echoed the US

Meeting German Vice Chancellor and Foreign Minister Joschka Fischer at the foreign ministers' meeting on the Iraq issue on February 14, 2003.

stand. The United Kingdom said that the peaceful disarmament of Iraq should be backed with military power.

Iraq refuted the American criticism.

A majority of the Security Council member states such as China, France, Germany, and Russia reaffirmed that the Iraq issue should be settled politically under the UN framework. They held that earlier inspections had yielded results and should be continued, and that the inspection mechanism should be reinforced. They also urged Iraq to improve its cooperation with the United Nations.

In my speech, I expressly agreed with the majority of the Security Council members that inspections were effective and needed to continue. Enough time should be given to the inspectors to implement Resolution 1441 and fulfill the mission assigned by the Security Council.

I stressed the need for a political settlement and the avoidance of war, describing peace and development as a common aspiration shared by the world population. As member states of the Security Council, we had no reason not to strive to realize it and to avoid war. Only by going in the direction of a political settlement could we meet the trust and expectations placed on the Security Council by the international community.

What impressed me most that day was the speech by French Foreign Minister Dominique de Villepin.

Mr. de Villepin was born in Rabat, the capital of Morocco. He is tall and slender, with wavy gray hair and an artistic temperament. He is indeed a prolific writer and poet, and his poetic stature brings great passion to his speeches and work.

On that day, on the platform of the Security Council, Mr. de Villepin delivered a passionate speech. In poetic words, he explicitly expressed France's opposition to the United States launching war against Iraq.

Meeting French Foreign Minister Dominique de Villepin at the UN headquarters in New York on September 14, 2002.

In his speech, Mr. de Villepin said that, although the war option might seem swift, the building of peace after the war would be a long and difficult process. Inspections, on the other hand, provided an alternative in moving forward day by day with the effective and peaceful disarmament of Iraq.

He emphasized that the path of war was no shorter than that of inspections, nor would it necessarily lead to a more secure, just and stable world, war always being the outcome of failure. In the present situation, the use of force was unjustified.

Finally, with deep emotion, he said that France was an old country that had never ceased to stand upright in the face of history and before mankind. Faithful to its values, France wished resolutely to act with all the members of the international community in the building of a better world.

Mr. de Villepin's speech drew prolonged applause from the audience.

It was clear that the Security Council members were split between the pro-war and the pro-peace camps, each sticking to its own viewpoint. Most countries stood in contrast to the United States and the United Kingdom, opposing the use of force against Iraq under the present circumstances. Countries like France and Germany publicly declared their opposing views.

It was very difficult for the United States and the United Kingdom to seek Security Council authorization for the use of force within a short period. They would probably settle for pushing through a new resolution derogating Iraq as a nation threatening international peace and security and setting a deadline timetable for Iraq to cooperate with the United Nations.

A Fourth Visit: Battling for Peace

TEN DAYS AFTER THE two organizations handed in the report to the Security Council, on the morning of February 25, 2003, Beijing time, the United States and the United Kingdom, together with Spain, presented a new draft resolution to the Security Council.

Just as anticipated, the draft explicitly stated that Iraq had not cooperated fully with the United Nations, and had breached the Security Council resolutions, posing a threat to international peace and security. It suggested that the Security Council take action in accordance with Chapter VII of the UN Charter.

As the core of the UN collective security mechanism, Chapter VII of the UN Charter determines the existence of any threat to the peace, breach of the peace, or act of aggression. It lays down clear and specific rules for determining any action to be taken to prevent the worsening of the situation, to apply military or nonmilitary sanctions in fulfillment of the Security Council resolutions, and the exercise of the right of self-defense. That is to say, under Chapter VII of the UN Charter, the United Nations can take collective enforcement action, including military action.

In this way, although authorization of the use of force was not spelled out in the new draft, it did identify Iraq as a country threatening international peace and security, against which action should be taken according to Chapter VII. If the draft were passed, it would be seen as tantamount to UN authorization of the use of force by the United States and the United Kingdom.

Though the cosponsors expressed that advice from other countries would be welcome, they stressed that they would make no substantive changes to this draft. From their attitude, we could tell that the United States was determined to go to war with Iraq and to overthrow the Saddam regime, and that its military deployment was in place. This meant that military action against Iraq was inevitable, irrespective of whether the new draft was passed.

At almost the same time, France, Russia, and Germany distributed a joint memorandum at the Security Council on strengthening UN inspections of Iraq's nuclear weapons, and clearly indicated their opposition to any new draft resolutions.

We were now at a stage at which the contending players had to show their hands.

China, of course, was against the new draft resolution.

Striving to the utmost for world peace, President Jiang Zemin and General-Secretary Hu Jintao talked to leaders of the United States, the United Kingdom, France, Russia, and Germany, emphasizing the necessity of further inspections and a political settlement of the Iraq issue under the UN framework, as well as the needlessness of a new draft resolution. President Jiang and General-Secretary Hu also stressed the peaceful settlement of the Iraq issue, and said wars would benefit no side. Though a political settlement might take longer, it would be the least costly option, and in the best interests of all concerned.

On March 7, the Security Council held an open meeting to hear an update on nuclear inspections in Iraq presented by UNMOVIC and IAEA.

The meeting had been originally convened at the proposal of the United Kingdom as a routine Security Council meeting, but was later upgraded to a ministerial-level meeting at the urging of France and Russia, whose purpose was to strengthen and expand the antiwar camp and to constrain the United States and the United Kingdom.

Originally, neither Colin Powell nor Jack Straw intended to attend the meeting, but they changed their minds. It seemed that all major powers were aware that the Iraq issue was at the stage at which all parties were showing their hands, and wanted to use this last opportunity to exert influence and win support.

In view of the importance of this meeting to all members of the Security Council, the central government decided to send me to the meeting. The timing happened to coincide with the Two Congresses (the National People's Congress and the Chinese People's Political Consultative Conference); therefore, deputies to the NPC and the media at home and abroad were paying great attention to the Iraq issue and China's position.

It is the usual practice each year for the foreign minister to hold a press conference during the two congresses to give a wide-ranging report on China's diplomatic work, and to answer questions from Chinese and foreign journalists on major international and regional issues. The press conference that year was held at the Great Hall of the People at three o'clock on March 6, the day before the third foreign ministers' meeting on the Iraq issue.

At that day's press conference, Iraq was the hottest issue, with questions raised by six reporters. I was mentally prepared for this.

The first question came from a China Central Television (CCTV) journalist. She first asked me to comment on and envisage

At the press conference for the "two congresses" at the Great Hall of the People on March 6, 2003.

China's diplomacy, and then inquired, "Iraq is now on the brink of war. In your opinion, can the war be avoided?"

This gave me the opportunity to explain China's position on the Iraq issue right at the start of the press conference, to describe China's efforts in maintaining world peace, and to announce that I was leaving for New York to attend the Security Council foreign ministers' meeting. I also declared that the purpose and objective of my attending the meeting was to make every effort to seek a political settlement of the Iraq issue.

Therefore, my answer to her question was that the Iraq issue was at the crossroads of a military or a political settlement. China's stand was clear to all: to seek a political settlement under the UN framework. It was under China's Security Council presidency in November last year that Resolution 1441 had been passed by the Security Council. The tasks stipulated in the resolution had not been fulfilled, so we should continue to step up the inspections to get a clear picture of the situation, seek a political settlement, and avoid war. Therefore, China did not think it necessary to pass a new draft resolution for the moment.

I told the journalists that after the press conference I would go to the airport directly and leave for New York. I would make it clear to the whole world at the foreign ministers' meeting that China, as a permanent member of the Security Council, would by no means give up the hope for peace. As long as there was a 1 percent possibility of a political settlement, China would make a 100 percent effort.

A journalist from L'Agence France-Presse (AFP) asked, "China has expressed many times its wish for a peaceful settlement of the Iraq issue, and you also have said that as long as there is a one percent possibility of a political settlement, China would continue its effort. Does this mean that China might use the veto at the UN Security Council? Will China take China-US relations into consideration when deciding on the use of veto?"

I replied that his question was still premature at this stage. In our opinion, there still remained the possibility of a political and diplomatic settlement. As for China's position on voting, when dealing with such issues, China had always been independent in making judgments on the merits of each case and in accord with China's diplomatic policies and principles and the fundamental interests of the people of China and the world at large.

That day's press conference was practically a special conference on Iraq. Even as I left the Great Hall of the People, many journalists were still surrounding me, asking questions about the issue.

I was driven directly to the airport for my flight to New York.

During the flight, I could not relax at all. Prior to this meeting, the United States and the United Kingdom had already made full military preparations: The arrow was on the bowstring. Now they were boosting public opinion and urgently needed the political support of the Security Council. Therefore, they would try their best at the meeting to push the passing of a new draft resolution to green-light their attack on Iraq.

We were facing a grave situation.

At about nine-thirty on the morning of March 7, 2003, when I arrived at the UN headquarters for the fourth time within a little over a month, seeing the national flags of the UN member states and the light blue UN banner fluttering in front of the building, I was overwhelmed by mixed feelings.

At the first UN General Assembly session in January 1946, New York was chosen as the location of the UN headquarters. Later, the Rockefeller family donated to the United Nations a piece of land beside the East River, which became the site of UN headquarters.

The complex, completed in 1952, consists of four adjoining buildings, including the thirty-nine-story Secretariat Tower, the Conference and Visitors Centers, the General Assembly Hall, and the Dag Hammarskjöld Library.

Fifty years later, the gray complex was still standing there, having played an irreplaceable role in maintaining world peace and promoting common development through changing times.

Today, as we were once more faced with such a major issue of principle—peace or war—would the United Nations stand firmly on the side of peace?

Eleven of the fifteen Security Council member states had sent their foreign ministers. The Arab League delegation had also changed their schedule and arrived in New York for the meeting. UN Secretary-General Kofi Annan was present that day. We could tell that all parties regarded the meeting as critical and most important.

The two inspection organizations gave a progress update, mainly providing facts, without drawing any conclusion.

The participants then began to speak. There was still a clear divide between the pro-war and the pro-peace camps.

France, Russia, Germany, and Syria did not support the use of force against Iraq. They maintained that since progress had been made in the inspections, we should continue with and enhance them, and finally disarm Iraq in a peaceful way rather than pass a new resolution. They also demanded that Iraq fully comply with the disarmament obligations stipulated in the Security Council resolutions, and cooperate more positively with the United Nations.

Mexico, Chile, Angola, Cameroon, Pakistan, and Guinea also advocated a peaceful settlement of the issue through multilateral endeavors. They stressed the significant role of the Security Council, and wished to find a solution by maintaining unity within the Security Council, in particular among the five permanent members.

Contrary to France's position, the United States, the United Kingdom, Spain, and Bulgaria held that continuation of the inspections would be meaningless. The Security Council should act decisively in order to maintain its authority and credibility. The United States expressly asked the Security Council to make a political decision, and to disarm Iraq by military means. It announced that it would soon ask the Security Council to vote on the new draft resolution.

I was aware that the United States was determined to resort to force in disregard of the results of the vote. Even so, the Security Council had to maintain its authority, uphold justice, and refuse to give the green light to the use of force. History would not allow us to do otherwise.

At my desk in the conference hall, with CHINA on the nameplate in front of me, I was aware that as the representative of China, we must grasp what might be the last slim chance of hope and make the utmost effort for peace.

At the beginning of my speech, I stressed that, four months earlier, Resolution 1441 had been passed unanimously in the spirit of unity and cooperation, which had reflected the Security Council's determination to destroy Iraq's WMD, and the common aspiration of the international community to seek a political settlement of the Iraq issue. The deed had been universally welcomed and supported.

I continued that it was an arduous task for us to implement the Security Council resolutions, and to thoroughly remove Iraq's WMD. According to the report from the two organizations, the implementation of Resolution 1441 was generally good, progressive, and effective. Problems and difficulties that had occurred during the inspection process proved the necessity of inspections. We believed that as long as we progressed in the direction of a political settlement, we would realize the goal of destroying Iraq's WMD.

I emphasized that what we now needed was not only determination and courage, but all the more patience and wisdom. Unity and cooperation had to be maintained in order to safeguard the authority of the Security Council.

I made clear China's position at the meeting. I said that we asked the Security Council to continue with its guidance and support of the inspection work of the two organizations, to carry on the inspections and size up the situation once the two organizations had completed their mission under Resolution 1441. Meanwhile, China also urged the Iraqi government to take further effective measures, enhance substantive cooperation with the UN inspectors, and create the necessary conditions for a political solution.

I pointed out categorically that we had no reason to shut the door of peace. China was not in favor of a new draft resolution, particularly a resolution containing the authorization of use of force.

I said that the Iraq issue concerned the peace and development of the Gulf area and the world at large. In resolving the issue, the common interests of all nations and the long-term interests of human development must be taken into full consideration. In the twenty-first century, peace and development remained the main theme of the times. All countries in the world were facing the same task of maintaining peace and promoting development and prosperity, and all countries earnestly desired a stable and peaceful international environment.

Finally, I said that we should take people as the foremost among all creatures, and harmony as the most precious among all things. Over the past few months, we had heard repeated strong appeals from most UN member states for a political settlement. Outside the hall, we had repeatedly heard the voices of the people of all countries for peace and no war. The powers of the Security Council came from all UN member states and their people. We had no reason not to be moved by their strong demands and voices. In view of the responsibility to history and the common interests of the peoples, the Chinese government strongly appealed to the Security Council to perform its responsibility in avoiding wars and seeking a political settlement unremittingly.

After the meeting, an internal Security Council consultation was held. The United States, the United Kingdom, and Spain elaborated on their amendments to the draft resolution, in which they were willing to give Iraq ten more days as an embodiment of flexibility. If, ten days later, it could not be concluded that Iraq had provided comprehensive, timely, positive, and unconditional cooperation, the Security Council should automatically determine that Iraq had missed its one last chance.

The United States and the United Kingdom set March 17 as the deadline, in effect delivering an ultimatum to Iraq.

This meeting was the last round of exploration and sounding out the opposition before all parties put their cards on the table, so fierce contests prevailed before and after the meeting.

It was clear that the United States would have great difficulty in getting its draft resolution passed at the Security Council.

I stayed for less than fourteen hours in New York, and returned to China immediately after the meeting, since prior to my departure the central leadership had instructed me to "hurry there and back."

On the flight back, we made a quick analysis and summary of the meeting that all parties were going to show their cards and that war would be inevitable.

As soon as we arrived in Beijing, I went to the Zhongnanhai, the central government compound, to report on the meeting to leaders of the party and the central government, and to present our analysis and conclusion. As later events proved, our conclusion was correct, and provided an important reference for the Central Authorities' preparations.

Justice Persists amid the Flames of War

HAVING FAILED TO WIN support from a majority of the Security Council member states by pressure, leaders of the United States, the United Kingdom, and Spain held an emergency consultation on Iraq in the Portuguese Azores on March 16.

After the consultation, a joint declaration was issued, reiterating that Resolution 1441 had given Iraq one last chance, but that since Iraq had failed to fully cooperate with the United Nations and was in material breach of the resolution, war against Iraq was the inevitable choice. However, the three countries also said they would make one final diplomatic effort.

On March 18, the United States and the United Kingdom announced that they would no longer ask the Security Council to vote on the draft resolution.

That night, US President George W. Bush appeared on national television, delivering an ultimatum to Iraq, demanding that Saddam Hussein and his sons leave Iraq within forty-eight hours.

On March 20, Bush made another television speech, announcing that "American and coalition forces are in the early stage of military operations to disarm Iraq."

The Iraq War finally began.

In the months leading up to the war, despite great pressure from countries such as the United States and the United Kingdom, the Security Council had withstood the pressure to the end and refused to give the green light to military actions against Iraq, thus upholding moral principles and justice.

That same day, China's Foreign Ministry issued a statement expressing serious concern over the military actions launched by the United States and the United Kingdom against Iraq, bypassing the UN Security Council. We reiterated our view that the Iraq issue should be resolved under the framework of the United Nations, demanded that the Iraqi government fully implement the relevant Security Council resolutions, and expressed our respect of Iraq's sovereignty and territorial integrity. We maintained that Resolution 1441 remained the important foundation for a political settlement. The statement also strongly appealed for the countries concerned to stop military actions and return to the correct path of a political settlement.

More than six years have now elapsed. Looking back, I am gratified by our consistent, firm, and clear-cut stand on the cardinal issue of peace or war on Iraq. We always adhered to our principles, safeguarded peace and opposed war, and spared no efforts in striving for the slightest possibility of peace at a critical time. Reality in Iraq has demonstrated who was right and who was wrong.

CHAPTER 4

Sino-Russian Negotiations over Heixiazi Island

H EIXIAZI ISLAND LIES AT the easternmost point of the territory of the People's Republic of China.

On October 14, 2008, China and the Russian Federation held a ceremony here to unveil the frontier markers for the eastern section of the China–Russia border. It was simple yet solemn; the national anthems of both nations were played and their national flags were raised. A wide backdrop screen stood amid the autumn fields. It was a fine day, with the sky cloudless and blue. At the conclusion of the ceremony, Chinese frontier guards entered Heixiazi Island to conduct their defense operations at this easternmost post along China's eastern border.

The frontier markers on Heixiazi Island were the last markers erected on the border between China and Russia.

When I saw this report on CCTV, I felt very excited that this thorny problem in which I intervened as foreign minister and state councilor was now finally resolved.

The events of those years flashed through my mind.

Raising the national flag of the People's Republic of China at the ceremony on Heixiazi Island unveiling the boundary marker for the eastern section of the China-Russia border, October 14, 2008.

The History of a Complicated Border Issue

THE CHINA-RUSSIA BORDER ISSUE was left over from the era of the Soviet Union. Following its collapse, the 7,600-kilometer boundary between China and the Soviet Union was now shared by China and four countries: Russia, Kazakhstan, Kyrgyzstan, and Tajikistan. The boundary between China and Russia stretched over 4,300 kilometers, most of which had been delimited through negotiations, leaving Heixiazi Island as the only outstanding land.

Heixiazi Island represented only 1.4 percent of the total length of the China-Russia border, a small proportion perhaps, but one of great strategic significance. As each side stuck to its own argument concerning the former boundary treaties and refused to yield,

it became the most difficult and sensitive issue of boundary negotiations between our two countries. China referred to it as "a hard
bone to chew" while Russia called it "a hard nut to crack."

Heixiazi in the dialect of northeast China means "black bear."
Locals explain that this island's name came about because it was
once the haunt of black bears. The western media translated it as
"Bear Island," a name I think both accurate and symbolic.

Heixiazi Island is also called the Fuyuan Delta. It is situated
in the east of Fuyuan County, Heilongjiang Province, and surrounded by three water courses: the Heilongjiang (Amur) River in
the north, the Wusuli (Ussuri) River in the southeast, and a channel in the southwest connecting the two rivers, which is known as
the Fuyuan Channel to the Chinese and Kkazakevichevo to the
Russians.

The Heixiazi shoreline measures sixty kilometers along the
north, forty kilometers along the southeast, and thirty-five kilometers along the Fuyuan Channel. Heixiazi comprises two major
islands and over ninety islets and shoals, whose numbers change as
the result of natural forces, such as water surges and tidal waves.

Covering 335 square kilometers, larger than the urban area
within Beijing's Fourth Ring Road, Heixiazi is a land of gentle
terrain, overgrown with weeds, bushes, and arbors typical of north
China. The waters around Heixiazi are rich in precious sea fish such
as salmon and sturgeon; black caviar of sturgeon and red caviar of
salmon are gourmet delights regularly seen on local tables.

According to Chinese historical records, Han, Hezhen, Ewenki,
and Oroqen ethnic groups used to live here. Some fired pottery
utensils, others ran taverns, and others even grew poppies.

Around the Revolution of 1911, a time of great chaos in China,
tsarist Russia took the opportunity to annex Heixiazi Island. Successive governments of China conducted repeated negotiations with
their Russian (Soviet) counterparts but to no avail.

In 1929, the Soviet Union occupied Heixiazi Island on the pretext of the Sino-Soviet Chinese Eastern Railway (CER) conflict.* For the following eighty years, Heixiazi Island remained under Soviet jurisdiction, with no Chinese inhabitants. All the buildings and facilities there were built by the Russians.

Heixiazi Island and Khabarovsk, a major city of the Russian Far East, face each other across the water. If you stand at the easternmost tip of Heixiazi Island, you can see the buildings in Khabarovsk quite clearly. For this reason, Heixiazi Island was regarded by Russia as both a natural barrier and gateway to Khabarovsk.

The Soviet Union (and Russia) never slackened its defenses on Heixiazi Island. They built many military installations, erecting a forty-kilometer barbed wire fence along the China-facing shore, and positioning gunboats, referred to by locals as "timber wolves," at the entrance to the Fuyuan Channel.

In 1974, the Soviet Union built a floating bridge over the Wusuli (Ussuri) River, twenty-six kilometers away from Khabarovsk. This 800-meter-long bridge is made up of 107 six-meter-wide pontoons linked, with bridge piers set up at each end. The bridge took vehicle traffic and also opened for one and a half hours daily between nine-thirty and eleven in the morning to allow vessels to pass. However, it was often closed by the Soviet Union for unspecified reasons, which obstructed the passage of Chinese ships, forcing them to anchor in midriver or turn back. China had made repeated representations to the Soviet Union about this issue.

For many years, the Soviets took advantage of their control over Heixiazi to exploit and make profits from its resources, building a factory and residential area, roads, and dairy farms on the

---

*In July 1929, Zhang Xueliang, the commander of the Northeast Army, regained by force the administration of Chinese Eastern Railway, and arrested a couple of Russians, including its general consul in Harbin. Russia, while lodging representations to China, sent its troops into Manchuria and sparked an armed conflict with the Northeast Army, which lasted for months. The Northeast Army suffered a crushing defeat, and the Chinese Eastern Railway fell back into Russian hands.

island. Every year, Russian residents would come to the island to cut grass, relax, and sunbathe. Their newspapers called it a "suburb of Khabarovsk."

Several years before the boundary demarcation, the Russian side planned to incorporate the development and building of Heixiazi Island into the Khabarovsk development plan under unified management, creating a nature reserve, an enclosed hunting area, and summer resort, developing tourism resources, further expanding agricultural production, and building bridges and roads.

Intense and Protracted Territorial Dispute

IN THE PAST FORTY years, China and the Soviet Union (Russia) conducted three rounds of border negotiations.

The first round of negotiations lasted from February to August 1964. The chief negotiator of the Chinese delegation was the then Vice Foreign Minister Zeng Yongquan, formerly a senior general in the revolutionary war. During the negotiation process, he argued fiercely with his Soviet counterpart, and as the Sino-Soviet relationship was beginning to openly deteriorate, no resolution of the border dispute was possible.

The second round of Sino-Soviet boundary negotiations began in October 1969. The first Chinese delegation leader was the then Vice Foreign Minister Qiao Guanhua. Those negotiations lasted for ten years, over which period the heads of delegation changed many times. The intense antagonism between the two countries during this period, plus the fierce armed clashes on Zhenbao Island even before these talks, meant that ten years of negotiations failed to resolve any of the border issues, still less that of Heixiazi Island.

However, the efforts were not completely fruitless. The process did at least establish a negotiation mechanism. The two sides began to act with restraint over border disputes, and armed conflicts like the Zhenbao Island Incident never recurred.

The third round of negotiations started in February 1987. The Chinese delegation was headed by the then Vice Foreign Minister Qian Qichen. In July 1986, Mikhail Gorbachev, general secretary of the Communist Party of the Soviet Union, made a public speech in Vladivostok, in which he said that China and Russia could demarcate their boundaries according to the thalweg (central line of the main channel) principle.

This was a positive signal to us. We responded quickly and agreed to restart negotiations.

This round of negotiations was most dramatic; at the outset, our rival negotiator was the Soviet Union, but by the end we were dealing with the Russian Federation. Maybe it was the unique moment that provided a historical opportunity: They were the most fruitful and most problem-solving of all negotiations so far. The two sides signed the Agreement on the Eastern Section of the Boundary between the People's Republic of China and the Union of Soviet Socialist Republics in 1991, and the Agreement on the Western Section of the Boundary Between the People's Republic of China and the Russian Federation in 1994, thus completing the delimitation of the overwhelming majority of the China-Russia border. However, the alignment of the boundary line in the areas of Heixiazi Island, despite repeated and intense arguments, made no progress and remained unsettled.

Later, the two sides resumed talks on this issue, but the negotiations made no headway, each one sticking to its own grounds and arguments over the years, each claiming full sovereignty over Heixiazi Island.

China claimed, according to the 1860 Treaty of Peking, that the boundary of the two countries was set along the Heilongjiang (Amur) and Wusuli (Ussuri) rivers. This being the case, it should be delimited along the central line of the main channel in accordance with recognized rules of international law. Since Heixiazi Island lay on the Chinese side of the main channel's central line, it should therefore belong to China.

Russia held that the map attached to the Treaty of Peking also formed part of the treaty. On this map, the red demarcation line was on Kkazakevichevo (Fuyuan Channel). Therefore, the Russian side maintained that border should be divided along this channel and that, accordingly, Heixiazi Island should belong to Russia. It also pointed out that, according to the Agreement on Delimitation of the Eastern Section of the China Russia Border signed in 1861 by tsarist Russia and the Qing government, a boundary marker had been erected on the Chinese side at the confluence of the Fuyuan Channel and the Wusuli (Ussuri) River. To the Russian government this was solid proof that Heixiazi Island belonged to Russia.

The boundary negotiations lasted on and off for almost forty years from 1964, and the ownership of Heixiazi Island still remained a contentious issue between the two nations.

History teaches us that border issues, if not properly settled, may become a hidden cancer in bilateral relations, leading even to war, and bringing trouble to both sides.

The Leadership Stepped In and Negotiations Moved Forward

BEFORE CHINA AND RUSSIA reached any agreement on the ownership of Heixiazi Island, Khabarovsk City intensified its efforts to develop the island and expand its influence westward.

What particularly caught attention was the building, between September 7 and November 18, 1999, of a twenty-eight-and-one-half-meter-high Russian Orthodox Church beside the Wusuli (Ussuri) River at the southern end of the Island. It was bright red and very eye-catching. Some high-ranking military, government, and religious representatives attended the groundbreaking ceremony. It was clearly intended to signal that Heixiazi Island belonged to Russia.

The more they exploited the island, the more difficult it would be for us to solve the problem, and this caused us serious concern. We made representations to Russia by various means but with no satisfactory results.

In March 2000, Vladimir Putin was elected president of Russia. A new administration was supposed to usher in a new era, and introduce new opportunities and practices, all of which might help settle this issue.

On July 17, 2000, at the invitation of Chinese President Jiang Zemin, President Vladimir Putin, in office for only three months at that time, paid a state visit to China. In preparing to receive him, we proposed using the opportunity of the summit meeting to push forward a settlement of Heixiazi Island.

Prior to the visit, the Foreign Ministry suggested to the Central Authorities that the two heads of state discuss the boundary issue at a tête-à-tête meeting.

Tête-à-tête meetings, as opposed to enlarged formal meetings, have become common practice in international exchanges. Virtually the whole entourage takes part in the latter, while tête-à-tête meetings are exclusive to state leaders and their key aides, with a strict limit on numbers. Generally, the topics of discussion are important and sensitive subjects on which both sides can have a direct and candid exchange of views, and even if no agreement is reached, it can still promote better mutual understanding without spoiling the atmosphere of enlarged formal talks.

On July 18, during the presidents' tête-à-tête, Heixiazi Island was discussed. Jiang said that the Russian local authorities' moves on the island, such as economic development, permanent infrastructure construction, and military activities, had aroused serious concern in China. He proposed that both sides should instruct their government departments to advance negotiations on the ownership of Heixiazi Island in the hope of finding a mutually accept-able solution and settling the China-Russia border issue once and for all.

President Putin's response was clear-cut. He said the unsettled border issue between China and Russia should be worked out as soon as possible, adding that he would instruct the departments concerned to negotiate with their Chinese counterparts.

The two leaders decided to write their principled position on the border issue into the Beijing Declaration between the People's Republic of China and the Russian Federation. The declaration summarized the results of the summit, and emphasized that talks should continue in order to speed up resolution of outstanding bor-der disputes.

In September of that year, the two leaders met again in New York while attending the UN Millennium Summit, and President Putin again talked with President Jiang about the border issue. He expressed the hope that border issues would no longer affect Sino-Russian relations in the new century.

Although the two heads of state showed their positive attitude towards the border issue, it was by no means easy to resolve it.

Subsequently, the two sides held two rounds of consultations, one at the deputy foreign minister level and one at the expert level. Both sides stood their ground: Russia still claimed the complete ownership of Heixiazi Island. China, of course, insisted that the island belonged to China.

Nevertheless, some talking was better than none.

Meeting Putin and More Discussion of Heixiazi

ON APRIL 29, 2001, at the invitation of Foreign Minister Igor Iva-nov, I paid a formal visit to Russia.

According to diplomatic protocol, when the foreign minister of a major nation pays a visit to another nation, he or she would meet with its head of state or government. As arranged by the Russian government, I would first hold talks with Igor Ivanov, then go to the Kremlin to meet with President Putin.

This was not our first meeting, but the first time I talked with him about the border issue.

Our first meeting had been one year earlier. I remembered meeting with him in the Kremlin on March 1, 2000, when I was invited to pay a formal visit to Russia and deliver a letter from President Jiang Zemin. At the time, he was the acting president.

Putin's story in Russian politics is quite extraordinary. Formerly chief of staff to the president, he rose within just half a year to the position of president itself. Before then, he had attracted little international attention.

He had spent years serving in security organs of the Soviet Union, and had worked in the Soviet embassy in the German Democratic Republic. He can operate many weapons and can pilot aircraft. He is also good at sports, holding a black belt in judo.

After entering politics, Putin first served as deputy mayor of St. Petersburg and was later appointed by President Boris Yeltsin as his chief of staff. During that period, the Kremlin witnessed the stepping down of three prime ministers within one year. Finally, Yeltsin appointed Putin as his heir apparent. On one public diplomatic occasion, he had praised Putin as modest and loyal. The Russians said that Yeltsin had done the right thing, selecting a good president for the country.

Vladimir Putin, less than forty-eight years old when he took the top office in the Kremlin, and became the leader of a vast country, soon caught the attention of the world, and became the focus of international media attention.

Mild in appearance but resolute in character, Putin was particularly loved by the Russian people and soon two catchy pop songs—"Putin Is My Kind of Guy" and "I Want a Husband Like Putin"—were popular among the public.

President Putin was prudent, calm, resilient, and decisive. After taking office, he took tough measures in key areas such as media, finance, and energy, addressed problems in social and economic development, and launched relentless strikes against Chechen terrorists.

Under his presidency, the Russian government remained stable, its economy recovered, its national strength increased markedly, social order was restored, and there was resurgence in Russian national pride and confidence.

I met him again in July 2000 during his China visit.

This would be our third meeting.

When their protocol officer ushered me into the office, the president got up from behind the wide desk and walked toward me, greeted me with a warm handshake, and invited me to sit by the oval table at the other side of the room.

The spacious second-floor office of building number one in the Kremlin, where President Putin worked, was the workplace of Russian presidents. Some have described it as "the powerhouse of Russia." The office was exquisitely decorated, in a color and style said to be Putin's favorite: light blue predominated, the décor was crisp and fresh, and the reception table, creamy with a gold trim, had a mirror-smooth surface.

I first conveyed cordial greetings and best wishes from President Jiang Zemin, then briefly described to President Putin the most recent developments in Sino-Russian relations since his visit six months earlier.

While I was talking, Putin looked me straight in the eye and listened attentively, nodding at intervals.

He expressed thanks to President Jiang for the greetings and also asked me to reciprocate on his behalf. Soon he shifted the topic to substantive problems in bilateral relations, to border issues in particular.

He said that over 98 percent of the demarcation work had been finished and that less than 2 percent of the boundary line remained unsettled. Despite the complexity involved, the Russian government still hoped that by pressing ahead with negotiations this could be resolved soon. In this way, it would be possible for both sides to move the focus to other important areas of cooperation.

Putin paused for a while before adding that he hoped an agreement in principle on the unresolved border issue could be achieved before President Jiang's visit to Russia, scheduled for July.

I instantly understood the meaning and importance of what he was saying.

I gave him an answer in principle right away. I said that the leaders of both China and Russia had shown concern and attached great importance to the settlement of border issues, had given their guidance, and pushed forward the process. China's Ministry of Foreign Affairs would consult with Russian counterparts and spare no effort in seeking an early settlement of the border issue on the basis of the important consensus by the two leaders.

Clearly, President Putin did not regard this meeting just as a courtesy reception but as an opportunity to make clear his viewpoint to China on the remaining border issues.

Frankly speaking, there were only two months before President Jiang's visit to Russia in July, and it would be really difficult to solve so complicated and sensitive a problem within such a short time. Prior to this, neither side had proposed a timetable to resolve this problem, but just tried to create the conditions to solve the problem when the time was right.

I was convinced that Russia's top leader did not talk without purpose. Our bilateral relations were moving forward fast, and things were entirely different from the period of the previous three negotiation rounds. In 1996, China and Russia had established a strategic partnership of cooperation, which created a sound political environment for the settlement of remaining border issues. Mutually beneficial economic ties had become closer and displayed unprecedented potential for further development. The popular aspiration for a better bilateral relationship was intense among people of both countries; the border area was no longer dangerously explosive, and border trade was in full swing. Our shared strategic interests and common ground demanded that both sides should strive to solve this residual historical problem as soon as possible.

Therefore, I thought our respective foreign ministries should strike while the iron was hot, pressing on with detailed negotiation arrangements.

An Exploratory Message from Russia

AFTER MY MEETING WITH President Putin, we sensed a change of attitude in the Russian Foreign Ministry with regard to resolving the outstanding border issue—a change for the better.

Their Foreign Ministry began to put out exploratory signals, suggesting that both sides should approach the problem from another angle rather than claiming "Heixiazi Island belongs totally to Russia or totally to China."

In light of this, I instructed our Foreign Ministry to work out every possible plan to address the issue.

On June 15, 2001, when President Putin came to Shanghai to attend the inaugural ceremony of the Shanghai Cooperation Organization, he gave us another constructive hint. He said to Jiang on one bilateral occasion that putting all of Heixiazi Island under Chinese administration would be like running a frontier through Shanghai, ceding sovereignty of Pudong on the east side of the river. Such a solution would be unacceptable. President Putin suggested working together with President Jiang to help the foreign ministries seek new solutions acceptable to both sides.

The message from the Russians made clear their basic approach towards the problem: Though they would not agree to drop all claims on the territory in favor of China, they would not insist on full ownership either.

Principles Defined, the Talks Begin

SOON, OUR RESPECTIVE FOREIGN ministries, based on the consensus reached by the two leaders, began negotiating the remaining border issue from a new perspective.

The first task was to define the negotiation principles to be followed in detailed discussions.

After several sessions, both sides finalized three negotiation principles: Namely, "the negotiations should be conducted on the basis of the treaties relating to Sino-Soviet (Russia) boundaries; in line with the recognized norms of international laws; and in conformity with the principles of being fair and reasonable, mutual understanding and accommodation, and mutual compromise."

They also agreed to ask the two leaders to confirm these principles in person. In terms of the specific approach, both sides agreed that the principles be proposed by President Putin during President Jiang's forthcoming state visit to Russia, to be confirmed by the latter then and there.

On July 16, 2001, President Jiang Zemin began a state visit to Russia at the invitation of President Putin. That same morning, the two had a tête-à-tête meeting at the Kremlin.

President Putin said that Russia and China had met with considerable resistance in their cooperation and that this might be due in large part to the unsettled boundary disputes. Some foreign forces had made every attempt to remind us of the border dispute in order to ruin the normal development of Russia-China relations. In his view, it was unjustifiable to leave the problem to the next generation, and he suggested that the two leaders give their political support to facilitate the successful settlement of border disputes before the spring of 2002.

President Jiang appreciated Putin's proposals. He said that since border disputes remained an unstable factor frustrating the progress of bilateral relations, the sooner the settlement, the better. The respective foreign ministers should be instructed to lose no time in negotiating, so as to find a final settlement acceptable to both sides within a year.

Here the two state leaders gave explicit commands. One said the border dispute should be settled before the following spring, and the other gave it a full year. Although there was a slight timetable disparity, both sides responded positively.

It was a lively and animated meeting, at which Jiang and Putin exchanged views intensely, encouraging everyone present. The firm resolution of the two leaders brought new hope and infused life into the border issue negotiations.

Yet, for some reason, President Putin did not bring up the three principles governing the settlement of border disputes as had been mutually agreed. Therefore, these principles failed to be confirmed by the two sides during this meeting.

Two months later, I accompanied Premier Zhu Rongji on a visit to Russia, where, once again, Foreign Minister Igor Ivanov and I held border talks.

Ivanov said that, according to the agreement reached by the two leaders, the remaining border dispute should be worked out within a year and that at present only ten months remained. We must fix the alignment of the boundary line, mark it on the map, and formulate relevant agreements with all possible speed during this period.

I agreed with him, emphasizing that both sides should seize

every minute to work it out. Then, I pointed out that there were some principles which should have been proposed by President Putin and confirmed by President Jiang during his visit to Russia, but that Putin had not brought them up. In order that the experts could steer negotiations along the right course, I suggested we should officially determine the guiding principles in the first place.

Ivanov informed me right away that the guiding principles previously defined by the two sides had been approved by President Putin. Putin had planned to put forward the principles at the tête-à-tête and ask President Jiang to confirm them. Yet, somehow, amidst the cordial atmosphere, the subject had inadvertently been overlooked.

Ivanov stressed that this had happened because of technical reasons and suggested there and then that there should be a prompt exchange of letters between the two foreign ministers, as written confirmation of these principles. I accepted his idea.

I received Ivanov's letter that same afternoon. He expressed in the letter that Russia would abide by the guiding principles concerning settlement of Sino-Russian border issues. I confirmed them in my immediate letter of reply.

Having confirmed the negotiation principles, we further exchanged views on the details.

Ivanov emphasized that the issue should remain highly confidential between us, considering its complex and sensitive nature. At the beginning of the negotiations, discussion should be limited to a small group from the two foreign ministries; only later, dependent on the progress of negotiations and only after mutual consultation between the two sides, should representatives from other departments become involved. Once talks were in the final stage, local representatives from both sides could also be invited to join in.

He was very insistent that information about the negotiations could be released to the news media only with the prior agreement of each side.

I understood his concern, aware as I was of the many dissenting voices in Russia. Therefore, I agreed that the negotiation should initially be confined to a small circle and kept highly confidential.

From then on, the Heixiazi negotiations entered the substantive stage.

Going Directly to Border Delimitation

DURING THIS PERIOD, I had frequent contact with Foreign Minister Ivanov, using the opportunity of bilateral and multilateral meetings to discuss and try to solve all the issues that arose in the course of the border negotiations.

A month after our meeting in Moscow, I again exchanged views with Ivanov on the border issue at the informal meeting of APEC held in Shanghai.

At the meeting, having decided that the negotiations could be conducted at expert level and vice foreign minister level, we exchanged lists of names. We also agreed that the two foreign ministers could negotiate directly if necessary.

After the meeting, I talked to him on the side.

I told him that since there were too many people around that day, I needed to speak to him one-to-one on a certain matter. What I had in mind was the negotiation approach to be accepted by the experts. In China's view, two approaches were possible: One was that each side should propose a boundary alignment for Heixiazi Island; the other was to reach consensus on the proportionality of division. China preferred the second option and asked the Russian side to study it.

Ivanov said that they would look into it and get back to us without delay.

Soon they informed us of their preference for the first option, that adjusting the alignment of the borderline was more acceptable.

With Russia's Foreign Minister Sergei Lavrov.

It seemed that Russia was very cautious. In fact, the issue of which negotiation basis to adopt was a purely technical one; resolving the border issue was the point. Either basis would do. In China's view, irrespective of what negotiation framework was selected, the crucial thing was to go to the heart of the matter and move the negotiations forward from the new perspective, rather than rehashing old arguments and ideas like frying up leftover rice.

Three Very Different Counterparts

AS THE BORDER NEGOTIATIONS moved into the substantive stage, I got a deeper understanding of my Russian counterpart, Foreign Minister Ivanov.

During my time in office I had dealings with three Russian foreign ministers: Yevgeny Primakov, Sergei Lavrov, and Igor Ivanov. I had had most to do with Ivanov.

Each was distinct from the others. Primakov was famous in Russia as an academic and expert in international studies, an experienced, insightful man with strategic vision. He was later appointed as Russia's prime minister. I called him "the patriarch."

Lavrov was appointed foreign minister in March 2004. By that time, I was already on the State Council and did not have much chance to meet him. He had been Russia's permanent representative to the United Nations, where he had a sharp tongue, was fast to respond, and acquired fluent American English.

On formal occasions, Lavrov looked very serious and reserved, but his grave exterior cloaked a very special brand of humor. He often made time to draw cartoons, and his drawings always captured the essential character and spirit of his subject. He once drew a picture of me. In 2004, at the Shanghai Cooperation Organization Summit in Tashkent, he sent me a cartoon. In the middle were the initials of the Shanghai Cooperation Organization, the name "Russia" on the left and "China" on the right, with "Tashkent June 17, 2004" at the bottom, all in Cyrillic letters.

Cartoon drawn and presented by Foreign Minister Lavrov.

The person with whom I had most dealings was Ivanov. He was born in 1945, and thus was seven years younger than me, and spoke good English and Spanish. An expert in European affairs, he was both shrewd and capable.

During his tenure as foreign minister, Ivanov faithfully implemented a "two-headed eagle—one facing east, one facing west" foreign policy. He attached great importance to the development of Sino-Russian relations. In 2002, he wrote an article, "Pine and Bamboo," for a Russian newspaper, extolling the relationship, likening it to the complementary natures of pine and bamboo, standing as firm as pines and as solid as bamboos. It was quite poetic. The *People's Daily* quoted and published it in China. On one occasion, I invited him to dinner in Moscow, and made a speech mentioning this article, much to his gratification.

I still remember the meeting in 2000 of foreign ministers of the Shanghai Five* held in Duschanbe, the capital of Tajikistan. Since I had to fly to Europe following the dinner, at Ivanov's suggestion all the foreign ministers gave me a sendoff, all the way to the airport and right up to the aircraft steps.

After leaving office as foreign minister in March 2004, Ivanov became secretary of the National Security Council, responsible for all the departments related to national security such as Foreign Ministry, Ministry of Defense, Federal Security Service, and the Ministry of Internal Affairs.

Ivanov was a straightforward person, and we got along well. We shared almost the same tenure as foreign minister. He was my opposite number in the negotiation of Sino-Russian border disputes, and my partner in promoting bilateral relations. In our respective posts, we were lucky enough to work hand in hand, each of us contribut-

---

*The predecessor of Shanghai Cooperation Organization (SCO), jointly founded by China, Russia, Kazakhstan, Kyrgyzstan, and Tajikistan in Shanghai in 1996.

With Russian Foreign Minister Igor Ivanov.

ing to the advance and development of the China–Russia strategic partnership of cooperation.

Fighting for Each Inch of Land amid Painful Progress

BOTH SIDES HAD REITERATED on more than one occasion that they were resolved to settle outstanding border disputes; the principles, scope, and framework of the negotiations had been identified. Practical steps should be the next stage.

Given that Heixiazi was fully under Russian control, we proposed that Russia should make the first accommodating move, since, "whoever started the trouble should end it." Russia emphasized both sides should move at the same time.

In the end, Russia took the first step.

The Chinese and Russian experts held consultations in Moscow from November 15 to 22, 2001. The Chinese delegation was led by Ambassador Sun Yanheng, an expert in Russian studies. He was also experienced in border negotiations, having been China's chief representative on the Sino–British Land Commission in Hong Kong, playing an important role in the successful settlement of land problems in the transitional period prior to the return of Hong Kong to the motherland in 1997.

In this negotiation, Russia put forward a proposal to give to China about eighty square kilometers of land in the west part of Heixiazi Island.

This fell far short of our goal, and acceptance was out of the question. Yet this area was of great significance, since it included the Fuyuan Channel, previously claimed by Russia to be the boundary river. That Russia was now willing to give it to China indicated that it was willing for this so-called China–Russia boundary river to become an internal river of China. In negotiation terms, this was a breakthrough.

From his rich negotiation experience, Ambassador Sun immediately recognized this as a very favorable turn, and that a major breakthrough could be anticipated. That said, the proposal on the table would not be the final one: This was just the first step, and the negotiations would be arduous.

Then, the Chinese side also worked out a demarcation line, proposing that sixty square kilometers of land in the east of Heixiazi Island, adjacent to Khabarovsk, should go to Russia. Naturally, this idea was not accepted.

Though neither side was satisfied with the proposals, never over the past forty years had such progress been seen in the Heixiazi Island negotiations. It was a very promising start.

As the saying goes, "well begun is half done." I believed that, provided we followed the guiding principles set by the two state leaders, we surely could hammer out a mutually acceptable boundary line.

Subsequently, the vice foreign ministers and experts held many more consultations. As border and territorial disputes bear on national interests, every move was taken with great caution and much haggling over details. Both sides were keenly aware that boundary negotiations were no trifling matter, and that once a boundary was defined, subsequent changes would be virtually impossible.

In one expert-level consultation, China and Russia each put forward six different demarcation lines, and the total discrepancy of territorial area involved in the twelve alternatives was fewer than seventeen square kilometers. Compared with the previous line, the new boundary propositions differed by less than one square kilometer only.

The going was extremely tough and the negotiations were marked by heated debate and flushed faces, with no one willing to give in. Nevertheless, we were working in the same direction, and the gap was gradually narrowing.

In expert-level negotiations held in Beijing from January 9 to 11, 2002, a considerable step forward was made. Russia suggested transferring to China 120 square kilometers of land in the west of Heixiazi Island, while China proposed that Russia keep ninety square kilometers in the east.

In the next round of negotiation ten days later, Russia proposed transferring to China 135 square kilometers in the west of Heixiazi Island (about 40 percent of the total area), and China suggested that 105 square kilometers in the east (about 30 percent of the total) should go to Russia. This was the biggest movement since the negotiations first started.

In the next month, no new proposals came from Russia, and the negotiations ground to a halt.

Things Deteriorate as Russia Makes a Volte-Face

THEN, THE UNEXPECTED HAPPENED. Just as we were awaiting developments, there were no new developments. On the contrary, Russia backed off.

On March 1, 2002, when China's Assistant Foreign Minister Liu Guchang and Russia's Vice Foreign Minister Alexander Losyukov were holding consultations in Beijing, Russia suddenly started talking tough, withdrawing the proposal tabled in the last negotiation round, and reiterating that since Heixiazi had been under Russia's control for so long, a maximum 20 to 22 percent of the island's area could be transferred to China, and that even this would be taking a huge political risk. Losyukov added that it was impossible for Russia to solve the border dispute regardless of the cost. If it could not be settled promptly, they might as well let the status quo stand.

Liu Guchang expressed his strong dissatisfaction with Russia's inconsistency and lack of good faith. He reiterated that proper settlement of border disputes would influence bilateral relations; he also stressed that the resolution of outstanding boundary disputes had been agreed by the two state leaders, and that it was the duty of the respective foreign ministries to implement their consensus and push forward the negotiations.

He made it plain that Russia's act was turning back the clock and that such disruption was totally unacceptable to China.

After this, Russia went even further, suggesting that they could transfer only 60 square kilometers to China—not even 20 percent of the island.

China then made repeated stern representations to Russia, stating that Russia was not taking the negotiations seriously and was ignoring the direction and principles set by the two leaders; China would not accept its latest proposals. We also made it clear that Russian occupation and control of Heixiazi Island did not mean that the buck stopped with Russia.

During this period, I too met with Foreign Minister Losyukov many times and on many occasions and consulted with him, but got nowhere on the issue.

A Turn for the Better

LATER WHEN LOSYUKOV CAME back to Beijing for consultations, he tabled no new proposals, but explained Russia's inconsistent stand. The Foreign Ministry, he said, was under "pressure from other departments and local authorities."

Perhaps this might be true, but we could not exclude the possibility that it was a negotiating ploy. No matter how Russia might change its attitude, we should stand our ground and continue working for further progress in the negotiations.

In our analysis, given Russian backpedaling, and the U-turn in negotiations, if we did not take measures promptly, negotiations might be broken off, and, if this happened, the border dispute would drag on indefinitely with no prospect for settlement. We had to do something to seize the initiative.

In order to get Russia to move forward, the central authorities approved that we propose a new formula, namely, dividing Heixiazi Island roughly evenly between the two countries.

Two weeks following the last negotiations, the head of the Russian expert delegation paid an unannounced visit to Beijing, declaring that Russia could consider transferring 40 percent of Heixiazi Island to China, leaving for further discussion how the area between the different demarcations should be apportioned. This implied that Russia was once more being constructive. With this turn for the better, brighter prospects opened up.

Three days later, on October 25, 2005, I met once more with Foreign Minister Ivanov, this time at the APEC Ministerial Meeting in Mexico. While exchanging views on the border issue, I told him that in order to move the negotiations forward, China was willing to consider the even-distribution principle to solve the issue of the land area between the two proposed demarcation lines.

Ivanov agreed that the two sides should continue discussions on this issue. He remarked that every time we met our two sides moved much closer together, and that, in his belief, when we met again in Moscow on November 23, we might be able to conclude the negotiations. He added half jokingly that we might one day find an Igor-Tang line on the island.

He seemed very confident that the outstanding border disputes would be settled while we were both still serving as foreign ministers.

Meeting with Putin Again, the Negotiations Bear Fruit

ON NOVEMBER 23, 2002, I went to Moscow for a meeting of foreign ministers of SCO member states. Though this was a multilateral diplomatic occasion, Russia specially arranged for me to meet with President Putin privately. I was the only foreign minister to meet with him alone, and we exchanged views on the border issue. He looked more relaxed than last time, smiling and talking freely.

In fact, Putin is a very eloquent individual. He held four major press conferences during his presidency, each one of them lasting for three or four hours. Journalists besieged and bombarded him with questions on domestic and foreign issues, some of them going to the point of provocation. Putin responded to them with ease, and the live broadcast elicited a warm public reaction.

Handshakes over, President Putin invited me to sit down, and told me he had been informed by Foreign Minister Ivanov of the important progress made by the foreign ministries in the border negotiations, and that he was pleased about this.

Meeting with President Vladimir Putin at the Kremlin, Moscow, November 23, 2002.

I agreed that there had been positive progress and that I had had a fruitful talk with Ivanov on the problem during the APEC meeting in Mexico, and would use the current meeting in Moscow to hear what he had to say.

I also added that a thorough settlement of the border issue would have a positive and profound effect on the expansion and deepening of the Sino-Russian strategic partnership of cooperation, a relationship of long-term stability, neighborliness, and friendship. I would like to work with Ivanov, trying our utmost to make the consensus reached by two leaders a reality.

President Putin smiled and nodded his approval. He remarked that the leaders of China and Russia were of one mind that the border dispute should not be left for future generations. He paused for a moment before saying clearly that he hoped further progress could be made by the time of his planned visit to China at the end of the year.

Yet again, in just a few words, he had given a clear indication of his positive attitude on the border issue.

My instincts told me that the negotiation might reach a satisfactory outcome during the course of this Moscow meeting.

Immediately after the meeting with President Putin, I dashed off to take part in a multilateral event organized for the six foreign ministers.

At five o'clock, I had another tête-à-tête on the border issue with Foreign Minister Ivanov, followed by a larger conference at which views on cooperation were exchanged.

These two meetings were held in a villa belonging to Russia's Foreign Ministry.

Their Foreign Ministry had a number of villas in Moscow, in beautiful, secluded surroundings amidst woods or by a riverside. The villa used for the talks was situated on a quiet street within Moscow's Second Ring Road, two kilometers away from the Foreign Ministry.

Built in 1898 and exquisitely decorated, the villa was once the residence of a Russian millionaire named Morozov. The splendid crystal chandeliers, stained glass, solid dark brown tables and chairs, delicate old paintings, tapestry, and comfy sofas were all indicators of its long history and the good taste of its owner. It has become the place for hosting state leaders and diplomats, and in a solemn or relaxed atmosphere, countless important and complicated problems have been solved here.

I have been here several times to communicate with my Russian counterparts on sensitive bilateral issues, and this villa has left a deep impression on me.

Ivanov and I held our tête-à-tête meeting in a small conference room here. He asked me to sit down and took a chair opposite. In view of our long friendship, he skipped the small talk and came straight to the point. He told me that he had reported to Putin the views we had exchanged in Mexico and that Putin had been very pleased.

Ivanov then told me in earnest that the Russian government had made a decision to realize the political settlement of our border dispute on the basis of the Mexico meeting. We could instruct our delegations and experts to continue their work and make a finalized version based on the consensus. Furthermore, we two could sign a memorandum specifying the demarcation parameters, and further negotiations could be conducted on the basis of this memorandum.

Ivanov finally stressed that President Putin hoped that all the outstanding boundary issues could be solved by December, when he was due to visit China.

I understood him perfectly: The Russian Federation was willing to settle the issue in line with the agreement at the Mexico foreign ministers meeting.

I instantly realized we were now at a crucial stage, and that meticulous care was needed to check every detail and eliminate any trace of ambiguity.

I then spelled out to Ivanov China's attitude toward the outstanding border issue as discussed at the Mexico meeting in October, namely to use the principle of shared distribution to apportion the land lying between the boundary line proposed by China and that proposed by Russia. My understanding was that Russia had studied this formula and approved it.

Ivanov responded, "Yes, absolutely."

I spelled out what I understood him to mean—that we had reached an agreement in principle, which in turn implied that the Sino-Russian border issue had been settled in principle. We should report to the state leaders about this success and urge the experts to press ahead with their negotiations along the line of this agreement in principle, and determine the specific alignment of the demarcation line without delay.

Signing the Memorandum with Foreign Minister Ivanov, Beijing, February 27, 2003.

I again confirmed with Ivanov that we had reached verbal agreement in principle on the border issue. We also decided that, during President Putin's visit to Beijing, the joint statement of the two heads of state should include a section about the agreement in principle to resolve the outstanding border issues. After that, the two foreign ministers would sign the memorandum providing the specific demarcation parameters.

Ivanov immediately indicated his agreement, and took out Russia's draft memorandum. Apparently, Russia had come prepared.

About ten days later, on December 2, 2002, President Vladimir Putin paid a formal visit to China. At the conclusion of the visit, the two heads of state issued a joint statement in which they noted "present conditions being favorable to finding a mutually acceptable solution. The foreign ministries should be instructed to bring negotiations to their conclusion as soon as possible."

This indicated that Heixiazi Island boundary demarcation work had been basically resolved and that negotiations were close to completion.

On February 27, 2003, I invited Ivanov to visit China again. He came primarily for the signing of the Memorandum on the Complete Settlement of Outstanding Sino-Russian Boundary Disputes by the Foreign Ministers of the Two Countries. This was the last important document I signed before leaving office.

Though it was just a memorandum and not a formal agreement, it constituted the basis of the settlement of the Heixiazi Island boundary issue.

Ratification by the Two Heads of State

THREE MONTHS LATER, DURING President Hu Jintao's visit to Russia, Hu signed another memorandum with President Putin concerning the border issue, confirming what had been stated in the foreign ministers' memorandum.

During this visit, the two heads of state spoke highly of the efforts made in handling this issue. They agreed that all the problems affecting bilateral relations were being gradually resolved, even boundary issues that had been left over for decades. This showed that with concerted efforts, all the problems could be solved. The thorough settlement of Sino-Russian boundary disputes would transform the long frontier dividing the two countries into a tie of peace and friendship linking both sides.

The memorandum signed by Hu and Putin was a milestone in the boundary negotiations, symbolizing that a final settlement was just around the corner.

The two sides finalized the alignment of the demarcation line in expert-level negotiations that took place from July 26 to August 2, 2004.

Based on the result of negotiations, the experts meticulously marked this red demarcation line on a 1:100,000 scale map, allowing no errors of negligence to slip into the process.

This red demarcation line was the consummation of painstaking work by countless people. It brought to an end long years of boundary disputes and presaged a brighter future for our bilateral relations.

The newly redrawn map, produced by high-tech surveying equipment, shows the total area of Heixiazi Island as 335 square kilometers, with 171 square kilometers going to China and 164 square kilometers to Russia.

On October 14, 2004, during President Putin's visit to China, Li Zhaoxing, China's foreign minister, and his Russian counterpart Igor Ivanov signed the Supplementary Agreement on the Eastern Section of the China-Russia Boundary Line, establishing the territorial settlements for the two countries. The borderline between China and Russia was now totally demarcated throughout its 4,300-kilometer length.

Presidents Hu and Putin attended the signing ceremony as witnesses.

As state councilor in charge of foreign affairs, I was also at the ceremony, and all kinds of thoughts welled up at this historical moment.

Although the Heixiazi boundary line represented only a small fraction of the China-Russia border, disputes over it had dragged on for decades without proper settlement. Historical experience tells us that border disputes, if unresolved, can be a hidden danger in bilateral relations.

Border disputes have also provoked many wars in history. For example, China and Russia had recourse to arms because of conflicts over Zhenbao Island, which is only three-fourths square kilometers in area, one four-hundredth of that of Heixiazi. Hence, had the demarcation of Heixiazi dragged on, it might well have brought trouble to bilateral relations. The Chinese are a peace-loving people, and in today's world, where peace, development, and cooperation prevail, we always advocate proper solution of boundary problems with neighbors through peaceful negotiations, and make unremitting efforts towards that end.

The settlement of the China-Russia border dispute has removed the hidden danger in our bilateral relations, and vividly demonstrated the constant improvement in our relations. It was also conducive to intensifying and promoting the China-Russia strategic partnership, and increasing mutual trust and friendship between us. Henceforth, both sides could devote all their resources to developing their national economies and raising the living standards of their peoples.

The proper settlement of the China-Russia border dispute has exemplary value for the settlement of boundary issues with other neighbors and great significance to conducting our periphery diplomacy and creating a sound external environment for our domestic economic development.

Solving sensitive and complicated boundary issues called for great political courage. The breadth of vision and decisiveness shown by the two leaders had created sound political conditions for a settlement. On thirteen bilateral and multilateral occasions, they stepped in and exchanged views in depth on the border dispute. By taking a broad and long-term view, each persistently protecting the national interest, while showing consideration for the other's concerns, seeking common ground and shelving differences, they were able to discover where respective interests converged, to give guidance at critical moments, and to steer the negotiations out of difficulties and towards progress.

Solving sensitive and complicated boundary issues also called for painstaking hard work. During the negotiations, my colleagues, undeterred by the intricacies and setbacks involved, resolutely implemented the policies of China's Central Authorities, adhering to principles while showing flexibility, working untiringly to the end. During this period, Ivanov and I held eight talks; there were eleven bilateral meetings at the vice foreign minister level, and ten bilateral consultations at the expert level. The positive outcome of such hard work—arriving at a solution acceptable to both parties— was really gratifying. I am happy to have been part of this team. My colleagues did their utmost for the national interests, and I am proud of them.

On April 27, 2005, the Supplementary Agreement on the Eastern Section of the China-Russia Boundary Line was examined and approved by the Standing Committee of the National People's Congress. In the Russian parliament, it was examined and approved by the State Duma on May 20, and by the Federation Council on May 25.

Following this, both sides started the boundary survey on Heixiazi Island. Its completion in October 2008 was marked by a bilateral ceremony unveiling the boundary marker.

Since then, images of Heixiazi Island have crossed my mind from time to time. I have always harbored a wish to take a look at this place, this piece of land into which we had poured so much effort, and to see the new boundary marker, standing tall and proud.

On June 22, 2009, I finally realized my dream and set foot on the island.

It had been raining cats and dogs the night before, but on the day of our arrival the weather changed and we were welcomed by a cloudless blue sky. I felt I knew the place well.

Three jeeps carried us from south to north along the newly delimited border. We bumped along the unpaved road amidst bushes that grew as high as a man.

One hour's drive later, we finally reached boundary marker 259/4(1). I approached, stroked the plinth on which it stood, and walked around it three times with a mass of surging emotions.

The boundary marker is made of solid gray granite, carved with

Standing by a boundary marker on Heixiazi Island, June 22, 2009.

the bright red national emblem of the People's Republic of China. Situated at 48°21'30.2" north, 134°46'03.7" east, it is now the easternmost point of our territory and the first part of China to get the first ray of sunlight each day. Hence, sunrise is visible in the motherland fifty-eight seconds earlier than before.

Heixiazi Island scene.

Several local friends told me that the spring here is very beautiful, and I believe it will become even more beautiful in the future.

Though still a wilderness and overgrown with bushes and grass, I believe this land will soon start thriving. Heixiazi will become a pilot area of China-Russian cooperation, a showpiece island of ecological conservation, common development, friendship, and harmony.

CHAPTER 5

Bombing of the
Chinese Embassy in Yugoslavia

O<small>N</small> M<small>AY</small> 8, 1999, in the early hours of the morning, when it was still dark, I was woken by the insistent, urgent ringing of the telephone. My heart sank. Years of diplomatic life had made me extremely sensitive to incoming calls at midnight or in the early hours. I suspected a serious emergency.

It was my secretary on the line. A little over ten minutes earlier, US-led NATO forces had flagrantly bombed the Chinese embassy in Yugoslavia, causing heavy casualties among embassy staff and severe damage to the building. Because of disrupted communications, detailed information about the damage was not yet clear.

Hearing the news, I was overwhelmed by feelings of shock, anger, grief, and anxiety.

Under the sudden blow of this tragedy, for a moment I could not believe my ears. What a gross outrage: attacking an embassy of the People's Republic of China!

Pulling myself together, I immediately ordered my secretary to inform relevant departments and get in touch with the embassy in Belgrade by every possible means. It was a top priority to get knowledge of our casualty situation and the degree of damage to the embassy premises.

I also told the secretary to inform department leaders to come immediately to an emergency meeting at the Foreign Ministry to evaluate the situation and discuss how to tackle it. I got up immediately and headed off to my office.

On the way there I made use of the time to marshal my thoughts.

During that period, the situation in Yugoslavia and Kosovo was one of the hottest issues under our attention. Despite our watchful eye on changes in the Balkans, no one could have predicted that the war flames there would inflict disaster on the Chinese embassy.

The Kosovo Issue Emerges amid SFRY Disintegration

YUGOSLAVIA WAS A NAME familiar to the Chinese people. In the 1970s, it had become famous in China after the screening of the classic Yugoslav movie *Walter Defends Sarajevo*.

Yugoslavia occupied a key strategic position in the Balkans, and was where the First World War broke out. During the Second World War, the communist Yugoslav partisans led by Josip Broz Tito put up a life-and-death fight against German and Italian fascists, making great contributions to the ultimate success of the anti-fascism struggle in the European theater of war. The well-known movies *Walter Defends Sarajevo* and *The Bridge* were both cinematographic accounts of the partisans' fight against fascism.

After the war, the Socialist Federal Republic of Yugoslavia (SFRY) maintained national unity and achieved significant economic and social development under Tito's leadership. Thanks to his glorious accomplishments, Tito was seen as the supreme leader hero by his countrymen.

Right through the Cold War, Yugoslavia once again became a focus of East-West rivalry.

Yugoslavia then was a multiethnic country composed of six republics and two autonomous provinces. Under the leadership of Tito, the country saw a stabilized political scene with the economy and national unity developing despite certain residual historical problems. For China, it served as a role model during the early stages of the reform and opening-up drive. The Poljoprivredni Kombinat Beograd (PKB), an agricultural complex in Belgrade, was a must-see for Chinese visiting groups. Locals joked that even PKB's cows could recognize Chinese faces and say "hello" in Chinese.

However, underlying problems began to emerge after Tito's death in 1980, and the SFRY finally broke up in the 1990s, influenced by the dramatic changes in Eastern Europe and the disintegration of the Soviet Union. In April 1992, Serbia and Montenegro, two of the SFRY's former republics, co-founded the Federal Republic of Yugoslavia (FRY). The federation suffered hard times right from the start and was constantly subjected to international sanctions.

And then the long-dormant Kosovo issue emerged.

Originally an autonomous province of the Republic of Serbia, Kosovo had an ethnic Albanian majority of 90 percent, which had a long history of conflict with the ethnic Serb community and had always sought independence from the Yugoslavia. When Slobodan Milošević took office in the Republic in the mid-1980s, a tougher line was adopted on the Kosovo issue.

Born in 1941, Slobodan Milošević was a controversial figure in Yugoslav history. Entering the world of finance as a young man, he once headed the Beobanka, one of Yugoslavia's largest banks. He entered politics in the early 1980s, became president of the Yugoslav Communist League's Serbian branch Central Committee in 1986, and was elected president of the Republic of Serbia in 1989. I had not met him in person, but according to many articles Milošević was an intelligent and eloquent person with a strong character, and even leaders of the opposition in Serbia acknowledged his charisma. Despite his operating a multiparty system in Serbia, Milošević was seen by the West as representing communism.

Conflicts between ethnic Serbs and Albanians intensified after Milošević came to power. In February 1998, severe fighting broke out between Serbia's military force and the Kosovo Liberation Army (KLA), an ethnic Albanian force claiming to fight for Kosovo independence, which resulted in many fatalities. The incident provided a pretext for Western intervention.

In October 1998, US-led Western troops advanced toward the Serbian border, demanding that the government grant a high level of autonomy to Kosovo. After several rounds of negotiations, Milošević was coerced into signing a treaty, conceding to Western demands to resume talks with the Albanians on Kosovo autonomy and admitting international observers to the region.

In January 1999, forty-five Kosovar Albanians were found dead in Račak, a Kosovo village. The US-led inspection group confirmed that these people were ethnic Albanian civilians killed by Serbian military force, and declared the Račak incident a "humanitarian catastrophe." Military action was threatened. This was the spark that ignited the Kosovo War soon after.

In February, the Serbian government was forced to have talks with a Kosovar Albanian delegation in Rambouillet, France, to seek political solutions to the Kosovo problem. Right at the outset, the American delegation presented to both parties a draft agreement the content of which was neither negotiable nor amendable and must be signed within a week.

The main contents of the nonnegotiable so-called agreement included a high degree of autonomy for Kosovo, disarming of the KLA, and a multinational NATO military presence in Kosovo. However, the Kosovar Albanian representatives insisted that Kosovo independence be written into the agreement and refused to disarm the KLA. As for the Serbian government, it flatly refused to allow NATO presence on its soil. Unable to bridge the gap, the talks closed without agreement.

However, when the negotiations reopened a month later, the Kosovar Albanian representative unilaterally signed the Rambouillet Accords under Western guidance, completely abandoning its initial firm stance. Serbia held its ground and refused to sign. The West, using this as justification, blamed Serbia for the failure at Rambouillet, and sent an ultimatum to government of the Yugoslavia.

On his trip to Belgrade on March 22, US Special Envoy Richard Holbrooke put his cards on the table with Milošević. All negotiation efforts had come to naught, and the clouds of war descended.

Protecting Chinese amid the Flames of War

ON THE NIGHT OF March 24, US-led NATO forces, bypassing the UN Security Council, flagrantly launched air strikes on the Federal Republic of Yugoslavia. The Kosovo War began.

The war constituted a serious violation of the UN Charter and norms of international relations, damaged the authority of the UN Security Council, and created an extremely perilous precedent in the history of contemporary international relations. The war intensified the imbalance of power in the Balkans, and had a serious impact on regional stability and world peace.

The international community reacted with vehemence. Russia's President Boris Yeltsin issued a statement expressing indignation at the NATO invasion of a sovereign state. Belarus, India, and other nations condemned NATO actions and pressed for an immediate end to its military operations. European countries like Greece and Austria openly expressed their opposition to the NATO action.

China has always been a supporter of justice, world peace,

and the authority of the United Nations. Responding quickly to NATO's brutal acts, the Chinese leadership, including President Jiang Zemin, chairman of the National People's Congress Li Peng, and Premier Zhu Rongji, repeatedly made plain China's principled stand on the issue. The Foreign Ministry expressed serious concern over the Kosovo situation, opposing the US-led NATO's air strikes on Yugoslavia without a UN mandate. It demanded forcefully that NATO forces cease their military operations immediately, and appealed for the concerted efforts of the international community and the parties involved to restore peace in the Balkans as soon as possible. In the UN Security Council, China actively called for an emergency meeting on the Kosovo issue.

While keeping a close eye on the Kosovo situation, we were also extremely concerned about the safety of our embassy staff and fellow Chinese in Yugoslavia.

In the early air raids, NATO forces concentrated their bombing on Yugoslavia's air defenses and military installations, hoping to finish the war quickly. Later, as the bombing intensified, civilian facilities became targets of attack. Many factories, schools, hospitals, and other civilian facilities were bombarded at will, resulting in many civilian casualties. The Kosovo War, launched in the name of protecting humanitarianism, actually produced Europe's biggest humanitarian disaster since WWII.

With the situation changing all the time, I had given repeated directives to our frontline embassy to be on the alert, not only to be watchful of their own safety, but also to protect local Chinese residents. I also ordered the planning of emergency measures and authorized the embassy party committee to determine evacuation plans on their own in case of emergency.

Under the leadership of Ambassador Pan Zhanlin, embassy staff worked out emergency plans despite extremely difficult living and working conditions. During that period, NATO's large-scale bombings often cut off water and power supplies in Yugoslavia, and food, including fresh vegetables, became extremely difficult to obtain. However, our embassy staff never forgot the duties with which they had been entrusted. With unyielding determination and dedication, they carried an even heavier workload than usual while risking their lives by venturing out during the bombing.

Even at the height of the war, the embassy never neglected the safety of Chinese people trapped in cities around Yugoslavia. Never having experienced war before, many were at the end of their emotional tether, asking to be transferred to safe zones through the embassy.

Understanding their anxiety, the embassy managed to calm them down despite all the difficulties, at the same time trying to find a way of evacuating the resident Chinese. After carefully mulling over the options, it was decided that they should be evacuated to neighboring Romania.

On the morning of April 3, a total of 211 students, company workers, and other Chinese living in Yugoslavia boarded four charter buses, which were lucky finds by the embassy, and arrived safe and sound in Romania two and a half bumpy hours later. The Chinese evacuees spoke highly of their well-organized retreat to safety, commenting, "As long as the embassy is with us, we feel safe."

Hearing what the embassy had done, I felt happy and relieved. I was proud of our staff's keen awareness of the interests of the country and the people at a critical juncture. At the same time, the issue of their safety also lay heavily on my mind.

I never dreamed that my deepest worries could become such cruel reality. The Chinese embassy, carrying out its peaceful mission and protecting the safety of so many, became a target of NATO bombings.

Sudden Disaster Strikes Our Embassy

As soon as I got to the office, I called an emergency meeting of leaders of the ministry and other relevant staff. Decisions were made on the spot and three working groups were set up to produce an immediate response to the incident.

After strenuous efforts, we finally managed to get into contact with the embassy and learned the details of the bombing.

That night, the Chinese embassy in Yugoslavia had been hit in a NATO air strike, and three people had been killed in their sleep. They were: Shao Yunhuan, a reporter from Xinhua News Agency; Xu Xinghu, a reporter from *Guangming Daily;* and his wife, Zhu Ying. Twenty more had been wounded, several of them seriously. The embassy building had also suffered serious damage.

Thirty people were then living in the embassy, including the staff and Chinese journalists in Belgrade who had moved in because the embassy was supposed to be the safest place in wartime. The tragedy was that they had fallen in the bombing of the embassy.

Because of the time difference, it was still late at night there, and confirmation of the specific details of the attack was difficult because of the ongoing NATO bombing of nearby targets. According to initial eyewitness accounts, the Chinese embassy had probably been hit by three missiles.

Later investigation showed that the strike had been carried out by a B-2 Spirit that had taken off from American soil. Rather than missiles, the stealth bomber had dropped five precision-guided heavy bombs, that is, Joint Direct Attack Munitions (JDAMs), on the Chinese embassy and the ambassador's residence from different angles, causing heavy casualties and serious damage to the embassy buildings.

The party's central leadership expressed deep concern over the incident and for the safety of our staff. In the shortest possible time, we compiled a briefing for the leadership, trying to include every

The Chinese embassy in Yugoslavia before the bombing.

detail of firsthand information, coupled with a strongly worded and evidence-supported draft government statement.

Later that morning, I reported to the top leaders in the Zhong-nanhai compound.

On my way there, I was heavy-hearted and flooded with thoughts and emotions.

As everyone knows, according to the Vienna Convention on Diplomatic Relations and established principles of relevant international law, a diplomatic mission is the representative organ of a sovereign state in a foreign country and is an inviolable territorial extension of that state, being strictly protected under the Vienna Convention and international law. For a nation or military alliance to bomb the embassy of another sovereign state is almost unheard of in diplomatic history, a barbaric act in blatant violation of the norms of international law.

I saw video footage showing the embassy after the bombing. From a number of different angles, the terrible damage to the building was very clear. It was an utter wreck.

The building had only been in use for three years. It was situated in a newly developed area of Belgrade, within a kilometer of the Yugoslav government building and just a few hundred meters from the River Danube. The complex comprised a main building and the ambassador's residence. The main building was a five-story structure with about six thousand square meters of floor space, and the ambassador's residence a two-story building about one thousand square meters in space. The buildings had gray granite-clad facades, green windows, and glazed-tile roofs, also green. An exemplary integration of Chinese and Western architecture, it had exhibited a stately appearance, gorgeous yet elegant.

An architectural landmark of Belgrade once completed, the embassy building won ardent admiration from visiting Yugoslav officials and diplomatic missions. It became an attraction for local people and tourists, too. However, none foresaw the destruction of these two buildings in a hail of NATO bombs.

All we knew at the time was that the building had been struck by three bombs. Information about damage to the interior was still unclear in the pictures, but it could be seen that most of the granite facades and glass had been completely destroyed and that the rear of the embassy and the flank adjacent to the ambassador's residence had collapsed.

Who could repress his righteous indignation at this appalling scene?

Faced with this bolt from the blue, China's collective leadership of the third-generation Party Central Committee, with Jiang Zemin at its core, in the midst of tremendous grief and indignation, immediately responded to the assault. Based on a comprehensive analysis of international and domestic circumstances as well as the nature and impact of the incident, the Central Authorities resolved to lodge a solemn representation in firm protection of our state sovereignty and national dignity, while taking into consideration the fundamental interests of the Chinese people and long-term development prospects for the nation.

On May 8, 1999, the Chinese embassy in Yugoslavia was destroyed by five JDAMs dropped by the US-led NATO forces. A side wall of the embassy completely came off.

I presented to the Central Authorities the draft statement on the issue, and this was approved on the spot for release to the press as a stern message from the Chinese government.

The Central Authorities also decided to lodge urgent, forceful representations and the strongest protest to the United States. A working group was immediately dispatched on a chartered plane to Belgrade to handle the incident on the spot, bringing home the remains of the three victims and those injured who could safely be moved.

This was the first time in my decades of diplomatic life to send an aircraft and a special group to handle an emergency case overseas, and it illustrated the high level of concern on the part of the Central Authorities. President Jiang Zemin told me solemnly, "You

Silent mourning: a bouquet presented at the doorplate of the Chinese embassy.

must ensure absolute safety for the flight and the people aboard. This is the responsibility of the Foreign Ministry." He even made phone calls in person to confirm the flight arrangements.

The Chinese government's official statement was immediately issued through Xinhua News Agency. The statement sent a stern message to the US-led NATO forces, condemning the atrocity of violating Chinese sovereignty, trampling over the Vienna Convention on Diplomatic Relations and norms of international relations, expressing the Chinese people's utmost indignation and the strongest protest. The statement pointed out that the US-led NATO alliance must bear full responsibility for the incident and that the Chinese government reserved the right to take further measures.

Vehement Condemnation and Passions Aroused

WHEN NEWS OF THE embassy bombing and the resulting Chinese casualties spread across China, there was an immediate and vehement reaction. Large numbers of people held street demonstrations, severely condemning the American atrocity. Wave upon wave of increasingly indignant protests put great popular pressure on the United States and NATO.

The world as a whole was astounded by the US-led NATO's blatant violation of international norms, and their action received strong condemnation from the international community. On May 8, Russia's President Yeltsin issued a statement strongly condemning NATO's brutal assault on the Chinese embassy, and two days later made a telephone call to President Jiang Zemin, reiterating his strong condemnation. In phone calls and letters to the Chinese leaders, state leaders of Asian, African, and Latin American nations also denounced US-led NATO's savage bombing, voiced support for the Chinese government, and expressed deep condolences to the victims' families.

However, the US-led NATO tried to evade responsibility, alleging that the bombing had been a "mistake." On the day of the incident, US President Bill Clinton, inspecting tornado damage in Oklahoma, told reporters that the bombing of the Chinese embassy was an unintended tragedy, and expressed regrets and condolences to the Chinese leaders and the people for the loss of lives and property.

In the light of strong domestic and international reaction, the Chinese government reiterated China's firm stand on the issue as well as maintaining overall stability in the country. On May 9, Hu Jintao, then member of the CPC Central Committee Politburo and vice president of the state, gave a television speech on the bombing, expressing deep condolences to the victims and strong protest against US-led NATO, demanding that the United States assume full responsibility and saying that the Chinese government reserved the right to take further action.

Hu also stressed that China would unswervingly adhere to its independent foreign policy of peace, persist in reform and opening up, defend state sovereignty and national dignity, and firmly oppose hegemonism and power politics. At the same time, in accordance with relevant international and domestic laws, China would ensure the safety of foreign missions and their staff in China, resident aliens and foreign nationals engaged in business, and educational and cultural undertakings in China. This message fully reflected the fine traditions of Chinese civilization.

Hu's speech won the firm support of the Chinese people and positive reactions from around the world.

Representations Intensify

HAVING REPORTED TO THE Central Authorities, I returned immediately to the Foreign Ministry to coordinate all the offices involved and determine implementation plans for decisions made at the meeting. The measures included: stern representations to the United States with the strongest protest and condemnation of their act; a series of measures on the bilateral front, postponing or canceling exchanges and dialogues with the United States; and lastly, urging the international community at the United Nations and other multilateral organizations to condemn the United States and NATO atrocity.

On the afternoon of May 8, our Vice Foreign Minister Wang Yingfan held an emergency meeting with US Ambassador James Sasser to officially lodge the strongest protest on the US-led bombing of the Chinese embassy in Yugoslavia using precision-guided heavy bombs.

The US ambassador was noncommittal, saying that China's representations would be reported immediately to the US government. He added that, despite the uncertainty as to who was responsible for the incident, he would like to express on behalf of the US government its deep regret for the loss of Chinese personnel and property.

The US side expressed condolences and regret, but neither President Clinton nor Ambassador Sasser had made an official apology for their act, so I decided to summon Mr. Sasser to reiterate a stern representation on behalf of the Chinese government.

Before summoning Sasser, I called in relevant staff of the Department of North American and Oceanian Affairs and instructed them verbally on the main contents of the representation, passing forward the Chinese government's four demands.

On May 10, Ambassador James Sasser arrived at the ministry at the appointed time.

I had met Mr. Sasser on various occasions, and had been impressed by his cordial attitude and pragmatic working style. A senior member of the US Senate who had served three terms, Sasser was no China expert; he had never visited the country before his appointment as US ambassador. In 1996, when he came to work here, Sasser began to acquire a deeper understanding of China. He believed that China would be one of the most important nations of the twenty-first century, and that the United States should accept China's development on its merit. As the US ambassador to China, Sasser felt his responsibility to promote the mutually beneficial development of US-China relations and the building of mutual trust between the two nations.

The atmosphere in the meeting room was grave. I reiterated to Sasser that the US-led NATO bombing of the Chinese embassy in Yugoslavia using precision-guided heavy bombs had resulted in heavy casualties and damage, and that this constituted a flagrant and disruptive violation of the UN Charter and the basic norms of international relations, as well as a gross infringement upon Chinese sovereignty. The Chinese government had already issued a solemn statement on the matter, in which it expressed utmost indignation and severe condemnation of the barbaric act, and lodged the strongest protest to US-led NATO, demanding that they take full responsibility for this incident. China would continue to pay close attention to the development of the matter.

I said, "On the afternoon of that day of the bombing incident, the Chinese Vice Foreign Minister Wang Yingfan held an emergency meeting with you, and lodged the strongest protest to the United States on behalf of the Chinese government. Now, on behalf of the Chinese government, I issue the following solemn demands to US-led NATO:

1. A public and official apology to the Chinese government, the Chinese people, and relatives of the Chinese victims;
2. A complete and thorough investigation of the NATO precision-guided bomb attack on the Chinese embassy in Yugoslavia;
3. Prompt publication of the detailed results of the investigation;
4. Severe punishment for those responsible for the attack."

I also stressed that the US-led NATO military operation against Yugoslavia had brought untold suffering to people in the region and that it must stop immediately, so as to bring the Kosovo issue back onto the track of political resolution as soon as possible.

Mr. Sasser said that he had listened carefully to my representations on behalf of the Chinese government, and that he would report the meeting to the US government immediately. He added that though he had previously expressed to my Foreign Ministry colleagues condolences on the tragic losses suffered by the innocent Chinese, he wanted today to offer his deep apology to me. He also expressed personal condolences to the Chinese people.

Finally, Sasser raised the topic of putting through a call from President Clinton to President Jiang Zemin. He explained that although President Clinton had issued a statement on the day of the bombing expressing regrets and condolences, he still wanted to apologize in person to President Jiang in a telephone call.

I told him that the immediate priority was to ensure that US-led NATO would address the representations and demands of the Chinese government seriously, that it must take effective action, and respond to the issue immediately.

In order to further stress our indignation to the United States, and make plain our position to the international community, we decided to take further action on the bilateral level: to postpone high-level exchanges between China and the United States; to delay China-US talks on nonproliferation, arms control, and international security; and to suspend dialogue on human rights. The decisions were announced by a Foreign Ministry spokesman on May 10.

International Condemnation of Brutality

AT FIVE-FORTY ON THE afternoon of May 8, on China's initiative, the UN Security Council held an emergency meeting for informal consultation on US-led NATO bombing of China's embassy in Yugoslavia.

Ambassador Qin Huasun, China's permanent representative to the United Nations, read out the Chinese government's statement, expressing utmost indignation and strong condemnation of US-led NATO's bombing of the Chinese embassy, which had resulted in heavy casualties and severe damage to the embassy premises. Qin also made China's firm demand that the UN Security Council president issue a statement to the press and call a formal meeting on the matter immediately.

During the consultation, the US and UK representatives raised objections, claiming that the situation was not clear enough for a press conference, and that there was no precedent for the UN president to issue statements between an informal consultation and an open meeting.

After rebuttals of these arguments by China, the council president ruled that the Security Council had the right to decide on its own working procedures and hold a press conference in these special circumstances. After another three hours of fierce debate, the council president issued a statement to the press, saying the United Nations was shocked and seriously concerned over the bombing incident and expressed sympathy and condolences to the Chinese government and the victims. The statement also said the Security Council would pay close attention to the development of the matter and was expecting investigation results from NATO.

A formal meeting was held on May 14 to discuss the bombing. In the consultation prior to the meeting, China had put forth a firm demand that the Security Council issue a presidential statement condemning the NATO act, and distributed copies of the draft statement. However, the United States, United Kingdom, and other NATO members tried to block the demand, opposed the inclusion of "condemning NATO for its violation of international law" in the draft, and insisted on the insertion of the words "accidental bombing."

This wording was categorically rejected by China and deleted by the council. Instead, the statement referred to internationally recognized principles, thus protecting China's interests and dignity to the greatest degree. Justice was done.

The presidential statement was finally passed and published at the May 14 meeting of the Security Council. In the statement, the Security Council expressed deep grief and regret over the bombing of the Chinese embassy and the loss of property and lives, as well as its most sincere sympathy and condolences to the Chinese government and victims' families. The council reiterated that, in accordance with established international norms, the safety of diplomatic personnel and the inviolability of diplomatic missions must be protected under all circumstances. It pressed NATO for a complete and thorough investigation of the matter and was waiting for its findings.

Upon China's request, prior to the start of the meeting, the Security Council unprecedentedly observed a moment of silence for the lives lost in the bombing of the embassy.

Rehabilitation and Mourning

WHILE MAKING REPRESENTATIONS TO the United States, the Foreign Ministry was coming to grips with coordinating and arranging the dispatch of a special working group to Yugoslavia to handle matters in the wake of the bombing.

On my way back to the ministry after reporting to the Central Authorities at Zhongnanhai, I was giving careful thought as to who should lead the group.

With the air strikes still continuing, it was a really tough decision for me to dispatch anyone, since it would entail sending a dear colleague to a war front.

The first candidate to come to mind was Wang Guozhang, a leadership member of the ministry, whose coordinating ability and skill met the needs of this demanding role.

As soon as I got back to the office, I called in Yang Wenchang, vice foreign minister in charge of personnel management. Yang was not aware of the decisions of the Central Authorities, but he was already considering what needed to be done.

He suggested that a group be dispatched and I told him that the Central Authorities thought the same way. When I consulted him about who should lead the group, Yang replied, "Given the circumstances, it should be either Wang Guozhang or myself."

Wang took on the task without a moment's hesitation, and, after consulting the other vice ministers, the matter was very quickly settled.

I then called an emergency meeting of heads of relevant offices and departments in the ministry, making further preparations and arrangement for the special group.

Many diplomats in the ministry signed up. Some had a heavy workload, some were not in very good shape, and some had family problems, but in the face of crisis, they all responded in disregard of personal risk and danger. I felt deeply moved by their selfless spirit.

In the meantime, under directives from the Central Authorities, the Beijing Hospital and the Civil Aviation Administration of China were putting together inexpert medical team and a flight crew. The Foreign Ministry liaised with them closely, and mapped out details.

The group rapidly took shape, comprising thirty-four professionals drawn from the Foreign Ministry, Xinhua News Agency, *Guangming Daily*, Beijing Hospital, and other units. At its head was Wang Guozhang.

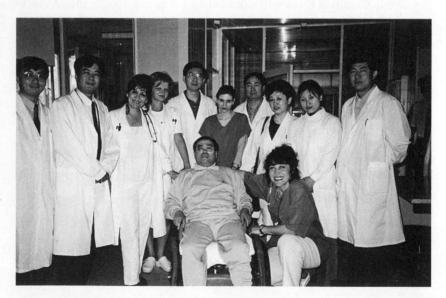

Chinese and Yugoslavian medical crews with the injured.

Meanwhile, as instructed by President Jiang Zemin, the Foreign Ministry and I were also working nonstop to ensure absolute safety for the plane and everyone aboard.

At the time, NATO was imposing an air blockade in Yugoslavia, and it would have been impossible to fly there without a NATO guarantee. To ensure a safe flight, I gave orders to our embassies in the United States, Belgium, and others to make representations to NATO, asking the latter to take all necessary measures to guarantee, not just verbally but in writing, absolute safety for the landing, takeoff, and stay of the Chinese government plane in Belgrade. We also demanded that NATO stop bombing the Yugoslav hospital where the embassy injured were being treated.

Worrying that things might not go as planned, I called the embassies personally, urging them to ensure absolute safety for the mission. I also told them I would remain in my office awaiting NATO's reply at any hour.

All I was thinking was to get NATO's warranty before the flight took off. My duty was to reassure our people on the mission and their families, making them aware of the Party Central Committee's care and concern for them.

Eventually, at around two-thirty in the morning on May 9, a written warranty came in from NATO.

I immediately called a group briefing at the ministry to boost morale. It was in the dead of night, but the group members had already been convened by Wang Guozhang and were waiting in the meeting room. The mood was tense and heavy as the team, busy but orderly, made the final preparations.

At the departure briefing, I listed four tasks for the special group: to convey to everyone at the front line the warmth and care of the Party Central Committee and the State Council, to treat and return the wounded and other personnel requiring evacuation, to arrange funeral and other relevant matters for the deceased, and to assist our embassy in deploying subsequent interior and exterior work. I also briefed the group about our demand for US-led NATO's written guarantee to ensure their safety during the mission.

In March 2008, after I had retired, I happened to meet Zuo Mingzhang, head of the anesthesiology department at Beijing Hospital, who had served on the medical team sent to Belgrade.

Reminiscing about the mission he said, "Actually, I had met you long before. That night, at two-thirty, you called us to an emergency meeting at the ministry to boost morale. We all felt reassured and warm at heart to learn how much effort you had made to get US-led NATO to guarantee our safety in writing. Thanks to your efforts, we also felt the concern of the Central Authorities. The Foreign Ministry did a really considerate and meticulous job."

Zuo's words stirred up memories. Nearly a decade had passed, but he could still remember the details of the meeting and my remarks. That night must have made a deep impression on him.

At daybreak on May 9, 1999, just fourteen hours after the decision to dispatch a group, the Chinese special working group boarded the charter flight to Belgrade.

During that period, staying up through the night was just part of the job. After the briefing, I decided to see the group off at the airport.

Standing by the ramp, I shook hands and bade farewell to each team member as they boarded the plane. We all knew the possible risks of the mission.

To outsiders, diplomats seem a genteel group attending ceremonious occasions in smart suits, wining and dining. In fact, their jobs often involve all sorts of difficult situations and unexpected dangers, sometimes matters of life and death. What is worthy of pride and gratification is that at every critical moment, my colleagues all prove themselves worthy of the trust of the country and the people, sparing no effort at the risk of their own safety. I feel truly proud of the Chinese diplomats.

Another life-and-death test lay ahead. Not only our diplomats

Solemn ceremony held to pay final respects to the victims at a chapel in Belgrade on May 10, 1999, which was attended by hundreds of people.

but every member of the special group proceeded to the front line of war without hesitation, setting aside all considerations of their own safety for the sake of China's national dignity and the people's interests. Not one of them said a word about personal or safety worries, and it was only later that I found out that some members had written their wills before boarding the plane.

I repeated to each one my hope that they would live up to the expectations of the motherland. Each one of them vowed to keep the people's trust at heart and do everything in their power to bring the mission to a successful conclusion.

As soon as the group landed in Belgrade, Wang Guozhang phoned to set my mind at rest. I asked him about details of the damage and casualties, and conveyed my respect and solicitude to our embsssy staffs. During our conversation I repeated the mission's top priority: careful management of the postbombing situation and bringing the relevant personnel back home safely.

In the days following, we were in constant hotline contact, which kept me informed of the local situation right up to date as to how things were being handled there. I would then promptly relay the information to the Central Authorities.

The working group brought with them medicine and medical instruments badly needed for the injured, as well as all kinds of instant foods and daily necessities. From the airport they headed straight to the hospital to visit the injured embassy staff, asking for details about the conditions and treatment of the patients. Medical checkups were done for all the embassy personnel. A solemn ceremony was arranged to pay final respects to Shao Yunhuan, Xu Xinghu, and Zhu Ying, who died in the bombing. The team also carried out careful inspections of the damaged embassy premises.

On the morning of May 12, 1999, having successfully completed their mission in Belgrade after sixty hours of uninterrupted work, the special group escorted the remains of the three victims, the six seriously injured, and some of the embassy evacuees to Beijing.

Hu Jintao, at that time vice president, met them at the airport on behalf of the Party Central Committee, the State Council, and President Jiang Zemin. Also present were heads of relevant departments involved and people from all walks of life in Beijing.

At ten o'clock sharp, the plane made a gentle touchdown at Beijing International Airport.

Sorrowful music played as the families of the victims descended the steps, carrying urns holding the remains of their loved ones. In solemn mood, Hu Jintao watched the escort of the ash urns to the hearse.

When stretchers with the wounded appeared, Hu stepped forward, took their hands in his and told them softly, "I am here to convey the concern of the Party Central Committee, the State Council, and President Jiang Zemin. The motherland is deeply grateful to you and welcomes you back home." He also hugged each of the less seriously injured who were able to walk down the ramp with the help of the medical crew, and comforted them: "You've

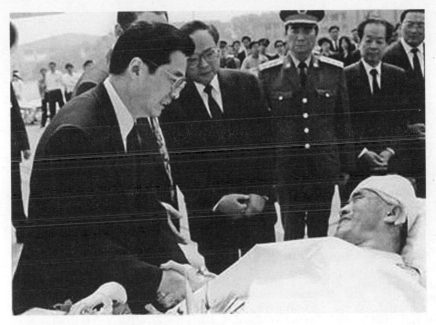

Hu Jintao meeting the injured at the airport on May 12, 1999.

really been put through the mill! The whole nation is waiting for your return." The scene moved many to tears.

On May 12, 1999, in memory of the victims, the State Council ordered that flags be flown at half-mast at Tiananmen, Xinhuamen, the Great Hall of the People, and the Foreign Ministry in Beijing, in front of the governments of all provinces, autonomous regions and municipalities, as well as the Hong Kong SAR and Xinhua News Agency Macao branch. Embassies of the United States, France, Germany, Italy, Egypt, and other countries in China also lowered flags to half-mast to express condolences.

That afternoon, party and state leaders paid a special visit to Xinhua News Agency and *Guangming Daily* to mourn the victims and extend condolences to their families.

On May 13, the Party Central Committee and the State Council held a solemn meeting at the Great Hall of the People in Beijing, attended by all Standing Committee members of the Politburo in

Beijing. Premier Zhu Rongji presided over the meeting, and President Jiang Zemin delivered an important speech. Shao Yunhuan, Xu Xinghu, and Zhu Ying were posthumously conferred the title of "revolutionary martyrs."

Tied up in Belgrade, Ambassador Pan Zhanlin could not return with the group, but directed the embassy at the front line with the remaining staff. Worried about his safety, I repeatedly told him to take good care of himself.

When he finally came back on June 11, 1999, I went to the airport to welcome him home in person, an uncommon thing for a foreign minister to do, as I recall. Later, I also hosted a reunion dinner in his honor, inviting all the ministry leaders.

Under Sustained Pressure, Clinton Officially Apologizes

BY 1999, PRESIDENT CLINTON had been in office for six years, during which period China-US relations had experienced ups and downs. Bilateral relations deteriorated seriously during the *Yinhe* incident* in 1993, Lee Teng-hui's 1995 visit to the United States, and the deployment of two US aircraft carriers near Taiwan in 1996. It was not until President Jiang Zemin's visit to the United States in 1997, and President Clinton's return visit to China the following year, that bilateral relations saw some light. But just a month after my visit to the United States, accompanying Premier Zhu Rongji, in April, the wholly unexpected bombing seriously disrupted the improving relationship.

The vehemence of China's series of responsive acts over the embassy bombing surprised the US government.

---

*On July 23, 1993, the United States claimed that the China-based regular container ship *Yinhe* was transporting chemical weapons materials to Iran. The US Navy forced the *Yinhe* to be searched at Dammam, a Saudi Arabian port, but nothing was found.

Initially, the United States tried to explain away its action by only offering deep condolences and regrets about the casualties and losses sustained by China. At the same time, they were suggesting that Clinton have a one-to-one telephone conversation with President Jiang Zemin, so that he could explain in person. Because of the US reluctance to make a formal apology, this request went unanswered.

Forced by China's firm stance and diplomatic pressure, by increasingly vehement domestic protests and international criticism, the United States was forced to change its attitude and apologized to China.

On May 9, President Clinton wrote a letter to President Jiang Zemin on the matter, expressing "apology for the tragic event at the Chinese embassy in Belgrade and sincere condolences to the victims." Clinton stressed the need for direct conversation between the two state leaders, hoping to talk to President Jiang at the Chinese leader's earliest convenience.

On May 13, President Clinton met with Li Zhaoxing, Chinese ambassador to the United States, at the White House. In the book of condolences that Li had brought along, Clinton expressed "deep condolences for the victims and sincere apology to their families and the people of China."

Considering the change of attitude by the United States, President Jiang Zemin accepted Clinton's request and a telephone conversation took place on May 14.

President Clinton went straight to the point. He said, "Mr. President, I would like to offer my sincere apology for the tragedy in Belgrade, especially to the wounded and families of the victims. I pledge a thorough investigation of the incident, and will let the Chinese people know the truth as soon as possible."

He reiterated the extreme importance of US–China relations, and said that he would do his utmost to deal with the "tragedy" so that bilateral relations might get back on track.

President Jiang restated the firm stand of the Chinese government, stressing that the Chinese government showed great concern over the safety of citizens and treasured the lives of everyone of its population of 1.2 billion. It was the Chinese government's duty to protect this fundamental human right.

He continued, "The assault on the Chinese embassy seriously hurt the feelings of the Chinese people. After the incident, Chinese people took actions of their own accord to express their indignation in various forms, and a wave of strong protests spread across the nation. This was only natural. The pursuit of justice by the Chinese government and people has won wide sympathy, understanding, and support from the international community and people around the world. US-led NATO must bear full responsibility for the incident, and the top priority for the US government is to conduct a comprehensive, thorough, and impartial investigation of the matter, and promptly make known the results of the investigation to satisfy all demands of the Chinese government and people."

Keeping Up the Pressure in Pursuit of the Truth

ON JUNE 16, THOMAS PICKERING, the special envoy sent by President Clinton, arrived in Beijing to report the outcome of the investigation into the embassy bombing. I met with him at the Foreign Ministry.

In the Clinton administration, Pickering served as under secretary of state for Political Affairs, the third top post at the US State Department. In a diplomatic career spanning more than four decades, Mr. Pickering had served as US ambassador to Russia, India, Israel, El Salvador, Nigeria, and Jordan and as US permanent representative to the United Nations. He had a good command of French, Spanish, Swahili, Arabic, Hebrew, and other languages.

He had the personal rank of career ambassador, the highest

honor in the US Foreign Service. Mr. Pickering once said in public that diplomacy was a lifetime profession, and he could not imagine a more attractive and remunerative career.

I had not made his acquaintance before, but later I learned that he had some acquaintance with China, having been to Beijing as early as November 1973 in the capacity of special assistant to Henry Kissinger on his visit to China.

Clinton's intention in sending over such a high-profile diplomat was obvious. However, the envoy was acting under orders; during talks and meetings he was very cautious, reading from written scripts and acting meticulously to avoid any possible slip.

When the meeting started, Mr. Pickering first handed me a letter from President Clinton to President Jiang. He said that, as President Clinton's representative on this important mission, he had notified the Chinese side of the details of the findings of the investigation carried out by the United States on the bombing of the Chinese embassy in Yugoslavia.

Pickering said the United States accepted responsibility for the incident, and that three mistakes had led to the tragic event: First, the technique used to locate the intended target, which was the headquarters of the Yugoslav Federal Directorate for Supply and Procurement (FDSP), was severely flawed; second, the US military and intelligence databases had not been updated with the correct location of the Chinese embassy; third, the target review process had failed to detect and correct these two mistakes, and the US departments concerned had not consulted people who knew the target was the Chinese embassy, not the FDSP.

He repeatedly stated that the bombing of the embassy had in no way been a deliberate act, for it would be completely against US principles and policies. In terms of policy, too, it would be totally unimaginable, being in fundamental conflict with US policy toward China. Furthermore, deliberately bombing the Chinese embassy would not be in line with the United States' objective of solving the Kosovo issue, since the United States saw China, as a permanent member of the Security Council, playing an important role in solving the Kosovo issue.

Pickering also said that internal investigations were still going on in the United States and that once these were completed, it would be determined whether any disciplinary action should be taken. The United States was ready to deal with compensation for China's losses of personnel and property, and was willing to exchange views with the Chinese side.

I solemnly told Pickering that China had noted a second apology offered by the United States and its promise to continue investigation into the incident. I also pointed out that the explanations so far supplied by the United States were unconvincing and that the conclusion of "accidental bombing" was not acceptable to the Chinese government and people.

I made it clear that in the US-led NATO's bombing of the Chinese embassy in Yugoslavia, China was the victim and NATO, in particular the United States, was the culprit. The US government must fully recognize the gravity of the incident from this perspective.

I repeated that a diplomatic mission is the symbol of a nation's sovereignty, and that its personnel and premises are inviolable under the protections of international law, which had always been a basic norm adhered to by the international community. However, the United States had bombed the Chinese embassy with five precision-guided heavy bombs, causing heavy casualties and serious damage to the premises. This was a gross encroachment on China's sovereignty and a willful trampling on the UN Charter and the basic norms governing international relations and international law. If the world allowed such crimes to go unchecked, it would definitely threaten the stability and security of the entire international community, and intensify international tensions. There would never be peace and stability in the world.

I further pointed out that the bombing had claimed the lives of three Chinese journalists, leaving over twenty diplomats injured. This incident had severely hurt the feelings of 1.2 billion Chinese people, and a strong wave of protests had swept across the nation. For the Chinese government and people, every individual life was precious. China must protect its national sovereignty and dignity as well as the fundamental human right, that is, the people's right to survival. It was only natural for the Chinese people to react strongly when their sovereignty and dignity were damaged.

I reiterated that the United States should bear all the responsibility for the bombing and the serious damage it had inflicted on bilateral relations. If the United States truly wished to eliminate the serious consequences of the incident, it should demonstrate its sincerity through practical action, fully acknowledge the gravity of the incident, give serious attention to the stern position and demands of the Chinese government, carry out a comprehensive and thorough investigation into the incident, and severely punish the culprits so as to give, with concrete action, a satisfactory account to the Chinese government and people.

Pickering listened attentively and took notes of everything I said. Finally, he told me that my speech had been most instructive and that he would report China's position and demands to President Clinton and Secretary of State Albright as soon as he returned to the United States. He also said that the United States agreed with China with regard to the need to respect and protect diplomatic missions, and that the United States had offered several apologies for the tragic mistake of bombing the Chinese embassy. The United States would make utmost efforts to tackle the incident in a practical way.

After the meeting, China made repeated representations to the United States on the matter, urging a prompt and positive response from the United States.

In Washington, on April 8, 2000, Pickering, representing the

US government, presented to Ambassador Li Zhaoxing an investigation report on the US bombing of the Chinese embassy in Belgrade. Unsurprisingly, the United States still stuck to its allegation, admitting only to an inappropriate targeting technique and failure at multiple levels to discover the mistake during target checking processes. He said that the United States had taken action against eight CIA officers involved, dismissing one of them. Pickering repeatedly stressed that the United States would offer compensation for the Chinese losses as soon as possible, and that he hoped this would bring the incident to an end and open up a new chapter in our bilateral relations.

In response, we restated the Chinese government's position that the United States bombing of the Chinese embassy resulting in heavy casualties and damage to property had seriously violated relevant international conventions and norms governing international relations. The act had constituted a gross infringement upon China's sovereignty, severely hurt the feelings of the Chinese people, and damaged bilateral relations. The Chinese government strongly demanded that the US government conduct a comprehensive and thorough investigation into the incident and severely punish the culprits so as to give a satisfactory account to the Chinese government and people.

Insistence on Just Compensation

NEGOTIATIONS BETWEEN CHINESE AND US delegations on compensation for Chinese casualties and property losses were initiated in Beijing on July 15, 1999. In the fifty years since the founding of the People's Republic of China, this was the first compensation case negotiated directly with a foreign government. Not only did the negotiations involve complex legal questions, but they had a significant bearing on the core national interests and feelings of the Chinese people. It was a serious political, diplomatic, and complicated legal tussle.

Altogether there were five rounds of talks, and each round was full of difficulties. The Chinese delegation, out of a strong sense of responsibility to the party, the country, and the people, and backed by an abundance of legal evidence, took the upper hand in the negotiations, forcing the United States to appear as an underdog throughout.

The first two rounds of talks took place from July 15 to 16 and from July 18 to 30 in Beijing. On July 30, an agreement was reached on compensation for the casualties and personal losses sustained by China. The two sides also agreed on further negotiations concerning property losses.

In August, the United States paid agreed compensation of 4.5 million US dollars to the Chinese government, which distributed the fund to the families of those killed and to individuals injured in the bombing.

Later, the two sides had three further rounds to negotiate compensation for China's property losses, and reached agreement in December.

Once agreement had been reached, China repeatedly urged the United States to fulfill its pledge and make the compensation funds available right away.

On January 17, 2001, the US government eventually compensated the Chinese government for property losses resulting from the bombing of the Chinese embassy in Belgrade, making a payment of 28 million US dollars.

In the wake of the bombing incident, the Chinese side made strenuous efforts to compel the United States, including President Clinton, to apologize to the Chinese people several times, to carry out investigations, and to pay compensation to China for its casualties and property losses. The United States had remained throughout in a passive and condemned situation politically and morally.

The biggest gain for us was the lesson we taught the United States: that today's China and its people cannot be bullied and will not be scared by evil forces. They are ready to fight for the defense of national sovereignty and dignity at all costs, and are resolutely opposed to hegemonic acts.

A Personal Visit to Yugoslavia to Pay Tribute

I WAS SCHEDULED TO visit some European countries in December 2000, and, since the Federal Republic of Yugoslavia was not too far off the itinerary, I decided to add a stop there, so as to get firsthand experience of the local situation, promote bilateral understanding and trust between the Chinese government and the new government of the Federal Republic, and facilitate the smooth transition and development of bilateral relations. I also wanted to visit my colleagues working there.

At the time, the political scene in the Federal Republic of Yugoslavia had undergone drastic changes. Milošević had lost the presidential elections and been replaced by the opposition party candidate Vojislav Kostunica. Owing to lack of contact in the past, the new leadership was not very familiar with China.

I arrived in Belgrade on December 2, 2000. Despite the great changes in their domestic situation, I still felt the profound friendship of the Yugoslav people for the Chinese people. The new government attached great importance to my visit and arranged for me to meet and talk with the president, prime minister, deputy prime minister, and foreign minister.

During these meetings and talks, I expounded on China's respect for the Yugoslav people's choice and our wish to continue developing bilateral relations, declared China's respect for Yugoslavia's sovereignty and territorial integrity, and our support for its policy of economic reconstruction. I clearly pointed out that China's policy on Yugoslavia was not based on ideological considerations, or support of any single party or individual, but on the pursuit and upholding of justice, as well as the protection of the fundamental interests of the Yugoslav people. The Yugoslav government was deeply moved, recognizing that my visit and announcement of China's principled position provided valuable support for their country. The Yugoslav government emphasized the strategic importance of developing bilateral relations, that its policy of friendly cooperation with China would not change, and that they expected such relations to develop and improve.

During my stay, accompanied by Ambassador Wen Xigui, I paid a special visit to the wreck of the embassy premises in Belgrade, and paid a solemn tribute to the three victims.

Standing on the land that had claimed the lives of my fellow colleagues, I could hardly contain my feelings. The embassy building was a miserable sight. As I walked into the ruins, treading where the bombs had fallen and where the victims had lost their lives, tears welled up in my eyes.

At the end of the visit, I presented flower garlands on behalf of the Foreign Ministry in front of the ruins, and wished that they rest in peace.

Ten years have passed, but emotions still surge up in me whenever the incident comes to mind. The US-led NATO's bombing of our foreign mission, a representative of national sovereignty, had resulted in heavy casualties and property losses. It was a rare and serious incident that shocked the world. How to deal with this bolt from the blue was a critical test of the Chinese government's capacity, and also proved to be an important issue for China's development, as well as for world peace and stability.

At the critical moment, the third-generation central leadership headed by Jiang Zemin made an accurate judgment of the international and domestic situation, and worked out clear and correct decisions, which not only protected China's sovereignty and national dignity, but also took into account our long-term development and the overall situation of reform and opening up. This was the fundamental guarantee for handling extraordinary incidents. Under the correct and forceful guidance of the Central Authorities from start to finish, our main concern was the overall situation and the interests of the nation and the people. Adhering firmly to our principles, we dared to tackle the situation and handled the incident on just grounds, to our advantage and with restraint. As a result, we protected our national dignity, and avoided disruption of the reform and opening-up process.

CHAPTER 6

Visit to Latin America
in the New Millennium

I N JANUARY 2009, FOREIGN Minister Yang Jiechi returned from
a visit to Brazil and sent me a photograph of a tree with a plaque
bearing an inscription in Portuguese commemorating its planting,
on September 23, 2000, by Tang Jiaxuan, foreign minister of the
People's Republic of China. The tree is an ipê, or trumpet tree, the
national tree of Brazil.

Seeing the photo, I remembered that prior to Foreign Minister
Yang's departure for Brazil I had mentioned planting a trumpet tree
by the Itaipu Hydroelectric Power Plant in Iguazu, during my own
visit to Latin America in 2000. Foreign Minister Yang was considerate enough to take a photo of that tree when he visited the power
plant.

What had been a small sapling had grown into a luxuriant tree
taller than an average man.

The photo always reminds me of my visit to Latin America.

In September 2000, I paid an official visit to Cuba, Mexico,
Brazil, and Chile as China's foreign minister. It was my first visit to
Latin America and the Caribbean since assuming the post. China's

The trumpet tree planted by the author on September 23, 2000, is quite tall now.

relations with Latin America at that time were developing steadily and smoothly, and the region attracted wide attention for its continuously emerging potential.

Close Friends Despite Long Distance

LATIN AMERICA, A TERM encompassing Latin America and the Caribbean, is a vast region covering an area of 20.7 million square kilometers. It is located in the Western Hemisphere, south of the United States, between the Atlantic and the Pacific oceans. It includes Mexico in North America, the Central American Isthmus, the South American continent, and the West Indies in the Caribbean. The line of the Equator crosses Latin America through Brazil, Colombia, and Ecuador.

In a broader sense, Latin America is a political and cultural concept related to its colonial history. The region was colonized by European powers, most notably Spain and Portugal, and hence is dominated by romance languages. With beautiful scenery and abundant resources, Latin America boasts great development potential. According to 2007 statistics, its population is estimated at 561 million and its GDP per capita at 5,540 US dollars.

The region has thirty-three independent states and thirteen dependencies, most of them Spanish speaking. Portuguese is the official language of Brazil, which was a Portuguese colony for over three centuries. English is the main language in most of the Caribbean countries, though some speak French or Dutch.

Despite the great distance between China and Latin America, their ties can be traced back over four hundred years, when Chinese merchants, artisans, and sailors voyaged via the Philippines along the Pacific trade routes to Mexico and Peru to do business or to work.

In the two decades following the founding of the People's Republic of China in 1949, China's relations with Latin America remained at a nongovernmental level. In 1960, Cuba became the first country in Latin America to establish diplomatic relations with China. In the 1970s and '80s, most countries in the region had established relations with China. Contacts and exchanges between China and Latin America kept increasing thereafter.

To date, China has established diplomatic relations with twenty-one of the thirty-three countries in Latin America.

With the growth of China's overall strength and international status, Latin American countries have attached greater importance to developing their relations with China. Mutual understanding and trust have deepened, and investment and economic cooperation have continuously expanded.

In 2000, the year I visited Latin America, the volume of China–Latin America trade reached 12.5 billion US dollars, exceeding 10 billion for the first time. In this context, it is worth mentioning the successful launch, in 1999, of the first Earth resources satellite jointly developed by China and Brazil—a model of South-South cooperation* in high-tech industries.

Years of fruitful contact had preliminarily prepared the ground for rapid and all-around development of China–Latin America relations in the twenty-first century.

Meanwhile, changes were afoot in Latin America in the new century.

In some Latin American countries, calls for reform were getting louder, and new left-wing forces were emerging.

After the economic turbulence of 1998–99, Latin American countries had reflected upon the problems emanating from neoliberalism,† including rising unemployment, widening of the gap between the rich and the poor, and sharpening of social contradictions. They actively promoted regional integration and at the same time focused more on developing their relations with the EU and Asia-Pacific countries.

Latin American countries cast their eyes towards China, and came to see China as an important cooperation partner in their self-development efforts.

China values its relations with Latin American countries

---

*South-South cooperation refers to cooperation among developing countries, also known as countries of the global south, mainly located in the Southern Hemisphere.
†Neoliberalism is a Western economic theory established in the 1920s and '30s. The term refers to a redefinition of classical liberalism and puts more emphasis on liberalization, privatization, and marketization. In the mid-1990s, neoliberalism became the dominant paradigm of Latin American economics. The term consists of four key elements: First, trade liberalization aimed at lowering tariff barriers and opening market access; second, financial liberalization aimed at deregulating government controls over financial institutions and attracting foreign direct investment through liberalizing financial markets, relaxing limitations on foreign investment, and allowing foreign capital into privatization; third, privatization of state enterprises through selling or listing the shares, purchasing equities by members of the management, joint venture, franchising, and leasing; fourth, marketization of economic system aimed at reducing direct state and government intervention in the economy and heightening the role of the market in economic development.

because they represent a key force in the world. Improving such relations accords with China's needs for its overall diplomacy and self-development.

After taking office as foreign minister, I deeply felt the necessity of a prompt visit to Latin America, with a view to furthering mutual understanding and cooperation between China and the region.

Because of the great distance, there were as yet no direct flights between China and Latin America. One had to change planes either in Europe or North America, and a one-way journey took at least twenty-four hours. The inconvenience of transportation had hampered to a certain extent the development of China–Latin America communications at all levels and in all fields. At the turn of the twenty-first century, both China and Latin America were actively exploring a development path suited to their own national conditions with the earnest hope to deepen mutual political understanding and trust, strengthen contact, and tap the cooperation potential.

I discussed my idea to visit the region with Vice Foreign Minister Yang Jiechi, who was then in charge of Latin American affairs. Mr. Yang's response was fully supportive and we started making preparations. With the consent of the Central Authorities, in 2000, I paid an official visit to four countries, namely Cuba, Mexico, Brazil, and Chile, each with its distinctive features.

Cuba is the only socialist state in the Western Hemisphere. Mexico is known for its culture and for its rapid economic development since joining the North American Free Trade Agreement (NAFTA). Brazil is the strongest country in Latin America in terms of overall national strength, and was the first developing country to establish a strategic partnership with China. Chile is a major trade partner of China in Latin America and an important cooperative partner in APEC.

Strengthening relations with these four countries, all of them representative and influential countries in Latin America, would be conducive to promoting China's relations with the Latin American region as a whole.

President Castro, a Caribbean Evergreen

ON THE MORNING OF September 16, 2000, after attending the UN General Assembly session in New York, I led the Chinese delegation for JFK International Airport aboard a chartered plane bound for Latin America and began an official visit to the four countries.

As it happened, 2000 was the fortieth anniversary of the establishment of China–Cuba diplomatic relations. So, my first visit to Latin America in my capacity of foreign minister started with Cuba.

Cuba is honored as the pearl of the Caribbean for its picturesque scenery and pleasant climate. With a population of 11 million and an area of 110,000 square kilometers, Cuba is also known for its prosperous sugar industry, its quality cigars, and its production of rum.

In the 1950s, Cuba's revolutionary leader Fidel Castro, as the head of twenty-eight followers, set out from Mexico on the yacht, and landed in Cuba to start a rebellion against the dictatorship of Fulgencio Batista. In 1959, the revolutionaries captured the capital, Havana, declaring the success of their revolution and the birth of a socialist country next door to the United States. The world was astounded.

Typical impressions of Cuba at that time in the memories of the Chinese were the romantic and legendary Cuban revolution, the bearded Castro in military fatigues, the resounding slogan "Cuba, Sí! Yankee, No!" Cuban sugar, and the popular Cuban song, "Beautiful Havana."

Like my contemporaries, I had always hankered to visit Cuba. This time, my first visit as Chinese foreign minister to Cuba would enable me to see the country close up and to meet Castro face-to-face.

During the flight, I carefully studied a map of America. The distance between Florida in the southern United States and the nearest point on the island of Cuba is less than a hundred nautical miles across the Straits of Florida. However, because of the US embargo against Cuba, the straits had become a barrier between the two neighbors on either side of its waters for over a half century: On one side one finds the biggest capitalist country in the world and on the other the only socialist state in the Western Hemisphere. I wondered how long the barrier would remain.

At one in the afternoon on September 16, 2000, the plane arrived on time at José Martí International Airport, where Cuban comrades and China's Ambassador to Cuba Wang Chengjia were waiting. As soon as we got off the plane, we received a warm and friendly welcome from the Cuban side. Cuba regarded China's visit on the fortieth anniversary of diplomatic relations as demonstrating the Chinese people's friendship towards Cuban comrades, and China's close attention to our bilateral relations.

On the way to the hotel, other members of the delegation and I enjoyed the enchanting scenery and agreeable climate of Havana and felt relaxed after the long flight.

The city indeed deserved its reputation as sung in "Beautiful Havana." Under the blue sky and white clouds was the boundless expanse of the Caribbean Sea. Royal palms, the national tree of Cuba, grew everywhere and soared high into the sky. Buildings of various styles were seen in the city. What a picturesque view!

Havana, an ancient city built by the Spanish colonialists in the sixteenth century, boasts a rich cultural heritage, and was listed, in 1982, as a UNESCO World Heritage site. A great many buildings surviving from the colonial period were preserved intact. The granite buildings, dotted widely about the city, were reminders of its faded colonial past. VW Beetles and vintage cars produced in the 1950s and '60s still ran on the city's streets, presenting a spectacle unique to Havana.

At four o'clock on the day we arrived, I held talks with my Cuban counterpart on the strengthening of China-Cuba relations. After the meeting, we signed an agreement on cooperation between China's Foreign Affairs University and Cuba's Institute of International Relations. Before leaving the Cuban Foreign Ministry, I was told that the commandante would host a banquet in my honor at the Palace of Revolution on that evening.

The commandante was none other than Fidel Castro: Cuba's president of the Council of State and the Council of Ministers. The Cuban people affectionately refer to him by his title Commandante-en-jefe (Commander-in-Chief) in the Cuban Revolutionary Armed Forces, which had overthrown the Batista dictatorship.

The Chinese people's knowledge about Cuba has mostly originated from the story of Fidel Castro. This much-esteemed leader of the Cuban people was born in 1926 on a sugar plantation owned by his father. It is said that, even in his youth, he already had a strong sense of justice and used to defend schoolmates from poor families against injustice. He went on to study law at the University of Havana, and, in the early 1950s, led a group of revolutionaries who shared his aspirations to launch attacks on the dictatorial Batista regime.

In 1953, at the age of twenty-seven, Castro was captured in his armed assault on the Moncada Barracks. During his trial, Castro delivered his famous defense speech "History Will Absolve Me," shaking Cuba and the entire world. Thereafter, his name was known throughout the world.

At the time of my visit, Cuba was in an extremely difficult situation due to more than forty years of US blockade and embargo and the loss of support following the collapse of the Soviet Union. However, President Castro had resolutely led the Cuban people in defense of their national independence and sovereignty, adhering to socialism, and forging ahead their own development path through self-reliance.

This would be my second meeting with President Castro in that single month. Before this visit to Cuba, I had accompanied China's then-President Jiang Zemin to the United Nations Millennium Summit in New York and had personally witnessed the Castro charisma on the international stage.

Many state and government leaders were to give a speech at the summit, so a time limit of five minutes per speaker had been set; a warning light at the podium would turn on when that time was up. When Castro, who was renowned for his long speeches, came to the podium, to the surprise of all, he covered the reminder light with a handkerchief to prevent being interrupted. This humorous action evoked much laughter in the audience. Everyone believed he was about to give a long speech, but in fact he spoke concisely and finished with time to spare. Before stepping down, he did not forget to remove the handkerchief from the reminder light. Once again, there was an explosion of applause and laughter from the audience.

Thus on the international stage of the UN General Assembly, Castro again demonstrated his ingenious sense of humor.

At eight o'clock on the evening of September 16, 2000, the Chinese delegation arrived at the Palace of Revolution at the appointed time. The Palace of Revolution, located by the Revolution Square, is the office of Cuba's Council of State. To its left are the offices of the Central Committee of the Communist Party of Cuba, and to its right the Council of Ministers. The palace is a magnificent and solemn building, where key party and state activities are held.

Castro had come down from his third-floor office to the main hall on the second floor ahead of time to await the Chinese delegation. When we entered, the stalwart president, dressed in his hallmark military uniform, was standing in the middle of the hall, full

Meeting with Cuba's President Fidel Castro, September 16, 2000.

of energy. He hugged me warmly and went straight into our talks, like chatting with an old friend.

Throughout our talks, Castro emphasized the importance Cuba attached to the development of its relations with China, and expressed Cuba's deep feelings towards China and the Chinese people. He recalled several times President Jiang Zemin's visit in 1993. He said gratefully that President Jiang was the only foreign leader to visit Cuba in 1993, at a time when many people assumed that Cuba would not survive. President Jiang and the Chinese people had given Cuba great political support and valuable help and strengthened its belief in the socialist path. The Cuban people would never forget China's support and help.

Castro expected China, as a major developing country, would play an increasingly important role on the international stage and saw China's prosperity as a beacon of hope for developing countries all over the world.

I replied that the Chinese people took a great interest in Cuba's development. Under his staunch leadership, the Cuban people had come through the hard times and were moving strenuously onto the path of recovery and growth. China believed that Cuba would certainly achieve greater success in its national construction. President Castro nodded in reply.

By coincidence, it was during my visit that the controversy over the Cuban boy Elián González arose and became a focus of media attention.

The president explained to me in detail the struggle to secure Elián's return to Cuba. Sitting erect, he explained to me all the twists and turns of the story, sometimes with a solemn expression and grave tone for emphasis.

In November 1999, six-year-old Elián González left Cuba in secret with his mother by boat for the United States. During the trip, their boat capsized and his mother died. Elián luckily survived, was rescued by fishermen, and taken in by his relatives in Miami. Some people with ulterior motives in the United States not only tried to prevent Elián from returning to his father in Cuba, but also used him as an anti-Cuba propaganda tool, labeling him a "little fighter for democracy." With support from the Cuban government, Elián's father strongly demanded the return of his son to Cuba, but was obstructed by the United States.

Excitedly, Castro told me he had led the Cuban people in staging million-people demonstrations for Elián's return. After seven months of unremitting efforts, Elián was returned to his homeland on September 6, 2000.

Finally, Castro declared passionately, "Elián is a son of Cuba, every Cuban's son! The Cuban people were destined to win this fight right from the start."

Fidel Castro is a legendary leader and a charismatic speaker. Throughout our meeting and banquet, the seventy-four-year-old president spoke with energy and eloquence on international affairs. His talk was full of vigor, witty remarks, and quotations from the classics. He was capable of talking animatedly on any subject.

Acquainted with China's revolutionary history, its current situation, and policies, he showed a keen interest in China's reform and opening-up policy and economic development. He delved deeply into many specific issues.

Our talks went on far into the night. Every time I tried to say goodbye for fear of delaying his rest, he persuaded me to stay on.

My conversation with this world-famous leader was imbued with enthusiasm and friendliness all along, lasting six and a half hours. Even at two-thirty in the morning, Castro was still eager to talk, but had to call a halt in view of the schedule for the Chinese delegation the next day.

Before leaving, every member of our delegation was given as gift a box of Cohiba premium cigars from the president. He joked that, since quitting smoking, he could only be a cigar salesman. He liked Chinese food and hoped that his Chinese friends would enjoy the Cuban cigars and remember him when smoking them.

After the meeting and banquet, I returned to my hotel and remained awake for a long time, thinking about Castro. I had gained more understanding of his personality through the meeting. A founding leader of the Republic of Cuba, Fidel Castro had profound feelings for the Cuban people and full confidence in the success of their revolution. His painstaking and tireless work in the interest of Cuba and its people had made Fidel Castro a figure of incomparable charisma in their hearts.

A Half Day at the Mayan Ruins

MEXICO WAS THE SECOND stop on my visit to Latin America.

As a major and ancient country in Latin America, Mexico is known across the world for its long history and splendid civilization. It is also the birthplace of the Mayan and Aztec civilizations, two of the three ancient Indian civilizations of the Americas.

En route between Havana and Mexico City, our delegation accepted Mexico's suggestion to make a technical stopover in Cancún, a famous coastal city in southern Mexico, due to some adjustment to our visit schedule. Since the schedule was extremely tight, we could stop here just for a half day. It was a rare and welcome opportunity to relax.

On September 18, 2000, we arrived in Cancún, the host city of the 1981 North-South Summit on cooperation and development. Cancún is known worldwide for its cultural tourism, in particular, its Mayan ruins.

In 1997, I had accompanied President Jiang Zemin to Cancún on his visit to Mexico, but I had hardly had time to enjoy the beautiful scenery and unique culture of the city. It was a source of regret that I could not see the Mayan site during that visit.

Cancún was still hot in September. At two o'clock on September 18, the chartered plane of the Chinese delegation touched down at Cancún International Airport. China's ambassador to Mexico, Shen Yun'ao, Mexico's ambassador to China, Cecilio Garza Limón, and officials of the Mexican Foreign Ministry and the Cancún government were waiting by the ramp.

In the airport VIP lounge, Ambassador Cecilio Garza Limón, on behalf of the Mexican government, extended a warm welcome to me. He said that the Mexican government set great store by this visit and had summoned him back from China to welcome the Chinese delegation to Mexico as an expression of friendship. The Cancún government had made the detailed arrangements for my visit.

After a short rest at the airport, we headed by car for the Tulum ruins.

The ancient city of Tulum, located 127 kilometers south of Cancún, is one of the major sites of Mayan culture in its postclassic period, from the tenth to early sixteenth century. Tulum is also one of the best-preserved coastal Mayan sites.

After a drive of over two hours, we arrived at Tulum, which, in Mayan, means "wall." The city faces the Caribbean Sea in the east, and is surrounded by stone walls in the other three directions, hence its name.

Tulum was a prosperous Mayan city and its citizens lived a comfortable and affluent life, but for reasons unknown the Mayans suddenly abandoned the city and went back into the forests. It still remains a mystery. Tulum was lost in the vast rain forest for four centuries until it was discovered intact in the mid-twentieth century.

The city and its surrounding structures extend six kilometers along the Caribbean coast. We left the car outside the city, and passed through a low gate for a walking tour around the city. It is said that the Mayans built the city gates quite narrow for security and defense considerations, allowing only one person to pass through at a time. The gates are obviously too low for modern people, who have to bend to pass through, but they were perfectly fine for the short-statured Mayans.

The low, narrow gate led to a broad, magnificent view. The first building in sight was the palace of the high priest. The palace was built with blocks and slabs of Cancún's characteristic lava rock. Its base platform bore relief carvings, on which the red color had faded due to long exposure to the elements. The palace, six meters wide, five deep, and three high, used to be the most sumptuous building in the city. The exterior of the palace remained majestic as ever, despite the passage of time, but the interior was empty. We had to rely on our imaginations to envision its past luxury and splendor.

Apart from the palace, everywhere inside the city there are civic and religious buildings, castles, temples, and altars, all in a fine state of preservation and with exquisite relief carvings on their walls. Despite the faded colors, the superb craftsmanship still demonstrates the extraordinary glamor of Mayan culture.

The views of that ancient city were breathtaking. We strolled around the city, bathed in the light from the azure sky and the blue

With our tour guide in the Maya city of Tulum, September 18, 2000.

3ca, and knowing about its remote history, our admiration for the achievements of Mayan culture grew even stronger.

That visit provoked many thoughts in me. Culture is an eternal common language for human communication. Despite the geographical distance between Mexico and China, both countries have long and splendid histories and cultures, greatly contributing to human civilization and progress. These venerable cultural traditions act as a bond for advancing mutual understanding and communication between the people of the two countries, and are an important basis for bilateral ties and cooperation. In the new century, China and Mexico's efforts in strengthening communication and cooperation would certainly benefit the people of both countries and make new contributions to world peace and progress.

Meetings with Incumbent and Outgoing Presidents

THE YEAR 2000 MARKED the start of a new millennium and a turning point in the history of Mexico.

In the presidential election, the ruling Institutional Revolutionary Party (PRI) had been defeated by its rival the National Action Party (PAN). The PRI had held power in Mexican politics for seventy-one years, since 1929. On December 1, 2000, the new president, Vicente Fox of PAN, officially moved into the presidential residence and workplace, Los Pinos, and took office as the sixty-fourth president of Mexico.

When we arrived in Mexico City on September 19, two months before the inauguration of the new president, intense preparations were going on for the handover from the old to the new administration.

We were not familiar with PAN or the new president. I decided to meet with both the incumbent president Ernesto Zedillo and the president-elect Vicente Fox during the course of my visit.

It was a rare opportunity to meet two presidents of a country in a single visit.

President Ernesto Zedillo was loved and esteemed by the Mexican people. Since taking office in 1994, he had led the Mexican people to overcome the problems arising from financial crisis and made great achievements in national construction and social progress. In 2000, the final year of his term, Mexico's foreign-trade volume and GDP ranked first and second, respectively, among Latin American countries. The Mexican economy had become one of the fastest growing in the region.

However, the constitution of Mexico states that a president cannot serve successive terms, nor can he or she stand for reelection. Ernesto Zedillo was no exception.

An old friend of China, President Zedillo put emphasis on building Mexico's relations with China during his six-year term. His visit to China in 1996 had greatly contributed to the advancement of friendly cooperation between the two countries.

On the afternoon of September 19, 2000, I set off from the hotel where I stayed for Los Pinos to meet President Zedillo. It was

Meeting with Mexico's President Ernesto Zedillo, September 19, 2000.

my fourth meeting with him: The first was in 1997 during Chinese President Jiang Zemin's visit to Mexico; the second and third times were in 1999, first at the APEC Informal Meeting in Auckland, New Zealand, and then during Zedillo's visit to China. The president was of medium stature with an urbane, academic bearing. He wore gold-rimmed glasses, and I could clearly see wisdom and resilience in his eyes.

Our meeting took place in an atmosphere of warmth and friendship. The president expressed friendly sentiments towards the Chinese people and good wishes for the lasting friendship between the peoples of China and Mexico.

President Zedillo stressed several times that Mexico and China, both as large, developing countries, shared similar views on many major international issues and firmly safeguarded the fundamental principles of international law. The Mexican people treasured their friendship with the Chinese people.

He sincerely promised to visit China again to meet his old friends there and continue contributing to China-Mexico friendship once he stepped down from the presidency by the end of 2000.

I replied that the Chinese people would always regard him as a respected and welcome friend. The meeting, though scheduled for a half hour, ran on for nearly a full hour.

Mr. Zedillo kept his word. After his presidency and during his tenure as chairman of the United Nations High-Level Panel on Financing for Development, and as director of the Yale Center for the Study of Globalization, he continued his efforts to advance China-Mexico friendship, and paid many visits to China, including participation in the Boao Forum for Asia in Hainan. He contributed enormously to the building of relations of mutual benefit and friendly cooperation between our two nations.

I maintained a good working relationship and a personal friendship with Mr. Zedillo. After he stepped down from the presidency, I met him again during President Hu Jintao's visit to the United States in 2004, and while attending the Boao Forum for Asia in 2006.

However, I had never met the incoming President Vicente Fox. The Mexican media had dubbed him the "Cowboy President," which aroused my curiosity.

On the day of our meeting, Mr. Fox strode towards us as our delegation entered his office. Mr. Fox, a tall man, with a neatly groomed mustache, greeted us in a warm, resonant voice, without putting on airs. We could hardly believe that he would soon become the president.

After being seated, I noticed that Mr. Fox, though wearing a business suit, was also wearing riding boots, decorated with traditional Mexican cowboy designs.

Later, Chinese Ambassador to Mexico Shen Yun'ao told me that Mr. Fox had grown up on a ranch in the state of Guanajuato, and always wore cowboy clothing. He wore a business suit only on

Meeting with Mexico's incoming president Vicente Fox, September.

formal occasions, but the boots were a permanent feature, a sign of intimacy to the people. His warmth and hospitality fully lived up to his fame as the Cowboy President.

During our meeting, I passed on President Jiang Zemin's invitation for him to visit China. Mr. Fox gladly accepted the invitation and promised that China would be the first stop on his Asian trip.

After taking office, he fulfilled that promise.

Although Mr. Fox and the PAN were coming to power for the first time, his friendliness towards China convinced me that our bilateral relation of friendship and cooperation would develop further in the twenty-first century.

Much Persuasion About China's WTO Accession

MEXICO IS A MAJOR economy in Latin America and its industrial structure is similar to that of China. Therefore, Mexicans were seriously worried about the potential impact of Chinese products on Mexican domestic markets due to China's accession to the World

Trade Organization. At that time, China was at the final negotiation stage for WTO accession. Bilateral negotiations had already been concluded with thirty-five of the thirty-seven WTO member states: Only Mexico and Switzerland remained uncommitted. China and Mexico had held four rounds of talks over the issue, but had not reached an agreement. One of the goals of my visit was to pave the way for a bilateral agreement on China's accession to the WTO.

I made this a focus of my talk with President Zedillo and discussed the issue with him in depth. I said that China, with its population of 1.2 billion, ranked ninth in the world in terms of foreign trade, and for seven consecutive years had absorbed the greatest amount of foreign investment among all developing countries. As a rapidly developing economy, China was an indispensable component in economic globalization. China's accession to the WTO would bring broader scope and increased vigor to the further development of economic globalization, thus benefiting both China's economic development and that of the world at large. Reaching a bilateral agreement as soon as possible would be in the fundamental interests of both Chinese and Mexican people, and would promote the long-term, stable development of their economic and trade relations, as well as make positive contributions to a multilateral trade system.

President Zedillo listened attentively to my words and told me that Mexico eagerly anticipated and supported China's accession to the WTO. He had instructed Mexico's Secretariat of Commerce and Industrial Development (today's Secretariat of Economy) to negotiate with the relevant departments of the Chinese government over the details and reach agreement as soon as possible. He added that he was willing to visit Beijing in person and seek a political solution if some problems could not be solved at the technical level.

In fact, President Zedillo was approaching the end of his term, and the technical details were too numerous to be solved within his term. However, the negotiations maintained momentum and resumed soon after President Fox took office. China and Mexico eventually reached an agreement on September 13, 2001, one year after my visit to Mexico.

The agreement marked the end of China's bilateral negotiations with WTO members and the success of China's fifteen-year journey to join the world trade body.

South-South Cooperation with Latin America's Giant

I IMMEDIATELY HEADED FOR Brazil after leaving Mexico City.

The last visit to Brazil by a Chinese foreign minister was in 1993, when Qian Qichen held the position.

In consideration of Brazil's position and influence in Latin America, I, before my trip, had done my homework on Brazil and the history of China-Brazil relations.

Brazil ranks first in Latin America in terms of territory, population, and overall strength. Moreover, its abundant resources, including land, forest, fresh water, mineral, and energy, are in the world's leading ranks, and provide Brazil with natural advantages for development.

Brazil has enjoyed long political stability and sustained economic development. In particular, Brazil's economy grew at 10.1 percent per year on average for eight consecutive years from 1967 to 1974, creating the Brazilian miracle.

In terms of foreign relations, Brazil is independent and progressive. It advocates world multipolarity and democratization of international relations, and makes active contributions to building a new international, political, and economic order that is fair and rational. Brazil also strives to play a more important role in international and regional affairs.

The history of China-Brazil relations is a process of two large, developing countries seeking and deepening mutual understanding and cooperation benefiting both parties under the prevailing trend of peace and development.

Brazil was the first developing country to establish a strategic partnership with China. During the visit of China's President Jiang Zemin to Brazil in November 1993, the two countries had achieved common understanding on key issues regarding the establishment of a long, stable, and mutually beneficial strategic partnership. Thereafter, China-Brazil relations had expanded and progressed in all fields.

The joint project that attracted great attention was the Earth resources satellite project, which, in the context of those times, was undoubtedly an event of great significance.

High-tech products like the Earth resources satellite had long been the monopoly of major capitalist countries. There were a few developing countries exploring in this field, but their technological level was generally low, so cooperation among them was out of the question.

The success of the China-Brazil Earth resources satellite program was very positive for relations between China and Latin American countries, and set an example for scientific and technological cooperation between China and developing countries.

The project began in 1988. Brazil's President José Sarney visited China and the two countries signed an agreement on the joint development of Earth resources satellites, thus initiating the bilateral cooperation in this project. The two sides agreed to use their individual technological strengths for the joint development of two Earth resources satellites.

This was the first high-tech cooperation between developing countries, and something of a trial venture in South–South cooperation. Geographical distance, language barriers, lack of funds, and other factors meant that it was far from plain sailing, and the project encountered some unforeseen difficulties, but neither country wavered in its faith in the project.

Thanks to the concerted efforts of both sides, the China–Brazil Earth Resources Satellite 01 was launched into orbit on October 14, 1999. Its successful launch ended the two countries' dependence on developed countries for satellite data and achieved an historic breakthrough in space technology of the two countries.

Encouraged by the experience and success acquired from the first satellite, China and Brazil soon started developing a second one. In addition, both sides expressed a strong desire for further cooperation in this field to develop more resources satellites and commercialize their use.

At the time of my visit to Brazil, China–Brazil satellite cooperation was going through a transitional period.

Friendly Cooperation

ON SEPTEMBER 21, 2000, I arrived at the Brasilia Air Base and began my Brazilian trip.

Brasilia is a young, modern city. Salvador and Rio de Janeiro were the first two capitals of Brazil. With a view to redressing the developmental imbalance between Brazil's interior and its southeast coastal region, safeguarding the nation's unification and security, its President Juscelino Kubitschek issued orders in 1956 to build a new capital city in the wilderness of Brazil's central-west region. Brasilia was completed in three years and officially became the capital of Brazil on April 21, 1960.

It was already one-thirty in the morning and dark outside when our plane arrived in Brasilia. We were rather sleepy and weary.

As soon as we emerged from the plane, a blare of bugles broke the silence of the night, startling every one of the delegation. I first spotted China's ambassador to Brazil, Wan Yongxiang. Behind him stood high-ranking officials of Brazil's Foreign Ministry and an honor guard of the Brazilian Air Force. Senior officials of the Chinese embassy and representatives of overseas Chinese in Brazil were also waiting at the airport to greet us.

Ambassador Wan Yongxiang, noticing my look of surprise, explained that Brazil set great store by this visit and that Brazil's minister of External Relations had specially arranged the airport ceremony of welcome that was usually reserved for heads of state and government.

I realized that Brazil attached great importance to this visit and the development of its relations with China.

It was my first visit to Brasilia, and its exquisite city planning left a deep impression on me. On December 7, 1987, UNESCO added Brasilia to the World Heritage list. This young city, just twenty-seven years old, won the honor mainly for its remarkable urban planning.

The city planning of Brasilia features a rational layout, ingenious and original architecture, and thought-provoking modern sculptures around the city. From above, the layout resembles a huge aircraft flying east. The north-south Highway Axis and the east-west Monumental Axis form the main framework, the Square of the Three Powers is its head, the federal and municipal government buildings are the body, and the modern highways and the commercial and residential zones are the wings.

Government activities are concentrated around the Square of the Three Powers, where the buildings are mostly steel-framed and glass-clad, lively and brisk in style. Across the Square of the Three Powers stands the National Congress building, where a pair of thirty-four-story office towers, linked to form an H, soars skyward. A Brazilian friend accompanying me during my visit told me that *H* was the first letter of the Portuguese word for human and that the shape conveyed the concept of people first.

Brazil's bicameral National Congress comprises the Chamber of Deputies and the Federal Senate, represented respectively by the dome and bowl on either side of the National Congress building. It is said that the bowl symbolizes collecting public opinion and the dome symbolizes summarizing public opinion. The presidential residence and the Supreme Federal Court stand on either side of the Square of the Three Powers. The seats of legislative, executive, and judiciary powers form a nearly equilateral triangle, a symbol of the separation of powers with checks and balances.

What Brasilia's city planning conveyed to me was that the city was pursuing a developmental concept of universal equality and harmonious coexistence between man and nature; perhaps it was one of the reasons that Brazil could rank among the emerging powers and possess great development potential.

On the morning of September 21, 2000, Brazil's Minister of External Affairs Luiz Felipe Lampreia and I held talks at the Itamaraty Palace, the headquarters of Brazil's Ministry of External Relations and where major diplomatic events take place.

The main building of the ministry has the appearance of a palace built of glass. In front stretches an enormous pool dotted with tropical aquatic plants. The glass wall and the pool reflect crystal clear images of each other. Seen from a distance, a gigantic rock seems to be floating in the pool, but it is actually a marble sculpture symbolizing the unity among the five continents.

Brazilian protocol officials told me that the Chinese delegation could enjoy the privilege of entering the Itamaraty Palace through the main door and being welcomed by a red carpet and a dragoon honor guard. Such treatment is usually accorded only to foreign heads of state.

The honor guards, wearing the military uniform of the Brazilian Empire period and holding flags, looked immaculate and imposing.

Brazil's Foreign Minister Luiz Felipe Lampreia, an old friend, was waiting for me at the main door of the Itamaraty Palace.

Mr. Lampreia became foreign minister in Fernando Henrique Cardoso's government in January 1995, and was reappointed in January 1999. He valued Brazil's relations with China and was hugely interested in China's economic development.

Our first meeting took place in 1998, when he visited China at my invitation. We held friendly and fruitful talks, and I hosted a dinner for him on the nineteenth floor of our Foreign Ministry building. I had learned before our meeting that he was interested in Chinese religion and culture, so I arranged for him to tour the Yonghegong Lama Temple in Beijing.

I was extremely happy to meet with my old Brazilian friend again. We had an in-depth exchange of views on bilateral relations and on international and regional issues of mutual interest, and agreed on enriching the China-Brazil strategic partnership in the new century.

We also discussed further expanding high-tech cooperation

Meeting with Brazil's Foreign Minister Lampreia, December 1, 1998.

between the two sides. I told my counterpart, with great earnestness, that China regarded its high-tech cooperation with Brazil as a strategy to promote South-South cooperation. The successful launch of the first Earth resources satellite jointly developed between us had set a good example for high-tech cooperation among developing countries, and thus had a political significance for South-South cooperation. China and Brazil should continue cooperation in the current field and expand exchanges and cooperation into other fields of advanced technology.

My views and suggestions were well received. He emphasized that Brazil attached great importance to its high-tech cooperation with China, and agreed that the two countries should build on the foundation of our successful cooperation in space technology to develop broader exchanges and cooperation in information, biotechnology, global climate change, environmental protection, and energy.

At the end of our talks, Foreign Minister Lampreia and I signed the Protocol on Cooperation in Space Technology between the Chinese and Brazilian governments. The two sides agreed to develop third and fourth satellites. The protocol established a legal framework for China-Brazil cooperation in developing second-generation satellites.

The Brazilian side held a grand signing ceremony that underlined the importance of the Earth resources satellite program to Brazil. Foreign Minister Lampreia invited over two hundred guests to the signing ceremony, including Brazil's minister of Justice, minister of Science and Technology, vice chairman of the National Congress Chamber of Deputies on External Affairs and National Defense Committee, and the president of Brazil's Space Agency. According to Chinese Ambassador Wan, it was rare for Brazil's Ministry of External Relations to hold a signing ceremony on such a scale.

Foreign Minister Lampreia and the minister of Science and

Technology delivered impassioned speeches and I, too, responded with a warm speech. The ceremony concluded in a friendly atmosphere.

That afternoon, I went to visit Brazil's President Fernando Henrique Cardoso at the seat of Brazilian government, called the Palace of the Plateau. It is so named because of the location of Brasilia on the central plateau of Brazil. It is a rectangular building supported on four sides by beautifully shaped pillars, magnificent and graceful.

This was our first meeting. The courteous, elegant president was a renowned scholar of sociology in the Latin American and international academic world. His work *Dependency and Development in Latin America* had been translated into Chinese, and was popular among Chinese readers.

I first passed on to President Cardoso the very warm greetings and best wishes from President Jiang Zeming and Premier Zhu Rongji, together with a letter from President Jiang.

I conveyed to him China's high regard for his years of active contributions to China-Brazil relations and admiration for the great achievements Brazil had made in its national construction.

President Cardoso was glad to receive President Jiang's letter. He was pleased to see that China-Brazil relations had maintained momentum since the establishment of a strategic partnership seven years earlier.

President Cardoso was also a leader with global vision. During our meeting, he stressed that peace and progress needed a multipolar world, for which the joint efforts of China and Brazil were necessary, thus Brazil prioritized its relations with China in its foreign policy. He explained to me that Brazil supported China's accession to the WTO, not only for our mutual trade and economic interests, but also for maintaining a global strategic balance.

Two Very Different Cities

AFTER BRASILIA, RIO DE Janeiro (commonly referred to as Rio) was my second stop in Brazil.

Rio is nicknamed "the Marvelous City." There is a saying that illustrates their affection for the city: "God created the world in seven days and on the eighth day, he created Rio de Janeiro."

Our embassy had briefed me that of all Brazil's cities, Rio had the best combination of natural, cultural, and historical settings, as well as socio-economic development. To Brazilians, it was the most Brazilian of cities.

Once there, I met with Anthony Garotinho, governor of the state of Rio de Janeiro. We conducted a friendly talk on strengthening China's relationship with the state of Rio and visited Brazil's landmarks, including the statue of Jesus on Mount Corcovado and the Maracana Stadium.

My last stop in Brazil was the world-famous city of Iguazu. *Iguazu* is the word in the language of native Guarani Indians for "great water." The city is located by the famous Iguazu Falls and the Itaipu Hydroelectric Power Plant at the border of Brazil, Paraguay, and Argentina, and the confluence of the Parana and the Iguazu rivers.

The Iguazu Falls, one of the five largest waterfalls in the world, was listed in 1984 among UNESCO's World Heritage sites. The Iguazu Falls extend for over three kilometers along the Iguazu River, consisting of 275 cataracts with an average drop of 80 meters. The cataracts crash down into the river, presenting a breathtaking spectacle.

I was impressed by the special nature of the tourism around the Iguazu Falls. The Brazilian government had built the Iguazu National Park while maintaining a proper balance between tourism and environmental protection. Brazilian aardvarks wandered around freely, looking for food, and stalls had been set up for Guarani Indians to sell souvenirs. Everywhere in the park was a scene of man and nature existing in harmony.

From there we drove to the Itaipu Hydroelectric Power Plant. *Itaipu* means "singing rock" in Guarani. The Itaipu Hydropower Power Plant used to have the largest installed capacity in the world until the completion of China's Three Gorges Dam project.

The power plant, fourteen kilometers south of the city of Iguazu, was jointly built by Brazil and Paraguay on the Parana River on the border of the two countries. It plays an important role in ensuring their energy supply and advancing their economic development.

During the construction of the Three Gorges power plant, China conducted many exchanges with Brazil over the technology of the Itaipu plant, which became further testimony to the deepening friendship between our two countries.

After the visit, we went to the garden nearby, where I planted the trumpet tree, symbolizing China-Brazil friendship. A Brazilian friend told me that the trumpet tree is a token of friendship and goodness.

Historic Correspondence Between China and Chile

ON SEPTEMBER 24, 2000, I flew from Iguazu to Santiago, capital of Chile.

Chile, located along the Pacific coast, is the longest and narrowest country in the world. Its territory is 4,333 kilometers long and an average of 180 kilometers wide, shrinking to 90 kilometers at its narrowest point.

In terms of overall economic strength, Chile ranks fourth in Latin America, behind Brazil, Mexico, and Argentina. The country is reputed as a window on regional economic development, by reason of its abundant natural resources, open economy, and sustained rapid economic growth.

Chile was among the first countries in Latin America to have contact and close relations with China. It was the first South American country to establish diplomatic relations with China. The year of my visit marked the thirtieth anniversary of China-Chile diplomatic relations. It is worth mentioning that in 1999 Chile was the first Latin American country to sign a bilateral agreement on China's accession to the WTO.

In preparation for my visit, I had been briefed by the Department of Latin American and Caribbean Affairs of our Foreign Ministry on the thirty-year history of China-Chile relations. My attention was particularly caught by this section of that history, as recounted by Li Jinzhang, director-general of the department.

After China and Chile established diplomatic ties in 1970, Chilean President Salvador Allende carried on correspondence with Chinese founding leaders Mao Zedong and Zhou Enlai. They often exchanged views on national economic and social development, bilateral relations, and international issues in their correspondence.

In 1973, Chinese Premier Zhou Enlai sent a letter to Chilean President Allende via Chilean Foreign Minister Clodomiro Almeyda, who was visiting China at the time. Premier Zhou wrote in his letter that developing countries should overcome difficulties and help each other, but mainly rely on their own resources because an economy that was not domestically based would be very vulnerable. He added that countries of the third world would have to wage prolonged and arduous struggles and pay some price on their way to developing an independent national economy. Premier Zhou's letter was published in Chilean newspapers and provoked the thinking of many people of vision.

Sadly, the original letter was lost in the ensuing coup in Chile, a coup in which President Allende was killed.

President Ricardo Lagos was in office when I visited Chile. He had served as a key aide to President Allende in the 1970s and was familiar with the history of the letter.

During a visit to China in 1998 as the leader of the Socialist Party and the Party for Democracy, Mr. Lagos mentioned this letter to the Chinese. He said that the letter bore testimony to the exchanges and contact between Chinese and Chilean leaders in history, and that its profound and significant content was a manifestation of the foresight and sagacity of the old-generation leaders of the two countries, as well as an important historical reference to the establishment and development of China–Chile relations. Mr. Lagos hoped that China could provide a photocopy of the letter and that Chile could keep it as a precious piece of historical information about its relations with China.

Li Jinzhang's account brought home to me the letter's historical and practical significance to China-Chile relations, and I asked the staff of the ministry's Department of Latin American and Caribbean Affairs to look for it carefully. Because of the technical limitations of the time, there was no photocopy of the letter signed by Premier Zhou Enlai, but we did manage to find a copy of the draft. I took along a photocopy of this precious historical document on my visit to Chile.

On the morning of September 25, 2000, I headed for La Moneda Palace to meet with President Lagos.

La Moneda, a typical neoclassical building, is the presidential residence of Chile. On September 11, 1973, a military coup was launched and La Moneda suffered severe damage from aerial bombardment. Following restoration, it still serves as the presidential palace.

Chile's Foreign Minister Soledad Alvear accompanied me to the presidential reception room on the second floor, where President Lagos was waiting for me.

President Lagos had a scholarly demeanor, with discerning eyes

A warm reception at the Chilean presidential residence, September 25, 2000.

and elegant taste. Already impressed by his tact and toughness in addressing the arrest and indictment in the United Kingdom of former president Augusto Pinochet, head of the military junta, I was looking forward to the meeting with even more anticipation.

First, I conveyed President Jiang Zemin's greetings to him. I commented favorably on the thirty-year history of China–Chilean relations and highlighted the memorable contributions of Chairman Mao Zedong and Premier Zhou Enlai and Chile's President Allende to the establishment and development of bilateral relations. I also mentioned that their correspondence was important testimony to the development of relations between our two countries.

At this point, I presented him with the photocopy of the draft letter from China's Premier Zhou Enlai to Chile's President Allende.

President Lagos was excited at seeing the letter and accepted it with happy surprise.

He welcomed my visit on the thirtieth anniversary of China–Chilean relations, then spoke at length about the letter. He thanked me for bringing the photocopy, which he regarded as a precious

Meeting with Chile's President Lagos, September 25, 2000.

piece of historical evidence of the friendship between Premier Zhou Enlai and President Allende. President Lagos recalled Premier Zhou's elaboration on the relationship of the internal and external factors and his view, expressed in his letter, that developing countries should rely on their own efforts to achieve development. President Lagos was an assistant to President Allende when the latter received the letter from Premier Zhou. President Lagos had always hoped to have a copy of the letter and, finally, his wish had been fulfilled.

President Lagos continued that, although the internal and external conditions had changed tremendously over the past thirty years since the beginning of China-Chile diplomatic ties, our bilateral relations had developed vigorously. He pointed out that, at the turn of the twenty-first century, both countries faced the dual task of integrating themselves into the globalized economy while developing their own economy and society. He further expounded that Chile kept developing its cooperative relationship with China and showing support for China's accession to the WTO, because the world could only be diversified with the active participation of major countries like China.

I expressed full agreement with President Lagos's remarks. I commented that Premier Zhou's letter to President Allende reflected the painstaking efforts made by the older generation leaders of China and Chile to establish and develop bilateral relations. I told him that the Chinese government and people honored the memory and spoke highly of President Allende's contributions to China-Chile relations. I stressed that our two countries should strive to boost our bilateral relations to a higher level in the new millennium.

Throughout our meeting, President Lagos had been holding in his hand the photocopy of Zhou Enlai's letter. After the meeting, he accompanied me right to the entrance to the palace to see me off.

During my visit to Chile, I met with my old friend José Miguel Insulza, the former foreign minister and the then-minister of the Interior, and with Soledad Alvear, the foreign minister.

After I was appointed foreign minister in 1998, Mr. Insulza was the first counterpart from Latin America that I met. He had given me his work *Ensayos sobre Política Exterior de Chile* (*Essays on Chile's Foreign Policy*), which helped me in understanding Chile's foreign policy and positions on major international issues. The reunion was a chance to refresh our friendship and exchange views on international issues.

Chile's incumbent Foreign Minister Soledad Alvear was a woman of extraordinary ability. I had first met her during the visit to China in July 2000 by the foreign ministers of Colombia, Mexico, and Chile, who form the Rio Group Troika. Her opinions and vigor left a deep impression on me.

Two months later, we met again in Chile. During our meeting, we both agreed that the current China-Chile relationship of equal-

Meeting with Chile's Foreign Minister Soledad Alvear, September 2000.

ity and mutual benefit, sustained stability, and comprehensive coop-eration was quite eligible to develop into an all-weather cooperative partnership in the twenty-first century.

Foreign Minister Soledad Alvear invited me to attend the first foreign ministers' meeting of the Forum for East Asia–Latin Amer-ica Cooperation to be held in March 2001. I gladly accepted her invitation and attended the meeting as scheduled.

Looking out from Valparaíso

DURING MY VISIT TO Chile, I delivered a speech entitled "China's Reform and Opening-up and China-Latin America Friendly Cooperation" at the headquarters of the UN Economic Commis-sion for Latin America and the Caribbean (ECLAC) in Santiago.

The ECLAC, an important economic commission in Latin

America, consists of forty-four member states, including the United States, United Kingdom, Brazil, and Mexico. China has been an observer since 1983.

In my speech, I presented China's tremendous achievements in social and economic development since adopting the reform and opening-up policy, and put forth China's views and propositions on strengthening its friendly cooperation with Latin American countries.

The over two hundred participants included Chile's Minister of Agriculture Jaime Campos and Deputy Foreign Minister Heraldo Muñoz, plus envoys to Chile from over twenty countries, including those that had not established diplomatic relations with China, such as Haiti, Paraguay, Guatemala, and Nicaragua. The participants spoke highly of China's reform and opening up and its economic achievements, and welcomed China's policy of developing friendly relations with Latin America.

The hospitable Chileans also arranged for me a visit to Valparaíso, their second-largest city.

Addressing the Economic Commission for Latin America and the Caribbean during the visit to Chile in September 2000.

Valparaíso is the seat of Chile's National Congress. I was told that the military junta had forced the National Congress to move here, so as to avoid protests against its regime by congress members. Even today, the separation of government and congress in two different cities still persists. I did not attempt to corroborate the story and just smiled.

Valparaíso, which means "paradise valley," is characterized by a pleasant climate and beautiful sunshine. The city bordering the Pacific Ocean is girdled by coastal mountains in the south and east like an eight-square-kilometer jewel set into a band of land between sea and mountains.

Valparaíso was built by Spanish colonists three hundred fifty years ago. Its old pubs, venerable churches, and narrow lanes still look as they were in the past. The city was listed in 2001 as a UNESCO World Heritage site.

Valparaíso, reputed as the gateway to Chile, was the first port in Chile. Until the opening of the Panama Canal, Valparaíso and San Francisco were the two most important ports in the western Pacific.

The container terminal of Valparaíso has an observation terrace, from where I cast my eyes beyond the Pacific toward China on the far side of the ocean. I was struck by my thoughts: With rapid globalization and sci-tech progress in the twenty-first century, the Pacific Ocean would no longer be a natural barrier between China and Latin America, but would serve as a link and channel for cooperation and contact between us.

Although my Latin American tour was not a long one, I was deeply impressed by the region's unique character, the friendliness and hospitality of the people, and the strong wish of those countries to develop relations with China. Chinese leaders of past generations had laid a good foundation for China–Latin America relations, which were widely supported by the people.

In the new historical context of the twenty-first century, China's relations with the world have undergone enormous changes and are closer than ever before. As China's overall strength has developed and its influence grown wider, the desire on the part of Latin American countries to develop comprehensive cooperation with China has grown accordingly. In these circumstances, it is all the more necessary for China to grasp the opportunity and blaze new trails to maintain and strengthen contact and exchanges with the region at every level and in all fields, to consolidate their traditional friendship and enhance mutually beneficial cooperation.

China and Latin America both have long history and ancient civilizations, as well as similar sufferings in modern history. However, contact between the peoples of China and Latin American countries has been limited by geography. Both sides should strive to create favorable conditions and adopt multiple flexible ways for facilitating exchanges, deepening friendship and mutual understanding, and solidifying and broadening popular support for cooperation.

It is now almost a decade since my Latin American tour. I am glad to see that over the past decade China's relations with Latin American countries have developed in all directions, at multiple levels and in a broad range of fields through joint efforts of both sides. Political relations between China and Latin America have been continuously reinforced, and this is manifested in increasing high-level contacts and mutual understanding and support on issues of core interest and major concern. In addition to Brazil, China has established strategic partnerships with Mexico, Argentina, Peru, and Venezuela; we have also set up mechanisms for bilateral high-level cooperation and strategic dialogue with a number of Latin American countries. The two sides have kept strengthening their dialogue on international and regional affairs, and deepening economic and trade cooperation. Trade volume has gradually risen, from 780 million US dollars thirty years ago to 143.39 billion in 2008. Two-way investment and cultural and sci-tech cooperation have kept growing. China and Brazil have developed and launched two more Earth resources satellites, bringing the total to four. In

October 2008, Venezuela's China-made communications satellite was launched successfully, marking a new breakthrough in China's high-tech cooperation with Latin America.

China–Latin America relations are thriving, like the trumpet tree that I planted in Brazil.

It is my firm belief that the friendship between the peoples of China and Latin America will continue to flourish and bear abundant fruit.

CHAPTER 7

Land Boundary and Marine Delimitation

Negotiations with Vietnam

I N EARLY AUGUST 2006, I went to Guangxi in southwest China to prepare for the summit commemorating fifteen years of the establishment of the dialogue mechanism between ASEAN and China. Taking the opportunity of being in the southwest, I set out from Nanning and stopped at Pingxiang to look at local China-Vietnam border trade. Then I drove a further eighteen kilometers to the Friendship (Youyi) Pass on the border between China and Vietnam.

At the square in front of the pass, I got out of the car and strolled around. The scene ahead was a familiar one.

The Friendship Pass stands above a valley between two mountains at a strategic point. To the left of the pass gateway is Zuobi Mountain, and to the right is Youfu Mountain. The two precipitous ranges curl in like two giant dragons, their heads meeting in front of the gateway.

Standing in the square, I saw the national flags of China and Vietnam flying above the border inspection post. The road by the post was busy with vehicles and people. It was a bustling, animated scene.

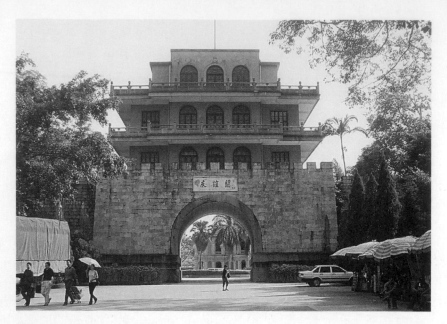

Tower of the Friendship Pass.

Turning around, I saw the white marble plaque on the gate tower, bearing the three-character inscription "Friendship Pass" standing out in red. The calligraphy was that of Marshal Chen Yi, a former vice premier and foreign minister.

The Friendship Pass is one of the nine famous passes in China.* According to historical records, the pass was built and named the Yongji Pass in the Han Dynasty (206 BC–220 AD). Later, it was given other names, like Jieshou Pass and Danan Pass. It was called Zhennan Pass in the Ming (1368–1644) and Qing (1644–1911) dynasties.

In 1885, the Sino-French War broke out. General Feng Zicai, despite being in his seventies, led officers Su Yuanchun and Wang Xiaoqi to fight the French aggressors here. They won the battle,

---

*The other eight passes are Shanhai, Juyong, Zijin, Niangzi, Pingxing, Yanmen, Jiayu, and Wusheng.

killing over 1,700 enemies. This victory turned the war in China's favor, whereas, in France, the Ferry Cabinet fell from power.

On December 1, 1907, China's revolutionary forerunner Sun Yat-sen led and directed the famous Zhennan Pass Uprising here, fighting against Qing troops for seven days and nights. Although the uprising was defeated owing to lack of food and ammunition, it undermined the rule of the Qing.

The Friendship Pass also symbolizes the friendship between China and Vietnam. In history, it was an important passage for China-Vietnam exchanges. Since the founding of the People's Republic of China in 1949, it has become a bond connecting the Chinese and Vietnamese peoples.

In 1953, approved by the Government Administration Council (former name of the State Council), the name of the pass was changed from *Zhennan* (conquering) Pass to *Munan* (good neighborly) Pass. In 1965, it was once again renamed, this time as Friendship Pass, in line with its Vietnamese name on the opposite side.

During the Vietnamese War of Resistance against France (1945–1954) and the Vietnamese War of Resistance against the United States (1954–1975), the pass was a strategic channel through which China transported supplies to Vietnam.

Over a half century, the Friendship Pass has played an important role in political, economic, and cultural exchanges between our two countries.

Looking at the gate tower, and reflecting upon its history, I could not help but remember the China-Vietnam border negotiations.

The Long History of Sino-Vietnamese Relations

CHINA AND VIETNAM ARE close neighbors, and the communication and friendship between the two peoples have a long history.

In modern history, the fates of our two countries have been linked.

The Opium Wars opened China's doors to Western invasion, reducing our country to semifeudal and semicolonial status. At the end of the nineteenth century, France launched an invasion of Vietnam, and our neighbor was reduced to the status of a French colony. From then on, the Chinese and Vietnamese peoples have gone through long and arduous struggles for their national liberation and independence.

After New China was founded, the first generation of leaders headed by Mao Zedong, in the spirit of internationalism and understanding of the two countries' common geopolitical interests, led the Chinese people to support and help the Vietnamese people in resisting France and the United States, and made huge sacrifices in the two wars of resistance. In those times, the two countries were like comrades and brothers.

At the end of 1970s, however, large-scale armed conflicts broke out in border areas between China and Vietnam, and the relationship dropped to a record low.

From December 3 to 4, 1990, Nguyen Van Linh, general secretary of the Communist Party of Vietnam (CPV), together with Do Muoi, chairman of the Council of Ministers, and Councilor Pham Van Dong of the CPV Central Committee visited China and met with Jiang Zemin, General Secretary of the Communist Party of China (CPC), and Premier Li Peng in Chengdu, Sichuan. The two sides achieved a common understanding to "end the past and create the future." This was a turning point in Sino-Vietnamese relations.*

In November 1991, at the invitation of Jiang Zemin and Li Peng, Do Muoi, the new general secretary of CPV, and Premier

---

*See *Peace, Development and Cooperation—Li Peng's Diary on Foreign Affairs*, published by Xinhua Press in 2008.

Vo Van Kiet led a delegation to China, where bilateral talks took place. The two countries then declared the normalization of their relations.

In the meantime, the Interim Agreement on Settling Border Issues between the People's Republic of China and the Socialist Republic of Vietnam (Interim Agreement) was signed. In this, the two sides decided to maintain the status quo and resolve border disputes by negotiation.

Both sides understood that to develop good neighborly and friendly relations, China and Vietnam must face up to and resolve border issues.

Complex and Sensitive Border Issues

IN MARCH 1993, I was appointed vice foreign minister in charge of Asian affairs. China-Vietnam relations were always among my major concerns.

China-Vietnam relations have a long and deep-rooted history, but are not without some grievances. Some issues involved national feelings and were complex and sensitive, particularly those relating to border areas. They were very difficult to handle.

Premier Zhou Enlai once said, to settle border issues, we need to study history and understand the causes and effects, so that we can tell right from wrong and find a good solution. Following this direction, at night I read many archives relating to China-Vietnam relations and got some ideas of the problems.

There were three dimensions to the border issues between China and Vietnam, namely the land boundary, delimitation of the Beibu (Tonkin) Gulf, and ownership of the Nansha (Spratly) Islands.

The first problem was a legacy of history.

The 1,347-kilometer land boundary between China and Vietnam starts at the junction of China, Vietnam, and Laos, winding southeastward following the Beilun River through Yunnan Province and Guangxi Zhuang Autonomous Region, and ending where the river flows into the Beibu Gulf.

The land boundary was a determined boundary, demarcated on the basis of the historical customary line and according to the Convention on Border Issues, its Supplementary Conventions, and other documents (hereafter, Sino-French Demarcation Treaties), signed at the end of the nineteenth century by the Qing court and the French colonial regime. The borderline in Yunnan is 710 kilometers long, running through high mountains and deep ranges, and is mainly on watersheds, with seventy boundary markers erected since the demarcation by the Qing court and French government. The borderline in Guangxi is 637 kilometers long, mostly in karst areas; it is mainly demarcated by ridgelines, with 240 boundary markers. Parts of the borderline are demarcated by rivers, ditches, and streams.

This boundary, demarcated in international treaties, had always been acknowledged by Chinese and Vietnamese authorities.

In general, the land boundary was clear. But, for some reason, the two sides had different understandings of the accurate location and specific alignment of the borderline, so there were some small sectors still under dispute.

After the founding of New China, the Secretariat of the CPC Central Committee and the Secretariat of the CPV Central Committee exchanged letters in 1957 and 1958, confirming that the border status quo be strictly maintained pending settlement of the issues through negotiation.

With the development of modern laws of the sea, coastal China and Vietnam extended their respective sovereign rights to the sea and their claims overlapped, giving rise to the issue of demarcating the Beibu Gulf.

An old boundary marker between China and Vietnam.

A semi-enclosed sea, the Beibu Gulf lies northwest of the South China Sea and is surrounded by China's and Vietnam's land territories on its eastern, northern, and western sides. It is 184 nautical miles across at its widest point and 112 at its narrowest.

Before the 1970s, there had been no dispute over the Beibu Gulf. The two sides had no conflict, each engaging in shipping, fishery, and maritime research in their respective waters. The two sides signed fishery agreements in 1957, 1961, and 1963, making stipulations for fisheries jurisdiction within three to twelve nautical miles of each country's territorial sea, and for fisheries cooperation. Waters beyond the three- and twelve-nautical-mile limits were regarded as a common fishing area for both countries, emanating the principle of freedom of the high seas, that is, both Chinese and Vietnamese fishermen were free to enter and fish in these waters according to traditional customs. Thus came into being the traditional fishing grounds and fishing rights for fishermen from both countries.

However, in the 1970s, with the development of modern laws of the sea, coastal countries extended their sovereign rights beyond their territorial seas, and gradually established legal systems about continental shelf and exclusive economic zones. As a result, both China and Vietnam claimed sovereign rights over other parts beyond their territorial seas in the Beibu Gulf. Their claims overlapped and collided. The Chinese government's view was that the problem should be settled through bilateral negotiations and according to international law and practice.

The Nansha Islands are the biggest group of islands and reefs in the South China Sea. Extending from 3°37' N and 12°40' N to 10°10' E and 119° E, the group comprises some 25 islands, 128 reefs (both above water and submerged), and 77 shoals (both above water and submerged).

The Nansha Islands have been an integral part of China's territory since ancient times. China has indisputable sovereignty over them and the adjacent waters. It was the Chinese people who first discovered the Nansha Islands; since then, the Chinese government has been exercising jurisdiction, and incorporated the islands into China's territory centuries ago. Historically, the islands were occupied by the Japanese, but were taken back by the Chinese government at the end of WWII. Until the 1970s, there had been no dispute in the international community about China's sovereignty over the Nansha Islands.

In 1983, the Chinese government renamed 189 individual islands, reefs, and shoals in the group, based on their previous names, and declared once again China's sovereignty over the group.

However, in 1975, Vietnam initiated territorial claims over the Nansha Islands and the Xisha (Paracel) Islands.

The Chinese government's position on this issue has always

been clear: China has indisputable sovereignty over the Nansha Islands, and the issue of sovereignty is nonnegotiable. In the meantime, we stand for shelving the differences and seeking joint development of the waters under dispute in the interest of safeguarding peace and stability in the South China Sea.

This was how China-Vietnam border issues stood when I took over responsibility for Asian affairs.

Looking Problems in the Eye and Starting Talks

IN THE 1970S, CHINA and Vietnam had held two rounds of border-related negotiations, mainly about the land boundary and the delimitation of the Beibu Gulf. The Nansha Islands issue was not discussed in the two talks.

At that time, for a variety of reasons, although they were described as negotiations, in fact they were a war of words, each side advancing its own reasoning. Neither the conditions nor the timing was right for resolving these border issues, and thus the two negotiations came to nothing.

Later, the continual wrangling over these border issues resulted in clashes leading to the spilling of blood and subsequent worsening of relations. Because of these territorial border issues, China and Vietnam resorted to arms and paid for the lesson in blood.

Actually, even after the normalization of Sino-Vietnamese relations, hostility still persisted among some officials and civilians, and disputes often arose. Maintaining peace and stability in the border areas, the Beibu Gulf, and the South China Sea was problematic.

We were aware that if conflicts in the three areas continued, they certainly would affect Sino-Vietnamese relations. Since diplomatic relations had been completely restored, it was put on the agenda to implement the agreement reached by both countries' leaders on normalization of relations and to settle border issues through negotiations.

In December 1992, Premier Li Peng visited Vietnam and met Vietnamese leaders. The two sides exchanged opinions on how to settle the border issues and agreed to start talks between the two governments as soon as possible on the basis of expert-level talks; reached consensus on the general principles for settling the border issues according to established norms of international law; decided to accelerate the talks based on these principles and to settle both marine and land boundary disputes at an early date; and agreed not to take any action that might complicate the border disputes prior to a negotiated settlement.

At that time, high-level leaders from the two countries reached an agreement on establishing and launching a mechanism for government-level talks at an appropriate time.

Actually, even before Li Peng's visit to Vietnam, experts from both countries had started the first round of talks in Beijing in October 1992. After the leaders reached agreement, experts from both countries held a new round of talks in Hanoi in February 1993, discussing the land boundary issue and the delimitation of the Beibu Gulf, and how to safeguard stability in the border areas and in the gulf. As a result of these contacts, each side had a better understanding of the other's position.

Later, based on the leaders' agreement and the talks, I organized experts, scholars, and officials from the Foreign Ministry and other departments, provinces, and autonomous regions to evaluate China-Vietnam relations and study the possibility of settling border issues through negotiations.

On the basis of a deep analysis, the Central Authorities approved the establishment of a governmental delegation, composed of members from the Foreign Ministry and other departments. I was appointed to head the group.

Establishing Principles and Working Mechanisms

THEN WE STARTED PREPARING for the negotiations.

After fully analyzing the previous stances of Vietnam, we made a Chinese draft for the Agreement on the Basic Principles for Solving the Problems of Land Boundary and Delimitation of the Beibu Gulf between the People's Republic of China and the Socialist Republic of Vietnam (Agreement on the Basic Principles). The draft covered the negotiation mechanism, steps for pushing forward the negotiations, political and diplomatic principles, and the basis of international law.

By means of this draft we hoped to send an important message to Vietnam: China adopts a positive, practical, and constructive attitude to the negotiations and the two sides can lay down a good foundation for the final resolution of the disputes.

In order to facilitate reaching consensus as soon as possible, we handed over the draft of Agreement on the Basic Principles to the Vietnamese delegation prior to the negotiations to give them enough time to study and send the feedback.

Even before the first round of China-Vietnam government-level talks on border issues officially started, the Vietnamese delegation responded to our draft in a positive way.

On July 22, 1993, in Singapore, China's Vice Premier and Foreign Minister Qian Qichen met Vietnam's Foreign Minister Nguyen Manh Cam. Qian Qichen said he hoped that the two sides would make concerted efforts, make progress in the government-level negotiations, reach agreement on some issues, and that, to signify their preliminary achievements, both sides should sign a document of principle on the resolution of border issues and call it Treaty of Basic Principles.

Nguyen Manh Cam agreed in substance.

From August 24 to 29, 1993, the first official round of China-

Talking to journalists in Beijing on China-Vietnam border issues, August 24, 1993.

Vietnam government-level talks on border issues was held in Beijing.

I was head of the Chinese delegation, and my opposite number was Vu Khoan, Vietnam's vice foreign minister. During those five days, the two sides held three plenary meetings and two individual meetings, and experts from the two sides held two meetings.

I presided over the first plenary meeting and spoke first, at the suggestion of the Vietnamese side.

First, I said that it was of great significance to hold government-level talks on border issues in the context of the great changes that had taken place in the international situation and the normalization of Sino-Vietnamese relations.

Then, I put forward China's tentative ideas for the negotiations. I said straightforwardly that we should operate on the principle of tackling the easier problems first, leaving the harder ones until later. The land boundary issue should be resolved on the basis of the Sino-French Demarcation Treaties, and the Beibu Gulf demarcated on the principle of fairness and according to international law and practice. For this, I made concrete suggestions, including the basic principles and steps for our negotiations.

As for the Nansha Islands issue, since it was very complex, I suggested that we could shelve our differences and jointly develop the waters under dispute and work together to safeguard peace, security, and stability in the South China Sea.

In addition, I made some suggestions about easing the differences. For example, the two sides should work together to safeguard peace and stability in the South China Sea, and not let the Nansha Islands issue affect our bilateral relations.

Vu Khoan responded positively to my suggestions. He said that Vietnam basically agreed with what the Chinese draft said about the land boundary and the delimitation of the Beibu Gulf. Thus, the two sides reached consensus on settling the land boundary issue on the basis of the Sino-French Demarcation Treaties. Vu Khoan also said that Vietnam agreed to negotiate with China on how to demarcate the Beibu Gulf, which in itself was a demonstration of Vietnam's greatest flexibility.

Vu Khoan was a career diplomat, with a thin face, polite manner, and elegant demeanor. As a young man, he had studied in Guilin, in China's Guangxi Zhuang Autonomous Region, and thus had a good understanding of China. He started work in Vietnam's Foreign Ministry in 1955 as a senior Russian interpreter; he accompanied Vietnamese leaders on visits to the Soviet Union many times, accumulating a wealth of diplomatic experience.

Vu Khoan was usually impassive, but, in the first round of talks, when talking about the importance of the Beibu Gulf to Vietnam, he became rather emotional. He described the Beibu Gulf as the mother of Vietnam, since it nurtured 15 million Vietnamese people in ten provinces. For this reason, Vietnam could not accept China's suggestion to demarcate the Beibu Gulf based on the principle of fairness.

Then Vu Khoan mentioned the Dao Truong Sa and Dao

Shaking hands with Vu Khoan in Hanoi at the signing ceremony of the border agreement between China and Vietnam on October 19, 1993.

Hoang Sa island groups, asking that these be written into the draft Agreement on the Basic Principles. Dao Truong Sa is the Vietnamese name for China's Nansha (Spratly) Islands while Dao Hoang Sa is Vietnamese for the Xisha (Paracel) Islands.

In response, I first summarized and affirmed our common views on the land boundary issue. I then expressed China's stance on the Beibu Gulf.

I too spoke with a degree of passion, declaring that the Gulf belonged to both countries, and though it might be very important to Vietnam, it was also crucial for China. Bordered by China's Guangxi Zhuang Autonomous Region, Guangdong Province, and Hainan Province, it nurtured 110 million people in an area of 450,000 square kilometers, and was an important sea lane for Guangxi and Hainan. The Beibu Gulf being geographically close to Vietnam, and also an extension of China's territory, it would benefit both countries and peoples to demarcate the Gulf according to the principle of fairness.

Then I defined China's position on the Xisha and Nansha islands. I made it clear that the Sino-Vietnamese border negotiations would not cover the issue of ownership of Xisha and Nansha islands. China's position on issues regarding territorial sovereignty is unalterable.

I asked Vietnam to take a realistic attitude. I said the dissension between China and Vietnam over the sovereignty of the Nansha Islands had arisen from Vietnam's contravention of its previous recognition of Chinese sovereignty over the islands. China had acted with great restraint on this issue, but would not agree to write the issue of the Nansha Islands into the draft.

After repeated discussions, the two sides finally agreed on the draft of the Agreement of the People's Republic of China and the Socialist Republic of Vietnam on the Basic Principles for Settling the Boundary Issue and signed a record of discussions.

On October 18, 1993, in the name of the head of the Chinese delegation, I went to Hanoi and signed the agreement with Vu Khoan, head of the Vietnamese delegation.

In this agreement, the two sides agreed to settle the border issues, both maritime and land, between the two countries on the basis of the Five Principles of Peaceful Coexistence;* and proceeding from the realities, agreed to "concentrate on resolving the land boundary issue and the delimitation of the Beibu Gulf, while continuing talks on the maritime issue, so as to achieve a basic and permanent solution."

Regarding the land boundary, the agreement says, "The two sides agree to determine all the alignments of the borderline based on the Convention on Border Issues signed by China and France on

---

*Referring to mutual respect for territorial integrity and sovereignty, mutual nonaggression, noninterference in each other's internal affairs, equality and mutual benefit, and peaceful coexistence.

June 26, 1887, its Supplementary Conventions signed on June 20, 1895 and other related documents, maps and border markers, so as to solve the issues of disputed areas and finally sign a treaty on border issues."

Regarding the delimitation of the Beibu Gulf, the agreement says, "The two sides agree to demarcate the Beibu Gulf through negotiations, according to the international law of the sea and international practice." To this end, "the two sides shall, based on the principle of fairness and taking into consideration all the factors about the Beibu Gulf, endeavor to achieve a fair solution."

The two sides also agreed to the establishment as soon as possible of two joint working groups under the leadership of the respective government delegations, one to settle the land border issue and the other to demarcate the Beibu Gulf. The two working groups would discuss and try to settle disputes, draft a border treaty and a treaty on the delimitation of the Beibu Gulf, and present them for signature by the representatives of China and Vietnam.

The agreement laid a solid legal foundation for the final settlement of the border issues between the two countries.

During the visit, I met with Vu Khoan and discussed the border negotiations and our bilateral relations. I also visited Nguyen Manh Cam, Vietnam's foreign minister.

I reached consensus with the Vietnamese side on two important points. First, we should follow the principle of tackling easier problems first and more difficult ones later, and try to settle the land border and Beibu Gulf delimitation issues through negotiations. Second, during the course of the negotiations, both sides should maintain peace in the land border areas and at sea and avoid the occurrence of unpleasant events.

Since it was my first visit to Vietnam, the Vietnamese arranged a trip for me to pay my respects to the late Ho Chi Minh and visit both his former residence and the Van Mieu temple while in Hanoi.

Chairman Ho Chi Minh was a great leader of the Vietnamese

people. I revered him as a revolutionary forerunner. I had read his poetry written in Chinese, and was aware of his love of traditional Chinese culture and his friendly feelings toward China. In his early years, he came to China and engaged in revolutionary activities, and had a deep friendship with Mao Zedong, Zhou Enlai, and other Chinese leaders of the first generation.

The Presidential Palace of Vietnam is a cream-colored French-style building set among green gardens. It is solemn and unadorned.

Ho Chi Minh's former residence stands in the compound of the palace. I was told by my Vietnamese escort that when Ho Chi Minh became Vietnam's top leader after the liberation, he did not move into the Presidential Palace; instead, he had a small house built in the woods behind the palace. He took command of state affairs from here and lived a simple life close to nature.

This visit gave me further understanding of Ho Chi Minh's virtue and his austere lifestyle; I held him in even higher regard.

In Hanoi, it is interesting to visit Van Mieu, a temple dedicated to the philosopher, thinker, and educator of ancient China: Confucius. The Van Mieu is a well-preserved architectural complex, covering an area of nearly three hectares. At the entrance to many of the buildings there are paired couplets hanging on each column of the gateway. These couplets are written in Chinese and I immediately sensed the presence of traditional Chinese culture.

The main hall of the Van Mieu enshrines a statue of Confucius. In the center, up high, hangs a horizontal board inscribed with characters meaning "teacher for all ages," and more characters indicating that the calligraphy was by Emperor Kangxi of the Qing Dynasty. In addition, the hall enshrines statues and memorial tablets of the sage's seventy-two disciples.

This visit brought home to me again the deep-rooted historical and cultural links between China and Vietnam, and the similarities between the religious beliefs, customs, and habits of our people. The friendship between the two countries, fostered by Mao

Zedong, Zhou Enlai, Ho Chi Minh, and some other old revolutionaries, is deeply rooted in the hearts of the two peoples. These are precious assets for developing Sino-Vietnamese relations, and we have the responsibility to build on the relations.

On the basis of the consensus and the Agreement on the Basic Principles signed by the two sides, China and Vietnam officially started boundary negotiations, and gradually set up a three-level negotiation mechanism.

The first level was government-level negotiation. China and Vietnam would each send a governmental delegation and each country would take turns to host the talks, which would be chaired by the head of delegation of the host country.

The major tasks of the government-level negotiation were to hold formal talks on major border issues, to direct the work of the joint working groups and the expert groups, and to examine and confirm the results of their talks.

This mechanism continued in operation after China and Vietnam signed the Treaty on the Land Boundary between the People's Republic of China and the Socialist Republic of Vietnam on December 30, 1999, and the Agreement between the People's Republic of China and the Socialist Republic of Vietnam on the Delimitation of the Territorial Seas of the Beibu Gulf, the Exclusive Economic Zones, and the Continental Shelf on December 25, 2000.

The second level was for the talks held by the Joint Working Group on the Land Boundary, Joint Working Group on the Delimitation of the Beibu Gulf, and the Maritime Problems Experts Group. The groups were subordinate to their governmental delegations.

The third level was for talks held between expert groups under the two working groups, including one group for marking the alignment of the land boundary, one for aerial surveying of the land boundary, one for demarcating the Beibu Gulf, and one for mapping the Beibu Gulf.

Land Boundary Discussions at Last Bear Fruit

THE JOINT WORKING GROUP on the Land Boundary and the Joint Working Group on the Delimitation of the Beibu Gulf held their first round of talks in Hanoi between February 22 and 25, then between March 22 and 25, 1994.

Hence the bilateral land boundary negotiations entered a stage for resolving specific issues.

The land boundary issue was simple in that it was a determined boundary based on old treaties; it was complex in that the treaties and supplementary maps had defects and that, over nearly a century, both human and natural factors had produced different understandings in China and Vietnam about the alignment of the borderline, thus giving rise to disputes.

In reality, these disputes manifested conflicts of interests, both national and local interests of immediate concern to people living in the border areas. An insignificant patch of land along the borderline could generate a household's grain ration or means of livelihood.

During the second round of talks between the Joint Working Group on the Land Boundary, the two sides exchanged their respective maps of the proposed borderline and determined that there were 289 points of disagreement covering a total area of about 233 square kilometers. Of these, 125 were the result of different mapping techniques, covering a total area of six square kilometers. These were still 164 places in dispute, covering a total area of 227 square kilometers. Most of these disputed places involved their inhabitants' real interests and so were difficult to resolve through negotiations.

When checking the alignment of the borderline, we made three suggestions.

First, determine the alignment of the borderline between China and Vietnam based on the Sino-French Demarcation Treaties, relevant supplementary documents and maps, and the boundary markers.

Second, for those places where, even after checking several times, the two sides could not reach agreement on the boundary alignment and the location of boundary markers, the two sides would make joint investigations on the spot, take into consideration local conditions, and carry out friendly consultation to seek fair and reasonable solutions in a spirit of mutual understanding and accommodation.

Third, having checked and verified the borderline, each country should in principle unconditionally return to the other side any place beyond its jurisdiction. For some places, the two sides could make fair and reasonable readjustments through friendly consultation in a spirit of mutual understanding and mutual accommodation, in order to facilitate border management.

Later, the Joint Working Group on the Land Boundary spent more than two years verifying the boundary alignment of 164 disputed places.

In July 1997, Do Muoi, general secretary of the CPV, visited China, and Jiang Zemin, general secretary of the CPC, reached an important consensus with him that both sides should work hard to achieve the goal of signing a land boundary treaty before the year 2000.

In February 1999, the CPV's new General Secretary Le Kha Phieu visited China, where he met with CPC General Secretary Jiang Zemin. They decided upon the policy for developing Sino-Vietnamese relations: "long-term stability, future orientation, good-neighborly friendship, all-round cooperation," thereby establishing the framework for developing Sino-Vietnamese relations in the twenty-first century.

The two sides agreed that it was in the fundamental interests of the two peoples, and their common wish, to resolve border issues as soon as possible. The two sides were determined to accelerate the negotiations, improve efficiency, sign a land boundary treaty in 1999, and work together to bring peace, friendship, and stability to the border areas.

The two sides also reached important consensus on solving the problem of settlements along the land boundary; namely, the boundary demarcation should avoid major shocks to the inhabitants of border areas, respecting their long-established residential, production, and living conditions.

The above consensus reached between the Chinese and Vietnamese leaders provided a reliable political guarantee and gave a strong impetus to the China-Vietnam land boundary negotiations.

Based on this consensus, I focused on pushing the Vietnamese side to make up its mind to negotiate with a realistic attitude for a solution to the issues in the disputed border areas, particularly problems of immediate concern to the inhabitants of border areas.

In May 1995, I wrote a letter to Vietnam's Vice Premier and Foreign Minister Nguyen Manh Cam concerning outstanding problems in the land boundary negotiations. In the letter, I expressed my wish that Vietnam would, in line with the consensus reached by our respective top leaders, proceed from the overall situation and the fundamental interests of the two peoples, follow a realistic and pragmatic approach in a spirit of mutual understanding and mutual accommodation, put forward solutions for the remaining disputed areas, properly solve the production and livelihood of inhabitants of border areas, reach an agreement with China on the boundary alignment in all disputed areas, and ensure that the land boundary negotiations would be concluded and the treaty signed within the time limit given by leaders of the two countries.

In regard to areas undisputed in history, I suggested that the two sides should verify them with a realistic and pragmatic approach, not widen differences, and not change any section of the borderline recognized by previous governments; in regard to areas in dispute, the two sides should strictly abide by the treaties, and determine the boundary alignment in accordance with the Sino-French demarcation treaties and their supplementary maps and boundary markers; for settlements, the two sides should strictly follow the important consensus reached by our leaders, that is, respecting the long-established residential, production, and living conditions of border area inhabitants and avoiding any major shock to them during the boundary demarcation.

Nguyen Manh Cam responded quickly. He reiterated Vietnam's commitment to resolving the land boundary problem and agreed with my suggestion of energetically pushing forward the land boundary negotiations. He said that the two sides should, in a spirit of mutual understanding and mutual accommodation and taking into full consideration various factors and each side's legitimate interests in national sovereignty, historical development, terrain features, jurisdictional requirements, and livelihood of border inhabitants, narrow the differences as soon as possible and seek mutually acceptable solutions so as to safeguard stability in the border areas.

Based on the consensus between us, I instructed Chinese negotiators that they must follow a realistic and pragmatic approach in negotiation, fully express their legal basis and reasons, and seek fair and reasonable solutions.

On July 25, 1999, during the ASEAN Ministerial Meeting, and again on September 11 during the APEC Summit, I met with Nguyen Manh Cam. In addition to regional and international issues, I seized the opportunity to contribute my efforts to the boundary negotiations.

On September 11, when I met with Nguyen Manh Cam in Auckland, I said that a realistic and pragmatic approach was essential for resolving disputes, and suggested that the Vietnamese side consider from a positive perspective an overall solution that could roughly balance mutual interests, so that the two sides could reach an understanding to direct the work of the Joint Working Group on the Land Boundary. Furthermore, I explicitly expressed my hope that the Vietnamese negotiators would strictly implement the important consensus reached by the two general secretaries regarding settlements.

Nguyen Manh Cam is a smart person. Born in 1929 in Vinh City, Nghe An Province, in the early 1950s, he studied Russian at Beijing Russian College (part of Beijing Foreign Languages Institute, which is now the Beijing Foreign Studies University); later, he became ambassador to Hungary, Germany, and the Soviet Union. A seasoned diplomat, he knows the art of negotiation.

Nguyen Manh Cam responded that Vietnam understood the Chinese view and was willing to put in more efforts to solving relevant problems.

Thanks to the hard work of the foreign ministers, heads of delegations, joint working groups, and expert groups, at the interim meeting of heads of the two governmental delegations in Beijing from October 20 to 28, 1999, Vietnam finally accepted my idea to balance the interests of China and Vietnam and to seek a package solution.

Following this, each side put forward its package solutions in the negotiations, including solutions to sensitive and difficult issues, and reached initial consensus on them, thereby making a breakthrough in land boundary negotiations. A further month of tough negotiations resulted in unanimous approval of the boundary alignment in disputed areas.

Thereafter, the joint working group and the treaty drafting group worked simultaneously, putting all their energy into making records of the negotiation results and drafting the land boundary treaty.

Over the following twenty days, negotiators from both sides worked closely together day and night, and finally agreed on the

中华人民共和国
和
越南社会主义共和国
陆地边界条约签字仪式

LỄ KÝ HIỆP ƯỚC BIÊN GIỚI TRÊN ĐẤT LIỀN
GIỮA
NƯỚC CỘNG HÒA XÃ HỘI CHỦ NGHĨA VIỆT NAM
VÀ NƯỚC CỘNG HÒA NHÂN DÂN TRUNG HOA

30 · 12 · 1999

Signing ceremony of the land boundary treaty between China and Vietnam, on December 30, 1999.

boundary alignment and all the articles in the draft treaty, and completed the text of the treaty and supplementary maps.

Before the formal signing took place, China and Vietnam held a ceremony for initialing the documents. The heads of the two governmental delegations signed their initials on every page of the treaty and on every supplementary map, their signatures constituting authentication of the text. Since there were many supplementary maps, the signing took over one hour.

On December 30, 1999, on the eve of the new millennium, I flew to Hanoi to attend the signing ceremony of the Treaty of the Land Boundary between the People's Republic of China and the Socialist Republic of Vietnam.

The signing ceremony was held that night at the Vietnam International Conference Center. I formally signed the treaty on behalf of China, and Nguyen Manh Cam did so on behalf of Vietnam.

I gave a brief speech at the ceremony, saying that the formal signing demonstrated that the two sides were bringing into the

The first new boundary marker erected on the China-Vietnam border.

twenty-first century a peaceful, friendly, and stable land boundary, which would not only bring direct benefits to people living along the border areas but would also be significant for promoting China-Vietnam relations, all-around cooperation, and local peace and stability.

On April 29, 2000, the 15th Meeting of the Standing Committee of the Ninth National People's Congress of China passed a resolution approving the treaty; on June 9, the Seventh Meeting of the Tenth National Assembly of Vietnam also approved the treaty.

On July 6, 2000, China and Vietnam held a ceremony in Beijing to exchange the instruments of ratification of the treaty. With this, the treaty formally came into effect.

In November 2000, in accordance with the treaty, China and Vietnam established the Joint Committee for Land Boundary Demarcation under the two government delegations. By the end of 2008, this committee had completed all the field survey work and had all the boundary markers erected. To this end, the two sides had spent eight long years.

China's First Marine Delimitation

IN THE BILATERAL BOUNDARY negotiations, the land boundary negotiations were conducted simultaneously with the negotiations on the delimitation of the Beibu Gulf.

Prior to this, China had signed land boundary treaties or agreements with ten countries, thereby amassing a wealth of experience in negotiating land boundaries. By contrast, negotiating marine delimitation was new to China's diplomatic corps. Therefore, bilateral negotiations on the delimitation of the Beibu Gulf constituted a new challenge.

The negotiations were a very tortuous process, requiring much effort to make every forward step.

The negotiations started in a good atmosphere. However, when it came down to concrete issues, conflicts of traditional positions and interests began to surface.

After signing the Agreement on the Basic Principles and embarking on the second round of talks, the China-Vietnam Joint Working Group on the Delimitation of the Beibu Gulf met with numerous difficulties.

In August 1994, before the second round of government-level talks were held, the two sides found themselves clearly at odds about the marine delimitation.

We had expected, following the signing of the Agreement on the Basic Principles and launching of the talks by the Joint Working Group on the Delimitation of the Beibu Gulf, that there would be fewer or even no clashes in the Beibu Gulf area and that tensions there would be eased.

However, that was not the case.

Within six months of the launching of talks by the Joint Working Group on the Delimitation of the Beibu Gulf, conflicts had increased and intensified rather than diminished. During this period, Vietnam expanded its actual jurisdiction over disputed waters in the gulf, and even denied the right of Chinese fishermen to fish in their traditional fishing grounds there, trying to create a fait accompli.

Before going to Vietnam for talks, I called together the Chinese negotiators and made a careful analysis of the situation.

At that time, we were no weaker than Vietnam in terms of naval strength and actual control in the Beibu Gulf. As long as we strictly abided by the international law, the United Nations Convention on the Law of the Sea, and the Agreement on Basic Principles we had signed with Vietnam, we were confident that, with time and patience, we would be able to persuade Vietnam back onto the right track.

The most immediate problem was that Vietnam kept seizing and detaining Chinese fishermen and fishing boats in their traditional Beibu Gulf fishing grounds. Since this concerned our fishermen's vital interests, we had to solve this problem as soon as possible.

We hoped that the two sides could sit down and have a thorough discussion and solve the problem.

Before leaving for Vietnam, I made a special trip to Hainan in early August, where I listened to the provincial governor Ruan Chongwu's views on the marine delimitation negotiations. During this trip, I visited the Gulf areas and made a field survey.

In Qionghai and Lingao, I visited fishermen's homes and went aboard some fishing boats berthed in the ports, hearing how their forefathers had worked at the traditional Beibu Gulf fishing grounds, and how their fishing had been seriously disrupted recently.

Standing on the quay, watching many fishing boats on the peaceful sea, and breathing in the smell of the sea, it took me some time to calm down. Territorial boundaries and state-to-state relations are not abstract concepts; rather, they are real issues closely linked with the people's interests. As a diplomat, I had to go to the grass roots and get to know people in order to fully understand the responsibilities I shoulder, to link the people's interests with my diplomatic work, and live up to the trust that the country and the people placed in me. In short, diplomacy must also serve to improve people's livelihood and safeguard social stability.

The second round of government-level talks between China and Vietnam on border issues was formally held in Hanoi between August 15 and 18, 1994. I led the Chinese governmental delegation.

Vu Khoan, head of the Vietnamese delegation, chaired the meeting and was the first to speak. He presented Vietnam's position and views on the land boundary, the delimitation of the Beibu Gulf and the South China Sea issue, and spoke highly of the progress made in the land boundary negotiations.

I was next to speak, delivering a long speech that focused on China's position on the Beibu Gulf delimitation.

First, I echoed Vu Khoan's praise of the progress in the land boundary talks. However, I also pointed out that, in order to maintain a good negotiating atmosphere, pending final resolution of the issues, both sides should maintain the status quo of border administration as it had been when the Interim Agreement was signed, and that local governments and relevant departments of the two countries should further educate their staff and border inhabitants accordingly.

Then I affirmed Chinese fishermen's Beibu Gulf fishing rights from the perspective of history, legality, international relations, and national practice. I pointed out that there was a fishing population of 1,380,000 in Guangxi, Hainan, and Guangdong, which meant that the fishing rights issue directly affected Chinese fishermen's livelihood and social stability.

In all seriousness, I told the Vietnamese side that before the two sides could reach agreement on the delimitation of the Beibu Gulf, Vietnam must respect Chinese fishermen's traditional fishing rights in the Gulf, including those in disputed waters. The Chinese government would not tolerate any seizure and detention of Chinese fishermen and fishing boats by armed Vietnamese vessels.

I pointed out that the two sides must consider Chinese fishermen's traditional fishing rights as an important factor in fair delimitation of the Beibu Gulf. Moreover, China and Vietnam needed to determine this right in some legal form, and make proper arrangements for cooperation in the fishing industry subsequent to delimitation.

On August 18, I met with Vu Khoan again and we exchanged views on bilateral relations and regional and international issues. After the formal meeting, I reminded Vu Khoan, as a friend, that safeguarding peace in the Beibu Gulf was vital to the land boundary negotiation and to the development of China-Vietnam relations, and we must properly deal with relevant problems.

During my visit to Hanoi, I met with Vietnam's President Le Duc Anh and Vice Premier and Foreign Minister Nguyen Manh Cam. Since I had previously accompanied President Le Duc Anh throughout his visit to China, he asked me during the meeting to convey a message from the Vietnamese leadership to President Jiang Zemin. He said that Vietnam and China had many things in common in terms of social system and current policies that the Politburo of the CPV Central Committee and people from all sectors of society agreed that Vietnam-China relations could only improve rather than deteriorate. Vietnam's leaders were determined and confident that this would be the case.

Much in Common, Either Side of the Border

ON AUGUST 19, 1994, we headed back overland.

In those days, it took ten hours to go by road from Hanoi to Nanning. In fact, there are only 180 kilometers between Hanoi and the Friendship Pass, but the journey took six or seven hours due to the poor conditions of Vietnam's roads. Yet, by going overland, we could see the provinces in northern Vietnam and make on-the-spot investigations in the border areas.

The day after the talks, we got up early and had a simple breakfast before setting out. Our convoy passed through the Hanoi suburbs, crossed the Red River Bridge, and left the city behind.

Soon we were on the plain of the Red River Delta. From the car I could see a wide expanse of flat land, a network of ditches beside the road, footpaths crisscrossing the fields, and orderly cottages.

We headed along National Highway 1, climbing as it went north. After traversing Bac Ninh Province, we entered the uplands of northern Vietnam, and our field of vision narrowed. Soon we were winding through mountain roads.

I noticed that many of the entrances to farmers' houses along the road had couplets hung at either side, some of which were in Vietnamese, and some in Chinese characters. Seemingly, putting up couplets was popular with Vietnamese people, too.

Beyond Bac Giang we arrived in Lang Son, which is very close to the border with China. The Vietnamese side had arranged for us to visit a farmers' market. Although it was not long since Sino-Vietnamese cross-border trade had started, it had grown fast. We saw quite a few products from China, mostly light industrial products. Locals told us that the most popular commodity here was Chinese beer.

Finally we arrived at the Friendship Pass at one-forty in the afternoon. I walked through the pass and returned to my motherland.

After a short rest, our delegation climbed up to Fort Barbette on Jinji Mountain to look at the China-Vietnam border.

Fort Barbette was built on cliffs that rise abruptly from the ground, southwest of the Friendship Pass. Its construction was supervised by Su Yuanchun, a Qing Dynasty general famous for his deeds in fighting French aggressors, and completed by his officers, soldiers and artisans. Fort Barbette is composed of three barbettes, each equipped with a Krupp cannon.

In the Qing Dynasty, Fort Barbette was part of a seventy-two-fort defense system in the Guangxi section of the border, and played an important role in the Sino-French War.

In the Qing Dynasty, when China and France delineated the boundary, all the areas where China had built barbettes were demarcated into China's territory. This was either recorded or marked in the text or maps of the Sino-French Demarcation Treaties.

Jinji Mountain is only 511 meters above sea level, but its towering and precipitous site makes it look commanding among the surrounding mountains. Standing to the right of the Friendship Pass, it is also called Youfu Mountain, and stands opposite Zuobi Mountain to the left of the pass.

Standing atop Jinji Mountain and looking into the distance, I could see clearly the borderline winding through mountain ridges from boundary markers fifteen to twenty, as indicated in the Sino-French Demarcation Treaties.

Since China and Vietnam are linked by rivers and mountains, it is essential to settle disputes, demarcate the boundary, and remove discord. This would be conducive to harmony between our two peoples and to our mutually beneficial cooperation, which would benefit future generations. This was a mission bestowed on us by history and reality, a weighty responsibility.

Agreeing on Demarcation, Transcending Differences

AFTER THE SECOND ROUND of government-level talks, the Beibu Gulf negotiations ran into severe difficulties.

During the talks, the Vietnamese negotiators claimed that the

Beibu Gulf had been demarcated by the so-called 108°3'13" E line in the Sino-French Demarcation Treaties, signed between the Qing court and the French authorities.

During the fifth round of talks by the Sino-Vietnamese Joint Working Group on the Delimitation of the Beibu Gulf from June 20 to 22, 1995, the two sides had a bitter quarrel and reached no agreement; this was the one and only instance during all the Sino-Vietnamese boundary negotiations.

On July 13, 1995, the third round of government-level talks on border issues officially got under way at the Diaoyutai State Guesthouse in Beijing. China being the host country, I presided over the talks. Right at the outset, I made clear China's stand on the issue of Beibu Gulf delimitation from the perspectives of history, reality, and law in an all-around, in-depth, and systematic way.

I pointed out that since the signing of the Agreement on the Basic Principles, Vietnam had unilaterally expanded its control over the Beibu Gulf, published the bid invitations for the development of certain sectors in the central area of the Gulf, and seized and detained Chinese fishermen and fishing boats conducting normal operations in China's traditional fishing grounds in the Gulf, thereby posing a severe threat to the lives and property of Chinese fishermen. Furthermore, Vietnam had again brought up the so-called 108°3'13" E line during the fifth round of talks by the Joint Working Group on the Delimitation of the Beibu Gulf, and China was most concerned over Vietnam's retrogression.

I urged the Vietnamese side to show sincerity and deal properly with the Beibu Gulf fishing disputes, and return to the path of negotiation for demarcating the Beibu Gulf.

Hearing what I said, Vu Khoan said that the signing of the Agreement on the Basic Principles in 1993 had actually broken the deadlock between the two countries in the 1970s on the demarcation of the Beibu Gulf. He assured China that Vietnam would not go backward or retreat from its position. Vietnamese leaders were determined.

During this round of talks, Li Lanqing, member of the Politburo of the CPC Central Committee and vice premier of the State Council, met with Vu Khoan. We arranged a trip for Vu Khoan to visit Shandong.

Having returned to Beijing from Shandong, Vu Khoan told me that he had visited Qufu in Shandong Province, the hometown of Confucius, and that the development of Shandong had deeply impressed him. After the visit, he wrote an article called "Visit to Confucius' Hometown," which was then published in the Vietnamese journal *International Weekly*. In the article, he said, "the tree of Sino-Vietnamese relations is deeply rooted in the fertile soil of history, and people of future generations have no reason not to make the tree more luxuriant."

The dispute over whether the Beibu Gulf had already been demarcated was not satisfactorily concluded until a visit to China by Du Muoi, general secretary of the CPV, in November 1995.

During that visit, the leaders reiterated that the two countries should properly settle the border issues based on the principles they had agreed upon during previous summit meetings, in the spirit of "taking into account the interests of the whole, mutual understanding and mutual accommodation, fair and reasonable treatment, and friendly consultation," according to international law and practices and through peaceful negotiations. The leaders agreed to help the two sides transcend previous differences, end the disputes over the delimitation of the Beibu Gulf that had persisted since the 1970s, determine the political framework for the negotiations and the direction for joint efforts, and bring the negotiations onto the right track.

On February 14, 1996, I went to Pingxiang/Dong Dang, a port on the China-Vietnam border, where I attended ceremonies marking the resumption of through services on the Guangxi–Vietnam

Railway. There was a joint ceremony in Pingxiang on the Chinese side followed by another in Dong Dang on the Vietnam side. The ceremonies were solemn and enthusiastic.

Vietnam's Vice Foreign Minister Vu Khoan and I each made speeches at the ceremonies. We both acknowledged the important role that the Guangxi–Vietnam Railway had played in China-Vietnam relations and in China's support for Vietnam in the wars against France and against the United States. We both believed that the resumption of through traffic indicated broader prospects for China-Vietnam relations.

After the ceremonies, I went to Lang Son, at the invitation of Vu Khoan, to discuss bilateral relations and border issues.

That was my second visit to Lang Son. It was a little more than a year since the first visit, but the border town looked very different, thanks to the development of border trade. I could see more shops on the streets, and the place was evidently more prosperous and busy. Many billboards along the streets were written both in Vietnamese and Chinese.

I met with Vu Khoan at the Jinshan Hotel in Lang Son.

I made three suggestions regarding the stagnation of the negotiations of the Joint Working Group on the Delimitation of the Beibu Gulf. First, during the negotiation, both sides should take as their guiding principle the consensus reached by their national leaders of "taking into account the interests of the whole, mutual understanding and mutual accommodation, fair and reasonable treatment, and friendly consultation," and take as the legal basis the Agreement on Basic Principles signed in 1993. Second, the two sides should continue exchanging views on the reasons behind their respective borderline claims and other factors. The Chinese side would put forward its borderline proposal at an appropriate time. Third, the two sides should reach an understanding between negotiators regarding the principle of fairness. At the same time, the two sides should make proper and reasonable arrangements for normal fishing operations from both countries in the Gulf throughout the negotiation process.

Vu Khoan basically agreed with my suggestions. He said Vietnam would stick to negotiation as the way for solving the gulf delimitation problems. As regards guaranteeing Chinese fishermen's normal operations in the Gulf, he said that Vietnam could consider this issue only after Gulf delimitation had been completed.

In response, I made it very plain that China could not separate the gulf delimitation from guaranteeing normal fishing by Chinese fishermen there, since the fishing issue was, in itself, an important part of the negotiations, and I expressed my hope that Vietnam would pay more attention to China's concern on this matter. I stressed that China's concern over the fishing issue had always been serious and that China would never sacrifice the interests of Chinese fishermen for the sake of delimitation.

From March 4 to 11, 1996, the sixth round of talks by the Joint Working Group on the Delimitation of the Beibu Gulf was held in Beijing. The two sides had an in-depth exchange of views on the principle of fairness, confirmed that this principle was the primary and most important principle for the delimitation of the Beibu Gulf, and agreed to exchange their borderline proposals as soon as possible. This brought the negotiations onto the right track again.

From September 18 to 23, 1996, I led the Chinese governmental delegation at the fourth round of government-level talks between China and Vietnam in Hanoi.

During these talks, I explained China's idea about fairly demarcating the Beibu Gulf from the perspective of international law. I pointed out that China and Vietnam were roughly in balance in terms of their general political and geographical relations in the Gulf, and this geopolitical reality was the primary condition that should be taken into consideration during the delimitation; the fact that each country had coastline on Beibu Gulf constituted the basis of their respective claims to maritime rights and interests.

I suggested that the two sides should consider the facts that China's coast and Vietnam's coast in the Beibu Gulf are adjacent and facing each other and that their gulf coastlines are of similar length, and thus try to achieve the goal of balancing the interests of the two sides. This goal was fair under the law, friendly in political terms, and reasonable in financial terms, and conformed to the fundamental interests of our two peoples.

Vu Khoan said he would report back in full to Vietnam's leaders about China's comprehensive and in-depth exposition of its thinking in regard to demarcating the Beibu Gulf. Then he stated Vietnam's views: Vietnam believed that the first thing to be considered in the delimitation should be geographical factors, including special natural features.

He also said that the Beibu Gulf was an estuary and an important line for international transportation in northern Vietnam; as such, it was of vital significance for Vietnam. He said when demarcating the Beibu Gulf, China's Hainan Island could not be mentioned in the same breath with mainland Vietnam.

Immediately, I pointed out that Hainan Island is China's second largest island next to Taiwan and that Hainan is a province of China. Hainan is only one of the islands on the South China Sea, but with respect to the Beibu Gulf, it is part of China's land territory and coast. According to international law and practice, Hainan Island should form part of the basis for China's marine rights and enjoy the same right in border delimitation as the coasts of Vietnam's and China's mainland.

Finally, I expressed my hope again that Vietnam would carefully study China's proposal and ideas about the gulf delimitation.

During this round of talks, the two sides agreed to establish a joint experts group, which would hold informal consultations on the proposed lines for demarcating the gulf.

On September 18, 1996, Vu Khoan and I held a discussion in

which we exchanged views on bilateral relations, and regional and international issues. The following day, Tran Tuc Luong, vice premier and member of the CPV Central Committee Politiburo, met with the Chinese governmental delegation and me.

From 1996 to 1997, the Joint Working Group on the Delimitation of the Beibu Gulf held another three rounds of talks, and informally exchanged views on the proposed lines. Major differences persisted, so no breakthrough was achieved.

In July 1997, General Secretary Do Muoi visited China. I held talks with the director of the Vietnamese Government Boundary Commission at the Diaoyutai State Guesthouse, mainly exchanging views on the difficulties in the delimitation negotiation process. I pointed out that the key reason for the lack of any breakthrough was that the two sides had not reached agreement on the goal of a rough balance of interests.

From August 13 to 15, 1997, as head of the Chinese governmental delegation, I chaired the fifth round of China-Vietnam government-level talks on border issues and a vice foreign ministers' consultation held at the Diaoyutai State Guesthouse.

During this round of talks, both sides reached agreement on launching a group for drafting a China-Vietnam land boundary treaty. As for the Beibu Gulf delimitation, there was an informal exchange of views on the lines claimed by each side; we agreed to expand common ground and narrow our differences as far as possible, and try to make our views closer, while maintaining the informal consultation mechanism for the joint expert groups, in an effort to work out a delimitation line acceptable to both sides.

After the talks, Vice Premier and Foreign Minister Qian Qichen met with Vice Minister Vu Khoan and his delegation.

The fishing problem involved in the Beibu Gulf delimitation had always been an issue of serious concern to me.

Since 1992, the year that China and Vietnam started boundary negotiations again, I had repeatedly talked about this issue with Vietnam, emphasizing that the two sides must solve the fishing problem when discussing the Beibu Gulf delimitation.

During the course of the Beibu Gulf negotiations, China had made several solemn representations to Vietnam about armed Vietnamese vessels seizing and detaining Chinese fishermen in the Gulf.

It was only at the final stage of the negotiations when the problem had obviously remained the largest obstacle to progress that the Vietnamese side understood why China had been so insistent that the fishing and delimitation issues should be resolved at the same time.

In fact, the reason we paid so much attention to the fishing arrangements was that the issue concerned the livelihood of Chinese fishermen and the responsibility of the state and government for the people. It was a political issue with implications for local social stability.

However, at that time, the Vietnamese negotiators could not understand why their Chinese counterparts would not give way on this issue.

In this connection, I had many brainstorming sessions with Wang Yi, who succeeded me as head of the Chinese governmental delegation. We both believed that we could make progress through the top leaders.

In February 1999, Le Kha Phieu, general secretary of the CPV, visited China and Jiang Zemin, general secretary of the CPC, met with him. The two leaders agreed that delimitation of the Beibu Gulf should be completed by the year 2000.

In December 1999, I went to visit General Secretary Le Kha Phieu after attending the signing ceremony of the Treaty on the Land Boundary between the People's Republic of China and the Socialist Republic of Vietnam.

During the meeting, I talked about the Chinese leaders' attention to and ideas about the fishing problem in the Beibu Gulf from

Meeting with Vietnam's Foreign Minister Nguyen Dy Nien in Shanghai at the APEC Summit, October 16, 2001.

the political perspective. In particular, I brought up the opinion expressed by Jiang Zemin to Le Kha Phieu: "The delimitation of the Beibu Gulf and the fishing arrangements should be solved in conjunction."

General Secretary Le Kha Phieu said that he had had detailed discussions with other Vietnamese leaders about this issue and wished to respond positively. He said that the fisheries departments of both countries could start discussing this problem right away, and that the two countries could hold negotiations on the fishing issues and on the Gulf delimitation simultaneously.

This statement by Le Kha Phieu was very important, giving the green light to immediate talks on fishing arrangements. It created the right conditions for solving both the Gulf delimitation and the fishing problem simultaneously.

On January 28, 2000, in a Vietnamese government reshuffle,

Nguyen Dy Nien became foreign minister, succeeding Nguyen Manh Cam, and Vu Khoan became minister of Industry and Trade. Shi Guangsheng, then minister of Foreign Trade and Economic Cooperation, and I sent congratulatory telegrams to the two new ministers.

Nguyen Dy Nien was very pleased to receive my telegram. On January 31, he told China's Ambassador to Vietnam Li Jiazhong that he hoped China would be the first country for him to visit as foreign minister, and that he hoped to meet with me and visit Chinese leaders. I promptly issued an invitation to him for the visit.

From February 24 to 26, 2000, Vietnam's new Foreign Minister Nguyen Dy Nien conducted a formal visit to China. Premier Zhu Rongji met with him at the Ziguangge in the Zhongnanhai and Li Peng, chairman of the Standing Committee of the National People's Congress, met with him at the reception hall of the Great Hall of the People.

On February 25, I held formal talks with him at the Diaoyutai State Guesthouse.

Nguyen Dy Nien is a gentle and cultivated man, with the air of a scholar. In 1954, he started working at Vietnam's Ministry of Foreign Affairs; in the 1960s, he studied and worked in India for nine years. He speaks fluent English.

During the talks, we exchanged views on bilateral relations, and regional and international situations. I emphasized the delimitation of the Beibu Gulf, saying that the two sides should work hard and focus on solving two problems: determining the proportion of China's and Vietnam's marine areas and making proper fishing arrangements.

I said that the Chinese leaders had proposed the idea of roughly balancing the interests of the two sides back in 1995 and that Vietnamese leaders had also made speeches to the same effect. Provided the two sides work in line with the consensus reached between our respective leaders to explore solutions in a realistic and pragmatic way, these problems could be solved.

I said that, frankly speaking, the Beibu Gulf delimitation would affect the traditional fishing operations of both China and Vietnam, which in turn would affect stability in the Gulf area; for this reason, the fishing issue had become an important political element in the Beibu Gulf delimitation negotiations. I hoped the Vietnamese side would launch a mechanism for negotiations on fishing as soon as possible, so as to solve the delimitation problem and the fishing problem together.

Foreign Minister Nguyen agreed with me on accelerating the negotiations on the Beibu Gulf delimitation and was willing to work together with me to this end. He said that the Vietnamese side was fully aware of China's concern about the fishing industry and that the two sides could draft a separate document about the fishing problem, but sign it together with the agreement on the delimitation of the Beibu Gulf.

In April 2000, China and Vietnam started talks by the fishing experts group within the framework of the negotiations on Beibu Gulf delimitation. However, the Vietnamese side delayed and postponed the talks again and again on technical pretexts, and refrained from holding substantive discussions with China.

On September 14, 2000, I went to New York to attend the 55th session of the UN General Assembly. During the session, I met with Minister Nguyen Dy Nien at UN headquarters and exchanged views with him on the Beibu Gulf delimitation.

I said that the negotiations were at a critical stage, and that the agreement by Vietnam to set up a common fishing area in the Gulf constituted important progress. The urgent necessity now was prompt bilateral discussion on the fishing agreement to ensure that this agreement would be signed together with the delimitation agreement. I also expressed the hope that Vietnam would make a political decision as soon as possible about the respective proportions of China's and Vietnam's marine areas.

Foreign Minister Nguyen said he would like to work with me to urge the two governmental delegations and the Joint Working Group on the Delimitation of the Beibu Gulf to work harder toward the goals proposed by leaders of the two countries. He also stated clearly that Vietnam agreed to sign the delimitation and fishing agreements at the same time.

On October 25, 2000, Wang Yi, head of the Chinese governmental delegation, and Le Cong Phung, his Vietnamese counterpart, held an informal meeting and reached an initial agreement on the tentative delimitation in the Beibu Gulf. This was a breakthrough.

The following day, I met with Le Cong Phung and confirmed the consensus reached between the two delegation leaders. I said that their meeting was highly significant, conducive to breaking the deadlock in or a favorable turn. I hoped that the experts could build on the agreement reached by Wang Yi and Le Cong Phung to work out a common delimitation line.

I also stated my concerns and views about the fishing problem. I hoped both foreign ministries would work together to ensure substantive progress in the fishing negotiations and complete the delimitation of the Beibu Gulf in one package.

On November 21, 2000, I wrote to Foreign Minister Nguyen about the Vietnamese fishing experts group delaying the negotiations. In the letter, I expressed my wish to speed up the negotiations on the delimitation of the Beibu Gulf, in particular the negotiations on the fishing issue. I wrote that the negotiations were at the final critical moment, and that the two sides should work hard from the political height to push forward the negotiations, particularly those relating to fishing, and ensure that both the delimitation agreement and the fishing agreement could be signed simultaneously before the end of 2000.

I also proposed a timetable, giving a deadline of December 5 for completion of all substantive talks on the delimitation and fishing problems. I hoped that he could work with me to push forward the negotiations from the political perspective and give clear instructions to the negotiators.

In his reply to my letter, Foreign Minister Nguyen said that Vietnam's leaders had made a decision to set up a common fishing area in the Beibu Gulf, and that Vietnam was ready to work with China and discuss the fishing agreement with a constructive attitude.

Thus driven by the two foreign ministries, the negotiators made the final push.

From December 12 to 14, 2000, Wang Yi, head of the Chinese governmental delegation, and Le Cong Phung, head of the Vietnamese governmental delegation, held the third informal meeting. After two days of tough talks, the two sides reached agreement on major problems involved in the delimitation of the Beibu Gulf, realizing a rough balance of interests and related areas between the two countries.

On December 18, the two sides determined the delimitation lines of the territorial sea of the Beibu Gulf, the exclusive economic zones, and the continental shelf. Agreement was also reached on the geographic coordinates of all the boundary points and all the documents on the delimitation of the Gulf.

Thus, after overcoming numerous difficulties, China and Vietnam finally completed all the substantive talks about the delimitation of the Beibu Gulf. To achieve this end, the two sides took into consideration all the related circumstances, acted on the principle of fairness, and resorted to friendly consultation.

At the same time as the delimitation negotiations bore fruit, the fishing experts group also solved the problem of postdelimitation fishing arrangements, including deciding the principles for long-term cooperation, delimiting a common fishing zone and transitional water area of over 30,000 square kilometers, and drafting the

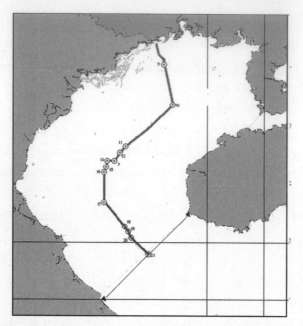

Delimitation lines of the exclusive economic zones and continental shelf in the Beibu Gulf between China and Vietnam.

Agreement between China and Vietnam on Fisheries Cooperation in the Beibu Gulf.

Looking back, the negotiations on the delimitation of the Beibu Gulf were very hard, full of twists and turns, lasting from 1992 to 2000. During those eight years, the two countries held two rounds of expert talks, seven rounds of governmental talks, three informal meetings between the heads of governmental delegations, eighteen rounds of talks by the Joint Working Group on the Delimitation of the Beibu Gulf, three informal meetings by the Joint Experts Group, six rounds of talks by the Fishing Experts Group, and seven rounds of talks by the Mapping Experts Group. China's diplomatic history has rarely witnessed negotiations requiring such a high number of meetings and so much input.

On December 24, 2000, President Tran Duc Luong of Vietnam paid an official visit to China, where he met with President Jiang

Zemin in a formal meeting held on December 25. The two top leaders spoke highly of the Agreement between China and Vietnam on the Delimitation of the Beibu Gulf and the Agreement between China and Vietnam on Fisheries Cooperation in the Beibu Gulf. The two heads of state then presided jointly over the signing ceremony of the two agreements.

The signing ceremony was held at the Great Hall of the People in Beijing. I, on behalf of the Chinese government, and Foreign Minister Nguyen Dy Nien, on behalf of the Vietnamese government, signed the Agreement between the People's Republic of China and the Socialist Republic of Vietnam on the Delimitation of the Territorial Seas of the Beibu Gulf, the Exclusive Economic Zones and the Continental Shelf. China's Agriculture Minister Chen Yaobang and Vietnam's Fisheries Minister Ta Quang Ngoc signed the Agreement between the People's Republic of China and the Socialist Republic of Vietnam on Fisheries Cooperation in the Beibu Gulf.

With the two agreements signed, China and Vietnam went through approval procedures according to their respective laws. On June 25, 2004, the Tenth Meeting of the Standing Committee of the Tenth National People's Congress of China approved the Agreement between the People's Republic of China and the Socialist Republic of Vietnam on the Delimitation of the Territorial Seas of the Beibu Gulf, the Exclusive Economic Zones and the Continental Shelf. Prior to this, on June 15, the Fifth Meeting of the 11th National Assembly of Vietnam had also approved the agreement.

In Hanoi, on June 30, 2004, Wang Yi, vice minister of Foreign Affairs and head of the Chinese governmental delegation, and Vu Dung, vice minister of Foreign Affairs of Vietnam and head of the Vietnamese governmental delegation, exchanged instruments of ratification of the Agreement between the People's Republic of China and the Socialist Republic of Vietnam on the Delimitation of the Territorial Seas of the Beibu Gulf, the Exclusive Economic

Zones and the Continental Shelf. In the meantime, both foreign ministries exchanged a note on the coming into effect of the Agreement between the People's Republic of China and the Socialist Republic of Vietnam on Fisheries Cooperation in the Beibu Gulf. The two agreements came into effect on the same day. The two sides also submitted to the United Nations for the record the Agreement between the People's Republic of China and the Socialist Republic of Vietnam on the Delimitation of the Territorial Seas of the Beibu Gulf, the Exclusive Economic Zones, and the Continental Shelf.

The Agreement between the People's Republic of China and the Socialist Republic of Vietnam on the Delimitation of the Territorial Seas of the Beibu Gulf, the Exclusive Economic Zones, and the Continental Shelf determined the Beibu Gulf delimitation line between China and Vietnam. It states that the line starts from the estuary of the Beilun River, the boundary river between China and Vietnam, runs southward, and ends at the closing line in the Beibu Gulf, with a total length of about 500 kilometers.

The Far-Reaching Significance of Reconciliation

ENTERING THE NEW MILLENNIUM, after working together for many years, and solving two important problems that had troubled bilateral relations, China and Vietnam signed the Treaty on the Land Boundary between the People's Republic of China and the Socialist Republic of Vietnam and the Agreement between the People's Republic of China and the Socialist Republic of Vietnam on the Delimitation of the Territorial Seas of the Beibu Gulf, the Exclusive Economic Zones, and the Continental Shelf. The signing of the two agreements was consistent with the fundamental and long-term interests of the two peoples and has had a far-reaching influence on the development of China-Vietnam relations.

The coming into effect of the two agreements signified that our two countries had brought into the twenty-first century a land boundary and a marine boundary of peace, friendship, stability, and cooperation. They substantiated the principles of "long-term stability, future-orientation, good-neighborliness, all-round cooperation," and laid a solid foundation for the healthy and steady development of bilateral relations in the new millennium.

The coming into effect of the Agreement between the People's Republic of China and the Socialist Republic of Vietnam on the Delimitation of the Territorial Seas of the Beibu Gulf, the Exclusive Economic Zones, and the Continental Shelf symbolized the birth of China's first marine boundary. China and Vietnam solved the delimitation of the Beibu Gulf through negotiations, and the practice accorded with the modern law of the sea system.

The delimitation of the Beibu Gulf fully demonstrated China's sincerity about solving marine delimitation with neighboring countries through negotiations, which will be conducive to building trust between China and neighboring maritime states, advance China's relations with them, and safeguard peace and stability in the surrounding areas.

The experience of China and Vietnam in solving the land boundary and marine delimitation disputes shows that we can achieve a win-win result, provided we adhere to international law and practice, respect history and reality, take into consideration the fundamental and long-term interests of the peoples, enter into consultations on the basis of equality, mutual understanding and mutual accommodation, and seek just, fair, and reasonable solutions.

To achieve win-win, the countries concerned must respect history and reality. These two things are not contradictory, but complementary. The aim is to understand the causes and effects and the prevailing situation, to clarify the differences and disputes, and to make an accurate judgment of the content, nature, and degree of the differences and disputes, thereby facilitating better solutions.

The criteria for gauging the success or otherwise of negotiations are whether the two sides' claims to rights and interests based on historical, geographic, sovereignty, jurisdictional, and political factors are fair, reasonable, and lawful, and whether their legitimate rights and interests are protected. In this sense, China and Vietnam acquitted themselves well with the Treaty on the Land Boundary between the People's Republic of China and the Socialist Republic of Vietnam and the Agreement between the People's Republic of China and the Socialist Republic of Vietnam on the Delimitation of the Territorial Seas of the Beibu Gulf, the Exclusive Economic Zones, and the Continental Shelf.

CHAPTER 8

The China-US South China Sea
Air Collision Incident

The Air Collision Incident

ON THE AFTERNOON OF April 1, 2001, I was in Nice, a beautiful coastal city in the south of France.

Having attended the ministerial meeting of the East Asia–Latin America Forum in Chile, I had flown to France for a visit and had to change planes at Nice.

Nice is known as the "Town of Sunshine"; it was a fine day with an azure sky and brilliant sunshine. After the tensions of the meeting and the long journey, I and the rest of my party felt rather tired and in need of a short break to recharge our batteries before the departure of our onward flight.

We were chatting in an airport lounge and enjoying a rare moment of relaxation when Chinese Ambassador to France Wu Jianmin hurried in. He had rushed down from Paris and was speaking in hushed tones before even sitting down. Ambassador Wu briefed us on the news that, that same morning, a US reconnaissance plane had collided into and destroyed a Chinese military aircraft near Hainan Island, and that the pilot of the Chinese plane was missing. He told us that the Chinese government was considering lodging solemn representations to the United States.

We immediately sensed the seriousness of the incident. The relaxed atmosphere in the lounge quickly became grave.

I asked Ambassador Wu to sit down and give us the details.

On the morning of April 1, Beijing time, an American EP-3 military reconnaissance plane once again entered the airspace over southeast of Hainan Island. The Chinese Navy sent two F-8 fighters to follow and monitor the US plane. At 9:07 A.M., the two Chinese aircraft were flying normally in an area 104 kilometers southeast of Hainan, when the US plane suddenly veered at a wide angle and rammed into one of the Chinese planes, which lost control and plunged into the sea. The pilot, Wang Wei, was missing. The damaged US plane entered China's airspace without approval, landing at Lingshui Military Airfield in Hainan. The Chinese made proper arrangements according to international practice for the twenty-four crew members on board.

From Ambassador Wu's briefing, I realized that the incident was a serious, sensitive emergency because it was the first direct clash between the Chinese and US militaries in the new world order after the Cold War, and it had had serious consequences, namely a lost plane and a missing pilot. In particular, the incident involved major matters of principle, including national sovereignty, territorial integrity, and national dignity. The proper handling of such a complicated issue would be by no means easy.

It seemed accidental, but actually it had a certain inevitability to it. Since the founding of the People's Republic of China in 1949, the United States had never stopped reconnaissance flights along the edge of China's waters. From the second half of 2000, the flights had grown more and more frequent and closer to China's territorial waters. China had repeatedly lodged representations to the United

States through various channels, demanding that the United States stop such reconnaissance activities, but the United States had turned a deaf ear to China's demands and stuck to its old ways.

I told Ambassador Wu that the incident was very complicated and sensitive, and would be a focus of our diplomatic work in the coming period. I also advised that the Chinese embassy in France should keep a close watch on how the incident developed, collect reactions, and clarify the facts.

Since I was to meet with French President Jacques Chirac in Paris the following day, and knowing that reporters might ask about the incident, I decided to take the opportunity to make China's position clear.

On the afternoon of April 2, 2001, after my meeting with President Chirac, I saw quite a few reporters waiting at the gate of the Élysée Palace. When I walked out, they surged forward and bombarded me with questions. As anticipated, the most-asked question was "What are China's comments on the air collision?"

Standing at the gate of the Élysée Palace, I spelled it out to the reporters: "I want to tell you that it was the US plane that hit the Chinese aircraft, rather than the other way around. The Chinese pilot is still missing. The entire responsibility for the collision lies with the United States and they should give a satisfactory explanation to the Chinese people."

Straight after the interview, I drove directly to Charles de Gaulle Airport and took the plane to China.

The flight from Paris to Beijing took nine and one half hours. Because of the time difference, it was nighttime all the way: Even so I did not feel like sleeping, my mind being totally preoccupied.

That time was a special period for the China–US relationship. Under the Clinton administration, despite a few confrontations in the early stages, our bilateral relations eventually began to improve. We had hoped that the succeeding Bush administration would continue to promote the development of China-US relations, given that George W. Bush had visited China before and that his father, George H. W. Bush, has a deep understanding of China.

However, once George W. Bush assumed the presidency, he readjusted the US foreign policy established by the Clinton government and, as Bill Clinton had done in his early days in office, began to adopt a tough policy toward China. In a televised election debate a few months before his inauguration, George W. Bush the presidential candidate had publicly declared that he would reposition US relations as regards China, and described China as a "strategic competitor" rather than a potential "strategic partner."

In foreign relations terms, *strategic competitor* and *strategic partner* have greatly different meanings. To a certain extent the word *competitor* implied the US position as being in opposition to China and it was disturbing to think about the possible adverse impact on China-US relations should the Bush argument become the China policy of the US government.

China-US ties are very important both for our two countries and for the world as a whole. Therefore, it was imperative that China should communicate with the new US government and urge President Bush and his administration to understand China-US relations and have a positive and pragmatic China policy, ensuring the healthy and steady development of China-US ties.

On December 14, 2000, George W. Bush was elected the forty-third president of the United States. On the same day, Chinese President Jiang Zemin sent him the usual message of congratulations.

In February 2001, shortly after taking office, President Bush wrote to President Jiang Zemin in a positive tone, expressing in his letter the wish to strengthen dialogue and cooperation with China and to resolve disputes with mutual respect and candidness.

President Jiang replied immediately, congratulating President Bush on assuming office and praising the positive attitude in his letter as regards the development of China-US relations. Furthermore, President Jiang expressed the hope for joint efforts with the United States in advancing healthy, steady, and sustained development of China-US relations in the new century.

At the end of March, Chinese Vice Premier Qian Qichen visited the United States and had face-to-face contact with senior officials in the new US government. US President Bush met with Vice Premier Qian and expressed how the US government valued its relations with China and that he was looking forward to attending the APEC Informal Summit Meeting to be held in Shanghai in October and to visiting Beijing at that time.

Vice Premier Qian's US visit achieved positive results and helped improve relations.

Then, suddenly, the air collision happened, the incident causing a severe strain on relations between the two countries.

Round One: Matching Toughness with Toughness

AT ABOUT TEN IN the morning on April 3, 2001, we landed at Beijing and I headed straight back to the Foreign Ministry, where I called Assistant Foreign Minister Zhou Wenzhong to my office. He was in charge of North American and Oceanian Affairs and very experienced in communicating with Americans.

Assistant Foreign Minister Zhou gave me a detailed account of what had happened over the previous two days. He told me that the Central Authorities regarded the air collision as extremely important and had formulated a series of strategic principles for dealing with the affair.

In line with the Central Authorities' arrangements, Zhou Wenzhong summoned US Ambassador to China Joseph Prueher for an urgent meeting on the day of the incident. Zhou lodged

China's solemn representations and strong protest, emphasizing that the United States bore total responsibility for the incident and must give the Chinese people an explanation.

The United States' response was highly arrogant, refusing to acknowledge any responsibility. Ambassador Prueher would not accept China's judgment regarding responsibility for the air collision and merely expressed "regret" about the loss of the Chinese aircraft and the missing pilot. Although the United States had offered to help in the search for the missing pilot, it was insistent on demanding the swift return of its air crew and reconnaissance plane, and even forbade the Chinese to board and investigate its aircraft.

Assistant Foreign Minister Zhou had immediately rejected the US argument and demand, stating that China reserved its right to pursue further the issues of its losses caused by the United States and of the US plane entering China's airspace and landing at a Chinese airport without China's authorization.

The United States is good at manipulating public opinion by getting its voice heard first. At about three in the afternoon on April 1, 2001, just six hours after the air collision, the US Pacific Command issued a brief statement on its website, making the collision public knowledge. In the statement, the United States demanded that the Chinese government abide by international practice to guarantee the safety of its aircraft and air crew and facilitate the prompt return of the crew and aircraft. Not a word was mentioned about the crash of the Chinese plane and its missing pilot.

In response to the unreasonable attitude of the United States, on the evening of April 2, Assistant Foreign Minister Zhou Wenzhong summoned US Ambassador Prueher again to reiterate China's solemn stance on the matter, urging that the United States face facts, acknowledge responsibility, and apologize to China.

Zhou told Prueher very firmly that the act of the US reconnaissance plane had constituted an infringement on China's sovereignty and airspace in violation of international law and provisions of Chinese law. According to both international and Chinese domestic laws, China had the right to investigate an aircraft that had entered China's airspace and landed at a Chinese airfield entirely without China's authorization. Zhou strongly urged the United States to seriously consider China's solemn representations and legitimate demands and give a prompt explanation to the Chinese government and people about the US plane's ramming of the Chinese jet and its violation of China's sovereignty and airspace.

Although Ambassador Prueher admitted that the incident was most unfortunate, he still did not accept China's view of American responsibility.

After Zhou's meeting with Prueher, the spokesperson of China's Foreign Ministry also made a statement to the media reiterating that full responsibility for the incident lay with the United States. He made clear that China had lodged solemn representations and protest to the United States and reserved its right to pursue the issue further.

In Washington, China's Ambassador to the US Yang Jiechi arranged an urgent meeting with US State Department officials and lodged China's solemn representations and protest.

For the next two days, however, the United States retained its tough stance.

President Bush delivered two successive statements: In the first, on April 2, he stressed that the priorities for the United States were the "prompt and safe return of the crew, and the return of the aircraft without further damaging or tampering." In the second, on April 3, he claimed that the United States had "allowed the Chinese government time to do the right thing," and that it was time for US servicemen to return home, and for the Chinese government to return the plane, and that the accident had the "potential of undermining our hopes for a fruitful relationship between our two countries."

In the meantime, the US Navy dispatched three destroyers to

cruise in the vicinity of Hainan and to remain in the South China Sea in the name of "monitoring the development of the situation."

The American attitude and actions aroused great indignation, both at the official level and among the Chinese public. On the Internet, many Chinese people suggested staging a protest demonstration outside the US embassy in Beijing, even urging the Chinese government to put the American air crew on trial.

In response to the tough, unreasonable attitude of the United States, President Jiang Zemin, during his meeting with Qatar's Prime Minister Abdullah Bin Khalifa Al-Thani on the morning of April 3, 2001, solemnly pointed out that the United States bore full responsibility for the incident, and said the United States should apologize to the Chinese people and put an immediate stop to all reconnaissance flights in the airspace over China's coastal areas. He emphasized, "What is most precious is human life. I am deeply concerned about the safety of the missing pilot and have repeatedly urged that no effort should be spared in the search-and-rescue work."

The next day, President Jiang's statement was covered by major media worldwide and met with a positive response.

Round Two: Getting an Upper Hand

ON APRIL 4, 2001, before President Jiang Zemin left for a six-country visit to Latin America, a brief send-off ceremony was held as usual in the Great Hall of the People, Beijing. Beforehand, President Jiang gave important instructions on handling the collision incident and designated Hu Jintao to take charge of this matter on behalf of the Central Authorities. He said to me, "The Foreign Ministry must seriously implement the Central Authorities' instructions and coordinate all the departments concerned. You must take personal charge of this to ensure the proper handling of the matter."

President Jiang told the media present that he was greatly concerned over the safety of the missing pilot, Wang Wei, and that all departments concerned must spare no effort in the search-and-rescue operation. He stressed that the United States should do something conducive to the development of China-US relations, rather than issuing statements confounding right and wrong and detrimental to bilateral relations.

After this, I kept in close touch with Hu Jintao with regard to the handling of the incident. I reported the latest information to him and often had meetings or talks in his office. Other leaders in the Central Authorities were also concerned about the handling of the incident.

I sensed the necessity to put more pressure on the Americans to enable them to have a clear understanding of the situation and come to a sensible decision. So, I called a meeting with US Ambassador Prueher.

Before Ambassador Prueher's arrival, I felt unable to suppress the memory of the US-led NATO bombing of the Chinese embassy in Belgrade, Yugoslavia, on May 8, 1999. Now, within less than two years, there was another incident resulting in the loss of Chinese life and property. This was really intolerable!

Despite China's repeated objections over the years the United States had kept on sending military aircraft on reconnaissance missions over our coastal areas, and I felt China had to win this diplomatic battle. I was determined to follow the guidance of the Central Authorities, to acquaint the United States with the strength of public indignation in China, so much so that an apology to the Chinese government and people would be absolutely essential.

In view of the United States' outrageous attitude, admitting no responsibility, offering no apology, no cooperation, and showing no signs of repentance, I decided to talk in depth with US Ambassador Prueher on four aspects of the situation.

At the appointed time, five-thirty on April 4, Ambassador

Prueher and several diplomats from the US embassy in China arrived at the Ministry of Foreign Affairs.

Joseph Prueher had served as an admiral in the US Navy and commander-in-chief of the US Pacific Command before being appointed ambassador to China at the age of fifty-eight by President Clinton in 1999. He was of great physical stature and had the bearing of a military man. This former admiral had served thirty-five years in the US Navy and could pilot over fifty different types of naval aircraft. He was said by the media to be calm, capable, pragmatic, and a good judge of priorities.

In normal circumstances, on diplomatic occasions, discussion of the real business is usually preceded by handshakes and greetings, creating an easy atmosphere in which the two parties can exchange views. However, these were not normal circumstances: Both Prueher and I looked very serious.

Prueher sat down, and I went straight to the point, saying that Assistant Foreign Minister Zhou Wenzhong had met with him twice to lodge China's solemn representations, and that today I would further and comprehensively clarify China's solemn stance on the collision incident. Then I talked on four aspects.

First, the United States should bear full responsibility for the incident. The US aircraft had violated the United Nations Convention on the Law of the Sea and had breached the consensus reached by the two countries in May 2000 on avoiding risky military actions in sea areas. The incident was the fault of the United States, and it should take full responsibility and issue an apology.

Second, the US attitude and actions subsequent to the collision were wrong, and greatly unsatisfactory to China. We had been taking a calm, restrained, and responsible attitude in handling the incident, hoping that China-US relations would not be affected or harmed. Out of humanitarian concerns, China had made proper arrangements for the US air crew, and had lost no time in arranging for diplomats from the US embassy and consulates to visit them.

The attitude and moves adopted by the United States had been quite the opposite. It was absolutely plain that the US reconnaissance plane, in violation of international aviation law, had rammed into a Chinese aircraft, illegally entered China's airspace, and landed at a Chinese airfield. These actions had severely infringed upon China's sovereignty and territorial integrity and posed a threat to China's state security. Furthermore, not only had the United States failed to respect the facts and own up to its responsibility following the collision, it had added insult to injury by acting in an overbearing, unreasonable way, confounding right and wrong, and making false accusations against China.

Third, there would be no release of the air crew until the United States apologized. China valued China-US relations and hoped for a rapid, proper settlement of the incident. If the United States admitted its fault and apologized, China would consider arranging for the US air crew to leave China as soon as possible. China's sovereignty and national dignity brooked no violation, and for the Chinese government and people, nothing could be more important than safeguarding state sovereignty and national dignity. The United States had to fully recognize the gravity of the incident, pay serious regard to China's solemn stance and demands, and cooperate with China in handling the issue. It should not make any erroneous judgments nor do anything that might escalate or complicate the matter. China did not wish to see continuous escalation of the situation, but if the United States insisted on doing so, we would take them on to the end.

Fourth, the United States must stop reconnaissance activities off China's coastal areas. Repeated US reconnaissance flights in the vicinity of China's coastal areas had been the root cause of the collision. The United States should take China's representations and Chinese people's solemn demands seriously, handle the issue with a responsible attitude, and adopt effective measures to prevent the recurrence of similar incidents.

Ambassador Prueher had been listening to me carefully. After I finished, he said seriously that US President Bush and Secretary of State Colin Powell also hoped for a quick, proper settlement of the dispute so as to avoid damaging China–US relations. Ambassador Prueher admitted that the US plane had entered China's airspace without China's authorization after the collision, but argued that the midair collision had occurred in international airspace and that, before landing, the US plane had sent out an S.O.S. signal and requested permission to land. He even claimed that, based on his years of flying planes, he could not agree with China's account of what had caused the collision, and that, as matters stood, the United States could neither accept responsibility nor apologize to China.

Ambassador Prueher also expressed the urgent wish that China could allow a further meeting between US personnel and the detained air crew, urging that they be released and the plane handed over with all possible speed.

I strongly refuted Prueher's argument, telling him that the crucial principle for handling this incident was respect for the objective facts. There was a mass of indisputable evidence showing that the incident had been completely the responsibility of the United States. In fact, the incident was a very serious political and diplomatic issue between China and the United States, rather than a technical issue, and it was wrong to oversimplify the matter to a dispute over piloting technique. The crew of the US plane that had caused the collision was military personnel who had entered China illegally and China was fully justified in investigating them according to international and Chinese laws.

I stated that China had never carried out any provocation against the United States since the establishment of diplomatic relations between the two countries, and that if either side had been guilty of provocation, it was the United States. Only two years earlier the United States bombed the Chinese embassy in Yugoslavia and now there was the destruction of a Chinese military plane. Over the past years, the United States had kept sending military reconnaissance planes close to China's coastal areas whereas China had never done the same thing off the west or east coast of the United States.

I emphasized to Prueher that China was unafraid of, and resolutely opposed to, such provocations. Over the years, facts had proved that more pressure from the United States could only provoke greater indignation on the part of the Chinese people. I requested the ambassador to report to the US government all of these representations of China and his findings in China, expressing the hope that he could play a constructive role in solving the matter.

Prueher promised to report China's requests faithfully to the US government.

On the same day, a spokesperson of China's Ministry of National Defense issued a statement clarifying the immediate cause of the air collision, backed with a wealth of supporting facts. The statement said that the United States should acknowledge full responsibility for the incident since the US reconnaissance plane, in violation of flight rules, had suddenly veered sharply toward the Chinese aircraft.

Over the next few days, Chinese people across the country expressed indignation and condemnation over the incident. The international community issued comments supporting China's stance and criticizing the US attitude. The newspaper *Nouvelles d'Europe* published a commentary denouncing the US government's hegemonistic behavior in handling the incident. America's *International Herald Tribune* carried an article pointing out that US reconnaissance flights directed against China were an insult to China. *The Australian* newspaper carried an editorial saying that "the United States should consider an apology for its surveillance plane bumping into China's fighter jet" and "the United States was engaged in spying activities."

All-Out Maritime Search for the Pilot

THROUGHOUT THE DIPLOMATIC STRUGGLE with the United States, China's concern had also been focused on the safety of the missing pilot, Wang.

Wang Wei had been an outstanding pilot and a squadron leader in the air force of the Chinese Navy. He had undergone rigorous training and was a superbly skilled aviator. Wang had often performed important flight missions and was a multiple recipient of awards for meritorious services. When executing missions, he was courageous, resolute, and calm. By April 31, 2001, he had completed 1,152 hours and 6 minutes of flying time and over two thousand flights, without incidents of negligence, oversights, or anything to indicate the possibility of an accident.

On April 1, 2001, immediately after the collision, the Chinese Navy and civilians started a full-scale search-and-rescue operation in the waters southeast of Hainan. The operation, lasting two

The Chinese military sent aircrafts and ships to search for the missing pilot in the waters southeast of Hainan Island.

weeks, involved 100,000 people and 115 flights, 113 searches by navy vessels, and 1,000 searches by fishery patrol ships.

On April 14, in consideration of all circumstances it was clear that there was zero possibility of Wang Wei having survived. That same day, the Navy committee of the Communist Party of China decided to honor Wang Wei as a revolutionary martyr. On April 16, Xinhua News Agency reported that Jiang Zemin, chairman of the Central Military Commission, had signed an order conferring upon Wang Wei the posthumous honor of Guardian of the Sea and Air.

Wang Wei's death meant the loss to China of an excellent Guardian of the Sea and Air. It also shattered the happiness of a contented family. On April 6, Wang Wei's widow, Ruan Guoqin, wrote President Bush a letter demanding justice. In his reply, the president merely expressed "regret" about the missing of her husband and "sorrow" for her pain, but offered no words of apology.

The United States Forced into a Concession

AFTER MANY ROUNDS OF resolute diplomatic struggle, the United States started to budge somewhat, shifting to a more pragmatic attitude.

On April 4, 2001, US Secretary of State Colin Powell issued a statement to the media at the US State Department expressing "regret" over the loss of the Chinese pilot. On the same day, Mr. Powell wrote Chinese Vice Premier Qian Qichen a letter in his own name, saying that the United States wished to join hands with China to put the incident behind them and move on in their bilateral relations.

The next day, in his speech at the American Society of Newspaper Editors Annual Convention, President Bush said, "I regret that a Chinese pilot is missing, and I regret one of their airplanes is lost. . . ." He said: "We should not let this incident destabilize relations. Our relationship with China is very important."

In order to make the United States fully aware of the gravity of the situation, accept its responsibility, and apologize, China had carried out hard struggles.

Between April 5 and 10, Assistant Foreign Minister Zhou Wenzhong conducted eleven rounds of tough negotiations with US Ambassador Prueher in Beijing, sometimes as many as three rounds in a single day. China insisted that the United States apologize for destroying a Chinese aircraft, causing its pilot to be missing, and for their entering China's airspace and landing at a Chinese airfield without China's authorization.

In Washington, China's Ambassador Yang Jiechi met intensively with US government officials, former important political figures, and key members of Congress, hoping that they could wield their influence and press the Bush administration to offer China an apology as soon as possible.

However, there were several outstanding challenges remaining. US public opinion showed no understanding that China's investigation of the US air crew to obtain evidence was completely legal, but claimed that China was detaining the crew members as hostages. With the US media fanning the flames, some Americans, families of the air crew in particular, were at an emotional fever pitch.

The Chinese embassy in Washington reported that the embassy and consulates had received quite a number of threatening phone calls and that organized demonstrations were happening outside. By day, yellow ribbons (symbolizing the wish for the safe return of loved ones) could often be seen tied to the trunks of trees nearby. By night, some Americans held candles and overnight prayer vigils outside the gate of the embassy. Some even blocked the way of Chinese diplomats in the street and shouted hysterically, "Why don't you let our people come home?" Certain anti-China forces in the

United States were restless, about to seize the opportunity to damage China-US relations.

Under such circumstances, Ambassador Yang Jiechi gave an interview to CNN. He explained the truth and made plain the Chinese position, trying to influence US public opinion by means of facts and reasoning. Ambassador Yang drew an analogy of the incident, to make it more understandable. He said that if a gang of people was always hanging around outside your gate, one of your family members would go out to check. However, if it turned out that your car was destroyed and a member of your family was unaccounted for, you surely had the right to find out what had happened and ask those people for an apology. This would be of great importance to your family. Ambassador Yang hoped that the American people would make their own fair judgment on the matter.

The broadcast interview had a positive impact on US public opinion. According to media reports, following Ambassador Yang's CNN interview, the proportion of Americans in favor of its government apologizing to China grew by a large margin, from less than 20 percent to above 50 percent. Families of the US air crew said they would support an apology to China if it could bring their people home.

Six Drafts of the US Letter of Apology

UNDER OUR SUSTAINED PRESSURE, the United States reluctantly began to give way.

On the evening of April 5, 2001, US Ambassador Prueher sent a letter to our Foreign Ministry addressed to me and in his own name, as a letter of apology from the US government to China.

We had suggested three requirements to the United States regarding a letter of apology about the air collision: One, the United

States must give an appropriately worded apology for the collision, for the loss of the Chinese pilot and aircraft, and for the US plane entering China's airspace and landing at a Chinese airport without China's authorization; two, the United States must admit that its plane had entered China's airspace without China's authorization; three, the United States should express gratitude for China's proper arrangements for the US air crew.

However, the first draft only casually mentioned "concern" for the missing pilot and failed to meet our two other requirements. China of course could not accept the letter. We immediately criticized the United States for lack of sincerity and pointed out that the letter could by no means serve as a basis for negotiation and that, unless the United States apologized, there would no need for further contact between the two sides.

In the light of our resolute attitude, the United States had to soften its stance again, and expressed its willingness to discuss revising the wording of the letter to satisfy our requests.

On the morning of April 6, the United States handed in the second draft. In this letter, the United States expressed regret for Wang Wei's family, friends, and colleagues, but claimed that the US government could not apologize for what they termed the "accident." Faced with this obstinate attitude, China rejected this letter too.

In view of the United States' reluctance to give China the apology demanded, on April 6, President Jiang Zemin issued a statement regarding the air collision during his state visit to Chile. President Jiang pointed out that the United States should apologize to the Chinese people for its reconnaissance plane colliding with and destroying a Chinese fighter, and that the leaders of the two countries should resolve the matter in the interests of their bilateral relations.

Vice Premier Qian Qichen stated clearly in his letter of reply to US Secretary of State Colin Powell that the United States ought to accept its responsibility, apologize to the Chinese people, and negotiate with China on how to avoid the recurrence of similar incidents. Vice Premier Qian added that respect for the facts and a positive, pragmatic attitude on the part of the United States were crucial to a prompt settlement of the matter.

China's firm stance, further strengthened by clear-cut statements by China's leaders, added to the pressure on the United States.

On the evening of April 6, the United States submitted the third draft letter and claimed that no further changes would be accepted, since US President Bush had approved the letter.

Although the third version showed some improvement, it still fell far short of what China had demanded. Therefore, on the morning of April 7, we again questioned the content of the letter and required the United States to rewrite it. We made it clear that China would never accept the letter if the United States did not revise it in line with our suggestions.

The United States had no choice but to revise its letter once more, and handed in the fourth draft that same afternoon. This version followed China's demand for an apology to the Chinese people, but on the condition that China should allow the United States plane to leave China no later than May 7. The United States actually had the nerve to impose conditions on us!

After studying the latest letter of apology, we agreed that the United States had made substantial concessions, but that the letter was still some distance from meeting China's demands. Furthermore, their demands and conditions were unacceptable. We decided to negotiate with the United States again.

On April 8, Assistant Foreign Minister Zhou Wenzhong conducted two negotiation sessions with Ambassador Prueher. Zhou required the United States to make further changes to its letter so as to meet China's demands in full and with no conditions attached.

Ambassador Prueher promised to report China's demands to the US government. That same evening, the United States submitted the fifth draft letter and used the expression "very sorry" to intensify the tone. In this letter, the United States also admitted that the US plane had entered China's airspace without China's authorization and acknowledged China's proper arrangements for the US air crew. The condition that "China should allow the US plane to depart China no later than May 7" was deleted.

The fifth letter met China's demands on the whole. Later that evening, the United States made further changes to some expressions in the letter as required by China and handed in the sixth version of the letter of apology.

The issue of apology lay at the heart of the struggle concerning the air collision incident. Therefore, appropriate wording for apology became an important and sensitive matter. In my view it was not simply a matter of semantics or rhetoric, but a political issue for history. So, I instructed the Department of North American and Oceanian Affairs of the Foreign Ministry to consult senior English-language experts on English expressions of apology.

Mr. Qiu Ke'an, honorary council member of the Translators Association of China, was then the most authoritative English expert in the Foreign Ministry, in addition to being one of the most famous translators in China. Mr. Qiu, already in his eighties, had a thorough knowledge of both Chinese and Western culture. An accomplished translator, he had long worked as a senior editor on the English translations of important state documents and diplomatic files, including *Selected Works of Mao Zedong*.

Mr. Qiu Ke'an and a few other English-language experts played an important role in judging the meaning and connotations of English expressions of apology.

After serious studies, the experts concluded that the Chinese phrase *dao qian* had but one clear, unambiguous meaning of expressing apology. According to the *Contemporary Chinese Dictionary*, *dao* means "express" and *qian* "feeling bad for having done something wrong to others." So *dao qian*, together, means to express such feeling.

English, on the other hand, has many expressions of apology. According to our language experts, the three most frequently used words were "apologize," "sorry," and "regret," with "apologize" as the most formal and "regret" the weakest in tone.

Two authoritative English dictionaries, *Oxford Advanced Learner's Dictionary* and *Webster's Encyclopedic Unabridged Dictionary of the English Language,* each said that "sorry" can be used to mean apologize.

Moreover, they concluded that *sorry* was certainly an expression of apology when used between governments of two countries, and was usually modified by *very* or *deeply* to intensify the tone.

Sadly, Mr. Qiu Ke'an passed away in August 2008 at the age of eighty-eight. I felt deeply grieved by the sad news and sent his family a funeral wreath in my own name and a telegram of condolences as an expression of my heartfelt grief and respect. I paid final respects to Mr. Qiu at the ceremony held by the Foreign Ministry at the Beijing Hospital.

Follow-Up to the Apology

HAVING REACHED CONSENSUS ON the content of the US letter of apology, the two sides agreed that on April 11, 2001, US Ambassador Joseph Prueher would, on behalf of the US government, formally hand over the letter to me as representative of the Chinese government.

Thanks to our arduous efforts, important progress was made in our initial diplomatic struggle by forcing the United States to meet all our demands and formally hand over a letter of apology. For the occasion, I chose to wear a dark suit. Even today, the memory of the handover remains fresh in my mind.

Beforehand, the US embassy had, of their own accord, provided the text of the apology letter to the Ministry's Department of North American and Oceanian Affairs for checking, and attached a letter guaranteeing that the content of the letter to be handed over to the Chinese would be exactly the same.

At five-thirty on April 11, Ambassador Prueher arrived at our ministry at the appointed time. In the Olive Hall, I received the letter of apology signed by him on behalf of the US government.

Ambassador Prueher first gave me a letter from US Secretary of State Colin Powell to Chinese Vice Premier Qian Qichen. This stated that Ambassador Prueher had been fully empowered by US President Bush as the plenipotentiary representative of the US government and had full authority to sign the letter.

After that, Ambassador Prueher formally handed me a letter of apology, the text of which said, "both President Bush and Secretary of State Powell have expressed their sincere regret over your missing pilot and aircraft. Please convey to the Chinese people and to the family of pilot Wang Wei that we are very sorry for their loss." It went on to say that it was "very sorry that the entering of China's air space and the landing did not have verbal clearance." The words "very sorry" were used twice. The letter also expressed its appreciation of "China's efforts to see to the well being" of its crew. Having received the letter, I told Ambassador Prueher that I noted that the US government had twice used the words "very sorry" in the letter. I pointed out that the United States should understand the seriousness of the incident and that the actions of the US military reconnaissance plane had seriously violated both international law and the provisions of relevant laws of China, and had broken the consensus reached by China and the United States in May 2000 on avoiding dangerous maritime military activities. The US plane had intruded into China's territorial airspace and encroached upon China's sovereignty, thus posing a threat to China's national security. It was entirely justified for China to demand a US apology to the Chinese people.

Despite the indignation of the Chinese government and people at the air collision incident, I told him, the Chinese side had, in the overall interests of China-US relations, all along handled this incident with calmness and restraint and in accordance with international law and relevant legal provisions of China. The Chinese side had, out of humanitarian considerations, treated the twenty-four air crew well and had arranged for them to meet with US diplomatic and consular officers several times. I noted that the US letter had expressed appreciation to China for all this. I formally notified Ambassador Prueher that the Chinese side understood the eagerness of the American people and the families of the crew to see the early return of the crew members and their reunion with their families. In view of the apologies offered by the US government to the Chinese people, the Chinese government had, out of humanitarian considerations, decided to allow the crew members to leave China once the necessary procedures had been completed.

Having heard my statement, Ambassador Prueher seemed to heave a sigh of relief. Seeing that, I decided to give him one more knock.

This was not the conclusion of the case, I told him, and the two sides should continue with negotiations on this and other related matters. The Chinese government and people demanded that the United States provide convincing explanations to the Chinese people on this incident, stop sending aircraft to the vicinity of the Chinese coast for reconnaissance activities, and take effective measures to avoid the recurrence of similar incidents. The United States must fully understand the gravity of the incident, take China's solemn stance very seriously, and properly handle this incident. It must not make any erroneous judgments that could further damage bilateral relations.

I finally stressed, "China's sovereignty, territorial integrity, and national dignity brook no infringement. It has been China's consistent position that state-to-state relations, including China-US relations, must be based on such basic norms governing international relations as mutual respect for sovereignty and territorial integrity, mutual nonaggression, and noninterference in each other's internal affairs. The Chinese side attaches importance to China–US relations. To develop friendly relations and cooperation between China and the United States serves the interests of both countries and the world at large. It is hoped that the United States will strictly abide by the three China–US Joint Communiqués and the basic norms governing international relations and refrain from doing anything more to impair bilateral relations. The United States should take a constructive attitude and work with the Chinese side to bring the bilateral relations onto the track of normal development." Ambassador Prueher listened to me carefully, without raising any argument, and said he would immediately report China's position and decision to the US government and Secretary of State Powell.

The US Crew Return Home

ON APRIL 12, 2001, at Meilan International Airport, Haikou, China, transferred to the US side the twenty-four crew members of the EP-3 reconnaissance aircraft. They were allowed to leave China from Haikou on board a commercial plane chartered by the US government. It was two days before Easter Sunday.

We had been considerate and reasonable in treating the US crew. However, on returning home, some of them complained that they had been subjected to strict surveillance and long interrogation, like hostages. They mistook their own status. They should have known they were neither tourists nor honored guests but intruders. They were US intelligence personnel who had posed a threat to China's national security and sovereignty, who had caused a Chinese military aircraft to crash and the death of a Chinese pilot. We had every right to set necessary constraints on them and to demand that they cooperate in the investigation.

Even so, out of humanitarian considerations and in accordance with the relevant provisions of the China-US Consular Treaty, we had arranged five meetings of the crew with US diplomatic and consular officers, let them call their homes, and keep in touch with their families by email, and passed on to them daily necessities provided by the United States. After the crew returned, President Bush acknowledged that "they are in good health, they suffered no injuries, and they have not been mistreated."

During the handling of the incident, our friends in the government of Hainan Province, especially those of the Foreign Affairs Office of the provincial government, made an important contribution. Chen Ci, head of the office, acted as the spokesman and kept in close touch with the media. His smart remarks, such as "The Hainan people welcome US visitors, but not US spy planes," were picked up and widely spread by the media.

As the US government had said "very sorry," the Chinese government decided, out of humanitarian considerations, to allow the air crew to leave China, a decision that won broad understanding and support in China. In the opinion of most international media, despite the negative impact on China-US relations brought about by the collision incident, it would not affect the overall bilateral relations, thanks to the calm, reasonable, and flexible handling of the case by the two sides through diplomatic channels.

Fruitful results have been achieved in the initial phase of our diplomatic contest. However, it was not the end; the next task was how to handle the issue of the US aircraft.

US Arrogance Deflated

STARTING IN MID-APRIL, THE Chinese delegation, headed by Lu Shumin, director-general of the North American and Oceanian Affairs Department of the Foreign Ministry, and the US delegation headed by Peter F. Verga, deputy under secretary of Defense, held repeated negotiations in Beijing concerning the handling of the US military aircraft.

Apparently, the US State Department and the Defense Department had different opinions regarding how the incident should be handled, and they vied with each other to be the lead player. When discussing the crew issue, the State Department was in charge. When it came to the aircraft, it was the Defense Department that took the lead. So this time, the US delegation consisted mainly of officers from the Department of Defense and the US Pacific Command, with only two officials from the State Department.

Having had no previous contact with China, these people assumed an arrogant air from the outset, their habitual attitude when dealing with other countries. Some even bragged of cases where US planes had made a forced landing on the territories of others, and the latter had compliantly handed back the planes and even had to refuel the plane for the United States.

They began the negotiations by accusing the Chinese side of being responsible for the collision, demanded that their aircraft be returned promptly, and that US personnel be allowed to examine and repair it. They also fallaciously defended US military reconnaissance flights off China's coast. Furthermore, they even did an about-face on certain specific issues that had been nearly solved or concluded by the two sides in the previous stage of negotiations.

On our side, we used reason to refute their fallacy, and we had to repeat what we had said in previous negotiations. Our negotiators reminded them that they must fully understand the seriousness of the incident, take a pragmatic and constructive attitude, and respond positively to the demands of the Chinese side, in the interest of finding a proper solution to the incident. Otherwise, there would be no point in continuing the talks.

Having deflated their arrogance, we proceeded to negotiate in earnest. Between April 23 and 27, 2001, Assistant Foreign Minister

Zhou Wenzhong conducted several rounds of informal talks with Ambassador Prueher. The two sides agreed to the United States sending a technical assessment group to Hainan in order to examine the plane at Lingshui Airfield. Subsequently, further rounds of negotiations were held on the return of the plane.

EP-3 Disassembled

ON MAY 10, 2001, the US technical assessment group finished their examination and asked to send US technicians to China to undertake repairs so that the plane could fly back from Hainan in one piece.

Just three days earlier, the United States had outrageously resumed its reconnaissance flights off China's coast, the first time since the collision. Chinese fighters immediately took off to track and monitor the American planes. In such circumstances, the United States was going too far in asking us to allow their plane to fly back to United States after repair.

Their demand was firmly rejected by the Chinese side.

The United States did not give up. They argued repeatedly that repairing and flying the plane back was the most convenient solution, saying that they would allow Chinese personnel to board the plane to monitor and prevent the reconnaissance devices from being started and, to meet China's security concerns, they would cut or dismantle the power supply to devices irrelevant to flying the plane. They also warned that delaying return of the plane would harm US–China relations.

We insisted that repairing and flying back the plane in one piece was out of the question.

We stressed that given the nature of the plane, the manner of its return was not just a technical problem, but a political issue with symbolic significance. The Chinese people would never agree to let the plane be repaired and leave China as if nothing had happened.

We told the Americans to cast away their illusions and consider other ways to transport their plane home.

We also pointed out that it was wrong to link the plane's return to other issues in China-US relations. The United States should take a pragmatic and cooperative approach to bring this issue to an early and proper resolution.

The plane, which had landed at Lingshui Airfield, had to be transported some 200 kilometers to Haikou Airport if it were to leave China. If it remained intact, the giant EP-3, measuring thirty-five meters long, ten meters high, with a wingspan of thirty meters, would not be able to leave Lingshui by either land or sea. The narrowness of the tunnel on the land route to Haikou meant the plane could not get through in one piece and, as for the sea option, a new road would first have to be built to transport the plane to the ship, and the United States would have to foot the bill for its construction.

In the end, and after much thought, the Americans had to suggest getting the plane disassembled and then transported by a commercial Antonov-124 cargo plane chartered from a Russian airline. We agreed to their plan and expressed our willingness to provide the necessary assistance.

During this period, Hainan was experiencing very changeable weather: scorching sun followed by gloomy rain with the prospect of typhoons. The US plane lying in the Chinese airfield lost its arrogance while waiting to be dismantled.

On June 15, 2001, the twelve American technicians sent to carry out the dismantling work arrived at Sanya's Phoenix International Airport.

The following day, the Antonov-124 flew to Lingshui, carrying forklift trucks, a crane, toolboxes, and packing equipment necessary for the disassembly. It took five deliveries to get all the equipment and devices to Lingshui.

The work began on June 18 and continued until noon on June 29.

The Antonov-124 transported the disassembled landing gear, antenna, and wings in separate consignments back to the United States.

On July 3, the Antonov-124 left Lingshui Airfield with its tenth and final load, carrying the EP-3 fuselage, the reconnaissance devices, and some of the dismantling equipment. One hour later, the US technicians left Lingshui and, the next morning, they left China from Sanya aboard a special plane provided by the United States, thus concluding the dismantling and transportation of the US EP-3 reconnaissance plane.

During the dismantling process an unexpected hitch occurred. Once the work had begun, a small number of foreign reporters came to Sanya. Though both sides had agreed to keep the work secret and to refuse media interviews, photos of the disassembly work soon appeared on the Internet, and kept on being updated as the work progressed. Clearly someone on the spot had photographed the work, and we had to remind the US team of the need for self-discipline to prevent any similar recurrences.

Postconfrontation Turn for the Better

DESPITE THE INCIDENT'S IMPACT on China-US relations, the two sides had to look to the future from the long-term view, so as to maintain the sound and stable progress of their relations.

I too was reflecting on how to earnestly promote improvement in China-US relations following the proper settlement of the incident and felt that a closer relationship with US Secretary of State Powell might be helpful in achieving this.

Colin Luther Powell took office as US Secretary of State on January 20, 2001, the first African-American in history to hold such a post. I sent him a telegraph of congratulations on his being appointed secretary of state by President Bush in December 2000.

I had never met him in person, but I knew of his fame in the United States. Born in the United States of Jamaican immigrant parents, he had joined the US Army and fought twice in the Vietnam War. He had held such posts as national security advisor in the Reagan administration, chairman of the Joint Chiefs of Staff under President Bush and President Clinton, and had retired as a four-star general. He was looked on as a hero by Americans for his performance in the first Gulf War.

In the eyes of the American media and some experts and scholars, Mr. Powell was a mild and pragmatic person in the Bush administration, and held a generally positive attitude toward the development of US-China relations.

At that time, despite the impact of the collision incident on bilateral relations, in the broader aspect our two countries shared common interests in many significant international and regional issues and needed to cooperate with each other. Hence, we maintained exchanges and coordination. Even during the handling of the incident, Mr. Powell and I had twice written to each other on the Iraq issue.

In diplomacy, struggle and cooperation go along in parallel. One should struggle when struggle is necessary, and cooperate when cooperation is necessary. One should not refuse cooperation because struggle is going on, nor give up struggle because cooperation is needed. Both struggle and cooperation are means to achieve the basic goal, namely safeguarding one's national interests.

On June 28, 2001, the United States notified us of Mr. Powell's intention to discuss the Iraq issue with me on the telephone. That was my first phone conversation with him.

Nowadays, direct person-to-person calls between leaders are ordinary practices, but a decade ago, telephone diplomacy was uncommon. Most diplomatic exchanges and communication were conducted via written letters and formal notes or via resident envoys. Leaders seldom called other leaders, except on important occasions. So, I knew I should grasp this rare opportunity to persuade Powell to go further in bilateral relations.

After a brief exchange of greetings, Mr. Powell came straight to the point. He said the United States hoped that China would support the US-proposed "Goods Review List" against Iraq, and that China would take a positive stand at the UN Security Council.

I explained China's principled stand regarding the Iraq issue. Then I went on to talk about China-US relations.

I said although China-US relations had encountered some difficulties earlier, China attached great importance to its relations with the United States and hoped to develop constructive cooperation with the United States. China was willing to work with the United States to make good preparations for the meeting of the two heads of state during the APEC Informal Leadership Meeting to be held in Shanghai that coming October, and for President Bush's visit to Beijing, so as to promote sound and steady development of bilateral relations.

My remarks met a positive response from Mr. Powell. He expressed his complete agreement and willingness to stay in close contact with me. He added that the recent difficulty in bilateral relations was now over and that he would be delighted to hold talks with me during the Foreign Ministers' Meeting of ASEAN Regional Forum (ARF) in Hanoi in July and that he looked forward to accompanying President Bush on his visit to China that coming fall.

In March that year, during Vice Premier Qian Qichen's visit to the United States, Mr. Powell had accepted an invitation to visit China. I underlined how we looked forward to welcoming him in China after the meeting in Hanoi, and he reaffirmed his pleased acceptance of our invitation.

Conforming to the Trend of the Times

THE FOURTH OF JULY is Independence Day, a US national holiday.

On June 29, the day after my telephone conversation with Mr. Powell, President Bush held a reception at the White House to which the ambassadors to the United States and their spouses were invited. At the reception, the president told Ambassador Yang Jiechi that he would call Chinese President Jiang Zemin immediately upon the return of the US aircraft.

This was an important signal. Mr. Yang immediately reported it to the authorities at home. Now that China–US relations had improved and the dismantling operation was nearly finished, we responded positively to the US suggestion.

On July 5, President Jiang spoke with President Bush on the phone upon request. This was the first exchange of telephone calls between the two heads of state after President Bush took office, and also their first direct communication after the collision incident.

President Bush first thanked President Jiang for sending a telegram of congratulations on US Independence Day, for agreeing to the telephone call, and for inviting him to visit China.

President Jiang said that China–US relations had earlier encountered difficulties, but bilateral relations had now improved thanks to positive steps taken recently by both sides. He had noted the president's frequently expressed readiness to build a constructive relationship with China and stressed that the Chinese government and people attached importance to China–US relations and wished for a constructive and cooperative relationship.

President Jiang pointed out that both China and the United States were influential states in the world, sharing great responsibilities for world peace and development. The existence of differences of one kind or another between the two countries was nothing strange, and they should work together for the stable development of bilateral relations on the basis of the three China–US joint communiqués.

President Bush said that US–China relations were of utmost importance and that there should be a frank exchange of views between the two countries. He said China was a great and important nation, and that he respected China, its history, and future. The United States and China could find wide areas for cooperation. He had always been a strong advocate of China's entry into the WTO, because that served the interests of both China and the United States. The two countries could work together on many international issues.

He again thanked President Jiang for inviting him to attend the APEC Informal Leadership Meeting that October in Shanghai and to visit Beijing thereafter. He was looking forward to having frank and fruitful talks with President Jiang.

This phone call delivered a clear and positive message to the public: China and the United States shared important common interests; the two sides were ready to strengthen dialogue and exchange, pushing bilateral relations back on the track of normal development at an early date.

First Meeting with Powell in Hanoi

AFTER THE PHONE CALL between the two leaders, in the interest of improving bilateral relations, both sides intensified preparations for the meeting in Hanoi of their foreign ministers, which had been in the offing for some time. As the first high-level direct contact since President Bush took office, and since the air collision, the meeting was bound to attract wide attention. It would also be my first meeting with Mr. Powell.

I took the meeting seriously and made careful preparations for it.

At that time, the United States had a sense of anxiety that its presence in the Asia–Pacific region would be impacted as a result of China's increasing influence in the world, especially in Asia, together with its growing overall strength and close relationship with the ASEAN countries. Some scholars even asserted that China was intending to squeeze the United States out of the Asia–Pacific region. With regard to their anxiety, I decided to give him a positive explanation of China's policies toward the Asia–Pacific region.

The Eighth ARF took place in Hanoi, Vietnam, from July 24 to 27, 2001, and on the afternoon of July 25, I met with Mr. Powell at the Daewoo Hotel.

He was taller and more robust than I had imagined. He wore a dark gray suit. He was solidly built and agile in movement, with the bearing of a veteran soldier.

We exchanged views on China–US relations, human rights, nuclear nonproliferation, and other issues.

I said that China–US relations were at a critical stage. After a period of difficulties, improvement and progress had recently been made thanks to the endeavors of the two sides. China had handled the collision incident with a forward-looking approach. The Chinese government had consistently held that the development of constructive and cooperative China–US relations was in the fundamental interests of the two peoples, and vital to peace and stability in the Asia–Pacific region and the world at large.

Then I switched topics and said that despite the great changes in the international situation, issues of common interests between us were on the rise rather than disappearing, and that areas for cooperation were expanding rather than shrinking. Our two countries had no reason to be enemies or adversaries. I knew that some Americans thought China was trying to squeeze the United States out of

Asia, but this view was groundless and at variance with the facts. We welcomed the United States playing a positive role in maintaining peace and stability in the Asia–Pacific region and were willing to strengthen cooperation with the United States.

Mr. Powell expressed his agreement and appreciation of these views, describing the EP-3 and other issues as bygones. It was time for both sides to look ahead and push bilateral relations forward. He also said that President Bush was looking forward to his China visit and that, even during the collision incident, the president had not dropped his plan to visit China, because he hoped and believed that the incident would be over.

On a subsequent occasion, Mr. Powell told me that he found my remarks very refreshing, and that it was the first time he had heard a Chinese senior official talking this way.

In fact, I was by no means the first to do so. Academics as well as Chinese officials had expressed these views. Mr. Powell's reaction made me realize that if we could grasp the opportunity for increased contact and purposeful communications, we could achieve the benefit of enhanced trust and reduced apprehension.

It was a good dialogue spread over one hour and more on the sidelines of the 8th ARF. Since we both had tight schedules, our meeting had to conclude, even though there was still much to be said. Mr. Powell told me he was looking forward to his upcoming China visit, and I said that I too was looking forward to talking with him in greater depth in Beijing.

A Second Meeting in Beijing

FOLLOWING THE ARF MEETING in Hanoi, Mr. Powell visited China from July 28 to 29. He was the highest official from the Bush administration to visit China thus far.

It was a whirlwind visit. July 28 was Saturday and his itinerary was packed. Besides meeting with senior Chinese leaders and me, he had also agreed to be interviewed at the US embassy by China Central Television and to meet the media at the St. Regis Hotel, where he was staying. Despite such tight arrangements, he showed not a trace of weariness.

President Jiang Zemin, Premier Zhu Rongji, and Vice Premier Qian Qichen each had a meeting with Mr. Powell, and expounded China's views on Sino-US relations from different perspectives. They stressed that, given the rich diversity of the world, it's not surprising that there exist differences between the two countries on some issues; the important thing was mutual respect and the search for common interests, while reserving the differences. Their message was that China attached great importance to China-US relations and hoped to work with the United States to develop constructive and cooperative relations on the basis of the three Sino-US joint communiqués.

On the morning of July 28, I met with Mr. Powell at the Diaoyutai State Guesthouse. The focus was still on bilateral relations. Since we had just talked in Hanoi, I thought long and hard about what to say and how to say it on this occasion.

In addition to expounding our principled stance on the development of bilateral relations, I thought I should urge the United States to take a positive attitude toward China-US relations in the twenty-first century from a strategic height, abandon the concept of strategic competitor, and join us in pushing forward bilateral relations.

At the meeting, I first extended our welcome to Mr. Powell for his visit to China and expressed the great importance attached by the Chinese government to China-US relations. Then I quoted President Jiang's sixteen-character guiding principles regarding the development of China-US relations, and had an in-depth exchange of views with Mr. Powell.

Meeting US Secretary of State Colin Powell on July 28, 2001.

The sixteen-character guiding principles of "enhancing trust, reducing trouble, developing cooperation, and avoiding confrontation" were first proposed by President Jiang Zemin in November 1992 when he received a visiting US Congress delegation. In 1993, he reiterated the sixteen-character guiding principles in a written message to US President Clinton. On April 5, 1993, President Clinton wrote two letters on the same day to President Jiang, one of thanks for his counterpart's congratulation letter on his election as US president, and one extending his own congratulations on Jiang's election as Chinese president. President Jiang promptly sent a verbal message to Clinton, saying that the two countries shared extensive common interests despite their different social systems and ideologies, and that the interests of the people of China and the United States, as well as the rest of the world, required that the two powers proceed from the overall international situation, viewing and handling bilateral relations via a long-term perspective. It was in this message that President Jiang raised the above principles. It played an important role in urging the newly established Clinton administration to look at China–US relations objectively, and be pragmatic in its dealings with China.

I stressed to Mr. Powell that these principles outlined by President Jiang still had practical significance for handling China–US relations, given the broader prospects for expanding bilateral exchanges and cooperation in the new century.

I told him that we knew that some US opinions advocated different policies regarding China. We appreciated how President Bush and Mr. Powell personally had reiterated that "the United States is willing to build constructive relations with China." Our own attitude had remained consistent and unchanged, namely that China was not, and had no intention of being, an enemy of the United States, and that we wished to join the United States in an effort to develop a constructive and cooperative relationship on the basis of the three Sino-US joint communiqués. Such a goal was in the interests of both countries and conducive to peace, stability, and prosperity of the world.

I pointed out that the two countries were facing new opportunities, as well as challenges in developing bilateral relations. The meeting between President Jiang Zemin and President Bush in the coming fall during the APEC Shanghai meeting, and President Bush's subsequent visit to China, would be of great significance to the direction of Sino-US relations in the new century. I expressed the hope that both sides would work together closely in making a success of the summit meeting and President Bush's first China tour.

Mr. Powell said that despite the ups and downs, the US-China relationship had gone forward on the whole; the two countries shared extensive common interests and had plenty of reasons to cooperate. Their relationship was both rich and complex, and could not be oversimplified as competitors or partners. The United States did not view China in a confrontational way.

He told me that the United States did not need, nor seek, an enemy, but hoped to build friendly relations with all countries, including China. The United States and China shared common views on some points and differed on others. The two countries were great nations and proud of their histories. He was confident that the two countries could find ways to solve their differences based on their common interests. He said President Bush was looking forward to his China tour scheduled in October and was coming with a positive and friendly attitude.

I could see how excited he was about his visit. He told me that he was impressed by the vigor and vitality in Beijing, and the tremendous changes compared to what he had seen on his last visit there as a military officer some twenty years ago. He congratulated the Chinese government and people on the great changes, and congratulated Beijing on winning the right to host the 2008 Olympic Games.

Mr. Powell invited me to visit Washington after attending the September UN General Assembly meeting in New York, and I accepted his invitation with gratitude.

Mr. Powell's statements during his visit made me feel that the United States had come to some new realizations about China-US relations, as they no longer labeled China a strategic competitor. This left scope for more constructive cooperation between our two countries.

Following Powell's visit to China, China-US relations had come out of a difficult situation caused by the collision incident, and we saw the emergence of a positive trend of improvement and development.

I met with Mr. Powell on several subsequent occasions. I was deeply impressed by his in-depth perspective and strategic vision on international issues and on China-US relations.

Since then, I have maintained a friendly working and personal relationship with him.

Visiting Washington in the Wake of 9/11

THE TERRORIST ATTACKS OF September 11, 2001, shocked the whole world. The World Trade Center buildings in New York collapsed amid terrified screaming, and several thousand people perished in the collapse and the fires.

The attacks of 9/11 left an indelible shadow in the hearts of all Americans. They also brought about tremendous changes in US foreign policy and concepts as well as in the international political situation. Looking back, it is no exaggeration to say that 9/11 has changed the United States and the world as a whole.

Ten days after the attacks, I paid a formal visit to the United States on September 20 and 21 at the invitation of Secretary of State Powell, before attending the 56th UN General Assembly meeting. It was the first US visit by a Chinese foreign minister following the Bush assumption of the US presidency.

By that time, China–US relations had seen some improvement, and high-level visits had gradually resumed. Through my visit, we hoped to strengthen contacts and interaction with the United States, promote further improvement in bilateral relations, and, specifically, to make political preparations for the meeting in Shanghai between the two heads of state and for the subsequent visit of President Bush to China.

During my visit, I held talks with Mr. Powell, and had meetings with President Bush, Vice President Cheney, National Security Advisor Rice, and some members of the US Congress. I expounded China's principled position on China–US relations, and exchanged opinions on the summit meeting and President Bush's visit to China. I expressed my belief that the summit and visit would strongly promote the advancement of China–US relations, and hoped the two sides would strengthen consultation and cooperation in our preparations.

Just ten days had passed since the events of 9/11. I made clear the position of the Chinese government on fighting terrorism, stating the Chinese government's consistent opposition to and condemnation of all forms of terrorist activities, and China's readiness to work with the United States and the international community to strengthen antiterrorism cooperation. The United States appreciated the Chinese position, thanked China for its sympathy and support in the wake of the 9/11 attacks, and hoped to strengthen consultation and cooperation in the fight against terrorism.

During my visit, I had extensive contacts with people from many walks of life. I made a speech at the banquet sponsored by friendship organizations, gave an interview to the *Washington Post*, and met with family members of the Chinese citizens who had died in the terrorist attacks, as well as with representatives of overseas Chinese. On these occasions, I gave a brief account of China's achievements following its reform and opening up, China's foreign policies, and our views on China-US relations and bilateral cooperation in fighting terrorism.

Before leaving Washington, I exchanged views with Ambassador Yang Jiechi and we agreed that 9/11 had forced the United States into a major foreign policy readjustment, and brought about a significant turning point for improving and developing China-US relations. We should grasp these opportunities and do a good job of advancing the sound and steady progress of bilateral relations.

Judging from subsequent reactions, it was a successful visit that created a positive atmosphere and conditions for a successful meeting between the two heads of state.

Following the events of 9/11, the United States' need for antiterrorism cooperation greatly increased, and it also accelerated the improvement of relations with China.

In October 2001, President Jiang Zemin and President Bush held talks during the APEC Informal Leadership Meeting in

Shanghai. They reached important consensus on building constructive cooperation and charted the direction for the China–US relationship.

In February 2002, President Bush paid a visit to China. Subsequently, as visits by leaders of our two countries increased, China–US relations got onto the right track of improvement and development.

Benefits of the Diplomatic Solution

SHORTLY AFTER THE AIR collision, former US Secretary of State Henry Kissinger wrote in *Newsweek* that confrontation with China should be a last resort, not the strategic choice.

When interviewed by *USA Today* in October 2004, Mr. Powell said that "with clever use of words and understanding one another's needs and positions, we not only were able to solve the problem . . . but we created the basis of talking to one another and how we should work with one another to resolve such problems

January 2009, meeting Dr. Kissinger during the seminar commemorating the thirtieth anniversary of the establishment of Sino–US diplomatic relations.

in the future. And we've been following that model for the last three and a half years, and it has put our relationship with China, I think, on the solidest foundation it has been for the 30-odd years of relationship." Later, he expressed his satisfaction at the resolution of the collision crisis through diplomatic channels, and his pride in the stability and improvement of US-China relations.

These remarks reveal the farsightedness of these two former US secretaries of state in their views about China-US relations.

In July 2006, Mr. Powell, then retired, visited China at the invitation of the Chinese People's Institute of Foreign Affairs. I met and arranged a banquet for him at the Yangquan Zhai (Sources Preservation Studio) in the Diaoyutai State Guesthouse. The Sources Preservation Studio is a complex of gardens and buildings in classical style. Mr. Powell showed great interest in the garden's classical rock arrangements and ponds, and the precious relics displayed inside the buildings. We also had our photos taken in front of the main hall.

I had planned the banquet menu to suit his taste. At the age of sixty-nine, Mr. Powell still looked as full of energy and moved as briskly as he had done at our first meeting. Clearly he felt more relaxed on this occasion, compared with the official meetings as secretary of state.

During the banquet, he again touched upon the collision incident. He said in all seriousness that since it had occurred in the very early days of the Bush administration, had we failed to handle it well, it might have blown up into a crisis between our two countries. But, thanks to our joint efforts, we had managed to turn danger into safety. The two sides' handling of the incident had been positive and effective. Despite differences and frictions, so long as China and the United States handled things properly in the spirit of friendship and cooperation, US-China relations would continue to develop.

Eight years have passed since the air collision. Looking back, we can say that the Ministry of Foreign Affairs and relevant departments, under the correct leadership of the Central Authority, had combined firm principles with flexible tactics and conducted the collision dispute with the United States on just grounds, to our benefit and with restraint. As a result, we succeeded in safeguarding China's state sovereignty, national dignity, and basic interests, and produced a timely shift of direction and improvement in China-US relations, an improvement conducive to maintaining and prolonging a period of strategic opportunities for China.

The handling of the collision incident shows that when managing important bilateral relations like those between China and the United States, we must see the bigger picture and take a long-term view. This is because our two countries both have enormous influence in the world and because global peace and prosperity need a long-term, stable relationship. The two sides should always view and handle bilateral relations from a strategic height and a long-term perspective, not distracted by individual sporadic incidents, and should strive to ensure that bilateral relations move forward along the path of constructive cooperation.

China-US relations have weathered the passage of thirty years. On January 12, 2009, the two sides organized events commemorating the thirtieth anniversary of the establishment of China-US diplomatic relations.

I attended and delivered a speech at the opening ceremony in Beijing of the seminar commemorating the thirtieth anniversary of the establishment of diplomatic relations between China and the United States. Before the meeting, I came across former US Ambassador Joseph Prueher in a lounge. He looked little changed and as strong as ever. We shook hands warmly and exchanged greetings.

In my speech, I said with emotion that, despite some unexpected incidents, including the air collision, China-US relations had in general maintained steady progress thanks to the efforts of both sides. This was the result of the endeavors of the leaders and the diligent work of people from many sections of society in our two countries, and we should all the more value this situation because it had been so hard earned.

Eight years have elapsed since the incident. Overall, the two terms of President Bush could be described as a period of steady development in China-US relations. For China, these eight years have meant a precious period of strategic opportunities. During this period we have grasped the opportunity and concentrated on development.

Today, China's overall national strength is growing, and its international status is on the rise. The China-US relationship today is beyond comparison to that of eight years ago, as is the importance of China in US foreign relations.

In the future, problems of one kind or another will crop up in China-US relations, and the US government's China policies will also see readjustments or changes of one kind or another. However, so long as we can learn from previous experience and continue to strengthen our dialogues, exchanges, and cooperation, expand the

January 12, 2009, addressing the seminar commemorating the thirtieth anniversary of the establishment of Sino-US diplomatic relations.

sphere of common interests, fully respect and take into account each other's core interests and important concerns, and properly handle our differences and sensitive issues in a calm and pragmatic manner, we have every possibility of pushing forward the development of our bilateral relations, thereby benefiting the people of China, the United States, and the rest of the world.

CHAPTER 9

The Maturing of China-EU Relations

Twists, Turns, and Improvement

RELATIONS WITH EUROPEAN COUNTRIES have always been a major component of Chinese diplomacy. After the founding of the People's Republic in 1949, Sweden, Denmark, Finland, and Switzerland were the first countries of the West to establish diplomatic relations with China at the ministerial level in 1950; in 1954, the United Kingdom and the Netherlands established ties at the level of chargé d'affaires. In 1964, France became the first Western power to establish diplomatic relations with China at ambassadorial level. By the 1970s, China had established diplomatic ties with all European countries except the Vatican.

At that time, our relations with Europe were largely at the level of individual countries. Relations with the European Community remained at a lower level, but we kept a close eye on the European integration process.

On May 9, 1950, France's Foreign Minister Robert Schuman initiated the famous Schuman Plan, proposing to integrate the coal, iron, steel, and other basic industries of western European countries including France and the Federal Republic of Germany (FDR), and to put them under the management of a supranational organization. His proposal was warmly supported by the FDR, Italy, Netherlands, Belgium, and Luxembourg.

In April 1951, those six countries signed the European Coal and Steel Community Treaty (Treaty of Paris), and officially formed the European Coal and Steel Community (ECSC) in 1952, marking the first significant step toward European integration.

In March 1957, the six countries signed the European Economic Community (EEC) Treaty and the European Atomic Energy Community (EURATOM) Treaty in Rome (collectively known as the Treaty of Rome). The treaty took official effect in January 1958.

In 1967, the major organs of the ECSC, EEC, and EURATOM merged and formed the European Community (EC), the precursor of the European Union (EU).

From the late 1980s to the early 1990s, European integration developed on a much bigger scale. Membership increased from the original six founders to twelve countries, and its power, status, and influence continuously expanded. Pushed forward by France and Germany, the twelve EC member states officially signed the Treaty on European Union in February 1992. The treaty was signed in the Dutch border city of Maastricht, so it is also known as the Maastricht Treaty. By this time, the EC had developed into the European Union (EU). Today, the number of EU member states stands at twenty-seven.

The progressive development of European integration provided the right conditions for China to build relations with the European countries as a collective entity. In the early 1970s, China had its lawful seat restored in the United Nations, and its international influence gradually increased. With the thawing of China-US relations, the EC paid increased attention to China's significance and influence in international affairs. The conditions for China to establish official diplomatic relations with the EC began to mature.

In the early 1970s, via many channels, the EEC made known its wish to establish relations with China, and at the end of 1974, the Chinese government made a strategically significant decision in principle to establish diplomatic relations with the EC.

At that time, most countries chose to establish ties simultaneously with all three organizations that composed the EC, namely the ECSC, EEC, and EURATOM, but China chose to establish ties with the EEC first on the basis of practical interests and needs.

From May 4 to 11, 1975, EEC Commission Vice President Sir Christopher Soames visited China at the invitation of the Chinese People's Institute of Foreign Affairs (CPIFA). Premier Zhou Enlai and Vice Premier Li Xiannian each met with him, and Foreign Minister Qiao Guanhua had an in-depth exchange of views with him on China-EEC relations. Both sides agreed to establish official relations between the PRC and EEC, and the Chinese government would accredit a representative to the EEC.

Subsequently, bilateral political and trade relations experienced quite a long period of sustained and stable development.

On November 1, 1983, pursuant to the further development of bilateral relations, China established overall diplomatic relations with all three EC organs, and for several years, China-Europe relations developed in a sustained and stable manner.

On the whole, China-Europe relations progressed smoothly and steadily, but it has gone through a period of twists and turns. After the 1989 political disturbance in Beijing, the EC imposed sanctions on China, and for several years sided with the United States to propose or cosponsor human-rights resolutions against China, thereby driving China-Europe relations to a low point.

With the end of the Cold War, the international political pattern entered a period of profound readjustment, and Europe wished to play a bigger role in building a new international political and economic order. At that time, China had overcome many difficulties of the tough post–Cold War period by persevering in reform and opening up, its economy kept growing rapidly, and its overall national strength was expanding. Accordingly, the EU paid more attention to China's status and influence, and took an ever more positive attitude to developing the China relationship. In 1994, the EU adopted a new Asia strategy, which emphasized the importance of Asia and putting forward a China-related policy framework.

In 1995, the EU issued its first China policy paper, "A Long Term Policy for China-Europe Relations." The paper states, "The rise of China is unmatched amongst national experiences since the Second World War," and advocates building a long-term and constructive relationship with China and comprehensively enhancing bilateral cooperation in political, economic, and other areas. This document sent a very clear signal about strengthening relations with China, but it also showed the EU's worries about China's human-rights issues. From its very inception, we can perceive the dual character of EU's China policy, which has been the root cause of many ups and downs throughout the development of China-Europe relations.

In 1996, the EU issued its second China-related policy document, "A New Strategy towards China."

Thereafter, through a variety of channels, the EU indicated its wish to further develop China-Europe relations.

Thanks to protracted and resolute struggle on our part, the human-rights resolutions against China proposed or cosponsored by the EU and the United States were repeatedly frustrated. In February 1998, the EU officially announced that neither the presidency country nor any EU member state would propose or cosponsor any resolution against China at the 54th Session of the UN Commission on Human Rights. This announcement broke the Europe-US alliance against China on human rights that had existed since the events of 1989, transformed confrontation into dialogue, and removed a political obstacle to China-Europe relations.

In March 1998, I was appointed minister of Foreign Affairs. During that time, I was always pondering how to encourage a more positive European attitude and to push the China-Europe relationship forward.

It was inevitable that China and Europe, as influential powers on the international stage, should strengthen their mutual strategic reliance. In this new situation, promoting relations with the EU and its member states became a significant part of China's diplomatic strategy, a strategy conducive to China's development and to world peace, stability, and prosperity.

Naturally, the ideological differences and economic disparity between China and Europe inevitably gave rise to disagreements and even conflicts on certain issues. However, we believed that all these issues could be properly resolved through dialogue, provided we all adhered to the principle of mutual respect and mutual benefit on an equal footing.

At this juncture, the EU proposed that the First EU-China Summit should take place during the Second Asia-Europe Meeting, (ASEM) to be held in London in April 1998. The rotating presidency of the EU at that time was held by the United Kingdom. Prime Minister Tony Blair played an active role in putting it into effect, and sent to Premier Zhu Rongji a warm invitation to attend. It was truly a good opportunity to improve China-Europe relations.

Between March 31 and April 7, 1998, Premier Zhu Rongji attended the Second ASEM in London and also paid official visits to the United Kingdom and France. During the visit, Premier Zhu met the British Prime Minister Blair and EU President Jacques Santer at 10 Downing Street, the official residence of British prime ministers, and had an in-depth exchange of views on further improving China-Europe relations, on the financial crisis in East Asia, and other issues of common concern.

After the meeting, China and the EU released a joint statement, agreeing that in the face of significant and profound changes in the international situation, the further enhancing of dialogue and cooperation between China and Europe conformed to the fundamental interests of both sides, and helped maintain world peace, stability, and development. Hoping to build a long-term and stable constructive partnership between China and Europe focusing on the twenty-first century, both sides agreed to maintain the momentum of high-level contacts, and would consider making the EU-China Summit an annual event.

The first EU-China Summit was of great significance in improving China-Europe ties. It defined the nature and orientation of China-Europe relations, institutionalized the leadership summit, and established a platform for high-level contacts between China and Europe.

From then on, China-Europe relations entered a stage of rapid growth.

Stepping Up the Pace

IN JUNE 1998, THE EU adopted its third China policy paper, "Building a Comprehensive Partnership with China," which emphasized that reinforcing relations with China was consistent with the EU's fundamental interests, and proposed the building of a comprehensive partnership with China and raising EU-China relations to the same level of importance as those with United States and Russia.

In 1999, a new European Union administration took office. Referring to EU organs, most people think of the European Commission. Actually, the European Union is composed of three major institutions, namely the Council of the European Union, the European Commission, and the European Parliament. The council, the EU's most important decision-making body, comprises the European Council and Council of Ministers. The European Commission, composed of representatives from each member state, is a standing executive body of the EU and is appointed by the council and approved by the European Parliament. The European Parliament is the supervisory, consultative, and legislative body of the EU. Members of the parliament are produced through popular elections within each EU member state according to its number of seats. The term of office of the European Commission and the European Parliament is five years in each case. Change of EU administration generally refers to these two institutions.

In September 1999, former Prime Minister of Italy Romano Prodi took office as the tenth president of the European Commission. The new generation of EU leadership, as represented by Prodi, took a more positive attitude towards China. Two years later, the fourth EU-China Summit was convened in Brussels, at the close of which the EU and China issued a joint statement establishing a comprehensive partnership between the two sides and pointing out the direction by which to further enhance EU-China cooperation.

Around the year 2003, there was a rare historical opportunity to develop China-Europe relations. We were aware of the EU's increasing strategic reliance on China and its growing enthusiasm to improve EU-China relations. EU officials revealed to China that EU had ranked China as a major strategic partner alongside the United States, Russia, Japan, Canada, and India.

At that time, we were having internal discussions about whether to issue China's EU policy paper, with reference to the EU policy documents towards China.

At the end of 2002, the Ministry of Foreign Affairs initiated the drafting of an EU policy paper. The drafting process involved some thirty revisions and took six months. In September 2003, China's first EU policy paper won official approval from the State Council.

It was China's first ever diplomatic policy paper openly issued towards a continent, a programmatic document of great importance. The paper established China's principles for developing China-Europe relations: to promote a sound and steady development of China-EU political relations on the principles of mutual respect, mutual trust, and seeking common ground while reserving differences, and contributing to world peace and stability; to deepen China-EU economic cooperation and trade on the basis of mutual benefit and equal consultation; to promote common development; to expand China-EU cultural and people-to-people exchanges on the basis of mutual appreciation, common prosperity, and complementarity; and to promote cultural harmony and progress between the East and the West.

While we were preparing China's first EU policy paper, the EU was incubating its fifth China policy paper, with the same hope of furthering China-Europe relations and boosting concrete cooperation between the two sides. If each side's policy paper were issued simultaneously, responding to and interacting with each other, this would undoubtedly send a much more positive signal to the world.

Therefore, I gave instructions to the Mission of the People's Republic of China to the European Union to coordinate with the EU on the release timing of our respective policy papers. Both sides agreed to issue their own document in October before the Sixth EU-China Summit, so as to create a favorable political atmosphere for the meeting.

On October 13, 2003, Xinhua News Agency issued the full text of China's first EU policy paper. The same day, the EU approved its fifth China policy paper, "A Maturing Partnership," which for the first time designated the relationship between Europe and China as a maturing "strategic partnership," and expressed the EU's hope to build an "equal, stable, long-lasting, mutually beneficial and comprehensive" EU-China relationship so as to boost peaceful, stable, and sustainable development.

On October 20, 2003, the Sixth EU-China Summit was convened in Beijing. After the meeting, the two sides issued a joint statement declaring that China-EU high-level political dialogue had been fruitful, that China-EU dialogue and consultation in all aspects had been enhanced, and that the China-Europe partnership was maturing. The two sides agreed to develop China-EU comprehensive strategic partnership.

In line with the summit consensus, we energetically promoted EU-China relations, making great strides forward. In the political field, the EU-China Summit was the lead mechanism of twenty-two dialogue and consultation mechanisms for maintaining close communication and coordination on major international and regional issues. In the economic field, a convergence of shared interests had already been formed. In 2004, the EU overtook the United States and Japan as China's largest trade partner.

During the short five years since the First EU-China Summit of 1998, China-Europe relations had taken three steps forward, from constructive partnership, to comprehensive partnership, to comprehensive strategic partnership. In both depth and scope, this was an unprecedented achievement.

On May 12, 2005, I attended the reception commemorating the thirtieth anniversary of the establishment of China-EU diplomatic relations, held in the Fangfeiyuan Banquet Hall of the Diaoyutai State Guesthouse. A happy and warm atmosphere prevailed at the reception, which was attended by more than three hundred honored guests, including the foreign ministers of the EU Troika.*

I met with the EU Troika foreign ministers before the reception. It was the first time the EU Troika had visited China together. The foreign ministers of the Troika at the time were: Foreign Secretary Jean Asselborn of Luxembourg, who then held the EU rotating pres-

---

*In diplomatic relations, the EU is usually represented by the Troika, comprising representatives of the current presidency state, the future presidency state, and the council and the European Commission, to demonstrate the integrity of the EU and ensure consistency in its policy.

Thirtieth Anniversary of China-EU Diplomatic Relations Reception, May 12, 2005.

idency; EU Commissioner for External Relations. Benita Ferrero-Waldner; and Britain's Ambassador to China Sir Christopher Hum.*

I told them that promoting China-Europe comprehensive strategic partnership was the common choice of both sides and a long-term strategy conforming to our fundamental interests. China and EU should treat China-Europe relations from a strategic height and long-term perspective, grasp the general direction of friendly cooperation, and push it forward unswervingly. Upholding the principle of equality and mutual benefit—equity—China and EU should take care of and seek resolution to each other's major concerns, making China-Europe relations better serve the fundamental interests of the two sides.

The maturing China-Europe relationship entered the best stage ever, shaping a situation of comprehensive, wide-ranging, and multilevel cooperation.

---

*EU's next presidency state, the United Kingdom, was busy at the time forming a cabinet after the general election and specially delegated the British Ambassador Sir Christopher Hum to represent the UK foreign minister on this occasion.

New Mission of the Last Governor

IN A CERTAIN SENSE, *diplomacy* means safeguarding the interests of one's country through communicating with people. My associations with the EU Commissioner for External Relations Chris Patten demonstrate this point to the full.

This name in its Chinese form, Peng Dingkang, is a familiar one to ordinary Chinese people. Patten was a veteran on the British political scene, and it was he who, as the last British governor of Hong Kong, had come up with political reform proposals, "the Three Violations,"* in order to oppose China. Even after returning to Britain, he had kept haranguing China on the issue of Hong Kong.

Later, he was appointed EU commissioner for External Relations, a different title with a different mission. His term as EU commissioner for External Relations coincided almost exactly with my time as China's foreign minister. Throughout the development of China-EU relations, my important opposite number was this last governor of Hong Kong.

In May 1999, the British government decided to recommend Chris Patten as the new EU commissioner for External Relations. As soon as the news got around, it aroused immediate attention and speculation from all sides. Many overseas reports said that Patten would adopt a "tough policy" towards China with blunt remarks on the issue of human rights in China, and assumed that his key position in the EU would have an adverse impact on China-Europe relations.

On June 27, 1999, the *Sunday Times*, a British newspaper, pub-

---

*In October 1992, with the support of the British government, Chris Patten abandoned China-UK cooperation and concocted political reform proposals that constituted "Three Violations": violation of the Joint Declaration, violation of the UK's commitment on ensuring that the development of Hong Kong's political system should be in conformity to the Basic Law, and violation of related agreements and understandings previously reached by the two sides.

lished an article entitled "China Vetoes Chris Patten's Position in EU," alleging that as a result of pressure from China, the European Commission was considering perhaps appointing Chris Patten as commissioner for Employment, Social Affairs and Equal Opportunities instead. I do remember, at that time, officials of the Delegation of the European Commission to China came to the Ministry of Foreign Affairs to sound out China's attitude, but we certainly would not interfere in the EU's internal affairs.

I was not particularly worried about Chris Patten. My experience was that things change and so do people. In diplomatic practice, the stance, words, and deeds of a diplomat represent the interests of his country or group, not those of himself. The diplomat must decide upon his stance according to his position, and in the interests of the organization that he represents.

Under the circumstances of the time, the EU wanted to keep expanding its relations with China, so Chris Patten, as EU commissioner for External Affairs, had to ensure that his words and deeds should conform to and serve the interests of the EU. As for Patten as an individual, we did not have to rake over the past; the important thing was how he performed now.

Chris Patten's attitude towards China had indeed undergone change. On September 2, 1999, at the hearing of the Council of the European Union about his appointment, Chris Patten said in reference to the EU's China policy, "China has a quarter of the world's total population. It is unimaginable to practice a policy of containment against such a country. We should develop a forceful and effective relationship with China." In his EU debut, Chris Patten sent a positive signal to China.

I thought it worthwhile to affirm those sentiments, so I sent him a congratulatory telegram on the day of his inauguration as EU commissioner. In addition to the regular formula, I made a point of adding this sentence: "I believe during your term of office,

China-EU relations, cooperation and communication in all areas will continue to forge ahead."

Patten replied expressing his thanks and the hope that we would meet soon.

In September, at the agreement of both sides, the China-EU Foreign Ministers' Meeting was held during the UN General Assembly. On the afternoon of September 20, I met with the EU Troika headed by the EU presidency state Finland's Foreign Minister Tarja Halonen at the Permanent Mission of the People's Republic of China to the United Nations. We exchanged views on China-Europe relations and issues of common concern, and reached consensus on the importance of improving bilateral relations.

Chris Patten attended the meeting representing the commission. This was our second meeting: The first had been at the Farewell Ceremony of the last governor of Hong Kong.

That day, Patten did not talk as much as the other two Troika members. I made a point of saying to him, "You're very famous in China." He smiled and courteously expressed the simple hope in principle of developing China-Europe relations. He obviously knew the reason for his fame in China, and I also felt the weight on his mind.

Three months later, Chris Patten accompanied President of the European Commission Romano Prodi to the Second EU-China Summit in China. Before setting off, Patten specially proposed a working meeting with me in Beijing, and I agreed.

The day before arriving in Beijing, Patten attended the Macao Handover Ceremony as a representative of the commission.

On the afternoon of December 21, 1999, President Jiang Zemin met Prodi at Zhongnanhai. The atmosphere was very friendly.

During the meeting, President Jiang talked about the significance of promoting China-Europe exchanges, making special mention of Chris Patten's attendance at the Macao Handover Ceremony.

President Jiang expressed his pleasure at being able to meet and communicate with friends from overseas on a frequent basis. Only the previous morning, for example, he had met with Commissioner Patten in Macao and was now meeting him again in Beijing. Referring to European culture, President Jiang especially mentioned William Shakespeare, and asked for the opinion of Chris Patten.

Quick-minded Patten picked up Jiang's theme and led the discussion onto European unity, soliciting President Jiang's opinion on EU construction and development. He said that President Jiang was very familiar with Shakespeare's works, many of which dealt with internal power struggles sabotaging unity. Unity was of equal importance to the European Union. Patten asked, since many European nations were hoping to join in the EU, if President Jiang were EU president, how, in his opinion, should the EU improve and proceed?

From this, we could see that Chris Patten was keen to make a good impression on the Chinese state leader.

Later, we had a working meeting at the Ministry of Foreign Affairs. I welcomed Patten at the Olive Hall. He was quite happy, and we chatted as we made our way to the meeting room.

Once we were seated, he first expressed congratulations on the smooth handover of Macao the day before. On the subject of China-Europe relations, he came straight to the point by quoting the Chinese saying "as interdependent as lips and teeth." He said he would try hard to rapidly and effectively push for implementation of the EU China-aid projects previously agreed upon by the two sides.

His metaphor indicated a degree of awareness on his part of the importance of China-Europe relations. I appreciated his positive attitude, emphasizing that China thought highly of the EU and would further develop relations with the EU on the basis of mutual respect, equality, and mutual benefit and sincerity.

We also exchanged views on China's accession to the WTO,

ASEM, and other issues. After the meeting, Chris Patten stood up and told me that he was very interested in traditional Chinese culture and arts, and hoped for further opportunities to visit China and build a good personal relationship with Chinese state leaders.

The year 2000 was the twenty-fifth anniversary of the establishment of China-Europe diplomatic relations. At the invitation of Commission President Romano Prodi, Premier Zhu Rongji visited the EU headquarters in Brussels from July 10 through 12.

During the visit, at the request of the EU, I had a working meeting with Chris Patten on the morning of July 10 in the seventh floor reception hall of the council's office building. We had an in-depth, candid, and thorough communication focusing on China-Europe relations, both sides believing we should try to settle disputes and conflicts on the principle of seeking common ground while reserving differences, to take a strategic forward-looking view in advancing China-Europe relations, and create more favorable conditions for boosting China-EU cooperation.

Inevitably, the talk turned to the issue of human rights. I took the initiative by outlining the progress achieved by the Chinese government in improving basic human rights, pointing out that China hoped to enhance communication through dialogue, clarify misunderstandings, remove prejudice, and expand consensus. Chris Patten said the EU would continue dialogue and cooperation with China in the area of human rights.

The meeting lasted over an hour as we went deep into these topics. Possibly as a result of being too engrossed in the conversation, Patten forgot to offer more tea to his guest. Having talked for over an hour, my throat was parched, so I teased him, "Since we're here talking about human rights, what about giving our own human rights a thought? We've been talking over an hour, but you haven't offered to top up my tea." He was stunned for a bit, and then we both laughed.

After the meeting, Chris Patten saw us out to the entrance gate.

It was drizzling. He escorted me to my car, holding an umbrella over me himself, and waved as he watched us drive away.

Through this and previous contacts, I clearly felt that Chris Patten was willing to push the EU to develop relations with China, and that he would like to contribute to this end. On many subsequent occasions, he said China was not a threat to the West, and that China and Europe would be key elements in maintaining world peace and security.

Soon after the China–US South China Sea air collision incident in April 2001, Patten told the press during his visit to Australia that the United States should not take China as a threat. In May 2001, he presided over the drafting of the EU's fourth China policy paper, and made many amendments and annotations himself. This document adopted a more positive tone than the first three in its proposal to develop a comprehensive partnership with China.

Some of the media caught the scent of change. The Hong Kong edition of *Newsweek* commented that the EU had not followed the US lead in treating China as a strategic rival, but had turned its focus toward China. The person who had helped bring about this shift was, ironically enough, none other than Hong Kong's last governor.

As time ripened, I put it on my agenda to invite Chris Patten to pay an official visit to China. On September 6, 2001, when I accompanied Premier Zhu Rongji to the Fourth EU–China Summit in Brussels, I took the opportunity of inviting him in person to visit China. He accepted with pleasure.

From March 28 to April 4, 2002, Chris Patten visited China together with his family. It was his first official visit to China alone as EU commissioner for External Affairs. Under the care of the party and state leaders, the Foreign Ministry made careful arrangements for Commissioner Patten's visit, giving him a warm and friendly high-standard reception.

President Jiang Zemin and Vice Premier Qian Qichen each met

with Chris Patten during his visit. They both affirmed his contributions to pushing forward China-Europe relations since taking office as EU commissioner for External Affairs. He was heartened by their remarks, saying that China's development benefited the EU and was in the interests of the region and the world, and that further enhancing China-EU relations was the only correct choice.

I held talks with Patten at the Ministry of Foreign Affairs. I spoke highly of mutually beneficial China-Europe cooperation in various areas, stressing that in the changing international situation, further deepening China-Europe relations conformed to both sides' common interests.

I also expressed great appreciation of all the steps taken by the EU to develop bilateral relations, saying that China wished to see the continued sound development of China-Europe relations in the new millennium.

The commissioner reciprocated my positive comments on China-Europe relations, describing the current relationship as going well and having promising prospects. The two sides shared common interests on a series of international issues and on building a multilateral international system.

He described the EU and China as both being at a critical development stage. For China, as the largest developing country with the fastest-growing economy, and EU as the largest group of developed countries, the sound development of EU-China bilateral relations would benefit both sides and the world at large. The EU endeavored ceaselessly to expand and deepen cooperation through greater political dialogue and consultation with China. Of course, we talked about human rights. Chris Patten said it was important that EU and China should handle the human-rights issue by means of dialogue instead of bickering.

After the meeting, I hosted a banquet for him in the banquet hall of the Foreign Ministry.

The hall is on the nineteenth floor of the Foreign Ministry office

With EU Commissioner for External Affairs Chris Patten at the Ministry of Foreign Affairs, March 2002.

building. During my years as foreign minister, banquets for visiting foreign ministers were usually held in this hall, both in order to save time and to make the guests feel at home. The chefs were all master chefs from the Diaoyutai State Guesthouse or on temporary transfer from other cities. They always won high praise from the foreign guests dining here. That day, I asked the cooks to prepare delicious dishes for Chris Patten that catered specially to his tastes.

To deepen his impression and understanding of China across the board, we arranged for him to meet with ministers in charge of commerce, public security, education, and labor, as well as with the chairperson of the Chinese People's Association for Friendship with Foreign Countries (CPAFFC).

Usually, we arranged only one or two trips to cities other than Beijing for our foreign visitors, but this time we made an exception and organized visits for Patten and his family to Shanghai, Suzhou, Yangzhou, and Nanjing as well.

In Shanghai, Patten visited the Xujiahui Catholic Church and site of the First National Congress of the CPC, and was interviewed by Shanghai Television. While in Nanjing, he paid a special visit to the mausoleum of Dr. Sun Yat-sen, the Memorial Hall of the Victims of the Nanjing Massacre by Japanese Invaders, and was interviewed for an English-language program on Jiangsu Television.

At the mausoleum, Chris Patten said with feeling that he got a deeper understanding of China's strong emotions on the Taiwan issue. Appearing very grave and solemn at the Memorial Hall of the Victims of the Nanjing Massacre, he wrote in the visitors' book: "This exhibition vividly demonstrated the most brutal organized violence in the 20th century. We should remember this period of history and firmly prevent the recurrence of such brutalities."

Commissioner Patten delivered speeches at the Party School of the Central Committee of CPC and at Fudan University.

This China trip left him with pleasant memories and a deep impression. He expressed on many later occasions that he had been very touched by China's goodwill, and that he had witnessed China's rapid economic growth during this visit with a deeper understanding of promoting China-Europe relations, declaring that "developing EU-China relations is our only right choice."

On his return, Chris Patten sent me a heart-warming letter of thanks saying that he could not remember a smoother, more exciting, and interesting diplomatic visit than his recent trip to China.

Of course, our ideological differences were obvious. In each of our meetings or talks, confrontations on human rights and other issues were unavoidable, and we two made no concessions on matters of principle.

In my opinion, Chris Patten is smart, principled, and tactful. I remember one year when a foreign minister of the EU presidency state headed the EU Troika delegation to China. From the very inception, the lady kept harping on human rights for quite some time. Of course, I retorted bluntly, saying that China's great achievements in human rights were obvious to all, that we were willing to have equal dialogue with the EU about human rights on the basis of mutual respect and equality, and were willing to listen to the EU's constructive opinions, but we were firmly opposed to forcing one's own ideas upon others and interfering in other countries' internal affairs in the name of human rights. When it was Christ Patten's turn to speak, he just made a brief reference to human rights and moved on.

In retrospect, Chris Patten's attitude to China changed a lot between his time as governor of Hong Kong and his time as EU commissioner for External Affairs. One factor in this transformation was probably the importance in EU's strategy of developing relations with China, but China's willingness to bury the past and treat others with respect also played a part.

Showing the Real Tibet

IN RECENT YEARS, CHINA-EU disputes on human rights became less acute. On the other hand, the Tibet issue became an ever more prominent one in China-Europe relations. Because of deep-rooted prejudice on the Tibet issue within EU member states, the activities of the Dalai Lama's group, and the interference of the press, the EU kept harassing China on the Tibet issue, the European Parliament being the worst offender in this respect.

The European Parliament differs from other kinds of parliament in its constitution and operation. Nominally it represents Europe, but since the Members of the European Parliament (MEPs) are directly elected by popular vote in the member states, they enjoy a high degree of independence. In emergency situations, illegally binding resolutions can be adopted if they are supported by more than half of the MEPs present. MEPs often kick up a shindy in order to get a public reaction.

Fully aware of this, the Dalai Lama's group tried every possible way to take advantage of the European Parliament as a political tool for anti-China activities. In response, a minority of MEPs often unreasonably denounced China on the Tibet issue.

The European Parliament vociferously encouraged the Dalai Lama group's disruptive overseas activities aimed at splitting China. In June 1988, in disregard of China's repeated stern protests, it obstinately invited the Dalai to deliver a speech at the plenary session of the European Parliament in Strasbourg, thereby providing Dalai the opportunity to dish out his so-called "Middle Way."

In June 2001, a joint conference of the European Parliament's political groups decided to invite the Dalai to address the European Parliament plenary session. Since this involved our struggle against the Tibet separatist activities and also had a bearing on our EP diplomacy, we once more lodged a stern representation with the European side.

In January 2002, the parliament elected as its twenty-fifth president Irish liberal Patrick Cox. Cox valued the development of relations with China, and had a different attitude from that of his predecessor on sensitive issues concerning China. In February, when Ambassador Guan Chengyuan, head of mission of the People's Republic of China to the European Union, visited Cox, the EP president indicated that the EP had previously adopted somewhat a negative attitude towards China, but would act more positively in the future.

Cox's positive stand on the Tibet issue provided a chance for us to work on the European Parliament.

For a long time, the European Parliament had taken a negative and confrontational attitude against China on Tibet. There were many reasons for this, but inadequate knowledge and understanding of Tibet's past and present was the overriding factor. Most MEPs had never been to China and still fewer had been to Tibet. Under these circumstances, it became a top diplomatic priority to take the initiative in improving contact and communication with the European Parliament.

In the meantime, China's National People's Congress and Tibet Autonomous Region were considering how to make the MEPs better informed about Tibet. We coincided in our ideas in this respect. In February 2002, the Ministry of Foreign Affairs and related departments requested that the Central Authorities authorize a visit to the European Parliament by a delegation of the People's Congress of Tibet Autonomous Region. This was quickly approved.

As to who should lead the delegation, we all thought of Raidi. As chairman of the Standing Committee of the People's Congress of the Tibet Autonomous Region, an ethnic Tibetan born into serfdom, a witness to Tibet's economic development and social changes since the peaceful liberation of Tibet, and knowledgeable in all aspects of the region, he was best qualified to speak about the Tibet issue.

The other members of the delegation were chosen as being representative, for instance, the renowned Tibetologist Lhagba Puncog, and the Living Buddha Chikukg for Tibetan Buddhism.

The Chinese Central Authorities paid great attention to the visit. Vice Premier Qian Qichen called me specifically, asking the ministry to assist the visit. I gave specific instructions to the Department of European Affairs and to the Mission of the People's Republic of China to the European Union.

In March 2002, the delegation of the People's Congress of Tibet Autonomous Region visited the European Parliament and Belgium. On March 25, the delegation arrived in the Belgian capital. Our colleagues in the Chinese Mission to the EU told us that it had been drizzling and gloomy in Brussels, but the day the delegation arrived, the sky turned sunny and cloudless, as if it had brought to Brussels the bright sunshine of Lhasa, the Sunlight City. Members of the delegation were all wearing dazzlingly bright Tibetan costume, and drew attention wherever they went.

The delegation made extensive contacts with the EU and people in all walks of Belgian society. Within just four days, the delegation took part in twenty-one talks, meetings, and other communication activities, to an enthusiastic response. At the European Parliament, the delegation met with EP President Patrick Cox, Vice President Joan COLOM i NAVAL Foreign Affairs Committee Chairman Elmar Brok, Head of Delegation for Relations with China Elly Plooij-van Gorsel, President of Group of the Progressive Alliance of Socialists and Democrats Enrique Baron Crespo, Vice President of Group of the European People's Party Ilkka Suominen, and Chef de Cabinet to Chris Patten, Anthony Cary. The delegation also met with a dozen representatives of the Belgium Federal Parliament including Pierre Chevalier, chairman of Foreign Affairs Committee of the Chamber, and Theo Kelchtermans, chairman of the Belgium-China Group; held talks with Frederic Renard, deputy director-general of Department of International Cooperation of Ministry of Foreign Affairs; gave interviews to Chinese and foreign reporters; and attended the opening ceremony of the Tibet Photo Exhibition.

During the talks, Raidi took President Cox by the hand and said that more bilateral communication was always better than none, and Cox completely agreed. The delegation met widely with and had in-depth dialogue with the parliament, and issued an invitation to MEPs interested in Tibet to come to see Tibet for themselves.

The highlight of the visit was the symposium with MEPs. Over forty MEPs attended and all stayed throughout the meeting, which lasted over three hours. This was exceptional by European Parliament standards.

The MEPs were very interested in the symposium and asked a lot of questions. The questions themselves showed that they knew little about Tibet, especially the tremendous changes that had taken place there. It was clear that most of their knowledge and opinions regarding Tibet were based on misinformation from the Dalai Lama's group.

Based on the contrast of their personal experiences in the past and present, the delegation members gave a comprehensive introduction of Tibet's historical development, tremendous achievements, and status quo on politics, economy, culture, ethnic groups, and religion, and answered questions from the MEPs. As the delegation members were all Tibetans from the Autonomous Region, their briefing of personal experiences was very convincing.

After the symposium, some MEPs said this was the first time Tibetan voices had been heard in the European Parliament building. Some agreed that it was a historical fact that Tibet was an integral part of China, and that Tibet would never return to feudal serfdom. Some admired the half century of achievements in Tibet and expressed their hope to visit the region. Some had begun to doubt whether Dalai's actions were in the best interests of the Tibetan people. Some openly admitted, "It seems that some resolutions we adopted in the past were, to say the least, inappropriate."

The Tibetan visit caused a strong response and got massive coverage in the main local newspapers *La Libre Belgique, Le Soir,* and *Le Point. La Libre Belgique* published a feature entitled "Another Voice from Tibet," an objective and truth-based report on Raidi's activities and speeches during the visit, noting that the visit of China's Tibetan delegation had "ended Dalai's monopoly over debate in the European Parliament."

"An Integral Part of China—the Tibet Delegation Visits Brussels," an article in *Le Point* said: "Belgium and the European Parliament received a delegation from the People's Republic of China. The Head of the People's Congress of the Tibet Autonomous Region and other members of the delegation said that the Tibetan people had achieved affluence under the guidance of the current government, and that the splittist Dalai Lama's group could not represent all the Tibetan people." The report also quoted a MEP, saying: "The Tibet delegation's visit to Europe has successfully cast doubt about the stance Europe has taken on Tibetans following Dalai Lama, and splitting Tibet from China as an independent state." European public opinion on the Tibet issue began to speak in our favor.

It was the first time China had sent a Tibet delegation to the European Parliament, and this significant breakthrough in European diplomacy made a great impact and got a favorable response. On April 7, 2002, I hosted a homecoming banquet at the Diaoyutai State Guesthouse for Raidi and the rest of the delegation. At the banquet, all were in the best of spirits, and Living Buddha Chikukg prayed for blessings by touching everyone on the forehead three times in a Tibetan Buddhist prayer ritual.

Following Raidi's visit to Europe, positive voices began to be heard within the European Parliament, and the blindly critical attitude gave way to active dialogue. At the same time, our contact and communication with the European Parliament began to increase.

Raidi told me that the People's Government of Tibet Autonomous Region kept in touch with everyone in the EP who had been to Tibet or had had contact with Tibet, so as to keep them up to date about the region. I found this quite inspiring. Our diplomatic work vis-à-vis the European Parliament was indeed full of difficulties, but solutions would always outnumber difficulties: The key was unswerving perseverance in seeking workable and effective solutions.

Despite certain successes, the European Parliament's attitude towards Tibet remained complicated and unpredictable, and was unlikely to change in our favor because of one or two visits. Following the March 14 Incident in Tibet in 2008, the European Parliament passed a strongly worded declaration on Tibet, launching an arbitrary attack on China. On December 4, disregarding China's repeated solemn and just representations, the European Parliament again invited the Dalai Lama to speak at the plenary session of the European Parliament in Brussels, causing new trouble in China-Europe relations.

All this illustrated the necessity of long-term, hard endeavor in our EP diplomacy.

Good relations with the individual EU member states are the cornerstone of China-Europe relations; sound bilateral relations with the member states boost the overall development of China-Europe relations, and the converse is also true. China's relations with the EU as an entity and with its individual member states are complementary parts of the whole.

The complicated operational structure of the EU has been likened to a twenty-seven-headed hydra, since each member state has a voice in policy-making. The United Kingdom, France, and Germany have powerful influence in the EU, and have played an important role in the development of China-Europe relations.

With the Shedding of Historical Burdens, China-UK Relations Revive

THE UNITED KINGDOM HAS had a glorious past in modern world history. Britain was the first country to undergo an industrial revolution, became the engine of modern science and technology, and nurtured a great many world-renowned scientists and thinkers including Newton, Darwin, and Adam Smith. Britain was a leading world power for a long time; its colonial territories covered a total area 111 times that of its home territory. It was described as "the empire on which the sun never sets."

In modern Chinese history, Britain had played a far from glorious role. The mention of Britain reminds the Chinese of many humiliations inflicted, including the Opium Wars, the Eight-Power Allied Forces, the burning of the Yuanmingyuan Imperial Garden, and a century's colonial rule over Hong Kong.

Shortly after the founding of the People's Republic of China in 1949, motivated by practical considerations of protecting its interests in China, the United Kingdom recognized the PRC as the legitimate government of China, the first major Western power to do so. In 1954, China and the United Kingdom established diplomatic relations at the level of chargé d'affaires, but Sino-British ties remained at a low level, and it was only in 1972 that they were upgraded to diplomatic relations at the ambassadorial level.

The Hong Kong issue was an historical wound hindering the development of China-UK relations. With the advent of the year 1997,* the issue must be settled as soon as possible.

In 1982, China and the United Kingdom started negotiations about Hong Kong. After two years of tussles, the countries signed a Joint Declaration on the issue of Hong Kong in 1984, and bilateral relations entered a honeymoon period. However, after the political disturbances in Beijing between spring and summer of 1989, and especially after the drastic changes in Eastern Europe and the disintegration of the Soviet Union, the United Kingdom miscalculated China's situation and development prospects. On the pretext of a crisis of confidence in Hong Kong, the British side attempted to reverse the agreement on such issues as garrison troops, direct elections, and the implementation of basic law. With this, China-UK relations started to go downhill.

In 1992, when Chris Patten assumed office as the last governor of Hong Kong, he made extensive changes in Hong Kong policies, and dished out political reform proposals, which violated three previously established understandings, thus severely undermining China-UK relations.

China-UK ties were conspicuously languishing, in contrast with the attempts of major world powers to improve their relations and cooperation with China.

China-UK relations remained tortuous and volatile until 1997.

At that time, China had undergone earth-shaking changes in

---

* The expiry date of an unequal treaty between United Kingom and China.

twenty years of reform and opening up; it was enjoying political stability, sustained economic growth, higher international standing, and huge development potential. When some Asian countries were hit by the financial crisis, China considered the overall situation and committed not to devalue the RMB, thereby making a great contribution to financial stability in Asia and the world. These things brought home to the United Kingdom China's boundless prospects for development and the unstoppable rise of its international influence.

In 1997, the British political scene was transformed. In the general election, the Conservative Party, which had long been in power, was trampled by the Labour Party. In May, the Labour leader Tony Blair became prime minister.

Blair was the youngest prime minister in British history, taking office at the age of forty-one. Energetic and quick-witted, he brought a breath of fresh air to the British political arena. Among the many new ideas he initiated, his Third Way had great resonance internationally. Soon after he came to power, he changed British foreign policy towards China, describing Hong Kong as "the bridge of UK-China relations," and was in favor of improving relations with China.

In 1997, Prime Minister Blair, in office for only two months, attended the Hong Kong Handover Ceremony. At the meeting with China's state leaders, Blair reiterated that the United Kingdom highly valued the development of UK-China relations and looked forward to a new start in the relationship.

With the smooth return of Hong Kong, China-UK relations shed a heavy historical burden and ushered in a new opportunity for all-around improvement and development.

During the first half of 1998, the United Kingdom assumed the rotating presidency of the EU. The Second ASEM was to take place in London from late March to early April, and Blair cordially invited China's state leaders to attend the meeting and to pay an official visit to the United Kingdom. He also proposed establishing and launching an EU–China Summit mechanism.

This was a positive signal from the British. It was a dozen years since the last UK visit by a Chinese premier. If it went ahead, the visit would not only set the tone for the development of the China-UK relationship in the twenty-first century, but would also push it forward and expand China's international influence.

On March 31, 1998, I accompanied Premier Zhu Rongji to the Second ASEM and paid an official visit to the United Kingdom. It was the first diplomatic visit of China's state leaders' since the forming of a new central administration, and the first official visit to the United Kingdom since the return of Hong Kong.

Thanks to the joint efforts of China and United Kingdom, Premier Zhu Rongji's UK visit was a great success, widely covered and favorably commented upon by the British media.

I summarized the results of this visit as the three news. First, China-UK relations had advanced into a new stage. The state leaders of both sides had held constructive meetings, and agreed to establish a sound constructive partnership oriented to the twenty-first century, pointing out the direction for the development of China-UK relations. Second, China-Europe relations had entered a new era. The China-EU Summit mechanism established and launched during the Second ASEM had built a platform for the sound development of China-Europe relations. As Blair's spokesman said, the China-EU Summit demonstrated that the EU regarded China as a major international force. Third, the political dialogue between Asian and European countries had created a new opportunity for regional cooperation in the new millennium.

I held counterpart talks with the British Foreign Secretary Robin Cook in the UK Foreign and Commonwealth Office.

It was my first meeting with Cook. He was an archetypal Scot, straightforward, quick-minded, and fast-talking. He was an influential figure within the Labour Party, and a man of high caliber in the cabinet. He was interested in, and well disposed toward, China.

The effect of our diplomacy on Cook would have a direct influence on UK policy towards China, so I put great weight on our counterpart talks. Prior to the meeting, I gave much thought to finding the right point of approach so as to make the meeting effective.

By that time, the human-rights issue had been a bone of contention between China and Western countries for eight years. Every year, the EU cosponsored US proposed resolutions concerning the so-called human-rights issue of China, but at the 1997 session of the UN Human Rights Commission in Geneva, the EU had decided to change its stance, a decision in which Britain, as the rotating president state of the EU, had played a positive role. Earlier, Blair had reiterated on various occasions that confrontation with China on the human-rights issue should be replaced by dialogue. It was a good point, so I decided to adopt this angle of approach in my conversation with Cook.

At the meeting, I spoke highly of the United Kingdom's efforts to improve Sino-British ties, and expounded my views on human rights in particular. I applauded the United Kingdom's performance at the Human Rights Commission, and further pointed out that disputes between us were only natural, given our historical, cultural, and institutional differences, but that we should seek ways to mend our differences by enhancing communication and negotiation. China was willing to engage in dialogue and cooperation based on equality and mutual respect.

Cook listened to me carefully, took notes every now and then, and frequently nodded in agreement. With this conversation, I established a sound working relationship with Cook, which laid a solid foundation for further diplomacy towards the United Kingdom.

This was my first trip to the United Kingdom, one that gave me some in-depth understanding of the country.

The United Kingdom is a country both traditional and modern. On the one hand, its magnificent ancient architecture and deep cultural background manifest the past glories of the British Empire. On the other, modern structures mushrooming everywhere are testimony to its prosperous business, highly developed finance, and vibrant economy.

Although the United Kingdom's present overall strength and international status are not what they once were, its economic strength remains considerable, and it has obvious advantages in science, technology, transportation, energy, finance, and other fields. Being a permanent member of the UN Security Council, the United Kingdom has significant international influence.

Sino-British relations are pivotal to China's overall diplomacy, and so should be seen, not simply as a bilateral relationship, but treated within the framework of China's overall diplomacy, which aims at the height of improving diplomatic relations with major powers. Consequently, our UK diplomacy called for farsighted vision.

In April 1998, one month after Premier Zhu Rongji's visit to the United Kingdom, the British informed us about Prime Minister Blair's wish to visit China before the end of the year.

While preparing for this visit, the British proposed issuing a joint declaration for the establishment of a comprehensive partnership between United Kingdom and China. I approved of this suggestion.

China and United Kingdom, as two nations with significant international influence, share extensive common interests in improving bilateral cooperation, safeguarding world peace, and boosting common development. Since the return of Hong Kong, high-level contact between the two countries had been achieved for the first time, bringing the improved China–UK relationship into a new historical stage. In this situation, it was necessary to clearly define the relationship between the two countries and to comprehensively plan for its long-term development.

I instructed my colleagues in the Department of West European Affairs to make good preparations for the reception of Prime Minister Blair, negotiate with the British about the contents of the joint declaration, and issue a good document.

From October 6 to 9, 1998, Prime Minister Blair visited China at the invitation of Premier Zhu Rongji. President Jiang Zemin met with Blair and Premier Zhu held talks with him.

During the meetings, both sides agreed that the smooth handover of Hong Kong had turned a new page in China–UK relations, and significant progress had been made in bilateral communication and cooperation in various fields.

Blair mentioned to us many times that he was the first British Labour prime minister to visit China since the establishment of diplomatic relations. Before taking office, Blair had stressed the importance of UK–China relations. He said to China's state leaders that China would rise to world power status in the twenty-first century, and that the United Kingdom hoped to become a partner of China and would like to contribute to China's development.

During the talks with Premier Zhu, there was an in-depth exchange of views on the economic situation facing East Asia. Prime Minister Blair expressed approval of China's measures in response to the Asian financial crisis, and appreciated the support and aid China had offered to its neighboring countries. The two sides also had an in-depth exchange of views on financial system reform, and reached a farsighted agreement on enhancing financial supervision mechanisms, reforming the international financial system, and improving financial transparency.

Before Blair's departure from Beijing, the two sides issued a joint declaration announcing the establishment of a comprehensive partnership between China and United Kingdom, and confirmed in the declaration that, at the invitation of Queen Elizabeth, President Jiang Zemin would pay a state visit to Britain during the second half of the following year.

This would be an historic event, the first state visit to the United Kingdom by a Chinese head of state.

A Right Royal Welcome

WHEN CHINA AND THE United Kingdom were negotiating on President Jiang's forthcoming visit to Britain, there were sudden changes on the international front.

In March 1999, the North Atlantic Treaty Organization (NATO) led by the United States bypassed the United Nations and launched a military attack against the Federal Republic of Yugoslavia. The Kosovo War broke out. It was the first time in its fifty years of existence that NATO had started a war against a sovereign state.

Prime Minister Blair's attitude on the Kosovo issue was aggressive. On many international occasions he took the line of new interventionism, asserting the "human rights above state sovereignty principle," described NATO's action as "a right move," claimed that "noninterference in internal affairs is conditional," and proposed establishing "new norms of international relations" with international intervention at its core.

In May 1999, the Chinese embassy in Yugoslavia was bombed by US-led NATO, which incensed the general public in China. These circumstances led to enormous concern among the Chinese general public as to whether President Jiang's visit to the United Kingdom would go ahead as scheduled.

After the bombing of the embassy in Belgrade, Prime Minister Blair sent two letters to China's state leaders and made a public apology. In the second half of 1999, when Vice Premier Qian Qichen was passing through the United Kingdom, Prime Minister Blair offered to meet with him and the reception arrangements were at a very high level. In the course of the meeting, Blair expressed his hope that the bombing incident would not affect President Jiang's visit and UK-China relations.

It was my view at the time, that although the ruling Labour government valued ideology by implanting new interventionism and other forms of power politics into its foreign policies, its China policy had always been positive, and it had repeatedly expressed keenness to develop UK-China relations. In spite of its prejudice in the areas of China's human rights and Tibet, the United Kingdom generally opposed confrontation with China and advocated cooperation and dialogue, and was gradually forming an objective understanding of China's social and economic development.

At that time, a comprehensive partnership had just been established between China and the United Kingdom, bringing Sino-British relations back onto a normal development track and into a crucial stage. We should stand high and take a long-term view on China's future overall diplomatic strategy, make our stance clear on significant issues through contact with the British side, and steer their foreign policies to be favorable to China-UK relations, and the democratization of international relations.

President Jiang Zemin would be the first Chinese head of state to pay a state visit to the United Kingdom. This visit would be a significant step in strengthening China's diplomacy vis-à-vis Europe and the United Kingdom, and in advancing China's overall foreign policies at the dawn of the new millennium. For these reasons, the visit should not be affected by the embassy bombing. I reported these opinions to the Central Authorities and they were approved.

In October 1999, President Jiang visited the United Kingdom as planned, and reached many significant areas of consensus with Prime Minister Blair on the development of China-UK ties.

President Jiang made clear China's stance about the principles of international relations, emphasizing that the norms of international relations established after the Second World War and widely accepted by the international community should be observed, especially the principles of mutual respect for sovereignty and territorial integrity, nonaggression, noninterference in each other's internal affairs, treating each other as equals, and settling international disputes and conflicts peacefully. These doctrines had helped to maintain peace over fifty years after the Second World War, thus proving effective. President Jiang also made it clear that the United Nations' authority should be reinforced, with its role fully respected and fulfilled in safeguarding world peace and security, and no country or group of nations should be allowed to defy the UN's authority.

Prime Minister Blair said the United Kingdom highly valued its cooperation with China on international issues. The world was indeed undergoing a process of establishing a political and economic order different from the old one, in which China was playing an important part. The United Kingdom paid much attention to China's future development and influence, hoping to make a joint effort with China to bring UK-China dialogue and cooperation in international affairs onto a new level.

During this visit, I had a second talk with Foreign Secretary Robin Cook, exchanged opinions, and reached consensus on many concrete issues in the China-UK relationship.

Seizing the Timely Moment

AFTER PRESIDENT JIANG'S VISIT, China-UK relations continued to develop smoothly, and there was a clear increase in communications between the two sides on international matters.

The two sides had agreed that I should visit Britain in March 2001, but, in February, we learned that the Labour Party government might move up the general election to summer, so I decided to postpone my visit.

I was not worried that the Labour Party would be defeated, but was thinking about how to work on the new cabinet. At that time, the Labour government was enjoying a constantly high approval rating. Its term of office was supposed to end in May 2002, but, considering the prevailing political situation to be advantageous, the Labour government decided to call a general election one year ahead. Even with a Labour victory, which looked likely, there would still be a cabinet reshuffle.

The purpose of my trip was to improve communications with key cabinet figures so as to further shape China-UK relations and reinforce international coordination. This being the case, it would be wiser to postpone the visit until after the election.

In the summer of 2001, Labour won the election by an overwhelming margin and Jack Straw replaced Robin Cook as UK foreign secretary.

Born in 1946, Straw had been a lawyer in his early years and had been home secretary in Blair's first cabinet. Known for his prudence and eloquence, he had a certain prestige within the Labour Party.

Not long after, the world was shaken by the terrorist attacks of 9/11 and the international scene experienced complex and drastic changes. At the same time, the international political pattern entered a period of readjustment, and relations between major world powers experienced a new round of interaction. In this situation, it was incumbent on China and the United Kingdom to further enhance communication and coordination in international affairs. Therefore, I decided to combine my visit to the United Kingdom with one to Africa in early 2002.

So, having visited Eritrea, Ethiopia, and South Africa, I paid an official visit to the United Kingdom from January 16 to 19, 2002.

This was my first official visit to the United Kingdom as China's foreign minister. During the visit, I called on Prime Minister Tony Blair, Deputy Prime Minister John Prescott, former Prime Minister Edward Heath, and former Deputy Prime Minister Geoffrey Howe, and also held talks with Foreign Secretary Jack Straw.

During the meetings, besides the exchange of views on the development of China–UK relations and trade cooperation, I went into in-depth discussion with the British side on the international situation and hot issues after the events of 9/11, elaborating on China's antiterrorism stance and underlining the extremely unusual start of the new century with the world-shaking terrorist attacks. The challenges facing international society were of a global nature. China vehemently condemned any form of international terrorism and actively supported and participated in international antiterrorist cooperation, hoping to make a joint effort with the international community in safeguarding world peace and stability.

I gave a positive evaluation of China–UK relations, highlighting the fact that 2002 was the thirtieth anniversary of the upgrading

Meeting with former British Prime Minister Edward Heath during the visit to UK, January 16–19, 2002.

With former British Deputy Prime Minister Geoffrey Howe during the visit to UK, January 16–19, 2002.

of China-UK diplomatic ties to the ambassadorial level. Thanks to the efforts of both sides, the relationship had maintained a good momentum of comprehensive development. I reiterated that China valued the United Kingdom's international status and role, and had made unremitting efforts to push forward the all-around development of China-UK ties from a strategic height. In the new situation, our two countries should step up consultation and cooperation to make the current bilateral tie even more fruitful.

The British side showed great enthusiasm for developing our bilateral relations. Prime Minister Blair spoke highly of UK-China relations, believing that in the complicated and volatile international situation, the United Kingdom and China should strengthen communication and coordination in international affairs and deepen bilateral cooperation. Recalling his visit to China in 1998, Prime Minister Blair said that the British government attached great importance to developing relations with China and that he looked forward to making a second visit.

During the meeting, Foreign Secretary Jack Straw also emphasized the British government's priorities in developing relations with China, and hoped for increased cooperation in bilateral and international affairs. He told me he was eager to deepen his understanding of China, but had not visited the country since becoming foreign secretary. I invited him to visit China as soon as possible, and Straw accepted with pleasure, indicating that he would start preparations right away and confirm the date within two weeks. His eagerness was obvious.

Meeting with former British Prime Minister Edward Heath and former British Deputy Prime Minister Geoffrey Howe, I praised their years of endeavor in promoting China–UK relations, facilitating closer bilateral contact at the nongovernmental level, and improving mutual understanding between our two peoples.

They said that China was a responsible power playing an increasingly important role in the world, and that there were many issues that could not be settled without the participation of China; that, as China's growth had brought significant opportunities to the United Kingdom, they would launch more active efforts in advancing the relationship.

I also attended a welcome banquet hosted by Asia House and delivered a speech entitled "Enhance International Cooperation to Jointly Tackle Challenges."

Asia House is a semiofficial organization in the United Kingdom, founded in 1995, which aims at introducing Asian culture and promoting cultural and commercial cooperation between United Kingdom and Asian countries. Asia House often invites senior government delegations from Asian countries visiting the United Kingdom to meet with British entrepreneurs, and give presentations on their respective government policies and economic growth.

Learning of my planned visit, Asia House made it known to

our embassy in London that they would prepare a welcome dinner for me, at which they hoped I would deliver an address. Seeing this as a good opportunity to introduce China to British business circles, I accepted the invitation with pleasure and decided to speak in English. For this, I sought coaching by senior translators in the Ministry's Department of Translation and Interpretation.

About 150 people attended the dinner that night, mostly well-known figures in British business circles. The dinner was permeated with a warm and friendly atmosphere.

In my speech, I presented China's perspective on the international situation and our diplomatic policies, making the point that China, as a developing country, treated economic development as a long-term mission. China's interests were tied up with the interests of other countries in the world, and China would safeguard world peace and promote common development jointly with the international community.

I also noted that China and the United Kingdom, as two permanent members of the UN Security Council, had strengthened

Addressing the Asia House welcome banquet during the visit to UK, January 16–19, 2002.

their cooperation on many international and regional hot issues. In the current complicated and volatile international situation in particular, China and the United Kingdom bore increased responsibilities and shared more common interests, so enhanced cooperation was essential.

Finally, I said that the future held promising prospects for China and the UK working in friendly cooperation, and that our two countries would make greater contributions to world peace and stability and to human progress.

The British had also arranged for me to visit Scotland. Scotland, in the northern part of the British island, has a reputation for science and technology, culture and arts. The Scottish people have unique ethnic traditions, music, arts, and traditional dress. Scottish bagpipe music tells the history of the Scottish people and their indomitable spirit. I appreciated the beautiful pastoral scenery around Edinburgh and felt the friendly affection of the Scots towards the Chinese people.

During this visit, I felt deeply convinced that developing China-UK relations was a common choice based on the strategic and realistic interests of the two countries, as well as the sincere and earnest aspirations of the two peoples. China–UK relations would definitely stride forward into a new stage of rapid development.

Coordination for Cooperation

IF THE PERIOD BETWEEN 2000 and 2002 can be described as a warm-up for China-UK relations in the twenty-first century, the relationship went into in-depth development in the post-2003 period. In July 2003, Prime Minister Blair paid a second visit to China. This time he witnessed the amazing social changes China was undergoing. During the visit, he repeatedly praised China's great achievements, expressed his high expectations and enthusiasm for developing UK-China relations, and invited Premier Wen Jiabao to visit the United Kingdom at the earliest convenience.

In preparation for Premier Wen's visit, Prime Minister Blair set up a China Task Force under the chairmanship of Deputy Prime Minister John Prescott, and invited celebrities from economic, cultural, and educational circles to join in.

Inspired by the British initiative, as an interactive response to the United Kingdom, we founded our China-UK Relations Task Force, with me as the chairman, and Vice Foreign Minister Zhang Yesui as secretary general. The secretariat was established in the Ministry of Foreign Affairs. The task force drew members from the ministries of commerce, science and technology, culture, and education. It was the first high-level interactive coordination mechanism in China-UK bilateral relations, and a rare practice in the diplomatic service of either side.

China Task Force Chairman John Prescott was an important member of Tony Blair's cabinet, and had been deputy prime minister since 1997. He was frank, straightforward, and friendly to China. An energetic advocate of developing UK-China relations, he frequently shuttled between the two countries, making a total of ten visits to China during his term in office, more than any other political leader in the West.

On February 19, 2004, Prescott wrote congratulating me on the founding of our own task force. His letter described the work being undertaken by the British task force and his views on developing UK-China relations, proposing that both sides should strengthen cooperation in the fields of trade investment, education, scientific technology, and environmental protection.

I paid much attention to Prescott's letter. On February 24, I summoned and chaired a group meeting to discuss the general scheme and key cooperation fields for promoting China-UK bilateral relations suggested in the letter. It was a lively brainstorming discussion, which ended in a consensus to further deepen cooperation in seven key fields, namely, trade and investment, finance, energy, science and technology, education, culture, environmental conservation, and sustainable development.

In the field of trade and investment, we should ensure the stable growth of bilateral trade volume, striving for an increase to 20 billion US dollars within three years and 40 billion US dollars by 2010, and establish a commercial information network to encourage bilateral cooperation between small and medium enterprises (SMEs).

In the field of finance, we should upgrade the China–UK financial dialogue mechanism to the ministerial level, so as to promote communication and consultation on the macroeconomy as well as financial stability, and encourage the British banking sector to participate as a strategic investor in the restructuring and institutional reform of China's banking sector.

In the field of energy, we should discuss with the British the possibility of energy cooperation in third countries for joint exploration of overseas oil and gas fields.

In the field of science and technology, we should set up a China–UK high-tech venture capital cooperation fund, a China–UK information and communications technology (ICT) cooperation mechanism, and a China–UK high-tech and innovation park steering committee.

In the field of education, we should set up a mechanism for regular consultation between our Ministry of Education and Britain's Department of Education and Skills so as to improve Chinese language education in the United Kingdom.

In the field of culture, we should make a success of the Chinese Culture Year to be held in the United Kingdom in 2004 in order to strengthen cultural, tourist, and media communication between us.

In the field of environmental conservation, we should actively consider the British proposal to set up the UK–China Working Group on Climate Change.

I wrote back to Prescott on March 1, 2004, with details of the China Task Force's proposals that had emerged from our group discussion.

These proposals later became an important part of the China-UK joint statement on building a comprehensive strategic partnership, and constituted key areas of bilateral cooperation.

This was my first letter sent to Prescott since the establishment of our task forces. Subsequently, during our chairmanships, we wrote to each other eight times and held four meetings, establishing a deep personal friendship.

The task forces of the two sides played an important part in Premier Wen Jiabao's successful visit to the United Kingdom.

In May 2004, Premier Wen paid an official visit to the United Kingdom. During the visit, the two national leaders had extensive exchanges of views on China-UK relations and international issues of common concern, and reached many important areas of consensus. The two sides issued a joint statement, announcing the establishment of a comprehensive strategic partnership and the annual China-UK exchange of visits at the prime ministerial level, and the decision to enhance cooperation in the seven fields mentioned. A dozen agreements and memorandums on trade, education, and science and technology were also signed.

With this, our bilateral relations were promoted once more, from comprehensive partnership to comprehensive strategic partnership.

It was originally planned that the China-UK Relations Task Force would be disbanded after Wen Jiabao's visit to Britain, but during our work, both sides became convinced of its irreplaceable role in developing China-UK relations, and so insisted that this mechanism be maintained.

During Prescott's visit to China from late November to early December 2004, I held talks with him about the China-UK Relations Task Force. It was our first face-to-face exchange of views on the work of our task forces since they were founded. We agreed to maintain them as an important mechanism for studying China–UK relations strategies and the implementation of agreements reached by the state leaders.

The Honored Guest Returns

IN THE SECOND HALF of 2005, the EU presidency rotated to the United Kingdom for a second time. Britain proposed times to invite President Hu Jintao for a state visit to Britain.

The United Kingdom receives only two state visits a year. The invitation to President Hu came only six years after President Jiang Zemin's visit to the United Kingdom. It was a rare historical example of the British queen entertaining a foreign head of state, and a clear indication of how the British valued UK–China relations.

At that time, China and the EU were expanding every area of cooperation with successful results, and there was a greater willingness among the individual member states to enhance their political and strategic coordination with China. Since the United Kingdom held the EU presidency at the time, improving diplomatic ties with the United Kingdom benefited not only China–UK relations but also China-EU relations.

From November 8 to 10, 2005, I accompanied President Hu on his state visit to the United Kingdom.

There, President Hu met with Queen Elizabeth II, leaders of the House of Lords and the House of Commons, and the chairman of the Parliamentary China Group, and held talks with Prime Minister Tony Blair.

The president and prime minister had an in-depth exchange of views on specific measures for promoting China–UK comprehensive strategic partnership, and reached consensus in many areas. Both sides agreed that the establishment of the China–UK comprehensive strategic partnership marked a new stage in China–UK relations, and agreed to maintain the sound momentum of high-level contact between the two sides, enhance political dialogue to further deepen bilateral cooperation, and focus on public health and the Olympics as two new key areas of cooperation. The prime minister said China's development had brought opportunities to the United Kingdom and the world, and that the two countries would conduct closer cooperation in trade investment, technology transfer, energy, and sustainable development, and other areas.

During the visit, I held counterpart talks with Prescott and exchanged views with him on the priorities of our task force work. We agreed that the priorities should be stepping up the implementation of agreements reached by our respective national leaders so as to bring effect to the outcomes of the state visit.

We both agreed that the two task forces should be in the vanguard in the development of China–UK relations, provide suggestions for promoting bilateral relations, and remain forward-looking, well-planned, and highly productive.

With British Deputy Prime Minister John Prescott at talks in the Great Hall of the People, February 21, 2006.

Prescott and I together signed the China-UK Joint Statement on the High-Level Dialogue Mechanism of Sustainable Development.

One particular event impressed me deeply. This was "China: The Three Emperors," an exhibition of cultural relics from the Palace Museum held at the Royal Academy of Arts. President Hu and his wife, together with Queen Elizabeth and Prince Philip, attended the opening ceremony and cut the ribbon.

The exhibition displayed over four hundred precious art relics dating from the period 1662–1795, covering the reigns of the Qing emperors Kangxi, Yongzheng, and Qianlong. They included court calligraphy and paintings, ceramics and ornaments from Beijing's Palace Museum, many on public view for the first time. It was the largest exhibition ever held outside China by the Palace Museum.

This exhibition became the highlight of President Hu's state visit. Lasting over five months, the exhibition received 320,000 visits, setting a record for an exhibition held by the Royal Academy. The British press gave it extensive, extremely favorable coverage.

The Magic of "China Now"

THE PALACE MUSEUM VISITING exhibition aroused great enthusiasm among the British people to learn about Chinese culture.

In 2007, Prescott told me during his visit to China that the British business circles were planning a large-scale cultural exchange event to be called "China Now." It would last for about six months, from the Spring Festival celebrations in February 2008 to the Beijing Olympics opening ceremony on August 8.

Over eight hundred events and performances were planned for more than twenty cities throughout the United Kingdom, with colorful events on various themes spanning culture, trade and economy, education, science and technology, sports, and many other fields. Examples included the Qin Terracotta Army Exhibition,

China Women's Weeks, "Chinese Gourmet Festival, China Design Now," and Traditional Chinese Medicine (TCM) Week.

In terms of its scale, duration, level of participation and the activities involved, China Now was an unprecedented event in the history of China–UK exchange.

Prescott invited me to attend the opening.

Considering it a significant occasion, I accepted his invitation with pleasure and wished it success.

I considered it significant for two reasons.

First, it would help the British public know more about China and enable them to identify more with Chinese culture. With the growth of China's comprehensive national strength and the development of China–UK relations, different sectors of UK society wanted to get to know China better, enhance cooperation with China, and benefit from China's development. However, the average British person in the street knew little about China. According to a July 2007 survey, the majority of British people stated that the only Chinese celebrities they were familiar with were Mao Zedong, Confucius, and Jackie Chan. Clearly such a large-scale cultural exchange event was badly needed.

Second, the scope of China Now went far beyond a simple cultural exchange activity. It would be a very effective platform for communication and exchanges in many disciplines. Via this event the charm of traditional Chinese medicine, traditional gourmet foods, costume, animated movies, and many other products would be displayed to the British public, giving them a deeper understanding of changes in modern China, and increasing communication between the two peoples.

I instructed my ministry colleagues to cooperate closely with the British to make this event a great success.

The Chinese Central Authorities gave full backing and support to the British for this event. Premier Wen Jiabao gave a special instruction that China Now would enhance communication and mutual understanding between the peoples of China and Britain, and hoped both sides would work together to make it a success. The Central Authorities approved my proposal to pay an official visit to the United Kingdom as state councilor and China–UK Relations Task Force chairman, and to attend the opening of China Now.

The British government cooperated actively. Soon after Prescott returned to the United Kingdom, Gordon Brown replaced Tony Blair as prime minister and Prescott resigned as deputy prime minister, but despite the political changes, the British government remained very positive about China Now. Soon after assuming office, Prime Minister Brown said that the event would be valuable and exciting.

I arrived in London on the night of February 16, 2008, for my second official visit to the United Kingdom.

On the night of February 18, I attended the opening ceremony of China Now, held in the Guildhall of the City of London. The Guildhall, an ancient building dating from 1411, has hosted a large number of major events.

The Guildhall was ablaze with lights, as over three hundred

Proposing a toast at the China Now opening ceremony, February 18, 2008.

people from all walks of life in China and the United Kingdom gathered to celebrate the opening of China Now. Foreign Secretary David Milliband attended the ceremony.

Milliband was appointed UK foreign secretary in June 2007 at the age of forty-two, and was a respected figure among young Labour Party leaders. It was our first meeting at the ceremony, and though we did not have an in-depth conversation, I could tell he was energetic, quick-minded, innovative, and friendly to China.

People at the opening ceremony all spoke highly of China's achievements, hoping to take this opportunity to expand China-UK communication and cooperation.

I was deeply impressed by the atmosphere. In my speech, I first warmly congratulated the organizing committee on the magnificent opening of China Now and spoke highly of the innovative spirit needed to launch and host this pioneering undertaking in the history of China-UK relations, which would promote heart-to-heart communication between the two peoples and advance bilateral cooperation in various fields. I said that the Chinese government attached great importance to and fully supported China Now, that China would take this opportunity to deepen understanding and friendship between our two peoples and make China-UK cultural exchanges a model for different cultures to learn from each other, seeking similarities rather than differences, and promoting human civilization, prosperity, and progress. Finally I expressed my sincere wishes for the success of China Now.

Prior to attending the opening, I had made extensive contacts with the key members of Brown's cabinet.

Gordon Brown is a senior UK statesman, enjoying the same reputation as Tony Blair as key reformer central to the creation of New Labour. As chancellor of the exchequer, Brown had been keen on reform and showed outstanding management talent, being praised by the British press as the most successful and authoritative chancellor of the exchequer over the past two hundred years. During his term as chancellor of the exchequer, the British economy maintained long-term growth at a rate exceeding that of any other G-7 nation.

Brown assumed office as prime minister in June 2007 and visited China in January 2008, an indicator of how he valued China. When I visited him at 10 Downing Street, he was still immersed in beautiful memories of his China visit the month before, and kept mentioning his experiences there. He spoke highly of China's development achievements, praising the outstanding contribution to world stability and development made by China's economic growth.

Having conveyed cordial greetings and best wishes from President Hu Jintao, Chairman of the Standing Committee of the NPC Wu Bangguo and Premier Wen Jiabao, I expressed my view on China-UK relations, talked about my current visit, and made suggestions on the further development of the relationship.

Prime Minister Brown said that he believed the relationship to be in its best ever period and that the United Kingdom would endeavor to deepen the comprehensive strategic partnership with China. He also wished the Beijing Olympics complete success.

Through my contacts with Brown, I found him a practical person who valued China's development and had confidence in China's prospects.

Before leaving the United Kingdom, I also met with Prince Charles. He had been a history major. Despite his interest in Tibet, he had scant knowledge of the facts and China's policies relating to Tibet. We used to have little contact with him, but it was he who called for the meeting and even rescheduled his diary to make it possible.

Considering Prince Charles's Tibet complex, I gave a detailed description of the history of Tibet and the social, economic, cultural, and religious development and changes there, making clear China's stand on the Tibet question, and hoping he would arrive

With Prince Charles at Clarence House during the visit to UK, February 2008.

at a correct understanding of Tibet. He outlined the major social community work in which he was engaged and hoped the funds under his management would increase communication with China.

Ten years have gone by since 1998. During these ten years, China experienced immense changes, and so did China–UK relations.

Having shed its historical burden, China–UK relations have continued to improve and develop, from comprehensive partnership to comprehensive strategic partnership. It is my sincere hope for the future that China–UK relations will grow in the right direction, towards healthy and stable development.

China-France Relations as a New Millennium Dawns

THE FIRST TIME I set foot in France was in April 1998, when I accompanied Premier Zhu Rongji on an official visit to France.

France is an ancient country with a long history and rich culture. From its voluminous political, philosophical, social, and literary works, we can see France's multifaceted society and form a distinct mental image of the country. France is a cradle of talents: Jean-Jacques Rousseau, Baron de Montesquieu, and Voltaire lighted the sparks of the Enlightenment Movement; François Rabelais, Honoré de Balzac, and Victor Hugo left unprecedented literary masterpieces; René Descartes, Louis Pasteur, and Marie Curie made great contributions to human science. France, baptized in blood and fire, is a country full of revolutionary spirit, inspiring many French people to lay down their lives for national revival movements such as the French Revolution and the Paris Commune. The Cathedral of Notre Dame, the Louvre museum, and the Palace of Versailles house a wealth of treasure. I had always looked forward to experiencing the extensive and profound humanistic charm of France and to deepening my understanding of French political and social affairs.

France is also an influential world power, a permanent member of the UN Security Council, and a founding state of the European Union, playing a significant role in EU and international affairs.

France was also the first Western power to establish formal diplomatic relations with the PRC. On January 27, 1964, Chairman Mao Zedong and General Charles de Gaulle made the historic decision to establish China-France diplomatic relations at the ambassadorial level, a decision dubbed by Western media a "Diplomatic Nuclear Explosion," and which had a profound impact on the world. Since then, China-France relations have on the whole been moving in the right direction in spite of some twists and turns.

France occupies an important place in our overall diplomacy, so I always saw our French diplomacy as an important duty on my part.

From April 5 to 7, 1998, Premier Zhu Rongji paid an official visit to France, after his visit to the United Kingdom and attending the First EU-China Summit and the Second Asia-Europe Meeting (ASEM) there. During the course of the visit, Premier Zhu held in-depth and concrete talks with President Jacques Chirac, Premier Lionel Jospin, and other French state leaders, met with Senate President René Monory, and delivered a speech at the joint breakfast meeting of Federation of French Employers and France-China Committee for promoting China-France trade cooperation.

On the morning of April 6, I accompanied Premier Zhu Rongji to meet President Chirac at the Élysée Palace. Situated on the north side of the Avenue des Champs-Elysées, the most flourishing street in Paris, the Élysée Palace dates back to 1718. It was originally an aristocrat's residence but became royal property in 1764. Subsequently, the palace had several changes of owners, including Napoleon Bonaparte and Empress Josephine, and became the presidential residence in 1848.

It was my first meeting with President Chirac. Over six feet tall, he was a smart thinker, elegant, and always laughing heartily. I was deeply impressed by his strategic thoughts on China-France relations, and by his passion for, and expertise in, Chinese culture.

During the cordial and friendly talks between Premier Zhu and President Chirac, Chirac said that France valued relations with China for political and economic as well as historical and cultural reasons, that he wished to develop a comprehensive relationship with China, and that he had been deeply impressed by his visit to China in May of the previous year.

Premier Zhu told him that the Chinese government would continue to treat China-France relations from a strategic height, wishing to enhance cooperation on bilateral relations and international issues, and contribute joint efforts with France for world peace, stability, and prosperity.

At noon, President Chirac hosted a sumptuous welcome banquet for Premier Zhu at his official residence. After the banquet, Premier Zhu held talks with Prime Minister Jospin at his official residence, the Hôtel Matignon.

Located in the 7th arrondissement, among a cluster of government offices, the Hôtel Matignon was built in 1721 as the residence of a French marshal, and has been the official residence of French prime ministers since 1935.

During the talks, Jospin said to Premier Zhu that China was playing an increasingly important role on the international stage, that the expansion of opening up had caused its economy to soar, both of which factors were beneficial for achieving balance in international relations, and that France as a friend of China was keeping a close watch on its development.

Premier Zhu praised Prime Minister Jospin's China-friendly policies, saying that China would, as ever, highly value its ties with France, and would join France in promoting mutually beneficial friendly cooperation in various fields.

Premier Zhu invited Prime Minister Jospin to pay an official visit to China before the end of the year. Jospin accepted the invitation with pleasure and the dates of September 24–26 were fixed.

Before we went to London for the Second ASEM, the French side had proposed holding counterpart talks between their Foreign Minister Hubert Védrine and China's new foreign minister accompanying Premier Zhu on his visit to France. I had been in the post for only a few weeks, and was keen to build direct contacts with France as soon as possible in order to do a better job.

On April 6, I went to the French Ministry of Foreign Affairs for counterpart talks with Védrine. He was a senior diplomatic official who had served the president for many years and who saw France-China relations as very important.

Although it was our first meeting, we found each other very congenial, and our exchange of views went beyond China–France relations on to major international issues.

Foreign Minister Védrine said that France-China relations were important for France's overall foreign policy, and that promoting relations with China was by no means a fashionable trend. Both France and China looked forward to a balanced, multipolar world and could play an important role in building it.

I said that China always looked at our bilateral relations from a strategic height, and that both countries bore great responsibilities, both as major world powers and as permanent members of the UN Security Council. Enhancing China-France cooperation would exert a positive influence in the changing international situation. I also urged further improvements in communication and coordination between our respective foreign ministries, permanent missions to the United Nations, and delegations to multilateral institutions. Védrine fully agreed.

Premier Zhu's visit was China's first significant France-directed diplomatic activity after the inauguration of China's new leadership administration, and Premier Zhu was the first Chinese state leader to visit France since the establishment of the bilateral, twenty-first-century-oriented comprehensive partnership. The visit also laid a solid foundation for the giant leap in China-France relations in the new century. President Chirac added that Premier Zhu's visit was a vindication of France's "constructive dialogue" policy towards China and had "commendable achievements."

Personally, I was deeply and favorably impressed by everything: France's diplomatic concept and attitudes towards China, its lovely scenery, the ancient buildings in Paris that breathed history, the charming and gentle River Seine, and the passionate, romantic, and eloquent character of the French people.

I subsequently paid official visits to France in 1999, 2001, and 2002, frequently accompanied state leaders to France, and met with many visiting French delegations, thus witnessing the entire rapid development of China-France relations.

My First Official Visit to France

BETWEEN JANUARY 15 AND 16, 1999, I paid my first official visit to France as China's foreign minister.

After I assumed office, the French repeatedly expressed the hope that I would pay a return visit as soon as possible, so as to maintain the mechanism of regular reciprocal visits of foreign ministers.

In 1998, there was a dramatic shift in the international situation, especially when the Iraq nuclear weapon inspection crisis broke out, and the United States launched air strikes against Iraq at the end of the year known as "Desert Fox."

China and France shared similar views on the Iraq crisis, among many international issues, and both promoted cooperation in the United Nations and other multilateral institutions. I believed our two countries needed to communicate and coordinate, and so, in early 1999, after a trip to Africa, I went on to France.

I reached Paris at midday on January 15, going immediately to discussions with Foreign Minister Védrine, in which we exchanged in-depth views on the international situation and the Iraq crisis. We were already on quite familiar terms, thanks to our previous meetings.

On the international situation, I commented on two major international trends since the end of the Cold War, namely world multipolarity and economic globalization. These trends had accelerated, but certain countries were reluctant to accept the fact of multipolarity and still clung to the Cold War mentality, thereby provoking the natural opposition of a majority of nations. China had constantly advocated a multipolar future, seeing it as an essential and inevitable world trend.

Védrine agreed, saying that France hoped for a multipolar rather than a unipolar world and for this a balanced and stable relationship between the poles was a prerequisite.

We agreed that our two countries, both being internationally influential, shared wide areas of agreement on many major inter-national issues, and hence should further strengthen cooperation in international affairs, thereby contributing to the establishment of a fair and reasonable new international political and economic order.

As regards the Iraq crisis that had caused wide international concern, I made China's stance clear, stressing China's consistent belief that any unilateral military operation without UN Security Council authorization would have a very adverse effect on settling the Iraq issue and would destabilize the international situation.

Védrine added that the US Iraq policy was centered on pun-ishment, while France believed it should aim at solutions. New approaches should be adopted to cope with the new Iraq situa-tion, while France and China should improve their coordination on enhancing the authority of the United Nations and the Security Council.

The next day, President Chirac met with me at the Élysée Pal-ace. This was my first one-to-one talk with him and he struck me as a world-class statesman, full of strategic vision, approachable, and agreeable.

I remember that President Chirac specially cut short a military inspection outside Paris and returned at dusk for our meeting. It started at five-thirty and was scheduled to last an hour, but Presi-dent Chirac was so engrossed in the conversation that it overran by half an hour.

He told me that further enhancing cooperation with China was the established government policy and that France would join China in boosting bilateral ties at a faster rate.

For my part, I pointed out that France had been the first West-ern major power to establish diplomatic relations with China, and that 1999 was the thirty-fifth anniversary. China had consistently valued its relationship with France and was ready to upgrade the cooperation to a higher level.

President Chirac also said how much he loved Chinese poetry, especially the poems of Li Bai and Du Fu. President Jiang Zemin had written out for him Li Bai's poem *Thoughts in a Tranquil Night* and he showed this to me, remarking that President Jiang's beautiful script was one of his favorite styles of Chinese calligraphy. After the meeting, President Chirac accompanied me in person to the front gate of his official residence, stood for the photo call, and saw me into my car. I knew this treatment stemmed from his warm feelings for China.

Doors Open for China

DURING MY VISIT, PRESIDENT Chirac told me he would like to invite President Jiang Zemin to France.

President Jiang had visited France in 1994, the first visit of China's head of state to a Western power since the formation of China's third-generation central collective leadership. This had turned over a new page for China-Europe relations. President Chirac paid his first state visit to China in 1997, during the course of which we had issued a joint declaration to build a comprehensive partnership oriented to the twenty-first century. Thereafter, bilateral cooperation in various fields had developed even faster.

Before bringing up the subject with me, President Chirac had written to President Jiang at the end of 1998, inviting him for a second visit to France. During our meeting, he made a point of inviting President Jiang to visit Corrèze, his native area, which was a very special courtesy in diplomatic protocol.

President Chirac's repeated cordial and sincere invitations to President Jiang within just a few months sent a clear diplomatic signal of his valuing France-China relations. He himself had said on many occasions that China would be an important pole in a future multipolar world, would soon rise as a world power, and that there should be closer communication and cooperation between the two countries.

Summit diplomacy was then less frequent than it is today. According to diplomatic practice, China's supreme leader rarely made more than one state visit to any one country while in office.

However, the world around us was changing rapidly. With the end of the Cold War, France hoped to maintain an independent foreign policy and play a larger part in international affairs. For China, developing and improving relations with France would benefit China-Europe relations, strengthen China's position and role in the international arena, and help form a multipolar world.

Our Ministry of Foreign Affairs submitted a report to the Central Authorities, recommending acceptance of President Chirac's invitation to President Jiang for a second state visit to France. This was approved.

France attached great importance to the visit of President Jiang. President Chirac personally scrutinized the schedule, and gave repeated instructions to the French Ministry of Foreign Affairs and other departments not to be restrained by protocol regulations and traditions, and to do their utmost in making good arrangements. Madame Chirac made a special trip to Corrèze, accompanying the Chinese advance team on a field survey, and made meticulous and considerate preparation for President Jiang's visit.

Diplomatic protocol is highly sophisticated. Particular reception standards are prescribed for different kinds of visits. Visits of state leaders are categorized into official, working, and private. A state visit is a form of official visit, one in which the leader of a nation comes at the invitation of the host country's head of state.

Normally, a state visit includes a welcome ceremony and formal talks and meetings held in the capital, with supplementary visits outside the capital. This time, however, to create the right conditions and ambience for direct communication between the two heads of state and to show their closeness, the two sides decided to arrange a private visit for President Jiang to President Chirac's hometown, to be followed by an official visit to Paris.

President Jiang, accompanied by Vice Premier Qian Qichen and me, paid a second state visit to France between October 22 and 25, 1999. During this visit, I was deeply impressed by the distinguished courteous reception arranged by the French, and by the in-depth exchange of views between the two heads of state on a series of important issues.

On the night of October 22, the special plane carrying President Jiang and his wife arrived in Lyon, the first stop on their French visit. Former French Prime Minister and Mayor of Lyons Raymond Barre met them at the airport, and held a grand welcome banquet at city hall in the heart of the city.

At noon the following day, having made a special journey from Paris, President and Madame Chirac hosted a banquet luncheon at the time-honored restaurant La Tour Rose for President Jiang and his wife and entourage, inviting the guests to savor the region's gourmet delicacies.

The highlight of this state visit was President Jiang's being invited to President Chirac's private residence, Château de Bity, in his native area of Corrèze.

Corrèze lies in central France on the Massif Central. Over 400 kilometers from Paris, it covers an area of 5,857 square kilometers with a population of 230,000. In 1964, Jacques Chirac bought the four-hundred-year-old Château de Bity when he was head of the personal staff of Prime Minister Georges Pompidou. It was the first time that Chirac received a foreign head of state at his private residence.

On the afternoon of October 23, the two presidential couples arrived in Corrèze aboard President Chirac's special plane and stayed at the Château de Bity while the rest of us stayed in a hotel not far away. President Jiang stayed in Corrèze for about twenty hours.

President Chirac accompanied President Jiang in all his activities here. They had in-depth conversations totaling more than ten hours, covering the international situation, China-Europe relations, China-France relations, and a broad range of sensitive issues such as Tibet, Taiwan, human rights, and the NATO bombing of the Chinese embassy in Yugoslavia.

During their talks, President Jiang stressed that the world is varied and multifaceted, and could not be unipolar, and hoped we would enhance bilateral cooperation in various fields.

President Chirac agreed, saying that within fifty years, China would definitely be a leading world power and a key pole in the multipolar world. France believed the world could be considered multipolar only if this was the case.

Both sides agreed to set up a China-France summit hotline for strategic dialogue, so as to urge the EU to lift its embargo on weapon sales to China. Chirac was the first leader of an EU member state to show his support for China on this issue.

On the subject of China-Europe relations, President Chirac painted a picture of the European situation, saying that having implemented the single market and monetary unification, the EU was now trying to promote a joint defense policy. For Europe to maintain its independence in the future multipolar world, it was vital to enhance joint defense. The EU and China, two important poles" of the future world, must strengthen dialogue between them.

President Jiang elaborated on Tibet's history and China's stand on the Tibet issue. President Chirac said that the Tibet issue was an internal matter for China, and that France saw Tibet as an indisputable, integral part of China.

On Taiwan, President Chirac said France would firmly uphold the one-China principle, and hoped that the Taiwan issue could be peacefully settled on the basis of one country, two systems.

President Chirac was the first state leader of a Western power to express clear support for the one country, two systems policy.

Concerning human rights and democracy, President Jiang said world opinion was completely wrong to claim that there was no democracy in China. The Party had always supported democracy before and after the founding of the People's Republic. However, democracy in China should be relative rather than absolute and should conform to Chinese conditions.

President Chirac observed that since France had modified its approach to the human rights issue in China he had seen the progress achieved in this area, and hoped that China would continue to move forward on human rights, of course, without jeopardizing its national stability.

The two heads of state also had an in-depth exchange of views on European and Asian affairs, reform of international monetary and financial systems, the Kosovo crisis, the comprehensive nuclear test ban, the Russia–Chechnya conflict, and the India–Pakistan situation, among other international issues.

President Jiang told the French president that Chirac was the first foreign state leader with whom he had had such long and in-depth discussions, and that these exchanges could be categorized as "enhancing friendship through complete candor, seeking common ground and setting aside differences." President Chirac agreed wholeheartedly.

On the afternoon of October 24, 1999, President Jiang arrived in Paris aboard President Chirac's special plane from Corrèze Airport. President Chirac held a grand welcome ceremony for the start of President Jiang's official visit to France.

In Paris, the two heads of state held official talks and called a joint press conference. President Jiang also met with French Prime Minister Lionel Jospin, National Assembly President Laurent Fabius, and Senate President Christian Poncelet, and delivered a speech at the Federation of French Employers.

President Jiang's visit to France was a significant diplomatic move towards Europe at the turn of the twenty-first century, having an enormous impact in France and Europe as a whole. President Chirac described it as "a major event in the history of France-China friendly relations, a sign of relationship entering a new development stage."

People from all walks of life in France widely regarded the visit as "extraordinarily successful" and as "exerting a profound influence on France-China relations." The French media paid great attention to the visit, and gave enormous, extensive, and objective coverage, saying: "France holds an important place in Chinese diplomacy, and is the only Western country to have received two successive state visits paid by President Jiang. China has become France's first preferred cooperation partner; their bilateral cooperation should look forward to the future and contribute to the building of a multipolar world."

During his reciprocal visit to China in October 2000, President Chirac reached many areas of consensus with President Jiang on the development of China-France relations, including setting up a summit hotline and promoting strategic dialogue, both being implemented through bilateral coordination.

Meanwhile, at the beginning of 2001, the international situation was facing new problems and challenges. In the United States, President George W. Bush took office and soon made great changes to American foreign policies, decided to promote the National Missile Defense (NMD) program, and launched air attacks against Iraq jointly with the United Kingdom. France was opposed to United States' developing and deploying the NMD system, and condemned the bombing of Iraq. France, China, and other peace-loving countries took similar positions, campaigning and striving for world peace.

This was how things stood when I accepted France's invitation to pay a second official visit from March 31 to April 2, 2001.

When meeting President Chirac, I told him that China-France

With French Foreign Minister Hubert Védrine in Paris, April 2, 2001.

relations had made new progress since his visit to China the previous October. The agreements reached between him and President Jiang had been implemented comprehensively. As China and France shared extensive common interests on a range of issues, enhancing bilateral cooperation not only benefited the interests of each country, but was also conducive to safeguarding world peace and stability.

President Chirac expressed his satisfaction with the current state of France-China relations, hoping both sides would join efforts to enhance dialogue and increase mutual understanding, thereby promoting communication and cooperation in political, economic, and cultural fields.

During my talks with Foreign Minister Védrine, he shared with me his views on the foreign policy of the new US administration, saying that the United States overrated its own strength, unaware of the need for negotiations or dialogue with the outside world, and adopted very tough foreign policies. He thought that the new administration would follow a unilateralist rather than an isolationist policy, and would do whatever it pleased.

Later, the launching of the Iraq War and other actions proved how accurate Védrine's analysis of the American attitude had been.

Visiting France After the World Expo Application

IN EARLY JULY 2002, I paid a special visit to France to give a presentation on China's bid to host the 2010 World Expo. China sent a high-caliber delegation headed by State Councilor Wu Yi, including the minister of Foreign Trade and Economic Cooperation, leaders of Shanghai Municipal Government, the China Council for the Promotion of International Trade, and me.

World Expos are also known as International Expositions or World's Fairs. The first ever was held in London's Hyde Park for a period of six months. Since then, many American and European cities, among them Paris, Vienna, Philadelphia, and Chicago, have hosted world expos more than once.

In November 1928, a meeting of representatives from thirty-one countries that frequently participated in world expos signed the Convention on International Exhibitions and decided to set up the Bureau of International Expositions (BIE) for coordinating and organizing the hosting of such events. Headquartered in Paris, BIE is an international governmental organization and each member state has a vote in the bidding to host the event.

BIE holds two conferences a year. In 2002, BIE had only eighty-nine member states, but the number has now grown to 155. China officially entered BIE in May 1993.

There are two types of world expo: Those with a comprehensive theme are usually held every five years and of six-month duration, for example, the 2010 Shanghai World Expo; the others have a particular theme and last for three months, like the 1999 World Horticultural Exposition in Kunming, China.

On July 13, 2001, Beijing had won the bid to host the 29th Olympic Games. In this situation, China also bid to host 2010 World Expo, seeing it as a grand event displaying economic, trade, and cultural achievements, and promoting international understanding and cooperation.

China had maintained twenty-three years of rapid economic growth, witnessing dramatic changes in various fields. The golden opportunity of hosting the 2010 World Expo would allow China to show its magnificent achievements to the world in a comprehensive fashion, and enhance its communication and cooperation with other countries. Every previous host country regarded the World Expo as an important platform to boost the national economy, expand foreign cooperation, and upgrade its international standing.

In May 2001, China submitted to BIE its official application to host the 2010 World Expo in Shanghai. The competitive bidding for this honor is done in the country's name. Hence, I, as foreign minister representing the Chinese government, officially signed the application letter on May 2, 2001.

South Korea, Argentina, Mexico, Poland, and Russia were also bidding. Winning the bid in the face of such powerful competition would be no easy task. It called for extensive work through various channels, including diplomacy. Therefore, I asked the Ministry of Foreign Affairs to cooperate closely and actively with the Shanghai Municipal Government and other departments for the bidding.

BIE would announce the name of the 2010 World Expo host country in December 2002, before which the bureau would carefully inspect each bidding city and hear presentations from each bidding country. An excellent bid presentation is crucial to winning the support of BIE member states.

The bid presentations for the 2010 World Expo were scheduled for the afternoon of July 2, 2002, between two-thirty and five, allowing thirty minutes per country. China's presentation was second in the running order.

My speech had to be in English rather than being translated from Chinese, so I really did spend a great deal of time preparing. In my youth, I had studied English for three years at Shanghai's Fudan University, but switched to Japanese and had subsequently been involved in Japanese diplomatic work for a long time. So, having had little chance to use my English, I was no longer as proficient. As soon as I got the script, I started making meticulous preparations for the speech. I consulted a colleague from the Department of International Organizations and Conferences who was skilled at giving English speeches, and I kept on practicing pronunciation, intonation, and articulation.

After State Councilor Wu Yi had given a general overview, I elaborated on the specific commitments of the Chinese government. I said that today's China had become a part of the wider world. China had formed a new opening-up pattern, one that was pandimensional, multilayered, and wide-ranging; it was dedicated to developing friendly and mutually beneficial cooperative relations on an equal footing with all countries in the world in political, economic, cultural, and other fields, and was looking forward to expanding cooperation with them in the interests of common prosperity and progress. The Chinese government pledged to give full financial support to a Shanghai World Expo, to provide special funds for developing countries' participation, to strictly implement the regulations of the 1928 Convention on International Exhibitions, and to provide every necessary courtesy and convenience to the staff and goods of all participating countries and regions.

Our presentation was applauded by the representatives at the meeting. BIE President Gilles Noghès said that China had shown its strength in the best possible fashion.

The bid presentation proved a great success, and laid a sound foundation for our victory several months later. At the 132nd BIE Congress held in Monte Carlo, on the night of December 3, 2002, Shanghai finally won the right to host the 2010 World Expo. China had won world recognition and respect for a second time, and Shanghai welcomed another precious development opportunity.

After making the bid presentation, I started my third official visit to France. One month earlier, a new French government had been formed.

On July 4, 2002, I held talks with the new Foreign Minister Dominique de Villepin in their Ministry of Foreign Affairs, where we had a candid and in-depth exchange of views on China-France relations and many international issues of common concern.

First, I extended my congratulations to Mr. de Villepin on his appointment, and said that during the forty years following the establishment of China-France diplomatic ties our relations had kept on moving forward. In 1997, China and France had established a twenty-first-century-oriented comprehensive partnership, creating a new milestone in the history of China-France relations. China had consistently valued France's position in Europe and the world, and was keen to maintain a long-term and stable comprehensive partnership. Facing the complicated and volatile international situation, China and France should enhance cooperation to keep on improving relations between the two countries.

He fully endorsed my evaluation of China-France relations, saying that developing relations with China was a priority of French foreign policy. France attached great importance to China's influence in international affairs, and wished to promote close cooperation and coordination with China in the United Nations and other international organizations. France would strive for comprehensive development of the France-China partnership by expanding communication and cooperation with China in fields such as economy, science and technology, education, and culture.

The next day, Prime Minister Jean-Pierre Raffarin met with

me in Hôtel Matignon, which was our first meeting. Raffarin had
been a provincial politician and not well known in national political
circles before becoming prime minister, and was dubbed a "genial
chap" by the press. My first impression was that he was bright, mild,
prudent, and friendly to China. Later, he proved an active and resolute promoter of China-France friendship, who came to the rescue
every time when our relations hit difficulties.

Prime Minister Raffarin said to me happily that I was his first
foreign guest since giving his inaugural speech, and this demonstrated the friendly relations between the two countries. He had
paid great attention to China's reform and opening up, and admired
the progress China had achieved.

I extended my thanks for the meeting, praised his friendly attitude to China, and said that China had consistently valued its relations with France as an influential power in Europe and the world.
We live in an increasingly multipolar world and growing economic
globalization, and the international situation was full of complexities. Under these circumstances, China and France should definitely
enhance cooperation in bilateral and international affairs to ben-

Receiving a traditional local welcome in France, November 24, 2002.

efit our two peoples and to contribute to enduring cooperation and world prosperity.

I exchanged views with Prime Minister Raffarin on China-France relations, China-Europe relations, and China-France cooperation in trade, economy, culture, and other areas.

Raffarin said that France-China trade and economic cooperation was based on a solid foundation, and had immense potential. In the future, the two sides should expand cooperation in culture, education, and other fields. Both countries were in favor of a multipolar world and had similar views on many major international issues. France would strive together with China to push forward the France-China comprehensive partnership.

After our talks, Prime Minister Raffarin told me that his previous visit to China had left him with a beautiful and profound impression, and hoped to visit China as soon as possible after taking office as prime minister. I immediately said he would be welcome.

Later on, both sides agreed to arrange Prime Minister Raffarin's visit to China for late April of the following year.

A Friend in Need Is a Friend Indeed

As an old Chinese saying goes, "Anything unexpected may happen any time." One month before Prime Minister Raffarin was due, China was struck by the severe SARS epidemic and was completely embroiled in combating the disease.

During that period, certain foreign state leaders suggested postponing their scheduled visits to China, but when we contacted the French to discuss Prime Minister Raffarin's visit, they told us Raffarin would stick to the original schedule.

One can imagine how difficult such a decision was for Prime Minister Raffarin. On arrival in Beijing, he told reporters there were loud voices in France trying to persuade him to delay his trip, but President Chirac had strongly supported sticking to the original schedule, and this had made him even more determined. Raffarin said he would never shirk his responsibility to strengthen France-China cooperation and that, when China encountered difficulties, France should show sympathy and friendship.

There were high expectations for Raffarin's visit both within and beyond China. I asked the Ministry of Foreign Affairs not to allow any slip in the reception work, but to make it better than usual.

The top party and state leaders paid great attention to this visit. Vice Premier Wu Yi, in charge of public health, presided over the reception work with the active cooperation of the departments concerned. Difficulties of all sorts were overcome, and meticulous and attentive preparations were made by 651 people working overtime.

On April 22, 2003, Vice Premier Wu Yi met with France's Ambassador to China Jean-Pierre Lafon, and described the SARS situation and our careful health security arrangements for Prime Minister Raffarin's visit, thereby winning the understanding and trust of the French side and laying a solid foundation for a successful visit.

At seven-thirty on the morning of April 25, an Airbus A310 taxied to the South Aircraft Parking Apron at Beijing Capital International Airport. Prime Minister Raffarin and his delegation of more than one hundred arrived in Beijing. As soon as he came down the gangway, Raffarin said he and his delegation would not wear protective gauze masks during the visit, as he believed China was capable of controlling SARS.

Perhaps inspired by Prime Minister Raffarin's spirit, it was not just the French delegation that wore no masks: Neither French nor Chinese reception staff wore them throughout the visit.

From his arrival in Beijing at seven-thirty in the morning on April 25 to his departure at one o'clock on April 26, Prime Minister Raffarin's schedule was packed tight. China gave him a special high-level reception. President Hu Jintao specially hosted a small-scale welcome banquet for him. Premier Wen Jiabao accompanied him to the National Grand Theater, which had been designed by a French architect. President Hu and Premier Wen had an in-depth exchange of views with Prime Minister Raffarin on bilateral relations and significant international issues, highly praising the French government's "true friendship tempered in adversity" to the Chinese people. A series of important cooperative agreements were signed.

China's warm reception contributed to the success of Prime Minister Raffarin's visit, and also left a deep impression on him. His second visit as prime minister in 2005 made him the only French prime minister in the history of China-France relations to pay two visits to China during his term of office. The Anti-Secession Law was released during his second visit to China. He repeated that France upheld the one-China principle and expressed his understanding of the formulation of China's Anti-Secession Law.

When he left office, Raffarin was elected senator, and continues to dedicate himself to France-China relations. In November 2005, he said with deep emotion at China Foreign Affairs University, "I have countless reasons to tell myself I must be a friend of China!"

In April 2008, when the Olympic torch relay passed through Paris, anti-China sentiment was becoming acute, giving rise to great trepidation in French political circles. Raffarin stood out to attend the starting ceremony of the torch relay at the Eiffel Tower, where he delivered a solemn speech to the press, saying that "the torch relay allows the whole world to bathe in the glory of the Olympic spirit. Olympics are great events to promote communication and friendship between sportsmen of all nations. In spite of the differences that exist among us, the Olympics enable us to seek common ground and set aside differences."

446 HEAVY STORM AND GENTLE BREEZE

Raffarin used practical actions to fulfill his commitments, resolutely supporting and safeguarding China-France relations. He has been a true and reliable friend of the Chinese people.

Successful Debut in Evian

DURING HIS VISIT TO China in 2003, Prime Minister Raffarin handed to President Hu Jintao an invitation letter from President Chirac to attend the South-North leaders' dialogue meeting during the G8 Summit to be held in Evian, France, on June 1, 2003.

The G8 was founded in 1975 by French President Valéry Giscard d'Estaing. G8 Summit themes were originally major global economic topics, but, with globalization and the rise of emerging nations, they have expanded to encompass international political issues. The combined GDP of the G8 countries once constituted over 60 percent of the world total GDP, hence it was dubbed the "rich nations' club" by the press.

The idea of a South-North leaders' dialogue meeting was initiated by President Chirac in 2003. France, the former G8 presidency state, wanted to invite China, India, Brazil, South Africa, and other major developing countries to discuss significant world issues such as globalization, trade, and economic growth. In this connection, President Chirac had sent two sincere letters of invitation to President Hu.

At first, there was little consensus in China about whether to accept. Some expressed concern that, as a developing country, Chinese contact with the "rich nations' club" would affect its international status. Furthermore, China was burdened with heavy domestic tasks, going through the toughest stage in the battle against SARS, and, on top of that, China had declined invitations from other G8 members many times before.

However, more believed that if President Hu could attend the

South-North leaders' dialogue, it would be the first overseas visit since China's new central collective leadership took office. In their view, attendance would be helpful for China to expound its views on major international issues and advance its relations with Western countries; it would have positive significance in improving China's international status and showing China's new central leadership.

I agreed with the second opinion. Besides, my consideration at the time was to pay equal attention to domestic and international situations. The fight against SARS did consume much of our state leaders' time and energy, but the G8 meeting would be a golden opportunity to show China's governmental capability and image to the international community. Moreover, our diplomacy should be adaptable to changed situations and should dare to be innovative.

In the first years of the new millennium, the international situation and China's international position experienced profound changes. Because of China's rapid economic growth, the other nations regarded China as a significant power in international political and economic relations. The theme of this South-North leaders' dialogue meeting was South-North cooperation. As the world's largest developing country, China's participation or absence would have a bearing on our international image and on major strategic issues such as building a new international political and economic order.

After comprehensive and repeated consideration, the Ministry of Foreign Affairs submitted the official proposal to the central government, advising President Hu to accept President Chirac's invitation for the South-North leaders' dialogue meeting in Evian. Approval came quickly.

President Chirac was delighted to learn that President Hu would attend the meeting and instructed the president's office and France's foreign ministry to spare no effort in the reception of President Hu, to give special courteous treatment to the Chinese side, and to arrange for President Hu to be the first speaker at the meeting.

Every year, the G8 Summit stirred up large-scale protest activities launched by world antiglobalization organizations. The tightened security effort is a big headache for every host country and brains are racked to find a tranquil venue. This was France's underlying reason for selecting Evian for the summit.

A holiday paradise with picturesque scenery, Evian is situated south of Lake Geneva (called *Lac Léman* in France), just across the border from Lausanne in Switzerland. Most people may not know of Evian as an actual place, but are quite familiar with its world-famous brand of mineral water. Evian is a small town with only 7,500 residents and accessible by only one expressway, thus it is very secure for land communications. Since Evian itself did not have adequate hotel accommodation, the various national delegations, ours included, stayed in Lausanne.

On June 1, 2003, I accompanied Present Hu on the boat journey from Lausanne, arriving at nine forty-five that morning at the Evian lakeside, where President Chirac was waiting at the dock. President Hu was the only foreign head of state that President Chirac went all that way to greet.

President Chirac, beaming with delight, cordially shook hands with President Hu, and exchanged greetings with me and the rest of the entourage before accompanying President Hu to the Evian Royal Palace for a bilateral meeting.

The two heads of state talked for over an hour in a relaxed and friendly atmosphere, and had an in-depth exchange of views on bilateral relations and the international situation. President Chirac said he was very happy to have President Hu at the meeting, which had great symbolic significance for China and the world. France would continue to take the lead in improving Europe-China relations while deepening bilateral cooperation with China.

President Hu said that the China-France comprehensive partnership had been increasingly strengthened and enriched through the joint efforts of both sides. China attached great importance to developing the partnership and had full confidence in the prospects for China-France relations. Despite the current complicated and changing international situation, peace and development remained the themes of the times. In the long run, the multipolar tide would not be reversed. There were about two hundred countries in the world with a total population of over six billion, having different traditions and customs, religions and cultures, economic capacity, and social systems, and it was not likely they would ever adopt a single form of culture, a single political system, or a single development pattern. China would join the other peace-loving nations and peoples in the world to safeguard world peace and promote common development.

During the meetings, the two heads of state made strategic plans on developing China-France bilateral relations and reached significant consensus, including the planned reciprocal visits between the leaders of China and France in 2004.

At one-thirty that afternoon, President Hu attended the informal South-North leaders' dialogue and was the first to speak, with the address "Promote Comprehensive Cooperation for Common Development."

President Hu said that accelerated economic globalization was the most conspicuous feature of the current world economic situation, but that economic globalization was both a great opportunity and a challenge. Human society should seize the opportunity, address the challenge, seek common ground, set aside differences, and expand cooperation in order to steer economic globalization towards common prosperity.

President Hu also made four proposals for promoting common human progress: First, take forceful measures to promote global economic growth; second, champion harmonious coexistence to maintain world diversity; third, enhance multilateral cooperation to build a new international economic order; and fourth, enrich the substance of North-South cooperation through increased endeavor.

President Hu's suggestions were highly regarded by the participating leaders.

This short visit lasted only thirty-five hours, but, in addition to the conference meetings, President Hu had extensive contacts and talks with eighteen heads of state or government, and five heads of international institutions attending the dialogue. It was extremely effective in promoting China's relations with the United States, France, the United Kingdom, and Japan, and other Western powers, and in enhancing solidarity and cooperation with developing countries.

President Hu took various opportunities to expound China's stance on the international situation and major world issues, especially on the importance and urgency of strengthening North-South cooperation. In addition, he responded positively to reasonable proposals and suggestions from developing countries, and gave realistic advice on promoting North-South cooperation, which was highly appreciated by all participants.

President Hu's frank description of China's fight against SARS won broad understanding and support. There was wide praise from state leaders and international opinion for the Chinese government's capability in bringing the situation under control, responding to emergencies, and overcoming difficulties.

Since the South-North leaders' dialogue meeting in Evian, it has become a practice for Chinese state leaders to attend G8 dialogue meetings with leaders of developing countries.

China-France Friendship Peaks

FROM JANUARY 26 TO 29, 2004, President Hu Jintao paid a state visit to France at the invitation of President Chirac. It was President Hu's first official visit to the West during his term of office. The visit made a huge impact, since it was arranged for the fortieth anniversary of the establishment of China-France diplomatic relations, and was the climax of the China-France Culture Year during the Spring Festival.

I remember clearly that we arrived at Paris Orly Airport by special plane at about two o'clock on the afternoon of January 26.

The temperature was pretty low that day, made worse by a chilly drizzle. When our plane landed, we looked out the window and saw President Chirac, now in his seventies, standing erect in the rain, with his wife behind him, holding an umbrella over him, waiting for President Hu and his wife.

As our colleagues familiar with French diplomacy were very aware, it was a special courtesy for President and Madame Chirac to welcome their guests at the airport. President Hu and his wife walked quickly down the gangway, and shook hands firmly with President Chirac and his wife, exchanging warm greetings.

From the reception at the airport it was clear that France attached great importance to President Hu's visit. During the visit, the two heads of state attended nine events together, and Prime Minister Raffarin went in person to Toulouse to wait for and accompany President Hu on a visit to Airbus SAS. This was unprecedented.

To create a good atmosphere, the Municipal Government of Paris approved a Chinese Spring Festival costume parade on the Avenue des Champs-Elysées. Jointly organized by the Beijing Municipal Government and the Association of Overseas Chinese in France, this was the first foreign cultural event ever held on the Champs-Elysées; in another first, the world famous Eiffel Tower was decked in Chinese red neon lights for five nights. During his two days in Paris, President Hu attended some twenty events, held two talks with President Chirac, and met with Senate President Christian Poncelet, National Assembly President Jean-Louis Debré, Prime Minister Jean-Pierre Raffarin, and other French senior political leaders. President Chirac, Senate President Poncelet, and Prime Minister Raffarin each hosted welcome banquets. President and

Madame Chirac held a special private dinner for President Hu and his wife at Le Jules Verne Restaurant in the Eiffel Tower. President Hu delivered a speech at the National Assembly at their invitation, met representatives of French business circles, and attended a welcome ceremony held by the Paris Municipal Government.

On January 27, the fortieth anniversary of the establishment of China-France diplomatic relations, the two heads of state announced the joint declaration entitled "Deepening the Franco-Chinese Strategic Global Partnership in Order to Promote a Safer World Characterized by Greater Solidarity and Respect for Diversity," which upgraded China-France relations from a comprehensive partnership to a comprehensive strategic partnership.

During the talks and meetings, President Hu and President Chirac, along with other French state leaders, had candid and in-depth exchanges of views on China-France bilateral relations, China-Europe relations, practical cooperation, international and regional hot issues, and reached extensive areas of agreement. President Hu's intensive talks with President Chirac on the Taiwan issue were particularly effective.

At the beginning of 2004, the Taiwan authorities, led by Chen Shui-bian, had flagrantly used the so-called referendum to try to pursue Taiwan independence, plunging cross-strait relations into a most critical and sensitive period.

During his talks with Chirac, President Hu elaborated on the cross-strait situation and China's stance, stressing that Taiwan was an integral part of China, and that it was a common wish shared by all the Chinese people to resolve the Taiwan issue as early as possible so as to realize the complete unification of China. Upholding the principles of peaceful reunification and one country, two systems, the Chinese side would spare no effort in achieving the peaceful reunification of China while firmly opposing Taiwan independence, and would never allow anyone to separate Taiwan from the motherland in any guise or by any means.

President Chirac said that China's population, culture, and history proved the one-China principle indisputable. No one should doubt that Taiwan was part of China. The one-China principle was conducive to peace, and should therefore be followed, so that the unification issue could be resolved gradually by the Chinese in their own way. President Chirac made clear France's objection to the referendum.

It was the most positive commitment made by a Western country on the Taiwan issue.

Besides, President Chirac reiterated at the welcome banquet, joint press conference, and on other occasions that any unilateral action, including the Taiwan referendum, that undermined current stability was risky and irresponsible. It would be a serious mistake leading to regional instability.

His statement was undoubtedly a heavy blow for advocates of Taiwan independence.

President Hu delivered a speech at the French National Assembly in the Palais Bourbon, which is situated on the left bank of the River Seine opposite Place de la Concorde. Since it became the official site of National Assembly in 1830, only thirteen foreign state leaders had made speeches there, and President Hu was the first Asian head of state to speak from the platform of the circular debating chamber in the National Assembly.

French government officials, members of the National Assembly, and celebrities from all walks of life totaling over six hundred people listened to President Hu's speech, giving him a standing ovation at its end. National Assembly President Debré praised the rich, profound, and convincing content of the speech. Many National Assembly members told me that President Hu's speech had sent a clear signal that France-China friendship was an inevitable continuation of history. France and China should jointly endeavor to create a more beautiful and equitable world.

President Hu's visit to France was a great success and had far-reaching significance. As President Chirac said during their talks, "President Hu chose France from all European countries for his first state visit, which is an important signal demonstrating friendship and trust between our two peoples, and an important new step in the long histories of China and France."

After President Hu's visit, the development of China-France relations gathered momentum each day.

Chirac's Great Love of China

PRESIDENT CHIRAC COULD BE described as a "family friend" of China. We met for the first time in 1998 when I accompanied Premier Zhu Rongji to France. Thereafter, we had many meetings, just the two of us, to discuss China-France relations and international issues.

During his twelve-year presidency, Chirac paid four state visits to China, and we released three joint declarations, which contributed to the quantum leap in China-France relations. Thus, Jacques Chirac was described by domestic and foreign media as a Western statesman most positive about developing relations with China.

In my opinion, in terms of relations towards China, President Chirac was the most farsighted and strategically minded French leader since General de Gaulle. He maintained good relations with Deng Xiaoping, Jiang Zemin, Hu Jintao, and other Chinese state leaders. As early as the 1970s, Chirac had keenly anticipated that China would rise to become a major world power. After he assumed office, he became even more aware that China, with its vast territory, huge population, and soaring economy, was becoming increasingly important and influential in the world, and would definitely become an indispensable partner of France and Europe in the twenty-first century. This drove him to be very active in developing France-China relations. In March 2007, on the eve of leaving

office, he made another important statement on China-France relations: "In a sense, France's future international status will depend
on its relations with China."

President Chirac gave us precious support on issues involving
China's major and core interests. In his early days in office, he over-
rode all objections and strongly advocated constructive political
dialogue with China and increased consultations on international
affairs. At his behest, France refused to cosponsor or support the US
resolution concerning China in the UN Human Rights Commission in 1996, and moved the rest of the EU to do likewise.

On the Taiwan issue, President Chirac consistently adhered to
the one-China principle. In 2004, he publicly declared his opposition to Taiwan independence and referendum, and his support of
China's one country, two systems policy. Chirac himself set the
tone for the section concerning Taiwan in the 2004 China-France
Joint Declaration.

President Chirac also paid great attention to cultural and youth
exchanges between the two nations. During a visit to Yangzhou
in 2000, he reached an important agreement with President Hu
on promoting bilateral cultural exchange and taking turns to host
China or France Culture Year. From 2003 to 2005, France and
China witnessed the grand openings, first of China Culture Year
and then of France Culture Year. In total, these festivals staged six
hundred activities given by both sides. The festivals had an important and far-reaching impact, and wrote a glorious new chapter
in the history of cultural communication between China and the
West.

From 2006 to 2007, eight hundred young people from China
and France exchanged visits, which acted as a forceful boost to
communications between the young people of France and China,
and as a solid foundation for enduring friendship between the two
peoples for generations to come.

If it was President Chirac's strategic vision regarding the position of China that set the general direction for developing France-China relations, then it was his persistent enthusiasm and profound study of Chinese culture that inspired him with the passion to promote the relationship.

President Chirac had a great knowledge and ardent love of Chinese arts, of bronzes in particular. He had perused all kinds of books on the subject, and his connoisseurship was on a par with that of Chinese bronze experts. His relationship with Shanghai Museum Curator Ma Chengyuan through bronzeware had become a much-told tale. During his visit to China in 1997, he had such a pleasant conversation with Ma that he delayed his flight. When Curator Ma passed away in October 2004, President Chirac, who was visiting Shanghai at the time, dispatched someone to present a wreath and condolences.

Another incident remains impressed on my memory. In October 2006, during Chirac's last visit to China as president, I accompanied President Hu at a small-scale banquet he was hosting for President and Madame Chirac in the Yangyuan Hall of the Diaoyutai State Guesthouse. During the dinner, the two presidents talked about the symbols on ceramics recently unearthed in Hunan Province. President Chirac said he believed them to be early Chinese characters older even than the oracle bone inscriptions, and that history would prove him right.

President Chirac's knowledge of Chinese culture was beyond the imagination of ordinary people, and astounded many Chinese scholars.

In the context of history, reality, or the overall situation of China-France relations, as a great French statesman, President Chirac's historic contribution to the development of China-France relations won full approbation from the two peoples, and will go down in the annals of history for all time. History will prove him right.

Because of Jacques Chirac's profound understanding and vast

With Jacques Chirac, recipient of an honorary doctorate at China Foreign Affairs University, April 29, 2009.

knowledge of Chinese culture and history, and for his great contribution to China-France relations, on April 29, 2009, Zhao Jinjun, president of China Foreign Affairs University (CFAU) and former Chinese ambassador to France, hosted a grand ceremony in the great hall of CFAU to bestow on him a CFAU honorary doctorate. As invited, Chirac gave a speech entitled "The Financial Crisis and New Global Governance" to some five hundred faculty and students of CFAU. I attended the ceremony and held talks with him. It was truly a cordial reunion of old friends.

Old Friends Look Back with Respect

SINCE RETIRING FROM THE State Council, I seldom attended diplomatic events.

One day in early 2009, I received an invitation letter from the Chinese People's Institute of Foreign Affairs (CPIFA) and Chinese People's Association for Friendship with Foreign Countries (CPAFFC). The invitation informed me that former French Prime Minister Raffarin would lead a France-China friendship delegation to China for a seminar commemorating the forty-fifth anniversary of the establishment of China-France diplomatic relations, and hoped I would attend.

I was very keen to meet my old friend, especially since China-France relations had encountered severe turbulence, because of President Nicolas Sarkozy's insistence on meeting with the Dalai Lama, in which I had taken a close interest. At this juncture, it would be exceptionally significant to have the chance to review forty-five years of China-France relations with Raffarin, along with friendly personages from all walks of life in both countries.

February 9, 2009, was the fifteenth day of the first lunar month, China's traditional Lantern Festival. That day, Beijing was filled with festival joy. The seminar commemorating the forty-fifth anniversary of the establishment of China-France diplomatic relations was being held in the Great Hall of CPAFFC in Taijichang Street.

I reviewed the disturbances in China-France relationship since its establishment forty-five years earlier. I said that China-France relations had encountered twists and turns, ups and downs, difficulties and hardships since then. However, provided both sides could see and handle their relations from a strategic height and long-term perspective while sticking to the basic principle of mutual respect on an equal footing and noninterference in each other's internal affairs, respecting and taking care of each other's core interests and major concerns, and settling disputes appropriately, China-France relations would maintain healthy and steady development.

My words were positively received by Senator Raffarin and the other speakers. He said the France-China comprehensive strategic partnership conformed to the common interests of both countries.

France highly valued its friendship with China, respected China's sovereignty, unification, and territorial integrity, and admired the courage and wisdom of the Chinese people, and would continue to promote dialogue and cooperation with China.

Before the seminar opened, I reunited with my long-lost friend in a meeting room of CPAFFC. Looking back on the good old days when we worked together, we were both overcome with emotion.

I had in-depth heartfelt talks with him on China-France relations in particular.

I said that in the severe international situation forty-five years earlier, Chairman Mao and General de Gaulle made the correct decision to establish China-France diplomatic relations, a decision reached through their strategic insight and long-term perspective and through their overall consideration of the fundamental interests of the two peoples and the inexorable trend of world development. It had been proved that the establishment of China-France diplomatic relations brought solid benefits to both countries and their peoples, and had exerted far-reaching influence on China-Europe relations and world peace, stability, and development.

China consistently advocated seeking common ground while reserving differences, harmony without uniformity, and treasuring peace. The key to handling relations between countries was to respect each other's core interests and major concerns. The Tibet and Taiwan issues both concerned China's core interests. Our conflict with the Dalai Lama group was not an ethnic, cultural, or religious one, but a matter of principle concerning separation or unification. At the current critical moment in China-France relations, we hoped the French side would respond with true sincerity to the difficulties we were encountering, and create favorable conditions to restore normal bilateral relations through practical and effective actions for the benefit of our two countries and peoples.

Senator Raffarin responded earnestly that France was convinced China was essential to world stability. The French govern-

中法建交45周年研讨

Colloque Célébrant le 45e Anniversaire des Relations Diplomatiques Sino-Fr

Speaking at the seminar commemorating the forty-fifth anniversary of China-France diplomatic relations, Beijing, February 9, 2009.

ment sincerely hoped that the issues between the two sides would be resolved as soon as possible. France had full confidence in overcoming the current hardships between the two countries and restoring normal relations with China.

Looking back over the past ten years, China-France relations made a giant leap, rising from the initial comprehensive partnership to a comprehensive strategic partnership. France was the prime mover in developing relations with China in various respects, and China was also determined to enhance China-France relations. One might say the two countries were fitting in easily with each other. China and France were the first countries to open strategic dialogues and to host culture year and youth exchange year alternately. In the high-tech field, there was wider and deeper bilateral cooperation, with good cooperation in energy, aviation, railway, and other strategic programs. It can be said that China's relations with France had always marched one step ahead of those with other Western countries.

Of course, because of the differences between China and

France, there would inevitably be disputes and disturbances in the relationship. Provided both sides could enhance political mutual trust and mutually beneficial cooperation, respect, and care about each other's core interests and major concerns, treat sensitive issues appropriately, and reinforce coordination and cooperation on international issues, China-France relations would definitely stride forward on a healthy and stable path.

Unremitting Efforts for China-Germany Cooperation

IN THE HEART OF Europe, between the high Alps, the North Sea, and the Baltic Sea, lays a country with a long history and splendid culture. This country is Germany. Germany came into being in the second half of the nineteenth century through unification by the Iron Chancellor, Otto von Bismarck, of a number of independent feudal states.

During the last century, Germany started and was defeated in two world wars. After WWII, the great perseverance of the German people created an astounding miracle that built their country into the world's third largest economy. In 1990, Germany, divided for over forty years between east and west, finally achieved peaceful reunification.

Germany has given birth to many philosophers, men of letters, and scientists that made great contributions to civilization. Philosophers such as Immanuel Kant, Georg Wilhelm Friedrich Hegel, Ludwig Andreas von Feuerbach, Karl Marx, Friedrich Engels, Arthur Schopenhauer, and Friedrich Nietzsche left a precious intellectual legacy; the works of Johann Wolfgang von Goethe, Friedrich Schiller, Heinrich Heinem, and the Brothers Grimm won universal appreciation; Johann Sebastian Bach, Ludwig Van Beethoven, Robert Schumann, and Johannes Brahms composed beautiful music cherished through the ages; Johannes Gutenberg, Alexander von

Humboldt, Carl Friedrich Gauss, Christian Goldbach, Wilhelm Röntgen, and Albert Einstein established Germany's outstanding reputation in the field of natural science.

Since China established diplomatic relations with the Federal Republic of Germany in 1972, bilateral relations have maintained sound development momentum. Germany is China's largest trade partner in Europe, as well as one of the biggest providers of aid to China.

China-Germany relations developed very well during my term of office, but not without twists and turns. We consistently treated the relationship from a strategic height and long-term perspective, and attached great importance to approaching German state leaders and people from all walks of life. Our unremitting efforts resulted in substantive cooperation between China and Germany, surpassing in both scope and depth our cooperation with other Western powers. When Germany tried to meddle in China's internal affairs, we fought back on just grounds, to our advantage and with restraint, thereby safeguarding China's dignity and core interests while ensuring the general sound and smooth development of China-Germany relations.

Gerhard Schröder: The Red Chancellor

IN MARCH 1999, THE Second ASEM foreign ministers' meeting was held in Berlin. I headed the Chinese delegation on what was also my first official visit to Germany.

At the time, Germany's new cabinet, composed of the Social Democratic Party (SDP) and Green Party, had been in power for less than six months. As the SDP was a left-wing party, the new cabinet was also known as the first national red-green government.

Gerhard Schröder became the first Red chancellor of a reunited Germany. The previous chancellor, Helmut Kohl, had visited China many times during his sixteen successive years in office, and knew China well, but the new Chancellor Schröder and Vice Chancellor and Foreign Minister Joschka Fischer understood much less of China than did Kohl. In particular, the strongly ideological Green Party cabinet members, brandishing the banner of peace, environmental protection, and human rights, were deeply prejudiced against China on the human-rights and Tibet issues.

I was eager to take this chance to meet the new state leaders of Germany, and build friendship and promote mutual trust, so as to push forward the smooth development of China-Germany relations.

There was another important fact in the background to the visit, namely the bombing by US-led NATO of Kosovo in the Federal Republic of Yugoslavia two days earlier, to which we were firmly opposed. Although Germany participated in NATO's related actions, it did not play a key role. After all, Germany was China's largest trade partner in Europe, and had a significant position in the EU. Maintaining long-term and stable friendly cooperation between China and Germany was in China's long-term and practical interests, and also conducive to pushing forward the process towards a multipolar world.

So, I started my first trip to Germany in early spring, 1999.

The German side attached great importance to my first contact with their new state leaders, and arranged for President Roman Herzog, Chancellor Gerhard Schröder, and Vice Speaker of the German Parliament Antje Vollmer to meet me. According to diplomatic protocol, Vice Chancellor and Foreign Minister Joschka Fischer would hold talks with me.

When I arrived in Berlin on March 26, the chill of bitter winter had already gone and spring was tiptoeing in. I arrived at two o'clock. Looking out the car window, I saw the streets in this European metropolis were full of vigor. Warm sunshine shone on people clad in heavy winter coats, and filled the busy yet orderly city with warmth and ease.

In the first half of 1999, it was Germany's turn to take the EU rotating presidency. Chancellor Schröder had hosted the EU Special Council Meeting for a straight thirty-six hours. Although exhausted, he met with the Chinese delegation immediately. Schröder was not a tall man by Western standards, but he exuded confidence, energy, and enthusiasm, showing not the slightest hint of fatigue after such a long and intense spell of work. His voice was mellow and attractive and his words were articulate and eloquent, amiable and convincing, possibly benefiting from his having studied law.

I first thanked the chancellor for meeting with the Chinese delegation despite his weariness, and expressed appreciation for the new German government attaching importance to developing relations with China and adhering to the one-China policy. I stressed that China also thought highly of Germany's status and role in Europe and the world and was eager to join with Germany in bringing our long-established and stable bilateral relations into the twenty-first century.

Chancellor Schröder showed a strong interest in China's political and economic development, expressing great admiration for the dramatic progress China had achieved through reform and opening up. The new government of Germany would remain consistent and reliable in its policies towards China. China-Germany and China-Europe relations should not be restricted to the economic field; political, cultural, and parliamentary cooperation should also be enhanced. He told me during the meeting that he would like to visit China in May in two capacities, namely chancellor of Germany and EU rotating president, together with a large number of business dignitaries.

Actually, China had been considering inviting Chancellor Schröder for a visit, so I immediately said he would be welcome.

Gerhard Schröder was born into a poor family, and his father died in WWII. He was intelligent, diligent, and adaptable, and showed a great interest in politics while still at school, all of which deeply imprinted his later political style.

Our first meeting confirmed this. Despite his capacity as leader of the SDP, he described himself as representing the New Middle Way, ideologically unconstrained, sincere, and practical, with a special focus on trade cooperation, and hoping to further enhance friendly cooperation between Germany and China.

After I returned to China, the Chinese and German foreign ministries started to prepare for Chancellor Schröder's first trip to China. This visit would definitely have a direct influence on the direction of the China policy adopted by Germany's new government.

Early in the morning of May 8, 1999, while both sides were busy with the preparations, the Chinese embassy in Yugoslavia was bombed by US-led NATO, an act that severely damaged China's relations with NATO member states.

As a NATO member state, Germany had taken part in this military attack against Yugoslavia. Germany was very worried that the bombing incident would cause a rift in China's relations with the West and have very negative consequences for China-Germany relations. Chancellor Schröder sent a message and a letter to Premier Zhu Rongji immediately that day, expressing the German government's deep sympathy in connection with the embassy bombing, the hope that the incident would not affect Germany-China relations, and that he would like to visit China as originally planned. On May 10, Chancellor Schröder demanded that NATO make a thoroughgoing and accurate investigation of the bombing incident to ascertain who was responsible. Considering the feelings of the Chinese, Germany proposed to change the planned official visit to a working visit and to condense it into one day with simplified protocol.

After careful consideration, we finally agreed that Chancellor Schröder should visit China as scheduled. Chancellor Schröder said at the cabinet meeting on May 11 that it was a very positive sign that the Chinese leaders were willing to receive a government leader from a NATO member state, and that it was very constructive for Germany and China to have dialogue during the current difficult time.

On May 12, four days after the bombing incident, Chancellor Schröder visited China on schedule, but the visit, originally planned for three or four days, was condensed into a one-day working visit, without spending even one night in China. It turned out to be a lightning visit in extremely special circumstances.

Chancellor Schröder's special plane arrived in the early morning at almost the same time of the arrival of China's special plane carrying the bodies of those killed in the bombing incident and the wounded survivors. That day was unexpectedly gloomy for the supposedly fine spring days of May, as if heaven was touched while mourning the spirits of those who had passed away. The reception parties awaiting the two planes were both in somber mood.

China's Ambassador to Germany Lu Qiutian specially returned to China to greet Chancellor Schröder at the airport, and reported to me at the very first opportunity. As soon as the chancellor stepped down the gangway, he solemnly and sincerely expressed unconditional apologies to the Chinese government and people on behalf of the German government and people and NATO.

On arriving at the Kempinski Hotel, where he was to stay, the chancellor suggested he might visit the injured victims at the hospital. Considering his tight schedule for this dozen-hour working visit, and that the injured were in great need of rest, we declined his request.

At that time, all China was immersed in grief and anger, and Chancellor Schröder could feel it. As chancellor of Germany, a key member of NATO, it was very courageous of him to insist on visiting China and to demand of NATO a thoroughgoing investigation of the bombing. Some German press called his visit to China a "confessional trip."

With German Chancellor Gerhard Schröder in Beijing, May 12, 1999.

In China, Chancellor Schröder apologized for the bombing incident many times on various occasions. During the meetings and talks with President Jiang Zemin and Premier Zhu Rongji, he said the main purpose of his visit was to extend a sincere apology to the Chinese government and people, hoping to make it known to more Chinese people. He said he would pay an official visit to China somewhat later that year, and would like to stay a few more days in order to get to know China.

I felt his candor for a second time during our meeting at Kempinski Hotel. Given the circumstances, our conversation could hardly be relaxed. His most frequently used words were "regret," "condolence," "sympathy," and "apology," and these constituted the theme of his visit. He said that he was not satisfied with NATO's explanation for the bombing incident, and had demanded that NATO Secretary-General Javier Solana look into the case thoroughly and clarify the responsibility of related staff so as to avoid the recurrence of anything similar.

In November 1999, Chancellor Schröder came to China again, this time for a four-day official visit. In addition to the political talks in Beijing, he also visited Shanghai, and got fairly comprehensive grounding in China.

In office, Chancellor Schröder announced that he would visit China at least once a year. Basically he kept this promise, thus becoming the most frequent visitor to China of all German chancellors. The German government under his leadership consistently adhered to the one-China policy, actively promoted relations with China, and refused to sell arms to Taiwan. On issues like recognizing China as a market economy and lifting the arms ban on China, Germany had a positive influence on the EU, and forcefully deepened China-Germany and China-Europe relations.

In October 2002, the so-called red-green alliance, headed by Chancellor Schröder and Foreign Minister Fischer, won another term of office. Only one month into the chancellor's second term, at Fischer's invitation, I paid my second visit to Germany and met Schröder during the course of my visit.

Time flies. It was three years since my last visit to Germany, and my last meeting with Chancellor Schröder took place on his third China visit one year earlier.

This was the fifth time we had met. Our bilateral relations had developed soundly, but on the international horizon the dark clouds of the Iraq War were gathering. During our meeting, Chancellor Schröder said that Germany-China relations were witnessing their best period ever. The two countries had established heart-to-heart mutual trust, sharing extensive common interests in international affairs, in particular the consensus on resolving the Iraq issue by political means, and bilateral cooperation was broader and deeper than anywhere in Europe. During this visit, I became deeply convinced that Germany was eager to enhance coordination with China in international affairs and to expand bilateral trade cooperation.

In December of 2003 and of 2004, Chancellor Schröder visited China, further deepening mutual understanding and friendship between the two sides.

Surrounded by local children during the visit to Germany, October 2002.

In autumn 2005, Schröder was defeated in the federal elections. That November, President Hu Jintao met with him during his visit to Germany. Schröder's role was now that of chancellor of the caretaker government. During his term of office, he persistently emphasized that Germany would never change its stance on adhering to the one-China policy, and reiterated that Germany would never do anything to threaten China's security. President Hu spoke highly of his statement, which constituted a solid political foundation of China–Germany relations, and also highly appreciated his unremitting efforts for boosting China–Germany friendly cooperation. President Hu also very much cherished his deep personal friendship with Schröder, and hoped he would visit China frequently after leaving office.

Chancellor Schröder said, movingly, that President Hu was the last foreign head of state he would have received as a German government leader, which symbolized the close ties between Germany and China. The new German government would maintain continuity, and actively promote and deepen relations with China as in the past, on the basis of the one–China principle.

Soon Chancellor Schröder left office, but continued to care about China-Germany relations. He visited China annually, continuing to play a constructive role in promoting bilateral friendship and cooperation.

Keeping up with old friends is a traditional Chinese virtue. I kept in touch with Schröder, who had faded from the political scene. In November 2007, I met with him and hosted a banquet for him in the Yangyuan Hall of the Diaoyutai State Guesthouse.

He was as eloquent as ever, brimming with energy, vitality, and mental agility. Perhaps because he had stepped down, he appeared much more relaxed and talked more openly about many topics. During his seven years as chancellor, he had paid six visits to China, and thus acquired a profound understanding of Germany's internal affairs and China-Germany relations. He talked freely and frankly about the policies of the SDP and the Christian Democratic Union (CDU), the two main political parties, reviewing the past and anticipating the future.

One month before this visit, his successor, Chancellor Angela Merkel, had met with the Dalai Lama at the official residence of the German president, which seriously disturbed and damaged bilateral relations. The subject came up in our conversation. Schröder and Merkel were rivals from different political parties and had completely different political ideas.

He admitted that he disagreed with Merkel's action, and believed she had made a mistake. He expressed his opinions frankly, two of which deeply impressed me. First, he said China had become too important a player in international affairs to ignore; no matter which political party came to power in Germany, it would definitely attach importance to German-China relations. Even Merkel's government agreed with, and would adhere to, the one-China principle. Second, he believed that the policies adopted by Foreign Minister Frank-Walter Steinmeier of the SDP basically followed the general principles he had implemented as chancellor. Therefore, he had a firm belief that the Merkel government would maintain continuity with regard to its ties with China, and there would be no reversal of the general trend for Germany-China relations to develop in depth and breath.

As a resourceful veteran of German politics, Schröder elaborated his views in an objective and practical way, giving full respect to his rival but not skirting around their differences.

I agreed with him. Actually, we had already come to the same conclusion as early as Merkel's election victory, and it proved to be correct through the later development of China-German relations.

Joschka Fischer: The Green Foreign Minister

THE SECOND KEY FIGURE in the Schröder cabinet decisive to the direction of Germany-China relations was Vice Chancellor and Foreign Minister Joschka Fischer. I locked horns with my German counterpart several times. I managed to cause some shift in his attitude to China by purposefully dwelling upon his particular points of concern.

Like Gerhard Schröder, Joschka Fischer came from a poor background, but he was more radical than Schröder. He had participated in the German student movement as a young man, and so had been dubbed the "street fighter" by the German press. Like Schröder, Fischer was also a great admirer of China's ancient culture, economic achievements, and opening-up policy, but was more of an ideologue than Schröder. Rather than being pragmatic, he focused more on divisive issues in Germany-China relations such as human rights and Tibet. He said many times that Germany and China should not be content with having close trade ties, but should go further to promote dialogue on human rights and rule of law. After taking up his appointment in October 1998, he met with first the Dalai Lama, and then Wei Jingsheng, and criticized China's human-rights situation at the UN Human Rights Commission in Geneva.

I made Fischer's acquaintance during my first visit to Germany in 1999. He was no stout fellow, but certainly not "barrel-shaped," as he self-deprecatingly described himself, but a little reserved. Our first talk lasted about three hours.

Catering to what interested him, I described China's ethnic and religious policies, stressing that relations between countries should be built on the basis of seeking common ground and setting aside differences, and seeking the greatest convergence of common interests. I also spoke positively about China-Germany bilateral dialogue on human rights and judicial cooperation.

Fischer first affirmed the importance of German-China relations, believing China had made remarkable contributions to world peace, stability, and prosperity, especially in the Asian region. But then his tone changed as the topic shifted to criticizing China's human rights and showing deep concern for the situation in Tibet.

It was only normal for China and Germany to disagree on various issues, given the differences in their history, culture, economy, social system, and other aspects. Fischer's comments came as no surprise, but his prejudiced, unwarranted criticism was not conducive to settling differences. I knew it would be hard going, but on issues of principle I had to refute his mistaken assertions. However, our approach must be carefully thought through and based on increased mutual understanding, so as to ensure the sound and stable development of China-German relations.

I expounded on the Chinese government's basic stance on the human-rights issue and our active participation in international human-rights cooperation, also describing China's remarkable achievements in poverty alleviation and legal construction. I elaborated on Tibet's past and present, backed up with real examples and precise figures, so as to show that the Dalai Lama was far from being the religious leader he claimed, but a political monk conspiring to split China. I also made clear China's consistent policy towards Dalai.

I told him about Tibet's formidable nature and geography. Having been to the Qinghai-Tibet Plateau, "the Roof of the World," several times, I was keenly aware of the living conditions there. The central government has been providing all sorts of assistance to Tibet for several decades. Tibet's dramatic economic, social, and cultural achievements were obvious to all and could not be ignored by anyone respecting objective facts.

I asked whether he had been to Tibet, and he said no, so I took the chance to invite him to visit China as soon as possible, and he accepted gracefully.

Diplomatic relations are a mixture of friendship and confrontation. At times of confrontation, a tough attitude is manifested in finely tuned wording rather than in tone of voice. Therefore, I consistently adopted a calm tone but uncompromising words in diplomatic negotiations. My first long talk with Foreign Minister Fischer was about a grave topic, yet the atmosphere was calm, because I believed that utmost sincerity and sound reasoning would be more effective.

In mid-December 2000, Fischer paid his first visit to China as German vice chancellor and foreign minister. Before that, he had been to China as a Federal Parliament member in 1985. We gave him a high-level reception. President Jiang Zemin, Premier Zhu Rongji, and Vice Premiers Qian Qichen and Wen Jiabao each met with him and I also held talks with my German counterpart. In addition, we made special arrangements for his visiting schedule, meetings, and talks.

The China-Germany Conference on Environmental Cooperation was a highlight of Fischer's visit. It was the highest-level bilateral environmental cooperation meeting ever held in China. Over one thousand representatives from Chinese and German governments, parliaments, research institutes, enterprises, nongovernmental organizations, and media attended the conference. The German delegation headed by Foreign Minister Fischer was four hundred strong. Vice Speaker of the German Federal Parliament Antje Vollmer from the Green Party and Environment Minister Jürgen Trittin attended the conference and delivered keynote speeches.

Unfortunately, because of an unexpected little accident, Fischer's special plane did not arrive in Beijing until after the conference opening ceremony, which the environmentally conscious green foreign minister bitterly regretted.

Anyway, the conference was a great success. China and Germany issued a joint declaration to further enhance environmental cooperation, identified cooperation subjects, and signed cooperation agreements, winning high appreciation from both sides. Premier Zhu Rongji stressed during his meeting with Fischer that the environmental conference had been a great success and was a big event for both countries. Fischer responded that its success had opened new fields of bilateral cooperation giving impetus to China-Germany environmental cooperation.

This time Fischer looked a little thinner than at our previous meeting but he was still full of energy. I was told that he had lost weight by long-distance running, and that his healthy way of slimming had set off a marathon craze in Germany.

During our talks, I gave him a second overall introduction concerning China's principled stand on the Tibet issues and Tibet's great achievements in various aspects. I patiently showed him the facts and used sound reasoning to try to convince him.

Fischer hoped the dialogue between the Chinese government and the Dalai would result in progress. I told him that we had been dealing with the Dalai for several decades, and thus had a deeper and more comprehensive understanding of his nature than did some Westerners. The Dalai's actions proved he was no simple religious leader, for how could any religious leader in the world set up a government in exile with functional organs and even its own constitution? The Dalai had won wide sympathy by cheating and two-faced dealings. Germany was among his major lobby targets in Europe. He had visited Germany more than twenty times, had accepted awards from those he misled, and gained courteous reception in various places. Everywhere he proclaimed himself as nonpolitical, but his intention to split the motherland had not changed in the slightest.

I told Fischer that, at each of our meetings, Tibet was an unavoidable platitude, since his knowledge of the true Tibet was limited and distorted. There was continuous progress in human rights in Tibet, which was in sharp contrast to the past under the Dalai's rule. This was undeniable fact. Did Westerners not see that the feudal serfdom of old Tibet was more backward and cruel than that of medieval Europe?

Judging from Fischer's expression, he seemed to be pondering my remarks. I continued that we appreciated the German government's position of regarding Tibet as an integral part of Chinese territory. We hoped the German side would see through the Dalai's ambition and conspiracy, and in the interest of safeguarding China-Germany relations, refrain from giving support to the Dalai's separatist activities.

Despite the fact that his visit was only two days, we organized a trip to Hangzhou's West Lake and the Oriental Pearl Tower in Shanghai to broaden his understanding of China's reform and opening up. Prior to the visit, Foreign Minister Fischer had suggested visiting the Nanjing Massacre Memorial Hall on December 13, the anniversary of the massacre, but his tight schedule made this impossible. Even so, his gesture impressed me.

Vice Speaker Vollmer, who visited China along with the foreign minister, later told us Fischer had been very satisfied with the meetings and talks with the Chinese and that the visit had been far more successful than he had expected. So, our unremitting efforts did bear fruit in the end.

On March 26, 2001, on my way to Chile for the Foreign Ministers' Meeting of the Forum for East Asia–Latin America Cooperation (FEALAC), I had to change planes in Frankfurt and stay there for half a day. Our Ambassador to Germany Lu Qiutian came from Berlin to see me, and advised me to spend this precious bit of leisure time seeing Heidelberg, the most beautiful city in Germany. Germany is not a huge country and Heidelberg is near Frankfurt, so we drove there.

It was early spring. We were impressed by the beautiful scenery along the drive, especially when we came into the center of Heidelberg. With a population of less than two hundred thousand, it is not a large city, but it has been blessed with a picturesque landscape and a rich accretion of cultural deposits. It was a frontier fortress of the Roman Empire in the first century BC, and its world-renowned ancient castle, dating back to the twelfth century, combines Gothic, Baroque, and Renaissance architectural style.

Heidelberg University, founded in 1386, was Germany's earliest university. Seven Nobel laureates studied there, and it was the alma mater of the famous philosopher Hegel and former Chancellor Kohl.

The Neckar River, gently winding between the red buildings and the green trees, the ancient castle, and bridges of this small city combine in a harmonious air of old-world charm.

As we strolled along the willow-lined Philosopher's Walk, where Kant and other thinkers had trodden, the talk turned to Fischer speaking at the UN Human Rights Commission in Geneva the following day. Having met him several times, I now knew him better and sensed a subtle change in his attitude on China's human rights and other issues.

Since I was here in Germany on the eve of his speech on human rights, I thought that I must seize the opportunity to do something.

I told Ambassador Lu my idea, and he agreed, so we began discussing the details. There was no time to arrange a meeting between us, nor could we get back to the Chinese embassy in Berlin, so the only feasible solution was to make a telephone call. For reasons of translation, we had to find a suitable place to call him on a landline phone. Therefore, we returned to Frankfurt immediately.

This was before we had a consulate general in Frankfurt, so the embassy staff took great pains to arrange this phone call. Finally, a certain Mr. Wu, the boss of a Chinese restaurant in a Frankfurt suburb, generously invited us to make the call from his place. He originated from Shanghai and had been in catering in Luxemburg before coming to Germany.

The restaurant was on the first floor, and Mr. Wu's private office was on the third. We went upstairs directly and dialed the number of the German Ministry of Foreign Affairs. On being informed that I would like to talk to him, Fischer stopped the meeting he was chairing and got me on the line.

I congratulated him on his successful visit to China three months earlier, and then went straight to the human-rights issue. I said it was normal for us to hold different views on human rights, and we both agreed on mutual respect and dialogue rather than confrontation. We really appreciated that the EU had refused to cosponsor the US resolution against China at the UN Human Rights Commission, and hoped the EU would not lobby on behalf of the United States.

I told him I had heard he was to speak at the Human Rights Council the next day, and hoped that in the overall interest of China-German relations and friendship, he would treat the related issues prudently and appropriately by following the consensus reached by China and Germany, so as to avoid any negative impact on our relations. Finally, I welcomed his forthcoming visit to Beijing for the ASEM Foreign Ministers' Meeting in May, when we could further talk about the issues in which we both took an interest.

Fischer said that his visit to China three months earlier had been a great success, that he had been deeply impressed by China's vigorous development, and that his understanding of the great country had been enhanced. He had planned to see western China but his tight schedule had prevented this.

He said Germany would like to deepen bilateral relations with China with a constructive attitude, but, as a friend, would not avoid disputes on human rights, and believed straight talking would do no harm to the development of bilateral relations. Besides, he acknowledged the great progress China had achieved in the area of human rights.

After putting down the phone, Ambassador Lu and I discussed the possible effects of this last-minute phone call. I thought we could not achieve our aim with Fischer in one move, and a quarter of an hour on the phone would not cause any fundamental shift of position. Nevertheless, considering that he had interrupted an important meeting to answer my call, I thought he was willing to get to know our attitude.

Just as we anticipated, Fischer's speech the next day contained presumptuous criticism of China's human-rights situation, but in a milder tone than usual and with modified wording.

A month later, Fischer came to Beijing for the Third ASEM Foreign Ministers' Meeting and we had a working breakfast together. I sensed that he was becoming somewhat more objective and positive in his attitude on the Tibet and human-rights issues.

He said that because of the increasing common ground and interests between Germany and China, both sides should enhance dialogue, communication, and exchanges. He spoke highly of China-Germany bilateral relations, saying that Germany as a reliable partner of China would make every effort to further improve the comprehensive cooperation between the two countries. He added that we could have a frank and sincere exchange of views on any issue, and hoped we would have more opportunities to meet.

In September 2002, I held another bilateral meeting with Fischer at UN headquarters while attending the UN General Assembly session. The Iraq War was looming, but China and Germany shared a similar stance on the peaceful settlement of the issue, both stressing the United Nations' leading role.

Fischer made it clear during our meeting that Germany was completely opposed to the United States resorting to force against Iraq, and hoped to continue close communication and coordination with China. Six months later, the United States started the Iraq War, an action unanimously opposed by China, Russia, France, and Germany. Just a couple of years earlier this would have been unbelievable.

One month after our meeting in New York, Fischer was reappointed as vice chancellor and foreign minister in the Schröder cabinet. In November 2002, just a month after Germany's new government came to power, I paid my second official visit to Germany at Fischer's invitation.

During this visit, I felt there had been a great change in Fischer's attitudes on human rights and Tibet. He made it clear in our talks that China had made great strides in human rights and the rule of law. Germany would continue to adhere to its one-China position against separatism. Judging from his statements, he had a more objective and deeper understanding of China's human-rights situation and the Tibet issue, and he was more positive and explicit in his attitude.

From my contacts with Fischer, this Green Party politician impressed me as erudite and quick-minded, and with an increasingly prudent and pragmatic political style. He had started to care more about Germany's long-term and real interests and pay increasing attention to China-Germany relations. His invited visits to China and the sincere dialogue between us on various occasions further enhanced his all-around understanding of our country, and brought about positive changes in his attitude towards China and China-Germany relations.

On the whole, the seven years of "red-green coalition" wit-

nessed the best China–Germany relations ever. Our friendly cooperation was deepened and widened, high-level reciprocal visits
remained frequent, trade relations kept reaching new heights, and
comprehensive cooperation became ever deeper.

In 2003, China and the EU established a comprehensive strategic partnership. When Premier Wen Jiabao visited Germany
in May 2004, the two sides decided to establish "a partnership of
global responsibility within the framework of the China–EU strategic partnership," raising China–Germany relations to a new height.

The Iron Lady of German Politics

IN 2005, CHANCELLOR SCHRÖDER decided to hold early federal elections in order to gain a workable majority in parliament and to
enhance his ability to govern. Unexpectedly, the coalition parties
(SDP and the Green Party) were defeated by a small margin by
the largest opposition party, a coalition of CDU and the Christian
Social Union (CSU). Schröder hence lost his position as chancellor.

Schröder's conqueror was Angela Merkel, the renowned "Iron
Lady" of German politics. She thus became the first ever woman to
wield supreme power in Germany. In November, the CDU-CSU
parliamentary group that she led and the SPD formed the second
grand coalition government in German history.*

Merkel was born in Hamburg, the port city in the northwest of
Germany, in 1954, and moved to the German Democratic Republic with her family when she was one year old. She grew up in a
strongly religious family, and her father was a priest. A physicist

---

*In Germany, the grand coalition refers to the government formed by CDU-CSU par-
liamentary group and SDP, Germany's two largest political parties. The first grand
coalition government in Germany was in power during 1966 and 1969, and Kurt
Georg Kiesinger of the CDU was elected chancellor.

before she became involved in politics, Merkel is known as a rational thinker. After the disintegration of the Soviet Union and drastic changes in Eastern Europe, Merkel threw herself into politics with great enthusiasm and soon became active in the CDU, a right-wing political party.

Merkel was less informed about China than Schröder, and had only been to China once, as environment minister in 1997. Moreover, her personal background and political beliefs aroused great concern about China-German relations once she assumed office. However, I believed she would pay attention to China and keep Germany's China policy consistent on the whole, but I was afraid that friction on human rights, Tibet, and Taiwan issues were inevitable.

In order to increase Merkel's knowledge and understanding of China, we made a point of communicating with her even before her inauguration.

In October 2005, on hearing of Merkel's election as chancellor, Premier Wen Jiabao entrusted our Ambassador to Germany Ma Canrong with conveying a verbal message of congratulations to her, indicating that Premier Wen believed the new German government she led would further improve friendly and mutually beneficial cooperation between China and Germany in various areas.

In November 2005, President Hu Jintao met with Chancellor Designate Merkel during his visit to Germany. President Hu congratulated on her coming inauguration as the first female chancellor in German history, emphasizing that the consensus on friendly cooperation between the two countries had never changed since the establishment of diplomatic relations thirty-three years ago, and that the two sides had built an all-around friendship. China had constantly regarded the China-Germany relationship as a priority in its foreign relations, and was eager to make joint efforts with the new German government to push forward the development of China-Germany relations.

Merkel warmly welcomed President Hu to pay a state visit to Germany, indicating that her government would pay great attention to Germany–China relations, and would continue to pursue active policies towards China and further enhance cooperation with the Chinese. She hoped to visit China as early as possible, and President Hu said she would be welcome.

It was at this event that I met Merkel for the first time. My first impression was that she was intelligent and capable, frank and straightforward, logical and clear-minded, perhaps because of her years in natural science research.

On December 1 at Zhongnanhai, Premier Wen Jiabao talked on the hotline with Chancellor Merkel, who had assumed office nine days earlier. Premier Wen congratulated her on being the first female German chancellor in history, indicating that the Chinese government would persistently attach great importance to developing relations with Germany. Premier Wen commended her indication on various occasions to continue Germany's positive policy towards China, and invited her to pay an official visit to China the following year at a mutually convenient time, so that she could witness the dramatic changes in China since her last visit in 1997.

Chancellor Merkel thanked Premier Wen for his congratulations, saying that the new German government would continue to improve close bilateral ties, and reiterated that the new German government she led would unswervingly persist in the one-China policy. Finally, she expressed her gratitude once more for Premier Wen's invitation to visit China, saying she would stay in touch with Premier Wen via the hotline.

As soon as the new German government was installed, Chancellor Merkel and Foreign Minister Steinmeier soon decided to visit China as soon as possible, explicitly describing the decision as "manifesting Germany's great attention to Germany–China relations."

However, the new German government also made some changes to its foreign policy, coming up with the so-called value-based diplomacy, enhancing its coordination and cooperation with the United States in a global range, and reinforcing its ties with Japan and India. On specific issues concerning China and the EU, the German side backed off from urging the EU to lift the arms ban on China and to recognize China's market economy. There was also greater criticism and pressure on China's intellectual-property-right protection, technology transfer, and environmental conservation.

I regarded these changes as probably attributable to Merkel's own subjective decisions and to some deeper-level reasons, the most important being that along with the growth of China's overall national strength these arose a certain ambivalence in Germany, a conflict between cooperation and protectionism, a fear that China might be a challenge to German interests.

In February 2006, Germany's Foreign Minister Steinmeier paid an official visit to China lasting only twenty-eight hours. During that time, President Hu Jintao and Premier Wen Jiabao each met with him, and Foreign Minister Li Zhaoxing held talks with him, which confirmed Chancellor Merkel's visit to China three months later, when the two sides would establish a strategic dialogue mechanism at the level of vice foreign ministers.

Chancellor Merkel visited China as scheduled during May 21–23. She had originally planned to visit Asian countries. including China, at the end of the year but instead moved up her trip and limited it to China. It was her first special visit to a non-Western country since her inauguration, bringing with her six important parliament members and forty financial leaders. This underlined the German government's attention to China.

China, on its part, set equal store by Chancellor Merkel's visit and put a great deal of thought into her schedule. For greater contact with ordinary Chinese, we arranged that she take a walk with

Premier Wen in Changpuhe Park, close to the Forbidden City. The two premiers made their way along winding paths to the secluded Tianqu Garden, where they had breakfast together. These special arrangements were the curtain raiser for this important visit.

After breakfast, Premier Wen and Chancellor Merkel held talks in the Great Hall of the People, where a wide range of topics was discussed in a frank and friendly atmosphere. Premier Wen issued an invitation via Chancellor Merkel for four hundred German young people to visit China. During her visit, Merkel reiterated that the grand coalition German government would continue to pursue positive policies towards China and adhere to the one-China policy.

Thanks to the support of the Central Authorities and careful preparations, Chancellor Merkel's visit was generally successful. On her way back to Germany, the elated Chancellor Merkel repeatedly told the press on board that it was the most successful visit she had ever paid; that though it had been only thirty-eight short hours, she was very happy with the rich content and the host's considerate arrangements. She hoped to visit China regularly in the future.

One year later, Chancellor Merkel paid a second visit to China on what was the thirty-fifth anniversary of the establishment of China-Germany diplomatic relations. While in China, she reiterated that the one-China policy was the political foundation for the relations between the two countries, and that Germany would further expand and enhance cooperation with China in politics, economy, culture, science and technology, and other areas. Chancellor Merkel went to Nanjing for the official launch of the three-year-long cultural event "Germany and China—Moving Ahead Together." In terms of scale and duration, this was the largest comprehensive overseas exhibition event Germany had ever staged. President Hu Jintao and Germany's President Horst Köhler both gave their support to this cultural event.

Reciprocating Premier Wen's invitation for four hundred German young people visit to China, Chancellor Merkel invited four hundred Chinese young people to Germany.

In general, this visit by Merkel also proved successful, in view of her positive and practical responses to a series of issues.

Unexpectedly, however, on September 23, only twenty days or so after her return from China, Merkel insisted on meeting with the Dalai in the official residence of the chancellor, disregarding the solemn representation of the Chinese. The meeting set a deplorable precedent of a German government leader meeting with the Dalai and plunged China-Germany relations to an all-time low. In response, we made a clear-cut stand and took a series of measures to fight back.

For years, under the cloak of religion, the Dalai Lama had intruded into one country after another, trying to disrupt China's relations with Western countries, carrying out his plot to undermine China's sovereignty and national unity. Therefore, the implications of Chancellor Merkel meeting with the Dalai at the chancellor's official residence went far beyond our bilateral relations. In my view, we had to tackle the issue from the broader perspective and put up a resolute fight.

In early November 2006, I met with former German Chancellor Schröder, who was visiting China at the invitation of the Chinese People's Institute of Foreign Affairs (CPIFA). He pointed out that Merkel's government had committed some policy mistakes, but believed that the German government would maintain continuity in its China policy.

I agreed with his evaluation of the Merkel government's China policy. Several days later, the news story "German Foreign Minister Backs Improving German-China Relations" appeared, confirming the accuracy of our views.

At the end of November, while attending an international conference in the United States, Foreign Minister Steinmeier asked his Chinese counterpart Yang Jiechi to convey Chancellor Merkel's greetings to Premier Wen, and her wish to speak on the phone with Premier Wen about bilateral relations. Steinmeier also indicated that he would like to write to Foreign Minister Yang about improving bilateral relations.

Meanwhile, I also noticed that the China policy conflicts between the two ruling political parties in Germany were out in the open. Some business leaders began publicly urging their government to mend relations with China, and Chancellor Merkel came under increasing criticism from the media and think tanks.

These things indicated that our recent struggle and endeavors were beginning to bear fruit. I immediately instructed our Ministry of Foreign Affairs to press on with the German effort while continuing to apply proper pressure, to handle relations with major European powers well, and to strive to maintain sound and stable development of China-Germany and China-Europe relations.

After much bilateral wrangling, Foreign Minister Steinmeier made it clear in his letter to Foreign Minister Yang that the German government put great value on its relations with China and would firmly uphold the one-China policy, that Tibet was a part of China, and Germany would not support or encourage any attempt for Tibet independence.

Based on these circumstances, China-Germany relations began to turn for the better from early 2008 and gradually returned to a normal track of development.

Rethinking China-Europe Relations

SINCE THE ESTABLISHMENT OF diplomatic ties over thirty years ago, China-Europe relations have achieved great progress and rapid growth, particularly during the last decade. We established comprehensive strategic partnerships with the EU, France, and United

Kingdom, and "a partnership of global responsibility within the framework of China-EU comprehensive strategic partnership" with Germany. The close high-level contacts and communication between state leaders of both sides have enhanced political mutual trust. We established political dialogue mechanisms at various levels with EU organs, the United Kingdom, France, and Germany, encompassing macro exchanges such as strategic dialogues, as well as specific consultations on human rights and arms control.

We can say that nowadays, for any issue between China and Europe, there exists an appropriate forum for dialogue. A mutually beneficial financial situation of convergent interests has taken shape. For many years running, the EU has been China's biggest trade partner, its biggest technology supplier, and fourth biggest investor in real terms. In 2006, the EU became China's largest export market, and its trade volume in 2008 reached US 425.6 billion dollars, almost six times over that of ten years ago. It is commendable that China-Europe trade maintained sound development momentum, despite the international financial crisis that started in 2008.

China-Europe cooperation maintained rapid growth in some fifty areas, including science and technology, energy, transportation, communications, environmental protection, health, tourism, and social security. Exchanges in culture and the humanities blossomed. Such communication and cooperation enhanced mutual understanding and drew the people of China and Europe closer together.

I should also mention that while promoting relations with EU organs, the United Kingdom, France, and Germany, we also made progress in improving relations with other EU member states. Among them are the Nordic countries, who were among the first to establish diplomatic relations with China; the South European countries who were friendly to China; as well as the original EU member states and the new EU members of central and eastern

Europe. Adhering to the principle of mutual respect and equality for developing relations with European countries, we promoted cooperation with them at different levels and in various areas, and thus reinforced the China-Europe relationship by enhancing bilateral relations.

I was sincerely happy about the great progress in China-Europe relations over the past decade, and I have come to realize after repeated thought, the strategic, distinctive, and complex nature of China-Europe relations.

First, the China-Europe relationship is a strategic one. The EU has a unique and key position in the current international pattern, with expanding regional and worldwide influence, and is a major power in a multipolar world. In the context of a complex and changing international situation, the tortuous movement toward multipolarity and increasing global challenges, the implications of China-Europe relations far transcend those of bilateral relations, and are becoming ever more globally significant. Therefore, we should safeguard China-Europe relations from a strategic height and long-term perspective, and should not shift our policies as the result of short-term disruptions or a single incident. Without consideration of the overall situation, China-Europe relations might go astray.

The development of China-Europe relations has great significance for us in building a moderately prosperous society in all aspects. China will be in the primary stage of socialism for a long time to come. Developing the socialist market economy and improving people's livelihood remain our top long-term priorities. The vast and populous EU has a world-leading position by virtue of its economic and sci-tech strength. Through the years of China-Europe cooperation, we have absorbed advanced technologies and considerable investment from EU member states, and learned much from their advanced management experience, which has provided strong support for China's modernization. Of course, China-Europe cooperation has benefited both sides. China's development was an opportunity for Europe, as the EU is well aware. The principle of "mutual benefit and reciprocity, mutual complementarity, and common prosperity" mentioned in China's EU policy paper of 2003 precisely illustrates this thinking.

The nature of China-Europe relations is also special and complex. The EU's organizational structure and operating mechanisms are complicated. There are EU organs formed through transfer of sovereign power by various countries, as well as the member states, each independent in its own national policies. Because of extremely different political systems, various historical, cultural backgrounds, and social values, and different levels of economic development, we often faced a complicated picture in our diplomatic dealings with Europe. While China-Europe relations continued to deepen, the dual nature of EU China policy tended to cause conflicts and differences from time to time, some of them quite conspicuous, particularly in the area of ideology.

We should take a dialectic approach to the complexity of China-Europe relations. In regard to important matters of principle affecting China's core interests, we should not be ambiguous and must wage a resolute and well-targeted struggle. However, we should also recognize that many disputes stem from inadequate understanding of each other. Lacking a comprehensive, objective, and accurate understanding of China, many Europeans have a mistaken impression of our country. Therefore, an important diplomatic task was to unremittingly enhance mutual understanding, forcefully promote cultural and people-to-people diplomacy, reinforce the political and social foundation for bilateral relations, and strive for the sound and stable development of China-Europe comprehensive strategic partnership.

Thirty years of diplomatic relations between China and Europe is merely a drop in the vast ocean of history: "the road is long and tortuous." Many tasks remain to be done between China and Europe.

Currently, China-Europe relations have recovered quite well. Adhering to the fundamental principle of mutual respect, equality, and mutual benefit, the relationship can achieve even greater progress. There are broad prospects for China-Europe relations. Of this, I am totally confident.

CHAPTER 10

The Nuclear Tests
by India and Pakistan

Indian Nuclear Tests Shock the World

ON THE AFTERNOON OF May 11, 1998, India's Prime Minister Atal Bihari Vajpayee announced at a press conference in New Delhi that India had successfully conducted underground nuclear tests in Pokhran, in the state of Rajasthan at three forty-five local time, detonating three fission, thermonuclear, and low-yield devices, similar to previous tests in May 1974. Immediately after the announcement, Vajpayee left the room without taking questions.

On the same day, the Indian Foreign Ministry also issued a statement that the tests proved India's ability to develop nuclear weapons, and that the test data would provide valuable support for its design of nuclear weapons of different yields and types in the future.

Rajasthan covers a vast desert terrain in northwestern India, which had become the subject of global attention when India conducted a nuclear device experiment there in the 1970s. Due to the high degree of secrecy on the Indian part, the outside world had no prior hint of the new test.

News of the detonations took the international community by complete surprise, since the act was totally at odds with the post–Cold War trend of global peaceful development. It also delivered a heavy blow to international concerted efforts on arms control and nuclear nonproliferation.

It was a very different climate than that of the Cold War, which had seen a protracted East-West military standoff led by the Soviet Union and the United States, and an escalating arms race, resulting in both sides amassing huge arsenals in excess of seventy thousand nuclear weapons. In the improving climate of the post–Cold War period, the American and Russian former Cold War rivals began reducing their own nuclear weapons, and work on international arms control and nonproliferation accelerated. Meanwhile, countries around the world were focusing on developing their comprehensive national strength through economic and sci-tech development. Peace and development were the watchwords of the day.

At the end of the 1960s, the international community concluded the Treaty on the Non-Proliferation of Nuclear Weapons (NPT), which came into force in 1970 for a duration of twenty-five years. By the mid-1990s, the international security landscape had stabilized considerably and, on May 11, 1995, the signatory parties decided by consensus to extend the treaty indefinitely and without conditions. In September 1996, the United Nations Assembly passed the Comprehensive Nuclear Test-Ban Treaty (CTBT), which had already been signed by some 150 countries. It was being actively put into effect before India's new tests took place.

Naturally, given this context, the Indian testing received unanimous condemnation from the international community.

UN Secretary-General Kofi Annan said he greatly regretted India's action. US President Bill Clinton gave a speech, saying that India had committed a terrible mistake, one that not only endangered security in the region, but also constituted a direct challenge to the international nonproliferation consensus. Clinton called upon India to publicly renounce further nuclear testing plans and to sign the CTBT immediately and unconditionally. Meanwhile, the United States imposed economic sanctions on India, canceling economic and military aid of all kinds, halting credit loans by its Import-Export Bank, and raising objections with the World Bank and the IMF against loans to India. Japan followed suit on economic sanctions, and Germany, Denmark, and some other countries also suspended aid programs to India. Canada, Australia, the Netherlands, and Norway announced either sanctions or cuts in aid. The international community and public opinion in various fields all pressed India to cancel further testing plans and to join the CTBT immediately.

As a permanent member of the UN Security Council, China carries a heavy responsibility in nuclear disarmament and other issues concerning international peace and security. China had always been a firm supporter of the comprehensive ban on and destruction of nuclear weapons, and resolutely opposed the nuclear arms race. We had to make our stance on India's act very clear.

When I heard about the testing, I gave immediate orders to the Foreign Ministry Information Department to issue a response making clear our position with all possible speed. Domestic and foreign media were already inquiring about China's attitude.

On the morning of May 12, a ministry spokesman set out China's position at a press pool briefing. The Chinese government expressed grave concern about India's nuclear testing, and pointed out that India's move contradicted the international development trend and jeopardized peace and stability in South Asia, at a time when nuclear disarmament efforts were making progress and the international community had reached consensus on the unlimited extension of the NPT and the agreement on the CTBT.

Unfortunately, ignoring all global objections, India pushed ahead with two further tests on May 13. Ominous clouds were gathering over South Asia.

Preposterous Finger-Pointing at China

EVEN MORE SURPRISING THAN its defiant testing of nuclear weapons, India turned the attack on China for its own action, saying it was trying to defend against the "China threat." This was plainly a feeble pretext for its nuclear testing.

The May 13 issue of the *New York Times* carried an astonishing item: On May 11, the day of the first tests, India's Prime Minister Vajpayee had sent a letter to US President Clinton citing as the major reason for India's testing its anxiety over the deteriorating security environment, in particular the nuclear environment. Vajpayee also made implications in his letter, saying that India had an overt nuclear weapons state on its borders, a state that had committed armed aggression against India in 1962 over an unresolved border problem, and that this state had materially helped another neighbor of India's to become a covert nuclear weapons state. The *New York Times* published the full text of the letter.

Although the letter did not specifically mention names, anyone with the slightest knowledge of international affairs would have known Vajpayee was referring to China.

As a matter of fact, in its May 11 statement, the Indian Foreign Ministry had implied that India conducted the testing because it was "deeply concerned as were previous governments, about the nuclear environment in India's neighborhood." India's Defense Minister George Fernandes had tried to stir up public opinion even before the testing, claiming in an interview on May 3 that the potential threat from China was greater than that from Pakistan. It was "India's number-one threat."

India's pointing the finger at China came from its need for an excuse—developing nuclear weapons had been a long-standing strategic goal and basic state policy.

India had started out early in its nuclear development. It

exploded the nation's first nuclear device in May 1974, and had been adhering to its nuclear development plan ever since. It had publicly denounced the NPT and CTBT as "discriminatory and unfair," and refused to be party to the two treaties on those grounds, an obvious tactic for future engagement in nuclear development. As one of the few countries opposed to the treaties, India had drawn constant criticism from the international community.

India's intention in nuclear testing after twenty-four years was crystal clear: it was internationally deemed as a hurried move on India's part to cross the nuclear threshold before the CTBT came into force, thus gaining equal status with the five nuclear weapons states. The five nuclear weapons states officially recognized by the CTBT were those that had manufactured and exploded a nuclear weapon or other nuclear explosive device* prior to January 1, 1967, namely the United States, Russia, the United Kingdom, France, and China. India was not a nuclear weapons state recognized under international law, but a nuclear threshold country—one with the capability and technology to produce nuclear weapons but not openly conducting nuclear testing and claiming to possess nuclear weapons.

Bolstered by the governments of the United States and Russia, the prospects for implementation of the CTBT were bright at that time. Once the treaty came into effect, India would face greater international pressure if it carried out more tests.

Back then, Sino-Indian relations had improved markedly, with bright prospects. High-level exchanges had flourished since the visit to China in 1988 of Prime Minister Rajiv Gandhi, and communication at various levels had also increased, with deeper mutual understanding and wider cooperation in different fields.

---

*Nuclear explosive device here refers to nuclear weapons or other explosive devices that release nuclear energy.

Under such circumstances, making China the reason for its nuclear testing, and depicting China as a threat, simply exposed India's ulterior motives. It was a totally untenable position.

China Explains Its Principled Position

RESPONDING TO INDIA'S NUCLEAR testing and subsequent acts, I called several meetings of Foreign Ministry departments to discuss countermeasures. It was unanimously agreed that India's nuclear testing not only endangered peace and stability in South Asia, but would also have a huge impact on international security, pose severe challenges to international arms control and nonproliferation, and might lead to a nuclear arms race in South Asia.

As a permanent member of the UN Security Council, China bears a major responsibility for maintaining world peace. It was necessary for us to take measures in bilateral and multilateral fields, make our position and attitude clear, and mobilize the international community into concerted action to demand that India stop its nuclear program immediately.

Besides, India's unwarranted attack on China and stain on our national image aroused great indignation and the conviction that we must react.

I reported the Foreign Ministry's opinions and suggestions to the central leadership, and with their approval, went ahead with our measures.

On May 14, 1998, the Foreign Ministry of China made a solemn statement on the Indian nuclear tests. The statement pointed out that the Indian government, despite strong objections from the international community, had carried out two further nuclear tests on May 13, following the tests on May 11. The Chinese government was shocked and strongly condemned the testing. India's act showed its blatant defiance of the common will of the international community on the comprehensive ban on nuclear testing. It had delivered a heavy blow to the international effort on nuclear non-proliferation, and would have serious consequences for peace and stability in South Asia and the world at large.

The statement also singled out that the malicious allegation that China posed a nuclear threat to India was utterly groundless and was a patent pretext for developing nuclear weapons.

That same morning, the Assistant to the Minister of Foreign Affairs Wang Guangya held an emergency meeting with India's Ambassador to China Vijay Nambiar, to lodge solemn representations concerning India's nuclear testing. Wang read aloud and officially presented to Nambiar the Chinese Foreign Ministry statement to be delivered to the Indian government, and told him that the statement, a rare act on the Chinese part in recent years, should receive the full attention of the Indian government.

As for India's groundless blaming of China, Wang especially stressed that such irresponsible remarks were unacceptable to China. India's actions had damaged Sino-Indian relations and cast a pall over the development of bilateral relations. India should take full responsibility for the consequences. Sino-Indian relations had reached their current stage of development thanks to the concerted efforts of both sides, and the improvement had been hard won. China demanded that India stop its nuclear weapon program immediately, stop using China as an excuse for its nuclear ambition, and stop vilifying China as a nuclear threat to India. China would pay close attention to the development of the matter.

Nambiar took a tough attitude, arguing that the international nonproliferation regime was discriminatory, that the international community's response to India's nuclear testing was unfair, and that India's restrained position on nuclear testing was praiseworthy.

On May 15, I wrote individually to the foreign ministers of thirty-three countries, urging the international community to take a common stance strongly demanding that India call an immediate halt to its nuclear program. These countries included all the Security Council member states, as well as nations with influence in international affairs, and representative of their continents.

The letter stated that India's act ran counter to the common will of the international community on the comprehensive prohibition of nuclear testing, undermined global nonproliferation efforts over the years, and fomented distrust between countries in the region. Whereas the world was developing in the general direction of peace and stability, India's nuclear testing brought about serious consequences for peace and stability in South Asia and the world at large. The top priority for the international community now was to take a common stance and make concerted efforts to demand that India stop its nuclear program immediately.

I also described India's malicious accusation of China posing a nuclear threat as totally without foundation and as simply a pretext for its development of nuclear weapons.

An Unstoppable Chain Reaction

IN NO COUNTRY WAS the reaction to India's nuclear testing more vehement than in Pakistan.

India and Pakistan had long-standing territorial, religious, and ethnic grievances, which had already erupted into armed conflict three times. Pakistan saw its neighbor as the biggest threat to its national security and had been trying to maintain strategic balance with India. Already at a disadvantage in conventional strength, Pakistan would have an even more difficult defense position if it were eclipsed by Indian nuclear strength.

Shortly after India detonated its nuclear device in 1974, Pakistan's Prime Minister Zulfikar Ali Bhutto said, "If India builds the bomb, we will also get one of our own, even at the expense of going hungry." He also said, "Pakistan will never be safe unless we have atom bombs able to counter India." In order to curb India's nuclear testing, Pakistan had suggested a nuclear-free zone in South Asia, but this was thwarted by Indian opposition.

Pakistan's nuclear policy was always inextricably tied to India. It had repeatedly indicated its willingness to sign the NPT and the CTBT, but only at the same time as India did so. If India signed, Pakistan would; if India did not, neither would Pakistan. Pakistani President Muhammad Zia-ul-Haq even offered that Pakistan would be happy to sign twice over, if India did sign the treaties.

The Indian tests unsettled the strategic balance in South Asia, putting the administration of Pakistan's Muhammad Nawaz Sharif under unprecedented pressure. Domestic reaction was intense, with political parties, the military, and the general public all demanding that Pakistan should launch nuclear tests of its own.

In response, Prime Minister Sharif made a public commitment that Pakistan was totally capable of safeguarding national security, and after the second Indian tests on May 13, a spokesperson for Pakistan's Foreign Ministry reaffirmed that Pakistan would take all necessary measures to deal with threats to national security and defend its national interests.

The possibility of a chain reaction caused general concern among the international community, which urged restraint on Pakistan. The United States, in particular, was worried about the possibility of Pakistan carrying out nuclear tests, for fear that once Pakistan had nuclear weapons that other Islamic countries, including Iran, might well take a similar course, with grave consequences.

Accordingly, the United States tried every possible way to dissuade Pakistan. In a phone call to Sharif, US President Clinton asked for restraint by Pakistan and urged it to abandon its nuclear option. To this end, he dispatched Deputy Secretary of State Strobe Talbott to Pakistan. The United States even proposed a security guarantee, conventional arms, and economic aid in exchange for Pakistan's not going ahead with testing.

The United States also worked on China, the closest neighbor on good terms with Pakistan. Through various channels, they made clear their urgent wish for China's help in persuading Pakistan to show restraint.

On the evening of May 13, US Secretary of State Madeleine Albright called me in the hope that China would work with the United States to put pressure on Pakistan. She said that the United States was deeply dismayed by India's nuclear testing, and was concerned that it might escalate a nuclear and missile race in South Asia, which would jeopardize stability in the region. The United States' top concern now was that the Pakistani government would succumb to internal pressure and respond to the Indian action with nuclear denotation or missile tests of its own. Albright continued that President Clinton had asked her to dispatch the deputy secretary to Pakistan, in an attempt to dissuade Pakistan from any action that might add fuel to the flames. The United States hoped China would make similar gestures, urging Pakistan to show statesmanship and leave India to face the consequences. She added that if Pakistan did take the same route, it would also face US sanctions.

In reply, I clearly stated China's principled position on India's nuclear testing, and pointed out quite candidly that US policy, which had created imbalance in South Asia, and its double standards in nonproliferation were not unrelated to the current situation. The top priority for the international community now was to make a joint effort to press India to change track. The United States should and could take responsibility if it was willing.

Albright totally agreed with my opinion that concerted effort by the international community was needed. She said the United States did not agree with India's assertion that its nuclear tests were

Meeting US Secretary of State Madeleine Albright at the Diaoyutai State Guesthouse in Beijing on June 22, 2000.

spearheaded against a threat from China, and believed that internal factors had actually led to its move. Nonetheless, she still expressed displeasure at my criticism of their imbalance strategy and double standard in nuclear affairs.

The first female secretary of state in US history, Albright was quick-witted and highly adaptable in dealing with international affairs. She had been US ambassador to the United Nations and had President Clinton's full confidence. Nicknamed the "Iron Lady" in international circles, she liked to wear bright red suits, which high-lighted even more her straightforward manner, tenacity, and asser-tive attitude, quite different from the more gentle approach of most diplomats.

The international community continued to work on Pakistan, but Sharif never made it plain whether Pakistan would carry out tests.

On May 25, China's President Jiang Zemin held an arranged telephone conversation with President Clinton.

Clinton said first that India had committed a grave mistake in testing its nuclear devices, and that the United States had imposed severe sanctions.

However, he quickly shifted the topic to Pakistan. Clinton said that he had already had three phone talks with Prime Minister Sharif, and believed that it was domestic pressure rather than his own will that was driving the nuclear test option. Clinton said he had informed Pakistan that if the United States helped Pakistan enhance its conventional weapons capability this would improve both its security and its economy, and that the support of neighboring and other countries for Pakistan's refraining from testing would be far superior to the short-term benefits of the nuclear testing option.

Finally, Clinton made clear his hope that President Jiang would personally join the effort and dissuade Sharif from carrying out nuclear tests.

President Jiang first set out China's position on the Indian nuclear issue. He said that, as a close neighbor of South Asia, China felt deeply uneasy about the situation in the region. India had carried out two rounds of nuclear testing in disregard of strong opposition from the international community, undermining the global nonproliferation effort, damaging peace, security, and stability in South Asia and the world, with possible serious consequences.

President Jiang suggested two top priorities for the international community: First, press India to stop developing nuclear weapons and sign up unconditionally to the NPT and CTBT; second, give practical consideration to Pakistan's proper security concerns, since simply urging restraint was inadequate. In this regard, China and the United States could work together.

Just as predicted, despite strong pressure from the outside world, Pakistan carried out five nuclear tests in the mountainous area of

Chagai, Baluchistan Province, on May 28, 1998, and a further test on May 30. Pakistan then announced it had essentially concluded its research and testing of nuclear devices and weapons.

UN Secretary-General Kofi Annan deplored the testing and urged restraint from both Pakistan and India. The United States, United Kingdom, France, Russia, and other countries also condemned the act, urging Pakistan to call off its nuclear testing immediately. We also expressed regret over the testing through a Foreign Ministry spokesman, calling for maximum restraint by the relevant South Asian countries and the immediate cancellation of their nuclear weapon programs.

International Concern, Major Power Coordination

HOW TO HANDLE THE nuclear testing by India and Pakistan became the focus of international concern. Some countries favored debating the problem in a meeting of the UN General Assembly, some favored taking it to the Security Council, and others favored collective intervention.

On the afternoon of May 29, the day after the Pakistan tests, Albright called me again to discuss the next move the United States and China should take.

Albright started by informing me she had exchanged views with the foreign ministers of the United Kingdom, France, and Russia on the nuclear tests and their impact on South Asia. The four nations were planning a conference in London two weeks later, which would involve the foreign ministers of the Security Council's five permanent members and of all the G8 countries.* The meeting would discuss international nonproliferation, the South Asia secu-

---

* The G8 consists of the United States, United Kingdom, France, Germany, Canada, Italy, Japan, and Russia.

rity situation, and the India–Pakistan dispute over Kashmir, before bringing into the discussion India, Pakistan, and a few other countries. Albright hoped for China's support for and participation in the meeting.

I told her that China felt deep regret over the two countries' nuclear testing, but it had been India that first pulled the trigger and created the current situation. As two major countries, the United States and China should uphold justice in this matter and discriminate between the roles played by India and Pakistan.

As for the proposed meeting of G8 foreign ministers, I expressed our clear view that continued nuclear testing by India and Pakistan and a nuclear arms race in South Asia had implications for regional and international peace and stability, and that the right place to discuss it was the UN Security Council. The five permanent members bore a special responsibility for world peace, and it would be inappropriate to discuss the issue in the G8 framework.

Albright then suggested first convening a meeting of foreign ministers of the five permanent members, before discussing the inclusion of other countries. She explained that involving the G8 had been President Clinton's idea, his thinking being that inclusion of Germany and Japan, two important countries without nuclear weapons, might help convince India that seeking major power status through the possession of nuclear weapons was a mistake. The United States worried that South Asia security problems, in particular the dispute over Kashmir, could not be addressed quickly and in depth within the Security Council. Moreover, the contents of the council's resolutions or statements, if any, might also be watered down in consideration of different stances.

Their worries were not unfounded. The member states of the full Security Council had long been at odds over major issues. Since the founding of the People's Republic of China, there had been no record of a foreign ministers' meeting attended by all five permanent member states to discuss major issues concerning world peace and security. Nevertheless, it was still inappropriate to discuss the nuclear issue, which concerned peace, security, and stability in South Asia, at a meeting with G8 foreign ministers. Such a meeting would undermine the status and function of the Security Council.

I told the secretary of state that the nuclear testing and the security situation in South Asia had already become a major international security problem, and was not just a matter concerning the five permanent members of the Security Council and the G8 nations. The foreign ministers' meeting she proposed could result in marathon sessions to no avail. It could also divert international attention and expectations from the role of the Security Council. This would complicate the situation and not be conducive to a genuine solution. More discussions were needed to decide on the form of the meeting.

Following the call, my ministry colleagues and I immediately analyzed the US proposal. We agreed that the nuclear testing by India and Pakistan actually proclaimed the failure of the American nonproliferation policy in South Asia. The United States was also worried that the tests might lead to an international chain reaction, that sanctions on the part of a few Western nations would be ineffective, which might bring about the collapse of the international nonproliferation mechanism it had orchestrated. The United States was also concerned that the tension engendered by the testing might lead to large-scale armed conflicts between India and Pakistan in Kashmir, leading to chaos in South Asia, which would threaten US strategic and security interests in southern and central Asia and in the Middle East.

I sensed from Albright's words that the United States wanted to take the lead in the nuclear issue, but was aware that help and support from other major powers, China in particular, was essential for proper handling of the problem. A common awareness and coordination between the United States and China would be crucial to solving the issue. This offered an opportunity for strengthening bilateral cooperation.

Having fully considered the US proposal, we decided that the most appropriate action was to call a meeting of foreign ministers of the five permanent members of the Security Council. If the United States insisted, we could also consider a meeting of the full Security Council at foreign minister level or expand participation to other countries, but reserving the right of decision to the five permanent members. I reported this idea to Vice Premier Qian Qichen, and got his approval.

I called Albright back that evening with the proposal of convening a foreign ministers' meeting of the Security Council permanent members soon. The discussion topics could include the nuclear arms race in South Asia, the nonproliferation effort, and maintaining peace and stability in the region. The meeting could release a joint communiqué to be submitted to the Security Council and the Kashmir problem could be discussed afterwards.

Albright immediately agreed that it was a good idea. She hoped that the meeting would result in a coordinated position among the five permanent members, giving a lead to the wider international community. She also suggested that, from this starting point and depending on how things went, participation could be expanded, bringing in other nations interested in the issues. Albright even offered to personally contact the foreign ministers of the United Kingdom, France, and Russia, and hoped she could report back with positive replies the same night.

Since Geneva was home to the Conference on Disarmament, we both agreed that the meeting should be held there.

At 1:30 A.M., May 30, 1998, Deputy Assistant Secretary of State Susan Shirk telephoned our Assistant Foreign Minister Wang Guangya, informing him that Britain and France had agreed to China's proposal for a foreign ministers' meeting. Though the Russian Foreign Minister Yevgeny Primakov had not yet been reached, Shirk said Albright was optimistic that he could be persuaded. Shirk also repeated Albright's gratitude for China's suggestion. On the night of May 31, Albright called again and we exchanged preliminary ideas about the meeting. The US side suggested three sections to the discussion: first, measures to urge restraint on India and Pakistan and avoid escalation of tension in South Asia; second, promote the settlement of major political disputes between the two nations, with the Kashmir issue as the final topic; third, a discussion of ensuing actions, such as inviting the participation of India, Pakistan, and other countries and establishing some sort of security mechanism in South Asia.

China's view was that there should be just two sections to the discussion, namely the nuclear issue and the South Asia security issue, and that Kashmir could be discussed as part of the latter.

I continued that the meeting should have clear goals, in this case, political and legal nonrecognition of India and Pakistan as nuclear weapons states. It should also establish a common stance on preventing a nuclear arms race in South Asia and on global nonproliferation. The Kashmir dispute was at the core of the South Asia security problem; it was crucial to urge both nations to use restraint on this issue, keep the status quo, resume dialogue and contact, and avoid the use or threat of force.

I also suggested a political statement be made at the meeting in order to send a clear and strong message to India and Pakistan as well as to the international community.

I reminded Albright that working together to bring the five foreign ministers together was highly important. The United States and China had extensive mutual interests as regards nonproliferation and restoring peace to South Asia, and we should strengthen our cooperation in these respects.

Albright responded that China and the United States shared many similar ideas, and proposed that, to ensure the success of the meeting, the five nations should send nonproliferation and South Asia experts to Geneva prior to the meeting to discuss the contents of the joint communiqué to be released afterwards. Before that, experts from China and the United States could arrive in Geneva even earlier so as to hold preparatory discussions.

Having reached consensus on the meeting, the next stop was implementation.

By convention, responsibility for coordination among the permanent members of the Security Council rotates between the five nations on a monthly basis. As it was China's turn to be coordinator in June, the arrangements for the foreign ministers' meeting became our responsibility.

On June 1, Wang Guangya held an emergency meeting with the ambassadors to China of the United States, Russia, United Kingdom, and France, officially notifying them that, after informal consultations, a meeting at foreign minister level of the Security Council's five permanent members was to be held on June 4 in Geneva, and that China's Foreign Minister Tang Jiaxuan had invited their respective foreign ministers to the meeting. Before the meeting, a discussion session with experts would be held at the residence of the Chinese mission in Geneva on June 3.

Permanent Members Reach United Stance

YEVGENY PRIMAKOV, THEN RUSSIA'S foreign minister, was a senior statesman whom I respected. On June 2, I wrote him a letter presenting China's opinions about the forthcoming foreign ministers' meeting, and expressed the hope that Russia would stand with China on the issue.

To fully exchange ideas before the meeting, I invited Primakov to take breakfast at the Chinese mission in Geneva on the morning

Meeting Russian Foreign Minister Yevgeny Primakov in Beijing on July 22, 1998.

of June 4. He accepted with pleasure, and rearranged his schedule to arrive in Geneva a day earlier.

The breakfast with Primakov actually served as an opportunity to talk business. I addressed him as a senior diplomat, and said that I was seeking his advice. We spent the next two hours sharing opinions in a cordial and friendly atmosphere on the nuclear issue and other problems of concern to the meeting. I stressed the core role of the five permanent member states in solving international peace and security problems. As he left, Primakov expressed complete agreement with China's views, and said that Russia, too, was highly concerned and would fully cooperate with China on the issues.

After I had seen out Primakov, I held another talk at the mission residence, this time with Albright, who had requested a preliminary talk with me on my arrival in Geneva.

Albright said that China's relations with India and Pakistan were very important in handling the South Asia problem. It was neither appropriate nor correct for India to conduct nuclear tests on the pretext of security concerns about China. Albright said the United

States understood China's feelings about this, but hoped China and India would take steps to settle their differences.

She also said that the United States hoped that China, as having influence with Pakistan, could inform Pakistan of the discussions after the meeting and dissuade it from taking any provocative action.

Albright was evidently worried that China's position in dealing with the nuclear crisis might be influenced by its bilateral issues with India, and that China might side with Pakistan.

I clearly pointed out that the India and Pakistan nuclear tests were a major problem with implications for world peace, security, and the international nonproliferation effort. China had always adopted a strategic view on the issue, which was why China had strongly condemned India's testing. On the other hand, India had used China as an excuse for its nuclear ambition, blaming China without justification. China had no choice but to respond to the charge and put the matter straight.

I also reassured Albright about China's position on Pakistan—that the historic friendship between the two countries would not disrupt China's principle on the nuclear issue, causing it to favor Pakistan. Objectively speaking, however, it was India that had initiated the nuclear arms race in South Asia, and the five permanent members should uphold justice, distinguishing between the respective roles of the two countries.

At five-thirty that afternoon, the foreign ministers' meeting of the Security Council's permanent members opened in the Council Chamber of the Palais des Nations in Geneva.

The Palais des Nations serves as the headquarters of the United Nations office in Geneva, and the Council Chamber is the traditional venue for major international security meetings and emergency sessions. The most magnificently decorated meeting room in the Palais, the Council Chamber features a painted ceiling showing five giant hands clasped together, symbolizing the solidarity of the five continents.

Many important international meetings have been convened here since the founding of the United Nations. In 1954, China's Premier and Foreign Minister Zhou Enlai attended the Geneva Conference discussions on Korea and Indochina in this room. As soon as I entered, a sense of historical responsibility and commitment welled up in my mind.

This was the first ever foreign-minister-level meeting of the five permanent members of the Security Council, and it was presided over by a Chinese foreign minister. The seating arrangement was different from that at the UN headquarters in New York: The Chinese minister sat on the platform presiding over the meeting, while the other four ministers and personnel sat alongside each other in rows below the platform.

In my opening remarks, I restated the special responsibility of the Security Council for maintaining world peace and stability, as stipulated in the UN Charter. The meeting was aimed at putting an end to the nuclear arms race in South Asia and restoring peace and stability to the region through the concerted efforts of the permanent member states.

During the formal consultations that followed, the foreign ministers of the United States, Russia, France, and the United Kingdom aired their respective positions. US Secretary of State Albright said that, faced with instability in South Asia and no promises from India and Pakistan to stop their nuclear tests, the group should put aside national interests and take a common stand on the issue.

Russia's Foreign Minister Primakov referred to the nuclear testing as the biggest post–Cold War challenge for the international community, apportioning equal responsibility to India and Pakistan for the severe crisis challenging the international nonproliferation mechanism.

France's Foreign Minister Hubert Védrine observed that, apart from their role in the Security Council, the participating countries were also major nuclear states and should therefore seek a far-sighted solution for the current crisis. He also brought up the issue of conventional arms, since, in the event of a conflict flaring up, conventional warfare would be the most likely scenario.

The British Foreign Secretary Robin Cook said that India and Pakistan's nuclear tests were a serious challenge to peace in South Asia and the world, which would deliver heavy blows to the international nonproliferation mechanism, unless the international community reacted promptly. The international community should urge the two nations to abandon their nuclear weapon development programs.

In my capacity as head of the Chinese delegation, I, too, addressed the meeting, setting out the Chinese government's basic views and recommendations with regard to the nuclear tests and the current situation in South Asia. I emphasized that the nuclear tests by both sides had embroiled South Asia in a dangerous nuclear arms race, and had delivered a heavy blow to international efforts in nuclear nonproliferation. I stressed that the most urgent thing now was to take measures and urge the two nations to stop nuclear testing, and promise not to weaponize the nuclear devices, not to deploy nuclear weapons, to join the CTBT and NPT immediately without conditions, and, lastly, to abandon their nuclear weapons development programs. I also suggested that the group should make it abundantly clear to the two nations that they would not be given the legal status of nuclear weapons state.

China, I said, had always adhered to a policy of friendship and good-neighborliness. As a close neighbor of South Asia, China earnestly hoped that tensions could ease and stability be restored to the region. China wanted to continue to play a positive, impartial, and constructive role in achieving that end.

For the informal consultations, I followed the international practice for multilateral occasions and invited Albright to take over. She was very pleased, and said it was the best meeting she had attended since taking office.

Afterward, I presided over the discussion of the joint communiqué, which was approved by all five participants. The communiqué expressed the five nations' condemnation of nuclear testing by India and Pakistan, and deemed it necessary to ease tension in South Asia created by the testing as soon as possible. The group demanded that India and Pakistan stop their nuclear programs and sign the CTBT immediately and unconditionally, and abandon their nuclear weapon development and deployment programs. The group also urged the two nations to join the NPT, stressing the nonrecognition of India and Pakistan as nuclear weapons states.

The communiqué called on India and Pakistan to establish trust through dialogue and peacefully settle the Kashmir dispute. The five members would pay continued attention to developments and promote the resolution of differences. The five would also work closely together to avert escalation of the arms race in South Asia and to strengthen the international nonproliferation mechanism.

The meeting lasted for about three hours and ended at eight-thirty. A half hour later, I chaired a press conference with the other four ministers. Albright and Primakov were on my right and Cook and Védrine were on my left.

First, I briefed the press about the main proceedings of the meeting. I said that peace and stability in South Asia had been seriously threatened, and that the top priority now was that both India and Pakistan should maintain calm and restraint, resume dialogue immediately, and seek ways of improving bilateral relations. As the coordinator state of the month, China had presided over the meeting with wide support and assistance from the other permanent members, and the meeting had achieved satisfactory results for all

The joint press conference held after the foreign ministers' meeting of the Security Council's permanent members in Geneva on June 4, 1998.

parties. China would continue to observe its independent foreign policy of peace and contribute its due share in maintaining peace and promoting development.

After the joint press conference, I called a separate briefing with the journalists.

By the time we returned to the residence for dinner, after a full day's work, it was ten-thirty .

The meeting was a big success. The five member states had achieved unprecedented unanimity, sending strong signals to the international community, and establishing the tone for the next step in handling the nuclear issue.

Two days later, the full Security Council meeting unanimously passed Resolution 1172, which recognized the joint communiqué passed at the meeting of foreign ministers. The resolution condemned the nuclear testing carried out by India and Pakistan, deeming that their acts posed severe threats for global nonproliferation and nuclear disarmament efforts. The resolution demanded that the two nations stop their testing and cancel nuclear development programs immediately, and urged other countries to halt exports of equipment, materials, and technology that would help with their nuclear weapon and ballistic missile programs. The resolution reflected the common will of the international community on the India–Pakistan nuclear issue.

Later developments proved that the meeting was crucial for the appropriate response from the international community, and that China played an important part in its success.

A Positive Turning Point in Sino-Indian Relations

INDIA'S BLATANT NUCLEAR TESTING and its unfounded allegation of a threat from China seriously disrupted Sino-Indian relations, which had previously been developing on a positive track. During this period, they had a major impact on high-level exchanges and communication, military cooperation, and in other fields, and the sense of friendship at a people-to-people level also deteriorated.

India was isolated on the world stage. Faced with strong international public pressure and China's stern response, India began to realize the severe damage it had done to bilateral relations with its groundless blaming of China and that its act would in no way benefit Indian interests. As the Indian government and various Indian sectors started to rethink the matter, there was a distinct shift in tone from Indian officials.

President K. R. Narayanan said in a public speech that at a time of disrupted bilateral relations, the urgent priority was that India and China should resume dialogue and improve mutual understanding, so as to return to a healthy track of bilateral development.

Via scholars, former ambassadors to China, its foreign ministry, and other channels, India delivered messages to our embassy in India looking for high-level contact with China.

At the same time, the voices decrying China got quieter.

The Foreign Ministers' Meeting of the Fifth ASEAN Regional Forum in Manila was due to start in July 1998, and, according to practice, I had been invited to attend it.

Prior to the meeting, the Indian embassy in China raised a meeting request, hoping to have talks with the Chinese foreign minister during the ASEAN event, which was to be attended by Jaswant Singh, deputy chairman of Planning Commission of India.

A moderate in the Bharatiya Janata Party (BJP), Singh was deeply trusted by Prime Minister Vajpayee. Singh had the reputation of being able to crack tough problems, an expertise demonstrated when the BJP had difficulties assembling a cabinet. After India's nuclear testing, Singh acted as a special envoy of the Indian government and had seven rounds of talks with US Deputy Secretary of State Strobe Talbott. In effect, he exercised the powers of a foreign minister.

I needed to make a comprehensive analysis with my colleagues at the Foreign Ministry before acceding to the meeting request: It was just two months after India's testing and feelings against India were still running high both internationally and within China.

Though it was still premature for bilateral contact, I considered that a multilateral occasion such as ASEAN might be a good chance for a face-to-face talk with India to show China's stance and leave room for mending relations. We could also take advantage of the meeting to warn India of the consequences of its act, and urge it to change its nuclear policy and have a correct attitude in Sino–Indian relations. Based on the above considerations, I gave my consent.

On July 27, 1998, I met with Singh at the Manila Hotel, where I was staying.

Tall and lean, with heavy black eyebrows, Singh appeared in traditional Indian costume. Throughout our meeting, he sat still and erect, with straightened back and without any change of expression. Later, when I got to know him personally, I asked him about his erect posture, which he answered with a smile, saying it was an old habit from his time as a cavalry officer in the Indian army.

Skipping preliminary small talk, we went to the heart of the matter.

I first looked back on the development of Sino-Indian relations, noting that India and China were the world's two largest developing countries, and that each boasted a long history and ancient civilization. The Five Principles of Peaceful Coexistence initiated by our nations' respective leaders had become a basic principle guiding international relations. China had always viewed developing friendly relations and cooperation with India as an important foreign policy, and had spared no effort to that end.

I then pointed out that India's using China as an excuse for its nuclear test in complete disregard of bilateral relations, and its unjustified allegation that China posed a threat, were absolutely unacceptable to China. India's regrettable actions had seriously disrupted the normal development of bilateral relations.

I made the point that whoever started the trouble should end it, and expressed the hope that the Indian side would draw a lesson from the disruption in bilateral relations and take responsible, concrete steps to bring relations back on the development track.

Singh did not say much in defense of the testing, but focused on Sino-Indian relations.

He said that India's nuclear testing was not targeted at any specific country, and that the recent disruption of relations between our two nations was unfortunate. India hoped that we could put aside our differences and work together with a forward-looking attitude to push forward bilateral relations.

He expressed India's wish to continue developing relations with China on the basis of friendship and mutual benefit, as well as expanding bilateral contacts and exchanges. He reiterated India's commitment to the Five Principles of Peaceful Coexistence, saying India wished to settle the outstanding problems through friendly negotiations with China.

From what he said, I sensed India's desire to ease international pressure and break away from isolation by mending relations with China. Nonetheless, its attitude on core bilateral problems was still not clear enough, nor had any necessary steps been taken.

Such being the case, we kept up moderate pressure on India in bilateral and multilateral areas, while implementing specific measures, which worked out well. Through a variety of channels, India repeated its wish to repair and develop relations with China.

After his official appointment as minister for External Affairs in December that year, Singh said publicly that mending relations with China was the top priority in Indian diplomacy.

In January 1999, Cheng Ruisheng, a former Chinese ambassador to India, led a scholars' delegation to India to attend the second China-India Scholars Dialogue. India received the group with exceptionally high distinction, and they met with President Narayanan, Prime Minister Vajpayee, and Defense Minister Fernandes.

President Narayanan said at the meeting that China did not constitute a threat to India, nor was India a threat to China. This was the first such statement from an Indian leader. Narayanan also said he wished to visit China as soon as possible.

Brijesh Mishra, the principal secretary to the prime minister, also expressed the wish that China could invite Singh to visit China before July.

In February 1999, at India's suggestion, a meeting was held in Beijing attended by foreign ministry officials of both countries. The directors in charge of Asian affairs of the two nations had an in-depth exchange of views on the problems in bilateral relations. During the event, the Indian side confirmed the Indian leader's speech stating that India and China caused no threat to each other

Meeting Indian Foreign Minister Jaswant Singh in Beijing on March 29, 2002.

as representative of the Indian government's policy and attitude towards China.

This explicit statement laid the political foundation for comprehensive improvement in bilateral relations, and made it possible to turn the corner. In response to India's positive message, we answered in kind.

Given the positive change of attitude on India's part as well as the progress made in nongovernmental and business exchanges, we decided to seize the opportunity and granted India's request. Singh's visit was therefore arranged for June 14 to 16.

During that visit, I held a formal meeting with him at the Foreign Ministry, during which we had an extensive and in-depth exchange of views on bilateral relations, India's nuclear testing, and other issues. In particular, we reached an important consensus on how to solve the problems facing Sino–Indian relations. The meeting, originally scheduled to last forty-five minutes, went on for two hours and fifteen minutes.

At the meeting, I made four points about Sino-Indian relations. First, the development of Sino-Indian relations was based on the premise that neither country viewed the other as a threat, and on the Five Principles of Peaceful Coexistence. Second, as the world's two largest developing countries, China and India shared similar histories and were both facing the arduous tasks of developing economy, eliminating poverty, and improving people's living standards. Our similarities far exceeded our differences. Third, China's top priorities were economic development and enhancing its comprehensive national strength, for which a favorable neighboring environment was essential. China needed to keep on good terms with its important neighbor, India. Fourth, differences of opinion on certain issues and a few unresolved matters existed in bilateral relations, but they should not become obstacles to the development of bilateral relations.

Singh expressed complete agreement. He restated that neither India nor China constituted a threat to each other, that what the two nations needed was stable bilateral relations, and dialogue rather than confrontation, and that there should be frequent dialogue at various levels. Singh also said that the Indian government regarded his visit as a turning point in the resumption and development of Sino-Indian relations.

During his visit, Singh was received by Premier Zhu Rongji in the Ziguang Pavilion, Zhongnanhai. Premier Zhu said that, for reasons known to all, Sino-Indian relations had been seriously damaged the previous year. Now that bilateral relations were improving, China hoped that the two nations could promote exchanges and trade, narrow differences, expand common ground, and strengthen friendly ties.

Singh replied that the Indian government attached great importance to developing friendly relations with China, and was willing to promote the resumption and improvement of bilateral relations based on the Five Principles of Peaceful Coexistence.

Following this visit, there was a gradual resumption of contacts in different areas. The time was ripe for comprehensive normalization of bilateral relations. The year 2000 marked the fiftieth anniversary of the establishment of diplomatic relations between China and India. With the continuing improvement in our relations, India wished to use the anniversary to take the improvement one step further. At the end of 1999, India expressed the wish for a state visit to China by President Narayanan.

Narayanan was an old friend of China. As India's first ambassador to China following the resumption of diplomatic relations in 1976, he had made outstanding contributions to the improvement and development of bilateral relations.

Narayanan was born in Kerala State to a poor family, but, by dint of talent and diligence, he achieved excellent academic grades and was recommended for a scholarship to the London School of Economics. In 1949, he began his diplomatic career, after retirement from which he went into politics and had held office as vice president of India. In 1997, he was elected president.

President Narayanan's state visit to China took place from May 28 to June 3, 2000. The event drew wide attention as the first high-level visit between the two nations since India's nuclear testing two years earlier.

Both China and India attached great importance to the event, and the schedule was meticulously planned. China's President Jiang Zemin welcomed his Indian opposite number with an arrival ceremony in the east square of the Great Hall of the People, and the two state leaders held talks afterwards. Then, NPC Chairman Li Peng, Premier Zhu Rongji, and CPPCC Chairman Li Ruihuan also held one-on-one meetings with him. Vice Premier Li Lanqing and his wife, Zhang Suzhen, accompanied President Narayanan and his wife to a joint performance by Indian and Chinese musicians at the Forbidden City Concert Hall. The Minister of Culture Sun Jiazheng attended the launch ceremony for the Chinese version of the first lady's anthology of poetry, *Sweet and Sour*. President Narayanan also delivered a speech at Peking University.

I attended President Jiang's meeting with Narayanan at the Great Hall of the People. The meeting proceeded in a friendly atmosphere and was concluded successfully.

President Jiang said that India and China were close neighbors with a long history of friendship. When the two nations established diplomatic relations in the 1950s, China's Premier Zhou Enlai and India's Prime Minister Jawaharlal Nehru had jointly initiated the Five Principles of Peaceful Coexistence. Despite ups and downs over the past five decades, the prevailing mood had been one of friendly relations between the two neighbors. The facts had proven that stable, healthy, and normal development of bilateral relations accorded with the common wishes and fundamental interests of the people of both countries, and were conducive to regional peace and stability.

He went on to say that at the turn of the new millennium, the leaders of India and China should steer the direction of bilateral relations from a strategic high ground, appropriately handle their differences, and strengthen the constructive cooperation partnership. Provided each side stood higher, took the longer view, and had a positive attitude, the prospects for the relationship were bright, and we two major powers could make due contribution to peace and development in Asia and the world at large.

President Narayanan expressed total agreement, noting that China and India had common interests in many areas. From every perspective, China and India were friends rather than rivals or enemies, and the two nations needed to further strengthen existing friendly ties. Sino-Indian cooperation, rather than rivalry or confrontation, would significantly strengthen the foundations of world peace and development. India's leaders were unanimous in hoping for more robust development of friendly relations, anticipating that the visit would mark a new chapter in Sino-Indian relations.

Narayanan's itinerary also included Dalian in northeast China and Kunming in the southwest. During his stay in Dalian, he commented on the very promising prospects for business cooperation and said that he wished, through his visit, to establish closer bilateral ties at the local level and promote further development of friendly exchanges and cooperation. He also met with Guo Qinglan, the widow of Dr. Dwarkanath Kotnis, a member of an Indian medical aid team to China in 1938.

President Narayanan's visit symbolized the normalization of relations between India and China, after the difficult times of India's nuclear testing.

As an important neighbor, with a long history of friendly exchanges with China, India was the first noncommunist country to establish diplomatic ties after the founding of the People's Republic of China in 1949. Despite subsequent major twists and turns, Sino-Indian relations have generally developed in a positive direction.

India and China are both influential countries in Asia and the world at large. As in the case of China, India is also experiencing fast growth and emerging as a new world power. Deng Xiaoping once said, "No genuine Asia-Pacific century or Asian century can come until China, India and other neighboring countries are developed."*

Developing good-neighborly relations with India is an important part of China's regional diplomacy. China has always valued friendly cooperation with India based on the Five Principles of Peaceful Coexistence. The existence of certain historical issues

---

*Source: "A New International Order Should Be Established with the Five Principles of Peaceful Coexistence as Norm" (December 21, 1988), *Selected Works of Deng Xiaoping Volume III*, (Beijing: People's Press, 1993).

should not obstruct the development of bilateral relations. China and India should not be rivals, but rather partners.

In the diplomatic dispute ten years ago, we expressed our strong objection to the Indian nuclear tests and made a necessary and appropriate response to India's groundless attack on China. Our moves were made in the interests of better development in bilateral relations, peace and stability in South Asia, and reinforcement and consolidation of the international nonproliferation effort.

In 2005, when Premier Wen Jiabao visited India, the two countries formally established the Strategic and Cooperative Partnership for Peace and Prosperity. With this, Sino-Indian relations moved into the fast lane of healthy development.

CHAPTER 11

The Beijing Summit of the China-Africa Cooperation Forum

A China-Africa Symphony

IN LATE OCTOBER 2006, Africa fever flared up in the capital as the Beijing Summit of the China–Africa Cooperation Forum (FOCAC) approached. Africa-themed billboards, banners, and streamers appeared everywhere along the city's main avenues; even in the suburbs one could see posters depicting giraffes wandering on the African savannah. Books about African politics, economy, culture, and history were selling like hotcakes. Africa-related movies and TV programs showed on screens throughout the city.

Downtown areas such as Tiananmen Square and Wangfujing Street were festively decorated. Floral displays were laid out across Tiananmen Square and from the midst of them rose up a huge billboard bearing the FOCAC logo, which symbolizes unity and cooperation between China and Africa.

Wangfujing, Beijing's main shopping street, was the venue for the exhibition Beautiful Africa. Pictures of Africa were displayed and African students studying in China performed drum dances on

The FOCAC logo towering over the floral displays in Tiananmen Square.

a specially erected stage. The exciting native dances attracted many passersby to stop and watch. Some of the audience even accepted the dancers' invitation to step up and join in, adding harmony and joy to the performance.

The upcoming FOCAC Beijing Summit was covered for days on end by major media in Beijing, China as a whole, and in the outside world, too. Leaders from nearly fifty African countries would gather at the Summit to discuss plans for the development of China-Africa cooperation.

As Confucius said, "What a delight it is to have friends coming from afar!" The entire city of Beijing was on the move. According to media reports, 250,000 car owners undertook not to drive during the period of the summit to ensure that traffic would run smoothly; Beijing traffic police invited African students studying in China to teach them African customs and etiquette; the hotels prepared for each African leader and spouse a presidential suite with bathrobes and slippers embroidered with their names. The local communities were also making preparations to welcome the African friends.

African students performing African dances on Wangfujing pedestrian street, October 31, 2006.

The FOCAC Beijing Summit was convened in the Great Hall of the People, between November 4 and 5, 2006.

In Chinese diplomatic history there had never been such a meeting; the summit was the largest and highest-level assembly ever, with the greatest number of state leaders attending.

The FOCAC, founded in 2000, is a new mechanism for collective dialogue and cooperation between China and African countries. The forum had held two ministerial conferences, in 2000 and 2003, blazing new trails for China-Africa cooperation. The Beijing Summit marked a new high point in China-Africa relations.

It was a significant event in China's diplomatic history and a memorable event in my own diplomatic career.

Prior to becoming foreign minister in 1998, I had handled Asian affairs, and this was when my connection with Africa started. In my ten years as China's foreign minister, I paid Africa ten visits, six of them official, and visited over thirty African countries. I was witness to, and an active participant in, the initiation, establishment, and development of the FOCAC. Therefore, I feel a special intimacy with the beautiful and distant continent of Africa.

My First Contact with Africa

AFTER I BECAME CHINA'S foreign minister in March 1998, I carried forward the tradition set by my predecessor Mr. Qian Qichen (then China's vice premier) of making Africa my first destination of visits abroad of the year.

Although I made a short working visit to Indonesia in April 1998, I reserved for Africa my first official visit as foreign minister. As soon as I took office, I asked Liu Guijin, director-general of the Department of African Affairs at the ministry, to recommend some African countries for my first official visit and to begin preparations.

Director-General Liu, who had been almost everywhere in Africa, was very experienced in African affairs and had a deep attachment to the continent. After leaving the post of China's ambassador to South Africa, he was appointed Chinese special representative for African Affairs. He was then mainly in charge of matters relating to Darfur, in Sudan, and so was also referred to as the Chinese special representative on the Darfur Issue. Director-General Liu advised me to visit West Africa, because the region was rarely visited by Chinese delegations, and China needed to strengthen mutual understanding with the region through visits. I immediately agreed. Then, the Department of African Affairs chose five countries as the destinations of my first official visit to Africa. They were Guinea, Côte d'Ivoire, Ghana, Togo, and Benin.

These would be my first-ever steps on African soil.

Since there were no direct flights available at that time, I flew to Guinea's capital, Conakry, via Brussels. On the plane, I perused the briefing materials about African politics, economy, history, geography, and customs prepared by the department. As I read the background material, I started conjuring up mental images of what these five African countries would be like.

My first stop was Guinea, the first independent francophone country in sub-Saharan Africa.

There is a story about how Guinea got its name. It is said that a Portuguese colonist was enthralled by its beautiful scenery and inquired of a local woman what the place was called. Not understanding Portuguese, the woman replied in Susu, her own language, with a word meaning "woman" but sounding like "guinée." The Portuguese mistakenly took her answer as the name of the place and called it "Guinea" thereafter. Later, the French named it "Guinée."

On the evening of June 10, 1998, I arrived at Conakry International Airport. A warm breeze embraced me as soon as the plane doors opened.

The Guinean people were very hospitable. Guinea's Foreign Minister Moussa Dadis Camara greeted me at the airport. He gave me a warm hug, and took me to see the welcoming performance of African singing and dancing.

This was the first time for me to see the ebullience of African singing and dancing. The dancers swayed their grass skirts to the insistent rhythm of beating drums, and the women ululated high-pitched calls of welcome for the Chinese visitors.

Foreign Minister Camara accompanied me to my room at the Grand Hotel de l'Indépendence.

The hotel, located on the Atlantic coast, offered wonderful views of ocean and sky. Before breakfast the next day, I took a walk in the vicinity of the hotel. Though the buildings appeared rather old, the streets were clean and lined with tall, lush mango trees. The scene was idyllic. Women wearing bright-colored African dresses and carrying trays, basins, and baskets of fruit, vegetables, and daily necessities on their heads made their unhurried way along the streets.

During my visit, I talked with Foreign Minister Camara and

Grass-skirt dancers at the airport to welcome the Chinese delegation on June 10, 1998.

with the Guinean president, the premier, and the speaker of the People's National Assembly. Guinea was the first country in sub-Saharan Africa to establish diplomatic relations with China and our countries enjoy very friendly relations. President Lansana Conté had been in power for a long time and was an old friend of China. During our meeting, he emphasized that China-Guinea ties had been a focus of Guinea's foreign relations and Guinea was honored to have the friendship of China, a world-respected major power.

At the time of my visit, China was assisting the building of Guinea's new presidential office. I met with President Conté at the old presidential office. During our talks, he asked me how construction was progressing, and I told him the Chinese company was making an all-out effort to complete the principal part of the construction by the end of the year and put it into use the year after. President Conté was delighted.

In the evening of June 11, Foreign Minister Camara held a welcome dinner for the Chinese delegation at which a whole roasted lamb was served. Most Guineans are Muslims, and lamb is considered the most prestigious dish when entertaining guests.

My thirty-hour visit to Guinea left me with pleasant impressions of Africa.

After Guinea, I began a visit to Côte d'Ivoire, known in English as the Ivory Coast. According to historical records, the Portuguese landed here in 1447, and a colonist called Fernán Gómez named it the Ivory Coast because of the thriving ivory trade along the littoral. Later, it became a French colony.

On June 12, 1998, I arrived in Abidjan, the economic and former official capital of Côte d'Ivoire. As the largest natural harbor in west Africa and one of the largest container ports in all of Africa, Abidjan has a developed economy. The political capital was moved from Abidjan to Yamoussoukro in 1983, since which time Abidjan has been known as the economic capital of Côte d'Ivoire.

I reached the city in the afternoon, but the weather was not as scorching as I had thought it would be. The broad streets were trimly lined with tall trees and buildings. The thirty-story Hôtel Ivoire, where I stayed during my visit, was the largest hotel in Africa at the time. It was a magnificent hotel, with a huge symbolic sculpture in ivory in the front. Sadly, violent civil war was to break out in this fine country and much of its glory would be lost.

During my visit, I met with Ivorian President Henri Konan Bédié, Prime Minister Daniel Kablan Duncan, and Foreign Minister Amara Essy. We exchanged views on international and African current affairs, the focus being on relations with China. To deepen political and economic cooperation between the two countries, I reached an agreement with the Ivorian side on establishing a regular consultative mechanism between our respective foreign ministries and the Economic and Trade Joint Committee. These two institutions later played an important role in developing bilateral relations between China and Côte d'Ivoire.

My third stop was Ghana, known in its colonial period as "the Gold Coast," for its extensive gold deposits. In March 1957, the famous national leader Kwame Nkrumah declared the independence of the Gold Coast, taking the name Ghana and becoming the first independent country in sub-Saharan Africa. Nkrumah advocated African unity and laid the foundations of pan-Africanism. He was on very good terms with China and paid several visits there, during which he developed a deep friendship with Premier Zhou Enlai.

During my stay in Ghana, I specially set aside some time to pay homage and present wreaths at the Kwame Nkrumah Mausoleum, located in downtown Accra, the Ghanaian capital. Covering an area of about five acres, the mausoleum grounds are planted with luxuriant trees and grasses. Before the mausoleum stands a bronze statue of Dr. Nkrumah in traditional Ghanaian robes, his head raised high, his gaze resolute, and his right hand pointing forward in heroic stance. It vividly embodies Dr. Nkrumah's heroic bearing in leading Ghanaians in their fight for independence.

Traveling overland from Ghana to Togo and Benin was more convenient than going by air, and, this being the case, I decided to travel to Togo's capital, Lomé, by car. The beautiful land unfolded a spectacle of undulating hills. There were other hills visible from the car—the smallest were the size of a basketball, the tallest stood as high as five meters. My companion, our ambassador to Ghana, Li Zupei, told me that these were Africa's renowned termite mounds.

I also spotted many strange trees with huge swollen trunks like beer barrels, which, as staff from our embassy in Ghana explained, were baobabs. Another common name for them was monkey-bread trees, because monkeys are said to eat their fruit. Its wood is light and soft, and therefore is useless as timber. However, Africans have a special love for baobab trees because they absorb and store water inside their trunks and thus provide a source of water during the dry season.

All the way, I kept on gasping at the biological diversity and wonder of nature, all so perfectly demonstrated in this land of Africa.

When we reached the Togo border, Togo's Foreign Minister Koffi Panou was there with a motorcade to welcome me.

During my visit, President Gnassingbé Eyadéma was running his presidential election campaign in his home area. Nevertheless, Togolese officials told me, the president had great respect for China, and would therefore meet the Chinese foreign minister despite the long distance between the capital Lomé and the president's home area. On June 17, President Eyadéma did interrupt his schedule and met with me at his presidential office in Lomé.

President Eyadéma was a legendary military statesman, who gained power through a military coup and escaped several assassination attempts. He held power for thirty-eight years, from 1967 to his death in 2005, making him one of the longest-serving rulers in Africa.

During our meeting, President Eyadéma expressed his views on human rights. He maintained that human rights should serve national development and suit the actual circumstances of each nation. He stressed that Togo opposed the Western countries' use of human rights as a pretext for interference in the domestic affairs of other countries, and that Togo upheld China's stand on the human-rights issue. I greatly admired his opinions in this regard.

On the evening of June 17, I concluded my visit to Togo and headed by car for Benin in the company of Jiang Kang, China's ambassador to Togo.

Benin's President Mathieu Kérékou left a particularly deep impression on me during my visit there.

President Mathieu Kérékou had served in the military and seized power in a coup in 1972. He enjoyed popularity among the people for his clean administration and affection for the people. Under pressure to move towards a Western-style democracy, he had been forced to practice a multiparty system. Mr. Kérékou lost power in the popular election in 1991, but regained the presidency in 1996, a rare thing to happen in Africa.

President Kérékou had a deep respect for China and great admiration for Chairman Mao Zedong. He put Chairman Mao's works *On the People's Democratic Dictatorship* and *On the Correct Handling of Contradictions among the People* on reading lists for Benin's government training at all levels, and often quoted Chairman Mao in his public speeches.

During our meeting, President Kérékou brought up the subject of the Asian financial crisis. He considered that it was in essence a financial war waged by the West, serving the same purpose as neocolonialism in Africa, namely to weaken the developing countries and transform them according to Western will.

President Kérékou also said that China's economic stability and steady exchange rate would be crucial to the Asian economy and provide spiritual support for developing countries.

He was, after all, a veteran statesman with a very clear understanding of, and incisive views about, the international political and economic situation.

Although my first African tour did not last long, it provoked my thoughts.

Objectively, with the exception of a few countries, the overall situation in Africa was still tough and backward. Many difficulties remained. All five African countries that I visited, including Côte d'Ivoire, where things were rather better, had a hot, humid climate and malaria was endemic. Life for ordinary people was hard.

Africa has incomparable advantages too, such as the abundant natural resources, spectacular natural scenery, and the people's simplicity, hospitality, and unfailing optimism.

I perceived that Africa had tremendous development potential. Though Africa would still face many pressures, challenges, and even conflicts and local wars on the road ahead, the continent was

Among the African youth.

on the whole moving towards peace and development, and playing an increasingly important role in regional and international affairs.

Africa is a land of hope and prospects.

During my first official visit to Africa, many African friends spoke highly of China-Africa friendship and cooperation and expressed gratitude for China's long-term selfless aid for Africa. They hoped that China and Africa could strengthen their cooperation in international affairs to safeguard the unity and interests of developing countries as well as in political, economic, sci-tech, and cultural fields.

Africa is the continent with the greatest number of developing countries, and a major constructive force for world peace and development. Africa occupies an important place in China's foreign policy.

After returning from Africa, I kept on seeking new channels

and methods to consolidate China-Africa friendship and to promote better and faster development of China-Africa relations.

Second Africa Visit

FROM JANUARY 13 TO 16, 1999, I made my second official visit to Africa. This time the itinerary covered Egypt, Kenya, Uganda, Tanzania, and Zambia.

Uganda and Tanzania are the two countries that made the deepest impression.

During my visit to Uganda, from January 8 to 10, I met with Uganda's legendary President Yoweri Museveni. Before assuming the Ugandan presidency in the mid-1980s, he conducted armed guerrilla struggles. An admirer of Chairman Mao Zedong, he had studied the chairman's thoughts, focusing on his theories about guerrilla warfare, and his public speeches often included quotations from Chairman Mao.

President Museveni had also read *Selected Works of Deng Xiaoping* for its theories of national development. On March 23, 1989, during a visit to China, he had consulted Deng Xiaoping on Africa's development path. He was the last foreign leader to have an official meeting with Deng.

During their meeting, Deng Xiaoping said to President Museveni, "After years of struggle, the international situation is becoming more relaxed, and a world war can be avoided. The African countries should take advantage of this favorable peaceful environment to develop. They should work out strategies and policies for development in accordance with actual conditions in each country, and they should unite so that all their people will work together to promote economic development. I agree that you do not practice socialism immediately after a successful revolution. I have told quite a few African friends that they should not be hasty about establishing socialism. They should not pursue a closed policy either, because that is not the way to develop. You are right in this respect."* Deng's thoughts had a great influence on Uganda's choosing its path of development on the basis of its actual conditions. Over the years, Uganda has maintained political stability and sustained economic development.

In 1997, on the death of Deng Xiaoping, President Museveni broke his practice of never attending events at foreign embassies in Uganda by going to our embassy in Uganda to offer condolences. In the same year, the Uganda Post Office issued a sheetlet of stamps in commemoration of Deng Xiaoping. The sheetlet had a half-length photo of Comrade Deng and bore the Chinese characters "悼念中国改革开放的总设计师邓小平 (Condolences for the chief architect of China's reform and opening up Deng Xiaoping) and the English words "CHINESE PARAMOUNT LEADER DENG XIAOPING (1904–1997)." The sheetlet also had a paragraph in Chinese and English about Deng's policy of opening up fourteen coastal cities as the forerunners of wealth creation and rebuilding the Chinese entrepreneurial spirit.

When Jia Qinglin, then a member of the Political Bureau of CPC and secretary of the Party's Beijing Committee, visited Uganda in July 2000, President Museveni put in a request for the English edition of *Selected Works of Deng Xiaoping*, and Jia Qinglin promised to give him several copies as a gift. President Museveni was glad to hear that his talks with Deng on March 23, 1989, had been incorporated in the third volume of the *Selected Works*. He emotionally recalled his meeting with Deng Xiaoping and expressed how eager he was to read this work.

---

* *Selected Works of Deng Xiaoping*, 1st ed., Volume III (1982–1992), p. 282, Foreign Languages Press, 1994.

President Museveni later received the books from our embassy in Uganda and mentioned the gift from his Chinese friends at the conference of Uganda's ruling National Resistance Movement (NRM). He commented that he had gained much enlightenment and benefit from many of Deng Xiaoping's theories and hoped that NRM leaders and officials would read the book.

To remind Uganda's top government officials of their roots and the hard life of its people, President Museveni took them to visit impoverished people in remote areas of the country on every fifth or tenth anniversary of the founding of the NRM. He named it the Long March. Although I never quizzed him about the origin of the name, I guessed it had to do with his years of studying the *Selected Works of Mao Zedong*.

During my visit to Uganda, President Museveni was conducting a Long March in the border areas of Uganda. Owing to the great distance between the border areas and Uganda's capital, our hosts had been uncertain whether President Museveni could meet me. By that time, I had already met with the vice president, the deputy prime minister, the foreign minister, and other important Ugandan officials, and, as a guest, I must suit the convenience of the host. If President Museveni had difficulty in meeting me, it was understandable in my view. However, his legendary life did fascinate me and I was really looking forward to meeting him.

By the evening of January 9, 1999, the day before my departure, the Ugandan officials had not yet confirmed a meeting with President Museveni, and I assumed it was now out of the question. In the early morning of the next day, we arrived at Entebbe Airport as scheduled and were waiting in the lounge for our flight to Tanzania. To my surprise, a Ugandan official told me that President Museveni would soon arrive at the airport. He had interrupted his Long March and taken a helicopter early that morning in order to meet me.

Meeting with Uganda's President Museveni, January 10, 1999.

Just as the official finished giving me the news, the lounge door opened, and a stalwart middle-aged man in camouflage coat and tall boots strode in. I was certain that this must be President Museveni, so I walked forward and firmly shook his outstretched hand.

President Museveni affectionately reminisced about his contacts with China. He said that Uganda had won its freedom struggle by gaining enlightenment from China's revolutionary history and from Chairman Mao Zedong's thoughts. As a student, he had paid close attention to Premier Zhou Enlai's visit to Tanzania in 1965. President Museveni admired the founding leaders of China and cherished his deep friendship with Chinese leaders of the second and third generations. The memory of his meeting with Deng Xiaoping remained fresh in his mind. He was also glad to have had the opportunity to meet with President Jiang Zemin in 1996.

President Museveni and I had a congenial talk on Africa's situation, economic construction, and the development path.

Then I left for Tanzania, one of the first countries in Africa to

Exchanging toasts with Tanzania's Minister of Foreign Affairs and International Cooperation Jakaya Kikwete, January 10, 1999.

win independence. Tanzania maintained long-term national unity and political stability after independence. Dar-es-Salaam, whose name means "Harbor of Peace," is Tanzania's largest city and its commercial capital.

Tanzania's Minister of Foreign Affairs and International Cooperation Jakaya Kikwete (now president of Tanzania) broke the conventional protocol and accompanied me throughout my visit to Tanzania. Before each event, he came in person to collect me at my hotel. I was deeply moved by his hospitality.

China and Tanzania have a deep friendship. Since the 1960s, China has sent to the country tens of thousands of workers, who have made selfless contributions to the economic development of Tanzania. Sixty-nine of that number lost their lives and were buried at a cemetery in the southwestern suburbs of Dar-es-Salaam. Some of those sixty-nine Chinese helped the local people with coal mining, agriculture, and water conservancy, but the majority gave their lives in the construction of the Tanzania-Zambia Railway (TAZARA).

As soon as I arrived in Tanzania, I inquired of Ambassador

Zhang Hongxi whether the Chinese workers' cemetery was far, since I wanted to pay respects to these compatriots. Ambassador Zhang explained that it was not far, but had not been included in the itinerary because of time constraints.

I told Ambassador Zhang that I wanted to make the visit and would happily sacrifice some sleep, get up very early, and make time for a visit to the cemetery. It would not only be a diplomatic activity but also significant for all the members of the delegation to pay homage to and remember them.

The embassy made rapid arrangements. On the morning of January 12, 1999, I led over two hundred compatriots working in Tanzania and all the members of the delegation, on behalf of the Chinese people, to present wreaths, and pay respects to those Chinese workers who had sacrificed their lives for China-Tanzania friendship. I said in my speech at the cemetery, "You contributed your efforts and lives to building a bridge of friendship that links China with Tanzania as well as the whole of Africa. Your motherland has never forgotten you. We are determined to carry on your wish and build better

Paying respects to Chinese workers who died assisting Tanzania, Dar-es-Salaam, January 12, 1999.

relations with Africa." Later, Ambassador Zhang wrote a report on our visit to the cemetery, which was published in the *People's Daily*.

Before going to the Chinese workers' cemetery, I visited the TAZARA station in downtown Dar-es-Salaam.

The world-famous TAZARA was China's largest aid project in Africa. In the early 1960s, Tanzania and Zambia aspired to build a rail link between the two countries to help develop their economies and support the national liberation of southern African countries.

During his visit to China in 1965, Tanzania's President Julius Nyerere formally brought up the request for aid from China to build the TAZARA. President Kenneth Kaunda of Zambia raised the same request during his visit to China in 1967. Although China was facing economic difficulties, China's founding leaders, headed by Chairman Mao Zedong and Premier Zhou Enlai, men of cour-

Visiting the TAZARA station in downtown Dar-es-Salaam, Tanzania, January 12, 1999.

age and vision, took full account of China's overall diplomacy and China-Africa friendship, and made the strategic decision to aid the building of the TAZARA. The railway represents not only China-Africa friendship, but is also a good example of South–South cooperation.

Construction of the railway started in 1970, and the railway opened fully to traffic in 1976. The railway is still playing an important role and is regarded as a milestone in China-Africa friendship.

Dar-es-Salaam is the first station on TAZARA's 1,860.5-kilometer journey westwards. Our African friends called it the "Railway of Friendship."

When I arrived there I was welcomed by a large number of people singing and dancing. They shouted "China" and "Thanks" in Chinese to express their heartfelt gratitude for China. The moving scene created an indelible impression on my mind.

It is worth mentioning that Tanzania was the only African country to participate in the torch relay leading up to the Beijing 2008 Olympic Games. The torch relay encountered disturbances in some Western countries, but Tanzanian officials assured China very definitely that no such unpleasantness would ever happen in Tanzania.

The Tanzanian leg of the relay started at Dar-es-Salaam railway station and ended at the sixty-thousand-capacity National Stadium of Tanzania, also built with aid from China, and another token of China-Tanzania friendship.

On the day of the torch relay, I was watching the live broadcast in Beijing. Tanzania attached much importance to the torch relay and had sent six cabinet ministers to carry the torch. I could see on television that the roads from the railway station to the National Stadium were lined with people waving Chinese national flags, running along with the Olympic torch, and shouting joyfully. I could not make out just what they were saying, but, after a while, the

Chinese reporter on the spot explained that the local people were shouting what they had just learned: "Go, China!" in Chinese.

The Chinese reporter, deeply moved by the scene, exclaimed, "Everyone in Tanzania is a torch bearer!"

Quite so. The torch relay was not just about passing the Olympic flame from hand to hand; it was also passing on friendship.

These two African tours conveyed to me the closeness of relations and depth of friendship between China and Africa.

China-Africa friendship was established and nurtured by Chinese and African leaders of several generations. Since the time of Chairman Mao Zedong and Premier Zhou Enlai, China has been making emphatic efforts to foster relations with developing countries, and with African countries in particular. Since the 1950s, China has provided human, material, and financial resources as well as moral support for the national liberation and economic development of African countries and helped African liberation organizations train a large number of activists. The wise decisions and earnest practice of China's founding leaders laid a solid foundation for China-Africa relations. Chinese leaders of later generations have adhered to this direction and blazed new trails in diplomacy.

Between 1963 and 1965, Premier Zhou Enlai paid three visits to Africa. During the December 1963–February 1964 tour, he visited ten African countries in succession. It was the first official goodwill visit of a Chinese leader to African countries and marked a new epoch in China-Africa relations. During this tour, Premier Zhou Enlai put forward the five principles guiding China's relations with the Arab and African countries, and the eight principles for China's foreign aid, which went on to play an important role in strengthening relations between China and developing countries, maintaining world peace and promoting common development.

China-Africa friendship was cemented in adversity and has stood tempestuous tests. The African countries have been China's all-weather friends. At the 26th Session of the UN General Assembly in 1971, the resolution for restoration of the lawful rights of the People's Republic of China in the United Nations was cosponsored by twenty-five countries, eleven of them from Africa. Of the seventy-eight votes in favor of the resolution, twenty-six were from African countries. When the resolution was passed, Tanzania's permanent representative to the UN, Salim Ahmed Salim (later to become Tanzania's foreign minister, prime minister, and secretary-general of the Organization of African Unity), was so excited that he began dancing at the Assembly Hall.

Learning the news, Chairman Mao Zedong remarked, "It is our African brothers who have carried us into the United Nations." This vivid, precise assertion has been passed down as a classic description of China's connections with Africa.

Deng Xiaoping also attached great importance to China's relations with Africa, and his views on Africa's development path were highly valued by many African leaders.

In 1996, President Jiang Zemin made a state visit to six African countries, the first such visit to Africa by a Chinese head of state. At the headquarters of the Organization of African Unity (OAU), President Jiang delivered a keynote speech, "Toward a New Historical Milestone of China-Africa Friendship," in which he put forward a five-point proposal for the development of a long-term, stable China-Africa relationship of all-around cooperation in the twenty-first century. His proposal established the guiding principles for our diplomatic work towards Africa in the new age.

From my two African tours, I perceived that the changing circumstances were presenting China-Africa relations with new development opportunities.

The world was changing. Against the background of economic globalization, Western powers, motivated by their own self-interests, locked horns in fierce competition for African resources and markets. On the other hand, African countries tended to be marginalized by globalization.

Africa was changing. In the late 1980s and early 1990s, Western powers forced the multiparty system on Africa, and the continent was swept by a wave of so-called democratization. African countries began to adopt more pragmatic and diverse domestic and foreign policies. In order to avoid marginalization, they allied and increased cooperation to strengthen themselves. As Africa's integration process moved steadily forward, there was a greater tendency for African countries to speak with one voice and act in concert in international affairs.

China was changing. Since the adoption of the reform and opening-up policy in 1978, China's overall strength and influence had been expanding. China had been devoted to developing cooperation with all countries, in particular mutually beneficial economic and trade cooperation with the developing world.

Under the new circumstances, in the interest of common development, China needed the cooperation and support of Africa; for its part, Africa had a strong need for China's help and support to maintain political stability and national development.

In the past, China-Africa cooperation had been conducted mainly at the bilateral level. Given the new world situation, it was my deep conviction that we must be innovative in our approach to Africa by establishing a mechanism for collective dialogue and cooperation. Such a mechanism would bring China and Africa together on a regular basis, or as needed, a mechanism that would help deepen mutual understanding, consolidate friendship, expand common ground, and increase cooperation. This would be conducive to protecting the lawful rights and interests of China and African countries and conducive to world peace, stability, and development.

Creation of FOCAC

WHILE I WAS PONDERING this issue I met with Madagascar's Foreign Minister Lila Ratsifandrihamanana during her visit to China in May 1999.

The brilliantly gifted minister, born into a literary family, had deep learning and broad vision. She was friendly toward China and set great store by China–Africa relations.

During our meeting, she said earnestly that as the international situation was undergoing immense changes, African countries eagerly hoped to establish partnerships with China, and hold consultations with China on peace and development issues of common concern. She suggested the establishment of a China–Africa forum.

Her suggestion coincided with my own thinking.

After Ms. Ratsifandrihamanana left, I asked my ministry colleagues with responsibility for African affairs, namely Vice Foreign Minister Ji Peiding and Liu Guijin, director-general of the Department of African Affairs, to conduct an immediate feasibility study of her proposal.

Director-General Liu reported back that the proposal had sparked fierce debate in the Department of African Affairs. Some were confident about it and others were uncertain. After thorough discussion, however, the colleagues had concluded that China should forge ahead and blaze new trails. They proposed convening the "Forum on China–Africa Cooperation—Ministerial Conference Beijing 2000."

Later, some foreign media mistakenly assumed that the forum had been initiated by China. Actually, it was the idea of our African friends.

Once the Central Authorities had given the go-ahead, we decided to proceed with convening the suggested forum in Beijing. We issued invitations to foreign ministers and ministers in charge of economic cooperation affairs from African countries that had diplomatic relations with China.

Two themes were established: First, in what way should we work toward the establishment of a new international political and economic order in the twenty-first century? Second, how should we further strengthen China–Africa economic and trade cooperation under the new circumstances?

In October 1999, President Jiang Zemin sent letters to the heads of state of all African countries that had established diplomatic ties with China, as well as to the OAU Secretary-General Salim Ahmed Salim. In his letter, President Jiang set out the background, purpose, and topics of the conference and requested the African heads of state to send relevant ministers to the conference. President Jiang invited former OAU chairman, Algeria's President Abdelaziz Bouteflika, incumbent OAU chairman, Togo's President Gnassingbé Eyadéma, incoming OAU chairman Frederick Chiluba, and OAU Secretary-General Salim Ahmed Salim to give speeches at the opening and closing ceremonies.

In February 2000, Shi Guangsheng, head of the Ministry of Foreign Trade and Economic Cooperation (today's Ministry of Commerce), and I sent a joint letter of invitation to relevant ministers of African countries for them to attend the conference.

The response in Africa was one of high praise for China's move, and one country after another signed up for the conference. It is worth mentioning that Tanzania's President Benjamin Mkapa offered to attend the conference in person.

As part of the conference preparations, I made my third tour of Africa in early 2000. This time I visited five African countries, namely, Nigeria, Namibia, Zimbabwe, Mozambique, and Seychelles.

I had a very clear goal for this tour, which was to solicit African opinions on the Ministerial Conference of the Forum on China–Africa Cooperation. Apart from giving positive comments on China's proposal, most African friends suggested that the forum should be characterized by substantive content on cooperation, and hoped that China could help African countries achieve development. After the tour, I advised my foreign ministry colleagues to use these opinions as a key reference when planning the content of the conference and to take into consideration both political and economic concerns.

From October 10 to 12, 2000, the Forum on China-Africa Cooperation—Ministerial Conference Beijing 2000 was convened in the Great Hall of the People, Beijing.

Attending the conference were seventy-nine foreign ministers and ministers in charge of economic cooperation, representing forty-four African countries that had established diplomatic relations with China. Even Somalia, mired in civil war for years, sent its representatives. Representatives of seventeen international and regional organizations, including the OAU, United Nations Development Program (UNDP), and United Nations Economic Commission for Africa (UNECA), were present as special guests.

At the suggestion of some African countries, we also invited African countries that had not established diplomatic relations with China to attend as observers. Malawi and Liberia attended with observer status.

As the conference chairman, it fell on me to declare it open.

Speeches at the opening ceremony were delivered by President Jiang Zemin, by the OAU troika—Abdelaziz Bouteflika, Gnassingbé Eyadéma, and Frederick Chiluba—and by Tanzania's President Benjamin Mkapa. All expressed the common aspiration to practically strengthen China-Africa cooperation under the new circumstances.

The three-day conference passed the FOCAC Beijing Declaration and the Program for China-Africa Cooperation in Economic and Social Development. These two documents established the new framework of China-Africa relations and outlined a blueprint for China-Africa cooperation in various fields. They won high praise from African countries and the world at large.

The African countries regarded the conference as an epoch-making event in the history of China-Africa relations and a new starting point for unity and cooperation between Asia and Africa. It was hailed as a "Bandung Conference for the new age."

Every new venture starts out with difficulty, and this conference was the first collective dialogue between China and African countries. We had no experience, but we did our best and made the conference a success.

Once the conference was over, I still felt a lingering excitement about finally having a platform for collective dialogue between China and Africa.

The FOCAC member states take turns hosting the ministerial conference. Ethiopia filed its request very early for hosting the second ministerial conference.

There was some discussion about the hosting of the FOCAC ministerial conference. Owing to African countries' limited conditions for hosting large-scale conferences and their different working habits, communication and coordination problems often occurred. Some suggested it would be more convenient if the ministerial conference were always held in Beijing.

I made my position very clear, namely that the forum belonged to both China and Africa. African countries wished to heighten their sense of involvement through hosting the ministerial conference, and their sense of involvement and ownership would be greatly diminished if the conference were always held in Beijing. I insisted that the hosting of the conference should alternate between China and one of the African countries in turn.

From December 15 to 16, 2003, the conference center at the headquarters of the African Union* (AU) in Ethiopia's capital Addis

---

*The Organization of African Unity was replaced by the African Union in July 2002.

Ababa witnessed the convening of the FOCAC Second Ministerial Conference.

China's Premier Wen Jiabao, thirteen African leaders, including Ethiopia's Prime Minister Meles Zenawi, AU Commission Chairman Alpha Oumar Konaré, and the representative of the UN secretary-general, delivered speeches at the opening ceremony. It was attended by seventy ministers responsible for foreign affairs and international economic cooperation from forty-four African countries, and by representatives of international and African organizations. Malawi and Swaziland, countries that had not established diplomatic relations with China, sent observers.

In his opening ceremony speech, Premier Wen gave a full account of China's Africa policy and put forward a four-point proposal on furthering China-Africa friendship and cooperation: first, continue to push forward the traditional China-Africa friendship through mutual support; second, promote democratization of international relations through intensified consultations; third, jointly meet the challenges of globalization through coordination of positions; fourth, start a new chapter in China-Africa friendly relations through enhanced cooperation. His concise and precise points met with a warm response and high praise from the African side.

The conference gave a strong impetus to the all-around development of China-Africa friendship and cooperation and to the establishment of the FOCAC mechanism. On the sideline of the conference, Premier Wen Jiabao and African leaders held fifteen bilateral talks and meetings where views on a wide range of issues were exchanged. Such concentrated diplomatic contact at national leadership level was unprecedented in the history of China-Africa relations.

The FOCAC Second Ministerial Conference was commonly recognized by African countries as a highly efficient and practical gathering. Premier Wen Jiabao's participation fully exhibited the self-confidence and practical style of China's new government administration.

Follow-up actions were effectively implemented. China adopted a series of substantive measures within the FOCAC framework, such as increasing aid to Africa, reducing and canceling debts owed by heavily indebted poor countries and the least developed countries in Africa, and expanding and reinforcing cooperation with Africa in the fields of tourism, science and technology, culture, education, and medical and health care. These measures propelled the development of China–Africa relations.

After completion and improvement through the two ministerial conferences, the FOCAC mechanism truly merited its name as a platform for collective dialogue and concrete cooperation between China and Africa.

Celebrating Fifty Years of Diplomatic Ties

IN ACCORDANCE WITH THE FOCAC's follow-up mechanisms, the Third Ministerial Conference would be held in Beijing in 2006.

This would be a memorable year for relations between China and Africa, since 2006 was the fiftieth year since the inauguration of diplomatic ties between China and African countries. On May 30, 1956, Egypt, resisting huge pressure from the West, was the first among African and Arab countries to establish diplomatic relations at the ambassadorial level with the People's Republic of China, thereby initiating the establishment of diplomatic relations with China among African countries. Fifty years later, forty-eight of the fifty-three African countries had established diplomatic relations with China, and, by the end of 2007, the number reached forty-nine, with the establishment of diplomatic ties between China and Malawi.

In 2003, after I had joined the State Council, the Ministry of Foreign Affairs reported to me that, since African countries placed high hopes on the FOCAC and were eager to strengthen its mechanisms and raise cooperation to a new level, there was a general wish among them for exchanges with China at a higher level, and that many African leaders had a strong desire to visit China. Some African leaders had proposed upgrading the FOCAC to a summit meeting of heads of state.

I asked the ministry to give the request active and careful consideration.

After some study, they reported back their opinion that a China-Africa summit would satisfy the desire to upgrade the FOCAC, would demonstrate China's regard for Africa, would be beneficial for introducing China's new China-Africa cooperation measures, and would facilitate direct communications between African leaders. Therefore, what they proposed was to make a special case of the Third Ministerial Conference of FOCAC by holding a summit meeting at the same time.

The Central Authorities approved the suggestion and decided to issue invitations to the Beijing Summit, in the name of President Hu Jintao, to leaders of African countries having diplomatic relations with China.

In August 2005, when President Hu Jintao met with Alpha Oumar Konare, chairman of the AU Commission, and Mwai Kibaki, president of Kenya, he told them China's idea of holding the Beijing Summit and both were enthusiastic. This was the first time that China had made the idea public.

African leaders were very happy about the summit. They believed that it would make FOCAC more dynamic and further promote friendship between China and African countries. One after another, they said they would be present, and some wanted to help China invite other leaders to the summit and ensure its success.

To commemorate the fiftieth anniversary of China-Africa diplomatic relations and to welcome the forthcoming summit, we published China's African Policy Paper in January 2006.

Before this, China's EU Policy Paper had been published in October 2003 to a warm response from China and foreign countries. The paper helped the international community to have a better understanding of China's EU policy.

With changes in the international situation and development of China-Africa relations, there was muttering in certain quarters about the relationship. Some said that China was developing its relationship with Africa because of its need for African energy resources; some even accused China of neocolonialism in Africa and spread rumors about China's threat to Africa. This being the case, we had to formulate a comprehensive Africa policy and present to the international community China's stance and plans for sincerely developing friendship and mutually beneficial cooperation with Africa.

China's African Policy Paper was completed in 2005, but since 2006 was the fiftieth anniversary of China-Africa diplomatic relations and the Beijing Summit of FOCAC would be held this year, we decided to delay its official publication until January 2006.

It was a fact that China-Africa relations were more and more valued. Even so, I was somewhat surprised that the paper received such attention from all sides.

In addition to publishing the paper in Beijing, we also held press conferences at the same time in a number of African countries.

As a powerhouse in the region, South Africa has an advanced, highly influential, news media, and its web-based media are second to none in Africa. On January 12, 2006, our embassy in South Africa held a press conference at the Sheraton Hotel in Pretoria, the South African capital, assuming that there would be fifty people present. Actually, more than 150 people arrived, including journalists from major South African TV and radio stations, newspapers and periodicals, locally based journalists from foreign press agencies, scholars, and government officials. The embassy had to contact the hotel immediately and switch to a bigger venue.

Some journalists' reports described the crowded press conference, noting that only China's African policy paper could have such a strong appeal and get such a warm reception, and that it would play an important role in the development of China-Africa relations.

The year 2006 was the Year of Africa. In January, China published the paper; in April, President Hu Jintao visited Morocco, Nigeria, and Kenya; in June, Premier Wen Jiabao visited Egypt, Ghana, Republic of the Congo (Brazzaville), Angola, South Africa, Tanzania, and Uganda. Seeing China's Central Authorities paying such attention and taking a series of Africa-related diplomatic actions, ministry officials working on Africa were inspired. We expected that the Beijing Summit of FOCAC to be held in December would take China-Africa friendly relations of cooperation to a new peak.

Summit Preparations Begin

In February 2006, President Hu Jintao sent letters to African leaders, inviting them to attend the Beijing Summit of FOCAC.

Holding the summit was an important strategic decision made by the Central Authorities in order to strengthen Africa-related work to meet the new world situation. It was also a major diplomatic activity for China that year. The Central Authorities attached great importance to the summit, and formulated explicit and specific policies. President Hu Jintao gave several important instructions and concerned himself with the preparations, and Premier Wen Jiabao instructed departments concerned to start Africa-related work around the task of successfully hosting the summit.

My many years in my diplomatic career have taught me that diplomatic work cannot proceed without the support and cooperation from all sides, and that every major diplomatic event is the result of concerted efforts. This was fully demonstrated during the preparations for FOCAC.

The first two ministerial meetings had been systematic projects completed with coordinated multilateral efforts. The Beijing Summit needed greater cooperation from all government departments. The Central Authorities decided that the Ministry of Foreign Affairs and Ministry of Commerce should carry out the preparatory work together, since the FOCAC involved China-Africa political relations and cooperation in many projects, and we could draw on our experience in arranging the first two ministerial-level meetings.

Preparations formally began soon after President Hu's invitation letters went out.

On March 9, 2006, officials from the two ministries came to my office and reported initial plans for the summit preparations. I confirmed their ideas and asked them to plan the preparation work from a macroscopic view. I stressed that the new measures to be announced would be the highlight of the summit, but that the content of those measures involve difficult coordination between the numerous departments and organizations concerned. I asked them to start the coordination as soon as possible and to work with perseverance to achieve success.

From the time the Central Authorities decided to hold the summit, I kept on thinking about all aspects of the preparations.

The Beijing Summit would be the highest-level and largest platform for dialogue between Chinese and African leaders, with the attendance of the greatest number of countries and leaders in the diplomatic history of the People's Republic. Planning and organizing such an unprecedented event was no easy matter. So, I kept reminding colleagues from the organizing ministries that, if the preparations were to be effective and orderly, the initial stages should make an overall arrangement, clarify the division of responsibilities, determine the schedule, and put forward requirements. If necessary, they could establish a preparatory committee consisting of all the departments and organizations concerned.

The two ministries immediately went to work with other ministries and departments to carry out the preparation work, making regular, detailed progress reports. I felt that the preparations were going smoothly, but it was still difficult for the two ministries to coordinate so many departments.

To ensure smooth preparations for a successful summit, in mid-July 2006, the Central Authorities approved setting up the Preparatory Committee of the Beijing Summit and the Third Ministerial Meeting of the Forum on China-Africa Cooperation. I was appointed director of the Preparatory Committee; Foreign Minister Li Zhaoxing and Commerce Minister Bo Xilai were vice directors. Other members were leading officials from the General Office of the CPC Central Committee, Ministry of Foreign Affairs, Ministry of Commerce, Ministry of Finance, Ministry of Public Security, Ministry of Culture, China Council for the Promotion of International Trade, and Beijing Municipal Government. Under the committee, there was a secretariat and working groups in charge of political affairs, economic and trade affairs, conference details, protocol, and so on.

On July 24, 2006, I presided over the first plenary meeting of the Preparatory Committee, where I conveyed instructions from President Hu Jintao and Premier Wen Jiabao about making a good job of the summit, and mobilized the preparation work.

The meeting adopted draft proposal documents concerning the summit preparation, and heard reports from different departments about progress.

According to the general plan, the summit theme would be "Friendship, Peace, Cooperation, and Development," and the summit would adopt the Declaration of the Beijing Summit of the Forum on China-Africa Cooperation and the Forum on China-Africa Cooperation—Beijing Action Plan (2007–2009).

The timetable was mapped out: Senior Officials' Meeting, November 1–2; the Third Ministerial Conference, November 3; the Beijing Summit, November 4–5. In addition, the High-level Dialogue Between Chinese and African Leaders and Business Representatives and the Second Conference of Chinese and African Entrepreneurs were to be held.

Since it was the first meeting of the Preparatory Committee and the preparation work was intense, difficult, and on a tight schedule, I put forward some concrete and explicit demands for each department.

I asked everyone to treat the Beijing Summit as a rehearsal for the Beijing 2008 Olympic Games. We had to make a success of it.

After the first plenary meeting, the preparation work went into greater details.

By mid-September, over a month before the Beijing Summit, our preparations reached a crucial stage.

The feedback from Africa had surpassed our expectations. The forty-eight African countries having diplomatic relations with China had signed up for the summit; over twenty international organizations had confirmed that they would send senior representatives as observers; and 1,600 people from African countries (excluding businesspeople attending the Conference of Chinese and African Entrepreneurs) had registered for the Beijing Summit, Ministerial Conference, and Senior Officials' Meeting. Over one thousand Chinese and foreign journalists had applied to cover the summit.

The enthusiasm from Africa and attention from international media was pleasing and exciting. It also imposed greater demands for preparation.

In order to have complete and in-depth control of progress, I decided to put aside time to hear the work reports of all the preparatory groups, examine and solve problems promptly, and push forward the preparation work.

The reports showed that though the preparations were going on smoothly, there were problems in two main areas: First, it was difficult to coordinate such a multiplicity of departments. The preparations were hard and we had no precedents to guide us; they involved economy, public security, education and other fields, and more than ten Chinese ministries. Second, in terms of protocol needs, it was extremely difficult to cater to such large numbers of high-level attendees, with so many activities. Moreover, the African side had rather high expectations of the summit.

In response, I asked our officials to have a stronger sense of responsibility, do a solid job, remain vigilant against potential challenges, and harness all their confidence and resolve to make the summit a success.

I made a point of reminding officials to pay attention to the following aspects.

First, pay attention to details. We should take into consideration the characteristics of our African friends and any possible problems, prepare in advance, strengthen cooperation and coordination within every individual link in the chain, and ensure smooth connections between all the links.

Second, do a good job of drawing up measures for practical cooperation with Africa. African countries had high expectations regarding business cooperation with China, and so our specific economic measures would be vital to a successful meeting. Considering the characteristics of Africa, we thought it essential to increase input into Africa in various forms, and we could use the summit to publicize specific measures. The Action Plan should have solid content rather than sheer rhetoric.

Third, prepare for the unexpected. We should carefully examine all potentially disruptive factors, and take preventative measures.

The Central Authorities always attached great importance to the Beijing Summit of FOCAC.

On September 28, 2006, General Secretary Hu Jintao presided over a meeting of the Politburo Standing Committee of the CPC, at which he heard a report about the preparations for the Beijing Summit and issued important instructions on doing a good job of hosting the summit and further strengthening Africa-related work. He made a particular point of stressing the profound and significant impact of the upcoming summit, asking us to make careful preparations and work together to ensure its success.

He reminded us that when receiving guests, we should treat them all evenhandedly, show warmth and hospitality, ensure their safety, emphasize practical results, and satisfy African leaders' wishes as much as possible.

What touched me enormously was Hu Jintao's willingness to meet with any African head of state or government attending the summit as long as he had time. This would demonstrate the spirit of equality between nations, irrespective of how large or small, rich or poor, strong or weak any individual country might be.

He also gave specific instructions on summit security issues and measures for China–Africa economic and trade cooperation.

Premier Wen Jiabao also made important suggestions on China–Africa economic and trade cooperation, government aid to Africa, the operation and management of government aid projects, preferential loans to Africa, and other issues.

The following day, I presided over the second plenary meeting of the Preparatory Committee and conveyed the instructions from President Hu, Premier Wen, and leaders of the State Council, making all the staff aware of our tasks and goals.

Seeking Perfection in Every Detail

THE WHOLE PROCESS OF the Beijing Summit preparations touched me deeply, the organizational details in particular.

It was really a big battle campaign that needed the cooperation of every department involved. In addition to substantive preparation work in areas of politics, economics, and trade, the organizing group had to take care of the accommodation, transportation, and registration arrangements for Chinese and foreign participants and the preparation of gifts and souvenirs; the protocol department made arrangements for large-scale activities and bilateral and multilateral meetings of unprecedented scale and complexity, and led several hundred liaison personnel and volunteers to receive all the guests; and the news department formulated and carried out a media program before, during, and after the summit, providing prompt and accurate information to the people of China and the international community.

The Ministry of Commerce, Ministry of Public Security, Ministry of Culture, Ministry of Health, and other departments worked on the preparations day and night. Departments of administration, finance, and logistics provided the underpinning. The Great Hall of the People, Diaoyutai State Guesthouse, and various hotels made meticulous arrangements for receiving the guests.

Staff of the Beijing city authorities cooperated with all the central government departments involved, and, with a strong sense of responsibility and great enthusiasm, made a good job of receiving the guests and guaranteeing their security. Incomplete statistics showed that during the summit, relevant city authorities put in 384,900 individual police shifts to maintain good public order. Between November 1 and 5, 2006, Beijing police received 122 criminal incident reports, 70 percent fewer than during the corresponding period in 2005. On November 4, a mere fifteen incidents were reported. In a metropolis with a population of nearly 20 million, such a rate was phenomenally low. One police emergency hot-line officer apparently joked, "During the summit, we were almost jobless."

In the run-up to and during the summit, leaders and officials of the General Office of the CPC Central Committee gave us guidance and full support. Their diligent, careful, enthusiastic, responsible, and meticulous work style set a good example to others.

To ensure the successful summit and smooth reception, our people were scrupulous and meticulous, dedicated to perfection in every detail. I have a few examples.

During the summit, we would have nearly fifty state leaders at certain meetings. But gathered at what kind of table? On this issue we were very particular.

None of the preliminary plans designed by the Protocol Department were satisfactory. To show the equality of all countries, especially that China and Africa are a united and harmonious family, we finally decided to use a round table. We could not find such a big round table and thus had one made to order. It was huge, twenty meters in diameter and sixty-two meters in circumference. To ensure mutual identification, we placed a name plaque in bold clear print bearing the name of the country in front of the seat of each head of state.

After the summit, many African leaders expressed surprise at this huge, round table, saying they had never seen one as large. It was put into service a second time during the Asia-Europe Meeting held in Beijing in October 2008.

I should also mention the carpet in the banquet hall. The banquet hall in the Great Hall of the People is one of the biggest of its type in the world, 102 meters long from east to west, 76 meters long from south to north, and covering an area in excess of 7,000 square meters. The carpet was bright Chinese red, with a traditional auspicious coiled grass design. The wooden floor of the banquet hall had been in constant use since the Great Hall of the People was built in the 1950s, and it was therefore looking rather old. To solve this problem, we decided to order a new carpet right away, but you can imagine the difficulty in weaving such a huge carpet in a short period. Fortunately, leaders from the General Office of the CPC Central Committee took up the matter and managed to get the carpet completed before the summit. The carpet was 6,800 square meters in area and nine tons in weight. Once the floor covering was installed, the banquet hall took on new splendor and won the approval of all.

After nearly a year of preparations, the long-awaited summit was now about to open. The first crucial test of the summit preparations was the welcoming arrangements.

Over fifty African leaders would arrive in Beijing within a two-day period, most of them heads of state or government. Diplomatic protocol stipulates that the host country should arrange a welcome ceremony for visiting foreign heads of state or government, but since there were so many leaders arriving in such a short time, it was unrealistic to hold individual welcome ceremonies on the square in front of the east entrance of the Great Hall of the People.

Thus, we designed a plan to hold a welcome ceremony for each African leader at the new special plane building at Beijing's Capital International Airport. The ceremony was simple but solemn, as we hung up welcoming banners, laid out the red carpet, raised the national flags of China and of the arriving African leader, played the national anthems, and reviewed the guards of honor, so that the leader could feel the friendship and enthusiasm of the host country immediately after disembarking. Eighteen leaders of ministries and departments greeted and saw off African leaders at the airport on behalf of the Chinese government.

During the summit, we arranged forty-two welcome ceremonies at the airport, thirty-four of which were on November 2 and 3; sometimes, several delegations arrived on the same flight.

The Military Band of China's People's Liberation Army was stationed at the airport for four days and nights. During the busiest two days, they worked from five o'clock in the morning till eight o'clock in the evening, not even having time to eat. With their superb performances, they expressed the Chinese people's boundless hospitality to honored guests coming all the way from Africa.

President Ellen Johnson Sirleaf of Liberia was the first African leader to arrive in Beijing and use the new special plane building of the Capital International Airport. She was the first female president in African history.

She arrived in Beijing on October 28, 2006, and stayed at the Diaoyutai State Guesthouse. The following day happened to be her birthday and, much to her surprise, when she walked into the dining hall, "Happy Birthday to You" suddenly sounded throughout the hall. The serving staff sang the song for her and gave her an exquisite birthday cake.

President Sirleaf was visibly moved at this surprise gesture. Her eyes welled with tears, and she said excitedly, "I'll never forget this birthday."

The Preparatory Committee secretariat held two large-scale rehearsals. In order to minimize the impact on Beijing's traffic, we held the two rehearsals at midnight. For simulation purpose, we arranged for foreign ministry staff to take the roles of leaders and their spouses.

The first rehearsal was very successful and we identified many points for improvement, for example, about foreign leaders arriving at the Great Hall of the People to attend the opening ceremony. Based on our experience of previous international conferences, we planned for leaders to arrive at one-minute intervals, so it took nearly an hour for about fifty "leaders" to arrive. This was clearly too long, so we decided to halve the arrival interval to thirty seconds.

I and all the other members of the Preparatory Committee took part in the second rehearsal. It was like a combat simulation, the entire process covering the arrival of the motorcade, welcome ceremonies, welcome banquet, variety show, roundtable meeting, luncheon, leaders reading out the Declaration of the Beijing Summit, and the group photograph. Virtually every element was rehearsed in the actual location, and journalists took photos at every stage, so that we could make further improvements on the basis of the actual results.

With the experience gained from the first rehearsal, the second went very well. The support and cooperation of Beijing's public security and traffic departments allowed us to shorten the arrival time to twenty-five seconds per leader, and thirty minutes in all.

On November 4, 2006, the day of the opening ceremony, the arrival ceremony took thirty-one minutes because one African leader was a bit later than scheduled. Although the time was one minute longer than planned, it was no easy outcome for such a large-scale event.

To enhance public understanding of and support for China-African relations and the Beijing Summit, I granted a written interview to a Xinhua News Agency journalist on October 23.

I talked about the long-standing friendship between China and Africa and our current all-round cooperation partnership; I explained China's response to the "China threat to Africa" theory that some Western scholars had been shouting about for a while, pointing out that economic and trade cooperation between China and Africa was on a mutually beneficial and win–win basis, and that China's development would provide more opportunities for Africa's development. The ideas they were trying to spread conformed neither with the facts of history nor with the actuality of China–Africa relations.

Of course, I did not avoid new problems that had emerged during the expansion of China-Africa cooperation, such as the trade deficit existing between China and some African countries, the

At the Exhibition on Sixth Anniversary of Forum on China-Africa Cooperation, November 3, 2006.

challenge to the African market of some Chinese products, and conflicts between some Chinese enterprises and local residents. I stressed that these were problems appearing in the process of development, and China was taking active measures and working with African friends to seek solutions. These problems, in my view, could be properly solved through cooperation and negotiations based on the principle of consultation on an equal footing, mutual understanding, and mutual accommodation.

I also clearly pointed out that China-Africa cooperation was transparent, open, and inclusive, and would not affect African countries' or China's cooperation with third parties, nor infringe upon the interests of third parties. On the contrary, expanded China-Africa cooperation and mutual development would provide a precious opportunity for countries around the world.

To supplement the summit and demonstrate the achievements of China-Africa cooperation, we held several exhibitions—Masterpieces of African Art, Stamps and Coins of African

Countries, and Six Years of China-Africa Cooperation—and issued commemorative stamps during the summit.

The exhibition Six Years of China-Africa Cooperation, held in the central hall of the Great Hall of the People from November 3 to 4, displayed 249 pictures, vividly showing how Chinese and African leaders had exchanged visits, how peoples had worked together, and how China-Africa cooperation had developed dynamically over the six years since the establishment of the FOCAC.

The exhibition opening ceremony took place on November 3, the same day as that of the Third Ministerial Conference. I officiated in the afternoon, cutting the ribbon and making a speech. Ministers and representatives of African countries went to the exhibition. They and I reviewed the development of China-African relations and the FOCAC, looking forward to the bright future.

Distinguished Guests Gather in Beijing

AT NINE IN THE morning on November 4, 2006, the northern hall of the Great Hall of the People was brightly lit, and the summit logo—"Joining Hands"—on its blue background was really eye-catching.

President Hu Jintao was there as planned, standing in the middle of the red carpet to welcome the African delegations attending the Beijing Summit of FOCAC. They entered in alphabetical order of country names, so the first to enter was Algeria's President Abdelaziz Bouteflika, who had attended the First Ministerial Conference. He was so excited that he opened his arms and hugged President Hu.

Next came Angola's Prime Minister Fernando da Piedade Dias dos Santos, and Benin's President Thomas Yayi Boni, followed into the hall by other African leaders. President Hu shook hands with them and greeted them one by one.

Over three hundred journalists made full use of every minute to record this historic moment on still or video cameras.

Liberia's President Ellen Johnson Sirleaf was the only female leader in this summit. Wearing a bright-colored Liberian dress, she was besieged by cameras as soon as she entered.

Then other African guests entered the hall and signed their names on the commemorative first day cover of the stamps for the Beijing Summit of the FOCAC. On main design elements were a red map of China, green map of Africa, and four white doves flying; on the upper right was a stamp with the FOCAC logo and the summit logo "Joining Hands."

The last to enter was Prime Minister Meles Zenawi of Ethiopia, co-chairman of the summit. President Hu and Meles walked into the hall shoulder to shoulder and also signed their names on the commemorative cover.

The arrangements were that, having signed, the leaders would enter the assembly hall and take their seats on the platform. Once up there, they would find many eye-catching big footprints on the floor, according to the seating order of these leaders on the rostrum, so that when the ushers guided leaders, it would be in order. These signs were to facilitate the dignified progress of each leader to the right platform place that had been specially designed by our Protocol Department. The rectangular big footprints each bore the name of a country and had a big white footprint at the center. They were bright and eye-catching. Since the order of these direction signs was the same as that of the seats, the leaders could find their seats quickly.

A warm and cordial atmosphere prevailed.

On the rostrum, the national flags of China and forty-eight African countries were ranged in order; on the blue backdrop "Beijing Summit of China-Africa Forum" was written in English and French, and from the second-floor balcony hung a horizontal banner, bearing the words "Friendship, Peace, Cooperation, and Development" in Chinese, English, and French.

Among the forty-eight African representatives, there were thirty-five heads of state, six government leaders, one vice president, and six high-level representatives; the chairperson of the AU Commission was also present. It was unprecedented. President Thabo Mbeki of South Africa said that some of the African leaders had not attended an AU Summit for years, but this time, they had all come to Beijing.

In addition, the United Nations Environment Program, World Food Program, International Monetary Fund, African Development Bank, Secretariat of New Partnership for Africa's Development, Southern African Development Community, and eighteen other international and regional organizations also sent observers to attend the summit opening ceremony and other activities.

When President Hu Jintao and African leaders stepped onto the platform and took their seats, over three thousand people in the hall stood up and applauded.

At ten o'clock sharp, I, as chair of the opening ceremony, solemnly announced the opening of the Beijing Summit of the Forum of China-Africa Cooperation.

It was an exciting moment.

President Hu delivered the keynote speech. His first sentence after greeting the guests was this: "Our meeting today will go down in history."

Before his voice had died away, thunderous applause filled the hall.

President Hu spoke highly of the important role of FOCAC in deepening China-Africa friendly cooperative relations and extolled the very substantial results achieved in the fifty years since the inauguration of diplomatic ties between China and African countries.

In the last part of his speech, President Hu declared that the

Chinese government would take eight measures to strengthen practical cooperation with Africa, including providing more assistance to Africa by setting up a China-Africa development fund; debt cancellation; further opening up the Chinese market to Africa, and establishing trade and economic cooperation zones in Africa; training African professionals; sending senior agricultural experts to Africa and setting up special agricultural technology demonstration centers in Africa; building hospitals, malaria prevention and treatment centers, and schools in Africa; dispatching youth volunteers to Africa; and increasing the number of Chinese government scholarships to African students.

The applause at the end of this speech took a long time to die down.

That reaction told me that President Hu's speech and the Chinese government's measures had won the hearts of African friends, had really communicated the sincerity of the Chinese people, and instilled belief that China would be a lifelong good friend, partner, and brother of Africa.

Premier Meles of Ethiopia, the copresiding country of the FOCAC, and President Denis Sassou Nguesso of the Republic of the Congo (Brazzaville), the rotating presiding country of the AU, each addressed the gathering. They expressed gratitude for China's great summit arrangements, in particular for the eight measures that President Hu had declared, which demonstrated China's sincerity about further China-Africa cooperation.

I noted that Sassou did not address President Hu as "respected chairman," which was the normal practice on diplomatic occasions; instead, he addressed Hu as "our dear friend" or "dear friend," which sounded more intimate and sincere. As one news report said, as rotating president of the AU, Sassou expressed not only his personal friendship with President Hu, but also the deep friendship of African countries and people for President Hu and all the Chinese people.

On that night, President Hu hosted a banquet for our guests at the Great Hall of the People. Members of the CPC Standing Committee and leaders of the State Council that were in Beijing all attended the banquet. It was rare in our history of treating foreign guests. The reason for the extraspecial treatment was that this was the largest and highest-level gathering of Chinese and African leaders, and the level of hospitality standard should be higher than normal.

The dishes served were not complicated nor were the ingredients extravagant; but they were exquisitely made, perfect in color, aroma, taste, and appearance. The menu was also exquisitely designed, like an artwork. The African guests kept on singing the praises of the food, and they liked the menu so much they all wanted to take it with them. In fact, not only the foreign guests, but also the Chinese people present at the banquet took the menus home, too. Thus, almost all the banquet menus "flew without wings."

During an interlude at the banquet, President Muhammad Hosni Mubarak of Egypt asked President Hu to autograph his menu as a memento of the occasion, but he left the menu behind after the banquet, only remembering it once he got back to the hotel. Mubarak immediately asked his people to return to the banquet hall and look for the menu. Fortunately, staff of the Great Hall of the People had found the autographed menu and handed it over to officials of the Protocol Department. When the Egyptian staff regained this menu, they thanked the Chinese staff again and again, saying how much President Mubarak cherished it and wanted it back. Now, they could rest easy.

After the meal, President Hu and African leaders watched a variety show involving some four hundred Chinese and African performers. The show was named "Ode to Friendship" and was in three parts: "Welcoming," "Gathering," and "Yearning."

Beijing Opera, original African art and modern art were presented one by one, the different cultural performances interacting and harmonizing on the stage.

"Distance counts for nothing, ten thousand miles cannot divide neighborly hearts." This ancient line of poetry was the best expression of the show's "Ode to Friendship" title.

After the show, many African leaders said that they could imagine how much the Chinese and African performers had practiced together and learned from each other to stage this show. They were impressed by the wonderful performances.

On the second day, November 5, the roundtable meeting of the Beijing Summit of FOCAC was convened.

Here Chinese and African leaders focused on the theme of the summit—"friendship, peace, cooperation, and development"—and exchanged views on developing a new type of strategic partnership and strengthening practical cooperation between China and Africa, and on major international and regional issues. The meeting adopted the Declaration of the Beijing Summit of the Forum on China-Africa Cooperation and Forum on China-Africa

The roundtable meeting of the Beijing Summit, November 5, 2006.

Cooperation—Beijing Action Plan (2007–2009); agreed to establish and develop a new type of strategic partnership between China and Africa characterized by political equality and mutual trust, economic win-win cooperation, and cultural exchanges; and mapped out mutually beneficial China-Africa cooperation for the following three years.

After the meeting, one African leader after another congratulated President Hu. They had high praise for the concrete, practicable, and clearly targeted eight measures he had announced, and believed they would help Africa to realize economic integration and independent development. They praised China as a true friend of Africa.

President Ahmed Abdallah Mohamed Sambi of Comoros described China-Africa cooperation as a model for cooperation, and Egypt's Foreign Minister Ahmed Aboul Gheit said that China and Africa had had fifty years of friendship in the past and predicted that China and Africa would maintain relations of peace and amity for five hundred years to come.

During the summit, Premier Wen Jiabao and thirty-three African leaders attended the opening ceremony of the High-level Dialogue Between Chinese and African Leaders and Business Representatives and the Second Conference of Chinese and African Entrepreneurs. In an important speech at the opening ceremony, Wen gave five suggestions on implementing President Hu's eight measures on practical China-Africa cooperation and raising the level: expand the size of China-Africa trade; increase cooperation in investment; upgrade assistance to Africa; promote cooperation between the business communities; and increase assistance to Africa in human resources development. At the Second Conference of Chinese and African Entrepreneurs, Chinese and African enterprises signed fifteen cooperation agreements totaling US $1.9 billion, and the two sides formally declared the establishment of China-Africa Joint Chamber of Commerce.

The summit strengthened communications, and provided a platform for better understanding and closer friendship between Chinese and African leaders. President Hu, Premier Wen, and other members of China's Central Authorities held a total of seventy bilateral meetings with African leaders. Before and after the summit, we arranged six state visits and nineteen working visits, thereby satisfying a strong desire on the part of African leaders to visit China and meet Chinese leaders, and enhancing mutual understanding and trust between Chinese leaders and the new generation of African leaders.

China–Africa relations became a hot topic in all sectors of Chinese society. The summit had brought back good memories of the long-standing friendship between China and Africa. Before the summit ended, there were many identical posts on the Internet: "Don't go, our African friends!"

There are many interesting anecdotes concerning African leaders in Beijing, during, before, or after the summit. One that impressed me was the story of South Africa's President Thabo Mbeki buying books.

President Mbeki was one of the leaders that paid an official visit to China after the Beijing Summit.

He is a representative of the new generation of African leaders. An advocate of African rejuvenation, he enjoys an excellent reputation among African countries. He became president of South Africa in 1999, selected as his successor by the country's first black president, Nelson Mandela. He loves reading, and is famous as a scholar president. I met him many times. He is restrained and gentlemanly, has great affection for China, and is eager to know and learn from China.

During his visit, President Mbeki asked to buy some books about China's reform and opening up and economic development at a Beijing bookstore. In the diplomatic history of New China, he was the first foreign state leader to want to visit a bookstore.

When foreign leaders visit China, for reasons of security, we usually do not add activities to the schedule, and during the summit, the schedule was tight. Initially, we suggested that relevant departments could prepare a selection of books to meet his requirements and deliver them to his hotel, but President Mbeki insisted on going to a bookstore to browse in person.

So, we went along with his wish, and the president went to the Xinhua Bookstore on Wangfujing Street accompanied by our ambassador to South Africa Liu Guijin.

President Mbeki was in high spirits, asking Ambassador Liu Guijin and the bookstore staff about recently published books concerning China's economic and social development. He selected carefully and bought more than ten books, including collected writings on China's reform and opening up and English books on China's rural and educational reforms.

Interestingly he bought a copy of *The Scholars*. Being a scholar himself, it is understandable that he was drawn by this title.

Leaving the bookstore, President Mbeki went directly to the luncheon meeting of Chinese and African entrepreneurs and made the keynote speech, to which he added an impromptu paragraph: "We have all been talking about learning from China, but to learn from China we should first know China. I wonder whether we in this audience know China. Our ambassador to China does somewhat, through working here. I know a little too, through reading books published in China. Usually what we learn about China comes from newspapers and magazines, and it is not comprehensive. I recommend that we all read some books published in China."

When Ambassador Liu Guijin told me about President Mbeki and the bookshop, I was really moved, thinking about the old generation of African leaders reading the *Selected Works of Mao Zedong* and the new generation browsing in Chinese bookstores. This, to my mind, was no coincidence: It illustrated Africa's ever-growing interest in China in the new world situation. It embodied the growth in friendship between China and Africa, and demonstrated that our communication and cooperation with Africa over the years had borne fruit.

Strong Response to the Summit

WORK ON THE BEIJING Summit was a huge endeavor involving a multitude of things; it was unprecedented in the diplomatic history of the People's Republic. Thanks to the importance attached to it by the central leadership, good teamwork between the departments concerned, and hard work by all the staff, every aspect went smoothly and was perfectly concluded, resulting in favorable comments from our African friends. In early 2007, when I accompanied President Hu on his visit to Africa, the summit was the first thing that many African friends mentioned to me, describing it as too impressive a gathering ever to be forgotten.

The Beijing Summit was an important milestone in the history of China-Africa relations. It was of profound significance for furthering the friendship between China and Africa, enhancing cooperation, establishing China's image as a responsible country, and expanding China's influence on the international stage.

The Beijing Summit aroused a great response internationally. Foreign media commented that its success demonstrated China's growing strength, as no other country but China could gather almost all African leaders at one meeting.

African governments and news media nicknamed the eight measures announced at the summit as the "Hu Jintao Plan." They saw the summit as giving a new impetus to China–Africa relations and China-Africa cooperation as becoming a model for South-South cooperation.

India, Malaysia, Ukraine, and some other developing countries commented positively on the eight measures and believed that stronger cooperation between China and Africa was in the interests of both parties.

Western countries also gave close attention to the Beijing Summit. Major Western media marveled at China's strong influence in Africa. The US *International Herald Tribune* said that this summit showed the appeal of China's development pattern. The *Guardian,* a British newspaper, said that this was only the start of Beijing amazing the world.

However, some Western media made irresponsible remarks on China-Africa cooperation. However, that was no surprise to us.

The Beijing Summit provoked a wide response, generating an Africa craze around the world. Following the Beijing Summit, the Europe-Africa Summit, suspended for seven years due to various factors, was held at the end of 2007. South Korea, India, Japan, and Latin American countries successively held the South Korea–Africa Forum, India-Africa Summit, the Fourth Tokyo International Conference on African Development, and South America–Africa Summit.

For this, African countries were grateful to us, believing that the Beijing Summit had resulted in the international community, major countries in particular, paying greater attention to Africa, and had enhanced Africa's status. For this reason, too, China then had more interaction with Africa and Western countries, and China and Africa expanded cooperation in international affairs.

Following Through After the Summit

THE BEIJING SUMMIT WAS a pioneering undertaking not only in the history of China-Africa relations, but also in Chinese diplomacy.

After the summit, President Hu Jintao met with representatives of the summit staff at the Great Hall of the People on the afternoon on November 7, 2006. He expressed sincere gratitude and regards to the representatives. President Hu said that the success of the Beijing Summit symbolized a new stage in China–Africa relations and that we should now shift the focus to implementing the outcomes of the conference.

To take the summit achievements to the people of Africa and demonstrate to Africa and the international community China's sincerity in cooperation, President Hu paid state visits to Cameroon, Liberia, Sudan, Zambia, Namibia, South Africa, Mozambique, and Seychelles between January 30 and February 11, 2007. I accompanied President Hu throughout the visit.

It was just nine months since President Hu's last visit to Africa, and three months since the Beijing Summit. This tour covered more countries than any of his previous visits and the president crisscrossed the continent, visiting countries large and small, rich and poor, according to the principle of regional balance. Apart from South Africa and Namibia, none of these countries had ever received a Chinese head of state.

The eight African countries attached great importance to President Hu's visit, and all accorded him the highest level of hospitality. The president of Cameroon welcomed President Hu at the airport and accompanied him to major activities, as did the presidents of Liberia, Sudan, Zambia, Namibia, Mozambique, and Seychelles. President James Michel of Seychelles told President Hu excitedly that Hu was the first foreign state leader to visit his country in twenty-three years.

The people of Africa welcomed President Hu enthusiastically. Thousands lined the streets, now singing, now dancing, and shouting and jumping for joy; it was exciting. By the side of the road taken by President Hu's motorcade, Sudanese had butchered camels, in what apparently is the highest honor accorded to guests there.

During his visit, President Hu exchanged views with African leaders and reached consensus on bilateral relations, particularly on how to put into effect the achievements of the Beijing Summit, and on some important issues of interest to both sides.

President Hu, being a very practical person, turned the eight measures into tangible cooperation programs according to local conditions in every country he visited. This won him a warm welcome wherever he went.

At the University of Pretoria in South Africa, President Hu delivered a speech, giving a comprehensive explanation of China's African policy, and elaborating on his ideas for strengthening China-Africa cooperation and helping build a harmonious world.

President Hu also met with people from the business, culture, education, and health-care sectors, particularly African youths, and did much work to strengthen the ties of friendship. He attended the opening ceremonies of facilities established with Chinese assistance, namely, the first malaria prevention and treatment center, the first agricultural technology demonstration center, and the first trade and economic cooperation zone.

This visit to Africa truly initiated the implementation of the eight measures, deepened friendship between China and Africa, consolidated and strengthened the social basis for China-Africa friendship, promoted affection between China and African countries, and demonstrated China's image of being true in word and deed. It was a journey of friendship, a journey of cooperation.

On November 4, 2007, the first anniversary of the summit, I invited high-ranking officials from ministries and commissions, and ambassadors of African countries to a reception at the Diaoyutai State Guesthouse to mark the first anniversary of the summit.

In the speech I delivered at the reception, I looked back on the year since the summit and on the new appearance of China-Africa relations. I stressed that advancing solidarity and cooperation with Africa was a long-term strategic decision on China's part, and a basic guiding principle of our Africa policy. China would continue

Addressing guests at a reception to mark the first anniversary
of the Beijing Summit, November 4, 2007.

to join hands with African countries to carry on the spirit of the
Beijing Summit, treat all as equals, deepen traditional friendship,
seek mutual benefits and promote common development, enhance
interaction of civilizations based on openness and inclusiveness,
promote solidarity and cooperation, and increase mutual support.
Building on the achievements of the Beijing Summit, China would
push China–Africa cooperation to ever-higher levels.

Cameroon's ambassador to China, Eleih–Elle Etian, also doyen
of the African diplomatic corps in China, who had lived in China
for nearly two decades, delivered a speech. He spoke highly of the
summit, and of China's follow-up measures in particular. He saw
the summit as a great innovation, one that had laid a new foundation for China's cooperation with African countries. He commended China's commitment to implementing the eight measures
and the progress achieved in carrying out the policies.

In February 2009, President Hu paid his fourth visit to Africa, visiting Mali, Senegal, Tanzania, and Mauritius.

Though I had retired from the State Council by then, I could see from the news that the people of Africa had again welcomed President Hu with the highest level of hospitality.

Actually, this visit was also an opportunity to examine the achievements of the summit. President Hu exchanged views with leaders of the host nations on how implementation was proceeding, and he visited some typical programs. The follow-up work of the Beijing Summit went on smoothly, and each of the eight measures toward Africa was being carried out.

When President Hu visited Africa in 2009, the global financial crisis had spread around the world and the world economy was facing severe challenges. During his tour, President Hu told each of the countries he visited that even though China too had met with some difficulties, we would, as a true friend of Africa, continue implementing the measures assisting Africa without compromising the timetable or the quality; we would not reduce any aid to Africa; instead, we would provide more assistance to the full extent of our capability; reduce or cancel their debt; expand trade and investment in Africa; and strengthen practical cooperation between China and Africa.

African countries were deeply grateful for China's energetic follow-through on the Beijing Summit achievements. In their opinion, China was a creditable and responsible major power, one that had always given honest help towards the development of African countries.

Even Western media prone to making irresponsible remarks on China-Africa cooperation had to admit that President Hu's visit showed China as living up to her word. Major media in Britain, France, and Germany mentioned that none of the four African countries on the visit itinerary was rich in energy or resources, showing that China treated all African countries equally without discrimination.

The facts gave the lie to China's so-called neocolonialism in Africa.

Harmony Between China and Africa

OVER SIX HUNDRED YEARS ago, China's famous navigator Zheng He made seven voyages to Southeast Asia, South Asia, and East Africa, collectively referred to as "the Western Ocean." He came to East Africa four times, bringing silks, satins, and chinaware and promoting the Chinese spirit of harmony in all the countries, thereby providing valuable experience for mankind's harmonious coexistence.

Every time Zheng He's deeds in Africa are mentioned, there is nothing but praise from African friends who suffered much under colonialism.

The greatest characteristic of history is that it can be handed down.

In modern times, similar historical experiences and aspirations have bound together the fates of Chinese and Africans. Hence, China-Africa relations have endured the tests of time and volatile international situations.

The China-Africa relationship is not an ordinary strategic partnership. As President Hu said, the Chinese have always seen African people as "all-weather" friends, and would always be their caring brother and partner. Friendship, brotherhood, and partnership are the essence of China-Africa relations. All this makes the foundation of the relationship solid and deep, a relationship of infinite potential.

Looking back, one word perfectly encapsulates the relationship. That word is *harmony*.

The building of harmonious China-African relations has

become an important element in China's theory and practice about building a harmonious world.

Looking back on the Beijing Summit, I can proudly say that it was a harmonious conference between China and Africa, a successful example in practice of building a harmonious world. The success of the summit complied with the common strategic needs of China and Africa, and has guided them in moving forward.

"A bosom friend afar brings a distant land near." It is my firm belief that, through joint efforts, China and Africa will write new and better chapters in the history of their harmonious relations.

POSTSCRIPT

I T TOOK OVER SIX months to complete this book.

Looking back, the task completed, I am struck once more by how rapidly China's overall strength has grown and how notably its international status has risen over the past decade. I am impressed, too, by the ability of China's diplomacy to address all the vicissitudes in the international situation, always making headway, turning challenges into opportunities, and achieving tremendous results.

At every important juncture and critical moment, China's central leadership has remained cool-headed, bringing accurate judgment to bear on every situation, resolutely making right decisions, pointing the direction, and laying down principles for our diplomatic work. This is the magic weapon for our successful diplomacy.

For our diplomatic work, China's development and strength provide a strong support; the interests of China and the Chinese people are its source of strength and objective. A contingent of high-caliber professionally trained diplomats underpins the implementation of foreign policies. Premier Zhou Enlai said that China's diplomats were actually a people's army in civilian clothes. In the severe tests of volatile international situations and diplomatic practice, China's diplomats have devoted their efforts, energy, and even lives to safeguarding the interests of the motherland and the people. Reflecting on this, I am confident about the future of China's diplomacy.

When writing this book, I had the help and support of many friends. First, I would like to thank State Councilor Dai Bingguo, and Yang Jiechi, Wang Guangya, and other leading friends from the Ministry of Foreign Affairs for their warm concern and support, and also the heads and staff of the Division of Policy and Planning of the Foreign Ministry for their selfless cooperation and support. Former Ambassadors or Consuls General Zhao Jinjun, Guan Chengyuan, Lu Shumin, Zhou Gang, Ning Fukui, Sun Yanheng, Zhao Xidi, Pan Zhanlin, Li Changhe, Lu Shulin, Qi Jianguo, and Liu Zhigang contributed in various ways to the planning or compilation of the content. My old colleague Wang Taiping was responsible for putting together and going over the whole book; Ou Boqian was responsible for organizing and coordinating the writing and compilation of the book and participated in checking the content; Yuan Luming was the editor in charge; Zhang Jinping, Liu Sipan, and my secretary Xiao Qian checked and proofread the draft and offered many valuable opinions and suggestions. It is thanks to the help of the people named that the publication of this book went without a hitch. Here I would like to express my sincere gratitude to all of them.

If there are any inaccuracies, the author would sincerely welcome criticisms and corrections from readers.

Tang Jiaxuan
October 17, 2009

ACKNOWLEDGMENTS

As the English edition of this book goes to press, I hereby extend my heartfelt gratitude to everyone who made a contribution

First I'd like to thank Mr. Zhou Mingwei, President of China International Publishing Group (CIPG), who offered dedicated support and vigorous assistance to the English translation of this book. Thanks also go to the CIPG translators, namely Li Yang, Han Qingyue, Liu Kuijuan, Wang Wei, Wang Qin, Xu Tingting, Jiang Xiaoning, Xu Xinge, Sue Duncan, Wang Mingjie, and He Jun, who worked diligently and efficiently to complete a high-quality English translation. My special thanks go to Ambassador Guo Jiading of the Ministry of Foreign Affairs, an expert in the English language, who played a key role in the final revision of the English translation, applying himself with professionalism and with a rigorous and conscientious attitude.

I also want to express my gratitude to Mr. Zhou Wenzhong, former Chinese ambassador to the United States, and Zhang Yesui, present Chinese ambassador to the United States, who provided enthusiastic support in the book's production.

My special thanks go to Mr. Brian Murray, President and Chief Executive Officer of HarperCollins, and his outstanding representative in China, Madame Stella Chou, for their support in ensuring a smooth path to publication.

Madame Ou Boqian, my authorized representative in charge of publishing coordination, played her role well as the communication bridge and hereby receives my acknowledgment.

Tang Jiaxuan
November 23, 2010